D1090970

A HUNDRED YEARS OF ECONOMIC DEVELOPMENT IN GREAT BRITAIN

A HUNDRED YEARS OF ECONOMIC DEVELOPMENT
in Great Britain

by

G. P. JONES, Litt.D.

Lecturer in Economic History in the University of Sheffield

AND

A. G. POOL, B.Sc., Ph.D.

Lecturer in Economics in the University of Sheffield

DUCKWORTH

3 Henrietta Street, London, W.C.2

FIRST PUBLISHED 1940
REPRINTED 1948

TYPE SET IN GT BRITAIN BY THE KEMP HALL PRESS LTD, OXFORD
PRINTED IN FRANCE BY GASTON MAILLET & Cie, SAINT-OUEN

CONTENTS

PART II. 1875-1914

PREFACE

In the pages which follow, an attempt is made to depict the economic character of what has been, in respect of its hopes and achievements, the greatest century in British history. Many will no doubt consider that other ages have burned with a nobler faith, flowered more excellently in the arts or rejoiced in a more widespread security and happiness. Edmund Burke, had he been able to foresee the century with which we have to do, might well have been more convinced than ever that " the age of chivalry is gone. That of sophisters, economists and calculators has succeeded; and the glory of Europe is extinguished for ever." The past century, nevertheless, has done more than any of its predecessors to help the weak, to free the captive and to teach the unlettered; it has been the first since the beginning of time to be able to postpone, for great masses of the people, the inevitable hour of death; and while it lengthened it also enriched their lives by adding to their leisure, freeing their movement and putting their destiny, to a great degree, in their own hands. That misery and squalor abounded in the hastily built towns of this period, while a new scope was given to sordid acquisitiveness in its industry and commerce, is plain enough; but what matters is that the existence of such evils was more frankly admitted than ever before and that the technique of bringing abuses into the light of day, as an indispensable preliminary to their removal, was elaborated and extended in a remarkable fashion. Despite its defects, the century showed, in social and economic questions as in others, an unprecedented faith in healing, if caustic, truth.

To describe all the economic developments of the past hundred years in a relatively small volume is manifestly impossible, and we have, accordingly, been compelled to say little on some topics and nothing at all on others. Our purpose has not been to write a general economic history, still less a social history, as those are commonly understood; and we have not, therefore, considered it necessary, even if space had permitted, to give any account of such subjects as poverty and the poor law or the development of economic doctrines; we have, also, dealt only incidentally with public finance. We are concerned broadly with changes in the methods of producing wealth and distributing goods and services, and in the types of organization and forms of association developed for those purposes, in what appear to us to be the more important industries and trades. It will be observed that our period is not to be rigidly interpreted, for neither 1839 nor the years immediately before and after it form a very satisfactory *terminus a quo*. One hundred years ago Queen Victoria and Sir Robert Peel fell out about appointments in the royal household; Bright and Cobden were organizing on a national scale the protest against the Corn Laws; Chartist demonstrators were being shot down in Newport, Monmouthshire; and Sir Rowland Hill was about to institute the penny post. Except, perhaps, for the last mentioned change, which was inaugurated in 1840, none of these events can be taken as significantly marking the end of an old order or the beginning of a new one, as the battle of Waterloo, the great Reform Bill, the Factory Act of 1833 or the new Poor Law of 1834 may be held to do. The economic condition and prospects of Great Britain a hundred years ago depended in part upon many trends and developments some of which had been in progress for a considerable time; thus, though we are in the main concerned with economic changes occurring between the end of the reign of William IV and the beginning of the reign of George VI, we must from time to time go back at least a few years for starting points. In tracing the changes with which we are concerned, we have thought it convenient to divide the hundred years into three main periods, though here also the boundaries cannot be rigidly drawn. First we are concerned with an era of marked changes and, at times, of great disturbance, between the later eighteen-thirties and the onset of what is commonly called the Great Depression. The second division covers the period during which Great Britain had to adapt herself to the loss of the industrial leadership of the world, between the earlier eighteen-seventies and the outbreak of the Great War. The third is the quarter-century of disturbance and complication since 1914.

So far, the general reader has not been very well provided with books covering the field which we attempt to survey. On the period of what is called the Industrial Revolution he has a choice of books; but most of them either stop short at or before the middle of the nineteenth century or treat the period after 1850 less thoroughly than the preceding period. The student is fortunate in the existence of Dr. Clapham's three volumes, the monumental *Economic History of Modern Britain*, to which we acknowledge a deep indebtedness, as all students must do for generations to come. It is our hope that the present volume may, besides serving as a guide for the general reader, be of use to undergraduates as a preliminary to the study of Dr. Clapham's work.

In order to save space and spare expense, we have refrained from giving in footnotes detailed references to all our authorities and sources; but we trust that the bibliography sufficiently indicates our major obligations to printed material and will be found useful. Readers will find in the following pages more statistical illustration than history books commonly contain; but that is required by the nature of the subject, in studying and treating which there is much to be said for going some distance with Sir William Petty, who desired "that no word might be used but what marks either number, weight or measure."

We have to acknowledge the willing assistance of our

colleagues in the preparation of this book. The advice of Professor I. C. F. Statham and Mr. E. Bevan enabled us to correct some errors and misunderstandings in connection with coal-mining. Professor Douglas Knoop was kind enough to read the typescript and to suggest numerous emendations.

The University,
Sheffield,
June 1939.

G.P.J.
A.G.P.

Postscript. Readers of this volume will understand that such expressions as " before the war," " after the war " and so on refer to the conflict of 1914–1918 and not to the present hostilities, which broke out while the book was being printed.

September 1939.

PART ONE

1837-1875

CHAPTER I

Population and Resources Before 1840

THE POPULATION AND ITS DISTRIBUTION

Queen Victoria, when she came to the throne, had about 17,500,000 subjects in Great Britain. If the Irish population, then larger absolutely and proportionately than later, be added, the population of the British Isles may be stated roughly as 25,750,000. This total was perhaps less by two or three millions than the population of Britain's ancient enemy, France, and about equal to that of her future rival, Germany. On the other hand, though the man power of both these countries was considerable, it was more thinly spread and industrially far less developed. France was still producing much of her iron by means of charcoal, a process which had been dying out in England for nearly a century; and Germany, politically divided and still preserving many relics of feudal serfdom, had only begun to free her industries from bondage to the forest and the stream.

Unlike France, whose population grew only very slowly, Great Britain was rapidly becoming more populous, and had been doing so, though the increase cannot be certainly stated or fully explained, for more than a century. It is probable that in the hundred years before the first census was taken, in 1801, the population of England and Wales rose from 5,500,000 or 5,800,000 to 8,872,000, an increase of 56 per cent. There is reason to believe that a specially rapid growth occurred in the central decades of the eighteenth century and again from about 1780 to somewhere between 1811 and 1821.[1] Thereafter the increase was

[1] T. H. Marshall, in *Economic History Review*, April 1935, p. 65.

slower but was nevertheless much faster than the eighteenth-century average, as the following table[1] makes plain :

POPULATION, 1801–1841 (000's neglected)

	1801	1811	Increase per cent.	1821	Increase per cent.	1831	Increase per cent.	1841	Increase per cent.
England	8,331	9,539	14.5	11,261	18·05	13,091	16·24	15,000	14·58
Wales	541	612	12.97	717	17·27	806	12·36	912	13·07
Army and Navy etc.	471	640	—	319	—	277	—	188	—
Scotland	1,599	1,805	12.92	2,093	15·93	2,365	13·0	2,620	10·78
Total	10,942	12,596	15.11	14,391	14·12	16,539	14·9	18,720	13·18

In times past the greater part of the population had been found in southern England but, though the metropolitan area continued to increase the number of its inhabitants at a rate which alarmed observers, the shifting of old industries and the rise of new ones had long tended to draw the population into the Midlands, South Wales, the textile areas of Lancashire and the West Riding and the mining districts of Northumberland and Durham. This trend was still active in the third decade of the nineteenth century. An indication of it is the difference between the rate at which population grew in a southern farming county, such as Huntingdon, and a northern manufacturing county, such as Lancashire. In the former, between 1801 and 1831, the population increased from 37,568 to 53,192, or roughly by 41 per cent.; in the latter, during the same period, the total rose from 672,731 to 1,336,854, an increase of more than 98 per cent. Similarly, during these thirty years, the almost entirely rural county of Anglesey increased its population by 43 per cent., while that congregated in the darkening valleys of Glamorgan increased by 77 per cent.; the inhabitants of pastoral Westmorland increased by 32 per cent. and those of coal-producing Durham by 58 per cent.[2]

[1] G. R. Porter, *Progress of the Nation* (1847), p. 8.

[2] For figures for the counties of England and Wales see J. R. McCulloch, *Statistical Account of the British Empire*, I. 401.

The remarkable rise in the population of such counties and, as will be mentioned later, of old and new towns, is only in part to be explained by an excess of births over deaths among the relatively old-established families in those areas. There was, besides, an influx from the neighbouring districts and from further afield. The population, more or less willingly, was on the move.[1] Some were lured from the fields to the factories by the hope of higher wages or driven by the loss or inadequacy of their holdings after enclosure; some were attracted by greater opportunities for the employment of their families; some were "transported," as they called it, by poor-law authorities eager to lessen the pressure of the rates. Scotsmen deserted the Highlands, the Lothians and the Lowlands for the mills and iron works of Glasgow and the Clyde; Welsh men and women came in large numbers from the counties of North Wales to form a more or less permanent section of the population of Merseyside and Manchester; the Irish poured into Wales and the western counties as seasonal workers in agriculture, and into Lancashire and parts of Scotland in repeated relays of low-paid industrial labour[2]; Englishmen from the western counties and the Midlands thronged into the iron works of South Wales. This mobility, which was evident as early as 1750, indicates that the barriers imposed by the law of settlement and removal cannot have been so effective as has sometimes been supposed, and, in any event, they were relaxed in 1795. By that time improved highways had facilitated transport, though long-distance travelling by coach must have been too costly for labourers and their families. Canal transport was cheaper; in 1835 adults were conveyed from Paddington to Manchester in four or

[1] The authoritative account of the mobility is A. Redford, *Labour Migration in England, 1800–1850*.

[2] Out of a population of 202,426 in Glasgow in 1831, 35,554 were Irish (R. Cowan, 'Vital Statistics of Glasgow,' in *Journal of the Statistical Society of London*, December 1840) and out of a population of 354,000 in Manchester and Salford in 1841, 34,000 were Irish born (*Manchester Guardian Civic Centenary Number*, 16 May, 1938).

five days at a fare of 14s.;[1] but canals were effective in redistributing population rather through the stimulus they gave to industry than by their usefulness, which must have been small, as a means of passenger transport.

This growth and shifting of population were accompanied by a process of concentration in what may be conveniently, if with incomplete propriety, called towns. Some of these were boroughs, a term hard to define before the reforms and uniformity begun in 1835; but, whether municipalities or not, they needed a good deal of improving before they could provide in anything like adequate fashion for the hygienic and moral needs of their inhabitants. The largest urban agglomeration was the metropolitan area, which in 1801 contained nearly a million inhabitants, or roughly one-ninth of the whole population of England and Wales. No other city or town in Great Britain then contained as many as 100,000 people. That was true of England and Wales in 1811 also, though Liverpool and Manchester, with Salford, were then both within a few thousands of that level. Edinburgh and Glasgow were a few thousands above it. By 1831 when the London area had over 1,400,000 inhabitants, six towns other than London had passed the 100,000 mark; they were Glasgow (202,426), Manchester (182,812), Liverpool (165,715), Edinburgh, including Leith, (162,403), Birmingham (146,986) and Leeds (123,393).

An indication of the increasingly urban character of the population is found in the number of towns having more than 20,000 inhabitants. Of such towns Great Britain had nineteen, excluding London, in 1811. Eight of them—Liverpool, Plymouth, Bristol, Portsmouth, Hull, Newcastle, Aberdeen and Dundee—were ports; another eight—Manchester, Leeds, Norwich, Nottingham, Leicester, Bolton, Rochdale and Paisley—were important textile or hosiery centres; Birmingham and Sheffield owed their growth to the metal trades; and Bath had no doubt been

[1] Redford, *op. cit.* p. 92.

made populous by Georgian fashion. By 1831 the number of towns of this magnitude had risen to forty-nine, of which eight, including by then Preston, Blackburn, Stockport, Oldham and Ashton-under-Lyne, were Lancashire textile towns. Only two, Leeds and Bradford, were in the West Riding woollen area. The relative lateness and slowness of changes in the woollen manufacture are indicated by the fact that in 1831 Bradford's population was only 23,200; Huddersfield had 19,035 and Halifax 15,382.[1]

It is not possible to determine precisely what proportions of the population were urban and rural in the earlier decades of the nineteenth century. One reason is that census returns were often made on the basis of parishes, which might include both urban and rural areas; another is the difficulty of determining the minimum population which a place ought to possess in order to be considered a town. If the figure be put as low as 2,000, it may be said that in 1801 there were in England and Wales 283 towns, with an aggregate population of 2,795,275, or approximately 31 per cent of the whole.[2] By 1831 the population of these 283 had grown to more than 6,000,000, and by 1841 to more than 7,450,000. That is, the inhabitants of these towns constituted about 46 per cent. of the population of England and Wales at Queen Victoria's accession. Two thousand is certainly rather low for an urban population; on the other hand, many of these towns had risen considerably above that level by 1841, so that 46 per cent., though probably excessive, is not a wildly exaggerated estimate of the urban population.

To say that out of every five persons in England and Wales three lived in the country and two in the town is not to say that 60 per cent. of the population was employed in or maintained by agriculture and that 40 per cent. depended on industry or commerce. The line between the two main

[1] For tables of the population of the principal towns in 1811, 1821 and 1831, see McCulloch, *op. cit.* pp. 405, 424.

[2] See T. A. Welton, 'On the Distribution of Population in England and Wales,' *Journal Royal Stat. Soc.* December 1900.

divisions cannot be drawn without some degree of arbitrariness, to include or exclude the engineers and artisans who made ploughs and threshing machines, the masons, bricklayers and carpenters who built barns and farm houses and the tailors who, in such areas as North Wales, travelled from farm to farm to make clothes for the inhabitants. Moreover there existed not only a large number of rural craftsmen—smiths, wheelwrights, saddlers and the like—but thousands of miners and quarrymen, about the industrial nature of whose occupation there can be no doubt, and who lived in areas which, though they might be populous, were not towns. The manufacture of textiles also, especially wool, had by no means been completely concentrated in towns and factories. Nevertheless, it is clear that the agricultural population, however it might be defined, was decreasing in proportion. In 1811 there were four English counties whose population was over 60 per cent. agricultural, and fourteen counties in which 50 per cent. or more of the population might be so described. By 1841, not a single county had a population 50 per cent. agricultural; in three the proportion was a little over 40 per cent. and in thirteen over 33 per cent.[1]

The declining proportion of the agricultural population cannot be satisfactorily traced from the beginning of the nineteenth century because the returns in the earlier censuses were on a different basis from that adopted in 1841. For the decade 1831 to 1841 the facts with regard to the occupations of males twenty years of age and upwards have been stated as follows:

Percentage employed in agriculture ...	1831	1841
In England and Wales	31·69	25·65
Scotland	30·4	27·88
Great Britain	31·51	25·93

If, instead of considering adult males only, we take into account the whole occupied population, the proportion will

[1] Porter, *Progress of the Nation* (1847), p. 58.

appear to be smaller. According to the census returns for 1841 the total occupied population of England and Wales was 6,706,920 persons, of whom 1,261,448, or approximately 18·8 per cent., were included under agriculture. For Scotland the percentage was 21·1. Even so, agriculture was far and away the greatest of British industries, at any rate in respect of the numbers employed in it. The next largest group of workers consisted of domestic servants, more than 999,000 in England and Wales in 1841, 765,000 being women and girls.[1] In comparison, the third largest group, the rapidly expanding cotton industry, seems small; it possibly contained 450,000, largely women, in 1835.[2] The building trades at that time may have included 400,000.[3] Mining, according to the 1841 returns, occupied 193,825 persons in Great Britain, of whom 118,233 were in or at coal mines. The same returns give the number of metal workers as 36,222 but the figure is incredibly small; of blacksmiths alone there were more than 97,000; of nail-makers more than 20,000; of brass-founders and the like over 13,000, and in the cutlery trades over 11,000.[4]

THE CONDITION OF THE PEOPLE

As we turn from the quantitative to the qualitative aspects of the British population, measurement becomes far more difficult; statistics tend to be scarce and imponderables to increase in importance. It is nevertheless necessary to attempt some estimate, for what kind of population then existed must in part have depended on the economic arrangements of the past and must also have influenced future economic development. The enactments of the Whig age of reform, especially the Factory Act of 1833 and the

[1] Porter, *Progress of the Nation* (1847), p. 50.
[2] Clapham I. 72. The returns for 1841 put the total for Great Britain at 377,662, of whom 197,283 were males. For the woollen and worsted industry the total is given as 167,296; for textiles as a whole, 800,246. See Porter, p. 74.
[3] Clapham I. 72.
[4] Porter, p. 79.

Municipal Reform Act of 1835, in time no doubt achieved a good deal of their purpose; but they can have brought about comparatively little increase in well-being before 1840. For the time being, at least, the need of reform was far greater than the means. It is indeed true that in some respects conditions had been improving for a long time. The plague disappeared after 1666 and smallpox, the eighteenth-century scourge, was far less frequent and fatal by 1836.[1] More scientific and productive farming during the eighteenth century, by providing more and fresher food and especially by making milk more easily obtainable during the winter, tended to reduce the death rate. Hospital treatment and medical knowledge had been improved, though in the organization of the medical profession and of training for it much remained to be done. On the other hand, there must be set against these factors tendencies in the opposite direction: the employment of larger numbers in industrial occupations, so far subject to little regulation; the more systematic and continuous employment of women; the more arduous labour in mines, mills and factories; and the crowding of people into towns.

The healthiness of country life, unless account be taken of rural poverty, can be exaggerated. "The sons and daughters of peasants," Malthus wrote, "will not be found such rosy cherubs in real life . . . the sons of labourers are very apt to be stunted in their growth and are a long while arriving at maturity. . . . And the lads who drive the plough, which must certainly be a healthy exercise, are very rarely seen with any appearance of calves to their legs, a circumstance which can only be attributed to a want either of proper or of sufficient, nourishment."[2] Still, that country life on the whole was healthier is clear from the difference between rural and urban death rates. In the Northumberland parishes of Chillingham and Chatton the average annual

[1] Porter, pp. 39–41.
[2] *Essay on the Principle of Population* (1798), p. 73.

mortality for the period from 1801 to 1837 was 1 in 165 and 1 in 112; in Alnwick, not far away, it was 1 in 49.[1] Glasgow, in comparison, was a death-trap; its mortality rate, which tended markedly to increase, between 1822 and 1839 never fell below 1 in 44·4 and in one year, 1832, rose as high as 1 in 21·7.[2] In areas with growing populations the mortality necessarily appeared higher, since the number of children was greater, and children in those times often had less than one chance in two of surviving infancy. At a time when, in England and Wales as a whole, 393 out of every thousand deaths were those of children under five, the proportion in Liverpool was 480 in every thousand; in Sheffield it was 506 and in Manchester and Salford, 517.[3] Those were days in which women might claim experience in the rearing of children because they had buried six. The heavy infant mortality reflected itself in the low average age at death and also, possibly, in the different averages for various social categories. Thus, for instance, in Bethnal Green in 1839, the average age at death in the families of gentlemen and the professional classes was forty-five years; in the families of tradesmen, twenty-six; and in those of mechanics and labourers, sixteen.[4]

Some of the heavy working-class mortality was attributable to the conditions in which particular trades were carried on. Sheffield grinders, for instance, commonly died of pulmonary phthisis. Of fifty-two London milliners and dressmakers dying in 1839, thirty-three perished of lung diseases at an average age of twenty-eight. Of tailors it was said that "a decline is the disease of which they generally die," an end to be expected when eighty of them might be found working in a room eighteen yards by eight at a temperature in summer-time twenty to thirty degrees higher

[1] *Journal Statist. Soc.* November 1838, p. 408.
[2] *Journal Statist. Soc.* October 1840, p. 265.
[3] G. Calvert Holland, *Vital Statistics of Sheffield* (1843), p. 104.
[4] *Report . . . from the Poor Law Commissioners on . . . the Sanitary Condition of the Labouring Population*, 1842, p. 159.

than the air outside.[1] Poverty increased the fatality from such causes. A competent observer wrote of Sheffield that "the deaths of hundreds in this town are to be traced to a deficiency of the necessaries of life. They may die of disease, but this is induced by poor living conjoined with laborious exertion."[2] The statement would doubtless apply to other towns both before and during the hungry 'forties.

Urban workers were not only subject to unhealthy conditions of employment; they and their families had also to put up with almost incredible filth and overcrowding in their homes. The appalling conditions of Manchester, as described by Engels,[3] were by no means unique. The same sort of gimcrack housing, hurriedly run up by speculative builders, existed in Sheffield[4] and a similar lack of sanitation in Liverpool and Leeds. Liverpool had indeed spent £100,000 in constructing sewers, but the working-class districts went without. Liquid refuse stagnated in courts and seeped into cellars. "In one cellar," it was said, "the filthy water thus collected measured not less than two feet in depth; and in another cellar a well, four feet deep, into which this stinking fluid was allowed to drain, was discovered below the bed where the family slept. . . . There are upwards of 8,000 inhabited cellars in Liverpool, and I estimate their occupants at from 35,000 to 40,000."[5] The condition of Leeds at its worst may be judged from a cul de sac containing thirty-four houses and 340 people, the Boot and Shoe Yard in Kirkgate, "whence the Commissioners removed, in the days of the cholera, seventy-five cart loads of manure, which had been untouched for years, and where there now exists a surface of human excrement of very considerable extent. . . . This property is said to pay the best annual rent of any cottage property in the borough."[6]

[1] *Report . . . from the Poor Law Commissioners on . . . the Sanitary Condition of the Labouring Population*, p. 98.
[2] Holland, *op. cit.* p. 111.
[3] *The Condition of the Working Class in England in 1844*, p. 45.
[4] Holland, *op. cit.* pp. 56–57.
[5] *Report . . . on the Sanitary Condition, etc.*, pp. 30–31.
[6] *ibid.* pp. 40–41.

It is thus evident that, from the point of view of economic progress, the condition of the working classes left much to be desired. Their working day was too long and their working lives were too short; their incomes and their productivity must have been considerably decreased by illness; and, despite the drastic changes in the Poor Law in 1834, there must have been a great loss in wealth through the sickness and death of heads and members of families, which threw them on the rates for support. It should, nevertheless, be remembered that, black as the picture was in Great Britain, there are grounds for believing that it was probably worse elsewhere. Between 1839 and 1842 the annual death rate in England and Wales was roughly 1 in 45 of the population; in France it is said to have been 1 in 40, and in Prussia, which must have suffered less from industrial diseases and urban overcrowding than this country, 1 in 36.[1]

To what extent the educational and moral condition of the population helped or hindered economic development, it is hardly possible to guess. The ideal working-man of the day, from the point of view of his betters, was one whose religion kept him sober, submissive to constituted authority, punctual and conscientious at work, thrifty and independent of parish relief; and it seems to be accepted that Nonconformity was especially influential in spreading an attitude of mind favourable to industrial development and unfavourable to political and social revolution.[2] On the other hand, it seems likely that, however strong its hold on the middle classes, it often had little attraction for those below them. A writer in 1840 declared, with little precision and possibly some exaggeration, that " the whole of the poorer classes are alienated from the Church . . . three-fourths or nine-tenths are neither church people nor of any other religion."[3] This indifference to organized religion was accompanied by a

[1] Porter, pp. 20–21.
[2] E. Halévy, *Histoire du Peuple Anglais*, I. 401.
[3] Quoted in J. L. and B. Hammond, *The Age of the Chartists*, p. 242.

high, if hardly measurable, degree of illiteracy. It was calculated that in Birmingham in 1838 over 51 per cent. of the children between 5 and 15 years of age were not receiving instruction either in day schools or in Sunday schools[1], and similar conditions existed elsewhere.[2] Inevitably, this degree of illiteracy hindered the attempt, then only in its early stages, to increase by education the efficiency of British industrial workers in accord with the technical changes which had been in progress for more than a century. The old system of apprenticeship was still practically the only means of passing on information and skill from one generation of craftsmen and professional men to another. It was indeed supplemented to some extent by printed manuals and other books; but these, even when relatively cheap, could have been useful only to a minority of workmen.[3] With the steam engine there came a need for new kinds of skill to deal with problems in which the ingenuity of millwrights was no longer sufficient. Some were settled by flashes of genius; but the discoveries of James Watt and others of his kind made necessary a host of pedestrian, if clever, craftsmen and engineers to construct and use new tools. Men of this sort, as well as artisans of genius, were trained in the workshops of such men as Boulton and Watt in Soho, Henry Maudslay in London and Richard Roberts in Manchester; but it was no part of the business of these firms to arrange for systematic and scientific instruction for their workmen. Occasionally, an exceptional workman might benefit by academic instruction, as Joseph Clement did from a course on natural philosophy at Aberdeen in 1812–1813[4]; but such courses were rare, and available in only a few towns; moreover, most

[1] *Journal Stat. Soc.* 1849, p. 25.

[2] In part of Newcastle, for instance, 31 per cent. of children between three and fifteen years of age could not read and 55·5 per cent. could not write (*Journal Stat. Soc.* 1839–40, p. 357). On the question of education see Hammond, *op. cit.* pp. 168 *et seq.*

[3] Some were more easily available because they could be bought in parts: *e.g.*, T. Sheraton's *Cabinet-Maker's and Upholsterer's Drawing-Book*, third edition, in forty-nine parts, £2 12s. 0d.; bound in boards, £2 14s. 0d.

[4] Smiles, *Industrial Biography*, p. 240.

workmen must have been incapable of following them, even had there been an opportunity, through lack of arithmetical and other knowledge.

This defect was realized by the workmen themselves who, with the assistance of benevolent employers and others, took steps to remedy it. Inspired by Neilson, the inventor of the hot blast, some employees of the Glasgow Gas Works formed an association to establish a library and lectures, and were provided with a room and light by the firm.[1] Dr. Birkbeck, in 1800, delivered a course of lectures for artisans in Glasgow and in 1823 founded the first Mechanics' Institute in London. Similar institutes were rapidly started in other towns; by 1850, there were 622 of them in England and Wales, with a membership of more than 600,000.[2] Nevertheless, the aims of the founders were far from being realized; in some centres especially the Institute did little but teach the three R's, and a large proportion of the members consisted of people who were not mechanics. Meanwhile, the State, whose assistance was vitally necessary, did little to further technical instruction and only moved at a snail's pace with elementary education. The Board of Trade in 1837 established a School of Design in London, and in 1841 government grants became possible for such schools elsewhere. Seventeen of them existed by 1852.[3]

THE LAND AND ITS PRODUCE

For their sustenance, in the unlikely event of a war and the utter cessation of foreign commerce, the seventeen and a half million people living in Great Britain in 1837 would have to depend on what could be produced from a total area of about 56,800,000 statute acres. Naturally, part of this would have to be deducted, as incapable of yielding anything more substantial than the delight of poets, artists and sports-

[1] Smiles, *Industrial Biography* p., 153.
[2] Abbott, *Education for Industry and Commerce in England*, pp. 14–15.
[3] *ibid.* pp. 23–24.

men. According to a calculation made in 1827,[1] some 3,256,000 acres in England, 1,105,000 in Wales and 8,524,000 in Scotland were unprofitable. There was, besides, much land which, though capable of yielding produce, was uncultivated. The estimate of 1827 puts the position as follows:

CULTIVABLE AREA IN ACRES (000's neglected)

	Total area	Cultivated	Uncultivated	Unprofitable
England	32,342	25,632	3,454	3,256
Wales	4,752	3,117	530	1,105
Scotland	19,739	5,265	5,950	8,524

During the eighteenth century, and especially since 1760, the cultivated area had been extended and farming improved[2] by successful experiments in the breeding of stock, by better systems of crop rotation, the reduction of fallow, the use of more and better manures, implements and drainage, and by the substitution of separate and enclosed holdings for the large open fields and the more communal system of cultivation which, in many parts of the country, had lingered on from the middle ages and which, here and there, as in the Nottinghamshire parish of Laxton, still survive. It was, no doubt, possible for enclosure to take place without the improvements which, in general, were the ostensible justification of it, and it had the unhappy social consequence of reducing the independence of the tillers of the soil. Nevertheless, an expert authority, taking a favourable view of the older system, cannot but admit that " for the balance of national advantage, it was necessary that the open fields should go."[3] The class of small-scale occupying owners had largely disappeared before 1780; thence to the end of the French Wars economic circumstances were more

[1] Porter, p. 158.

[2] For an account of the improvements, which are outside the scope of the present volume, see, *e.g.*, Lord Ernle, *English Farming Past and Present*, chapters VIII to X.

[3] C. S. Orwin, in *Econ. Hist. Rev.* May 1938, p. 134.

favourable to them; but after 1815 decline set in once more.[1] In the early nineteenth century, therefore, British agriculture had reached a stage of organization which it retained throughout the century and which distinguished it from the agricultural systems prevalent over large parts of the Continent, where peasant proprietorship was the rule. In Great Britain, on the contrary, the large mass of occupiers of land consisted of tenants on lease, often a short lease. The size of their farms varied a good deal; many were small; in 1831 there were nearly 95,000 occupiers of land who employed no labour, other than that of their families probably. The number of occupiers who did employ labour was 141,460; but not all of these were resident farmers or lived by farming alone. The average size of the farms cultivated by people who made that their sole or principal business may have been as high as 150 or 160 acres.[2]

In the absence of censuses of production, little can be said about the yield of British agriculture in and before 1837, though there is good ground for believing that in general British farming was in advance of that ordinarily practised on the Continent. An indication of that is the greater importance of wheat in comparison with rye, then and later the main bread-crop of Germany. In parts of Wales and Northern England, especially Durham, miscelin, or wheat and rye in various proportions, was still sown; barley bread was not uncommon, being the ordinary bread in Wales and the Lake District. Elsewhere, in Norfolk, Suffolk, Bedford, Leicestershire, Nottinghamshire, Warwickshire, Shropshire and part of Herefordshire, though a good deal of barley was grown, it was raised chiefly for malting or for cattle food. Oats were extensively grown in the northernmost counties of England, in Lancashire, Wales, parts of Cheshire, Derby and Stafford and in Northamptonshire, as well as the counties of Huntingdon, Cambridge and

[1] E. Davies, in *Econ. Hist. Rev.* January 1927, pp. 112–113.
[2] McCulloch, *op. cit.* I. 446–447.

Norfolk. In Scotland, where oats could be grown more successfully than other cereals, the proportion of oats to other grain was at least seven to one.[1] There, as in some parts of England and Wales, much of the crop was consumed in the form of porridge and oatcake foods, on which the inhabitants of Scotland and the Cumberland dales throve the more easily because they had milk and butter with them. In England, as Dr. Johnson observed, oats were largely used as provender for horses. That was probably even more the case in the earlier nineteenth century, when horses were superseding oxen in agriculture, and road transport and communication were developing rapidly. It has been computed that in 1839 there were at least 1,500,000 horses in Great Britain; and their sustenance must have amounted to a great deal.[2]

Wheat, by the nineteenth century, could be grown with success in many parts of Great Britain, from the Moray Firth down to the English Channel; but the wheat counties *par excellence* were all in the south, and most of them in the south-east; they were Kent, Essex, Suffolk, Rutland, Hertfordshire, Berkshire, Hampshire and Herefordshire. Thence, no doubt, came the bulk of the grain which until comparatively late in the eighteenth century not only sufficed for home consumption but in good years left something for export. The growth of population and the difficulty of getting foreign supplies stimulated the production of wheat in this country during the Napoleonic wars; but the importation during the first ten years of the nineteenth century was on the average more than 600,000 quarters a year, or sufficient for the consumption of from 600,000 to 800,000 people. In the second decade, the importation decreased; but it rose markedly in the third and fourth. Between 1831 and 1840 the average was over 900,000 quarters, which would suffice for somewhere between 900,000 and 1,200,000 persons. In the first four

[1] McCulloch I. 479.

[2] *ibid.* p. 484.

years of the "hungry forties" the rise continued, showing clearly that, when all allowance has been made for variations in the weather and in harvests, the population and its standard of corn consumption was increasing more rapidly than the capacity of the country, with the arts of husbandry as they then were, to supply it.[1]

The situation, in the eyes of some contemporary observers, was not serious, or was the less so, because they believed that the gap could be filled by means of potatoes. Weight for weight, it was admitted, mealy potatoes contained far less nourishment than wheaten flour; on the other hand, the yield per acre was far greater. In Cheshire and Oxfordshire, for example, potato crops might average over 350 bushels to the acre,[2] while very good wheat crops could not amount to much more than 45 to 50 bushels on the same area. If, as was then believed, 1 lb. of wheat could be regarded as equivalent to 4 lbs. of potatoes, the greater utility of potato-growing is clear. It is certainly true that the cultivation of this crop, which was hardly possible under the old open-field system, was widespread by 1837. But Cobbett, in 1832 as earlier, regarded the increase as a loss. Where, as in Northumberland and Durham, he found few potato fields, he regarded their absence as "a certain sign that the working people do not live like hogs."[3]

The staple food of the people, he considered, should consist not of potatoes but of bread and meat; but to what extent they could obtain the latter is anything but clear. There can be no doubt that improvement of breeds, and the use of turnips and clover as cattle food, had greatly increased the numbers and weight of cattle and sheep. Of the former there may have been in Great Britain some 5,200,000 in 1839; rather more than 1,300,000, besides cattle imported from Ireland, were annually slaughtered for consumption.[4]

[1] For import figures see Porter, pp. 137–9.
[2] McCulloch I. 476.
[3] *Rural Rides* (Everyman), II. 291.
[4] McCulloch I. 490.

To a modern view, however, the increase in cattle may be most significant not as providing more beef but as the source of vast quantities of milk and butter. London alone, it was computed, required over 38,000,000 quarts of the one and 29,000,000 lbs. of the other in the earlier years of Queen Victoria's reign. Of sheep, Great Britain had perhaps thirty-nine or forty millions, the breeds varying a good deal in weight and fineness both of fleece and mutton. Broadly speaking, the experiments of Bakewell and others had greatly improved the latter at the cost of some deterioration in the former.[1] Nevertheless, though large quantities were imported at various times from Spain, Germany and other countries, the wool of British sheep was vitally necessary for the looms and mills of the West Riding. It seems impossible to determine the home production with exactness. It was perhaps about 130,000,000 lbs. in 1846; in 1849, over 76,700,000 lbs. were imported, including nearly 36,000,000 lbs. from Australia.[2]

MINERALS

In the course of the nineteenth century Great Britain was driven to draw the bread and meat of its population in large part from the ends of the earth, a development possible only because of its vast subterranean riches, especially in coal and iron. In Scotland, where coal was dug as early as the eleventh century, that mineral was found in a rich field stretching across the country from the Clyde to the Forth and especially in the counties of Fife, Midlothian, Lanark and Ayr. The importance of these coal measures was increased by their proximity to the carboniferous or Black Band ironstone, discovered by David Mushet in 1801, though it was not until Neilson had patented the hot blast in 1828 that this ore could be satisfactorily treated. In the northern counties of England the coal-fields are separated by the Pennines:

[1] McCulloch I. 496.

[2] Thomas Southey, *The Rise, Progress and Present State of Colonial Sheep and Wools, etc.* (1851), pp. 4, 6.

on the western coast of Cumberland was the relatively small field in which Workington and Whitehaven were the chief centres; while on the eastern side was the much larger field of Northumberland and Durham, whose coal had perhaps warmed the legionaries who kept the Roman Wall and which, almost until the last decade of the nineteenth century, was to remain the most productive in the country. Near to the Cumberland coal there existed supplies of haematite iron; near the Northumbrian, the Cleveland ore, worked extensively only after 1850. Further south, the coal measures of Lancashire and Cheshire, on which Burnley, Wigan and St. Helens stand, were more than counterbalanced by the large coal-field stretching from a point north of Leeds down to the confines of Nottingham. To the west of this were the small fields, in the counties of Stafford, Shropshire, Worcester, Warwick and Leicester, on which the industries of the Black Country were based; and south of these again, the coal of Bristol and Somerset and of the Forest of Dean, with its ancient organization of free-miners. Wales had two coal-fields, one in Denbighshire and Flintshire, and the other, far richer and more extensive, including parts of the counties of Monmouth, Glamorgan, Caermarthen and Pembroke.

Newcomen's engine, in the early eighteenth century, and Watt's steam engine, more effectively after 1775, stimulated coal-mining by overcoming the difficulty caused by water in the pits, and Sir Humphrey Davy's lamp, after 1815, provided adequate illumination with safety. The improvement of canals was especially important in giving the coal of the inland fields ready access to areas hitherto supplied, with greater difficulty, by sea and land carriage.[1] After the

[1] " Vast quantities of coal are annually sent out of the counties of Derby and Nottingham southward, by means of the Cromford, Derby, Erewash, Grantham, Leicester, Melton Mowbray, Nottingham, Nutbrook and Trent canals or navigations, and others with which these connect " (John Farey, writing in 1811, quoted in 1871 Coal Commission Report, Vol. III, p. 34). The Erewash canal carried over 250,000 tons in 1803, over 316,000 tons in 1833 and over 330,000 tons in 1843 (*Ibid.* Vol. III, p. 33).

opening of the Stockton and Darlington line in 1825 and the Manchester and Liverpool in 1830, the railways gave a further impetus, both by their own demand for fuel and for iron and steel and by their services as coal carriers. At the same time, the use of coal gas for lighting, an improvement adopted in London after 1807, raised a new and increasing demand. It is not possible to trace the effects of these developments on the total British output of coal during the earlier nineteenth century; indeed, the estimates for as late a date as 1854 are very uncertain. But there is some ground for believing that between 1800 and 1839 the total output of the United Kingdom rose from about 10,000,000 tons annually to about 31,000,000 tons.[1] Neither France nor Belgium in 1839 raised 3,000,000 tons, and Prussia in 1837 yielded only a little over 1,500,000 tons. It may thus be said that the coal mines of Great Britain a century ago provided approximately four times as much as the three most important coal-producing countries on the Continent.

Among minerals of less, but still of considerable, importance were tin, copper, lead and salt. The output of Cornish tin rose from 2,522 tons in 1800 to 4,180 tons in 1834.[2] The same county was the main source of copper, producing 5,187 tons in 1800 and 11,527 tons in 1838; by that time the Parys Mountain copper of Anglesey, once considerable and energetically exploited by Thomas Williams, was nearing exhaustion.[3] Salt, the production of which was stimulated by the reduction of the excise in 1823 and its removal in 1825, was found mainly in the Cheshire "wiches," though brine springs existed also in Staffordshire and Worcestershire. The increase in output is indicated by the growth in the quantity sent down the River Weaver, 180,236 tons in 1803 and 390,480 tons in 1838.[4] Of the

[1] 1871 Coal Commission Report, pp. 32, 61; for French, Belgian and Prussian outputs see pp. 208, 211, 219.
[2] In 1827 it reached 5,316 tons; see Porter, p. 273.
[3] Dodd, *The Industrial Revolution in North Wales*, p. 162.
[4] Porter, p. 287.

output a little more than half was exported. In marked contrast to the minerals so far noted, lead, which in past times had constituted an important export, was declining in Derbyshire,[1] Somersetshire[2] and in the Welsh counties of Flint and Denbigh.[3] The chief reason appears to have been the plenty of foreign ore available at a time when the British workings were deep and costly.

HIGHWAYS AND WATERWAYS

Though, by Queen Victoria's accession, the first modern railway had been running for twelve years, the railway time-table had by no means made unnecessary its forerunner, the road-book.[4] How useful that kind of compilation was in its day, and how important the highway was at the end of the pre-railway age, may be gathered from the pages of Cary's *New Itinerary* in, for instance, the edition of 1821. In that official publication, as in a map of Roman Britain and the modern *Bradshaw*, the predominance of London is plain. From 51 metropolitan centres, nearly all of them inns, no fewer than 795 mail and other coaches set out for various destinations. Some of these inns, such as the White Hart in St. John Street, provided a terminus for only two or three coaches; but others saw the departure of dozens. From the Golden Cross in Charing Cross fifty-six coaches set out; the departure of these, with the arrival of others travelling in the reverse direction, meant a great and almost continuous bustle from before half-past six in the morning until after nine at night. A considerable, if lesser, activity occurred at the Angel in the Strand, with its twenty-three coaches, the Bull and Crown in Holborn, with twenty-five, the George and Blue Boar in Holborn, with twenty-nine, the Cross Keys in Cheapside, with thirty-four, the Bull and

[1] *V.C.H.* Derby, II. 247.
[2] *V.C.H.* Somerset, II. 378.
[3] Dodd, *op. cit.*, p. 176.
[4] In 1837 there appeared the sixth edition of *Leigh's New Pocket Road Book of England and Wales.*

Mouth, with thirty-seven, and the Spur, in the Borough, with thirty-nine.

From London there radiated a vast net-work of roads, in which the main routes were connected by innumerable cross roads, and both at the ends and junctions there were provincial centres whose coach traffic, if less than that of the metropolis, was still of the same kind. Gainsborough, apparently, was served by only two coaches of its own; Hereford managed with half a dozen; Cheltenham provided business for sixteen; Liverpool required no fewer than ninety-eight.

For more than a century the highways had been undergoing improvement—patchy and piece-meal, but, in the aggregate, considerable—through active justices of the peace, the pressure of the Post Office, which was concerned about its mails, and of the Board of Agriculture, anxious to give farmers better access to markets. The development of a new type of authority, the turnpike trust, many as the faults and difficulties of such bodies were, had given the better methods of road maintenance and administration evolved by Telford and McAdam a chance to spread; in consequence, the transport facilities existing in the age of the Reform Bill, poor and slow as they may appear by modern standards, were remarkably good in comparison with the facilities of 1750. Then, Manchester had one coach running to London and taking four days and a half for the journey, though the Flying Machine was advertised in 1760 as covering the distance in three days, "if God permit."[1] By 1837, the mail coach travelled approximately the same distance, from London to Chester, in just over seventeen and a half hours, that is, at a pace of nearly eleven miles an hour. Over a longer distance the pace was, naturally, not so good; the 396 miles between London and Glasgow took forty hours and forty minutes, so that the average speed was 9·9 miles to the hour.[2]

[1] Smiles, *Lives of the Engineers* (1874), I. 163.
[2] Mail time-tables are given in *Leigh's New Pocket Road Book* (1837), pp. 454 *et seq.*

To supplement road transport there existed a system of inland navigation which, by 1830, included—besides about 800 miles of open river—such as the Severn, Mersey and Humber—some 3,400 miles of waterway.[1] The growth of this network, the construction of which began in earnest with the collaboration of the Duke of Bridgwater and James Brindley on the Worsley canal, opened in 1761, lies outside our present purview; but it is necessary to consider the usefulness of the system when complete. After allowance has been made for the difficulty of construction in this country, which, unlike Holland, the classic land of canals, is not flat, the extent of the system is not unimpressive. Brindley's canals and others joined the Thames, Severn, Mersey, Trent and Humber. The Pennines were crossed at three points by the Leeds and Liverpool, the Rochdale and the Huddersfield canals. Scotland was crossed by the Forth and Clyde and the Caledonian canals. South of Durham, it was said, there was no point more than fifteen miles from water transport of some kind. The stimulus which canal construction gave to industry was especially evident in the Potteries, which previously had only been able to bring in their clay and send out their china and earthenware expensively by horse or mule transport; after the construction of the Grand Trunk canal the output, and the population, increased rapidly. Perhaps the greatest advantage of inland navigation lay in easing and cheapening the distribution of coal, both for industrial and for domestic consumption; but the cheapening applied to the carriage of other goods as well. "The cost of inland transport," according to Baines[2], "was reduced to about one-fourth of the rate paid previous to the introduction of canal navigation. . . . Wheat which formerly could not be conveyed a

[1] This consisted of 1,927 miles of canal and 1,312 miles of improved and straightened river in England and Wales, together with 183 miles of canal and other navigation in Scotland. See Knowles, *Industrial and Commercial Revolutions*, p. 243.

[2] Thomas Baines, *History of the Commerce and Town of Liverpool* (1852), p. 440.

hundred miles . . . for less than 20s. a-quarter, could be conveyed for about 5s. a-quarter."

Nevertheless, however well it may have answered the needs of the eighteenth century, the system of inland navigation was in several respects inadequate for the nineteenth, largely because it had not been thought out as a whole and in relation to probable future developments. Thus the various acts enabling parts of the system to be constructed had not imposed uniformity in depth or breadth, with the result that a consigner could not be sure of sending his goods in the same vessel if they had to pass from one canal to another on the way. Indeed, not only was uniformity lacking as between one canal and another, but, with regard to the dimensions of locks, it might be lacking between different parts of the same canal. Reliance on optimistic private enterprise resulted, in some instances, in very heavy costs being undertaken in cutting canals where there was insufficient prospect of remuneration. It is thus not astonishing that, even before railway competition began, some canals made very small profits or none at all. To this fault—the lack of plan and control—which might have been avoided, another was inevitably added. Since the earlier canals were cut before Watt's engine had been patented and long before Stephenson's locomotive had been invented, the possibility of steam traction could not be foreseen, and the depth and breadth of canals in general were calculated only for horse traction.

CHAPTER II

Fifty Years of Progress in Transport and Communication

RAILWAY DEVELOPMENT, 1825–1850

In its complete and modern sense, a railway must have at least three characteristics: it must possess a special kind of road or track, must use locomotive traction upon it, and must, ordinarily, be the only carrier operating over its own line. These three developments came at different times and were by no means indissolubly linked when what is regarded as the first modern railway, the Stockton and Darlington line, was opened in 1825. The special track was then more than two hundred years old, for coal was transported in that way from Wollaton to the Trent Bridge near Nottingham as early as 1609.[1] That early railway probably consisted of nothing more elaborate than wooden planks, and a similar method was used much later, as, for instance, in the two-mile tramway laid down in 1774 by the agent of the ninth Duke of Norfolk for the carriage of coals to Sheffield.[2] Wooden rails, however, gave way to iron ones about 1738,[3] and the Coalbrookdale firm was making cast-iron rails for its own traffic in 1767.[4] The greater ease of transit on such tram roads, whether flat or inclined, led to their increasing use, especially in the coal-mining regions of Northumberland and Durham and in South Wales and the Forest of Dean; in these areas there were 450 miles or more of railway, in some instances constructed at great cost, before

[1] *Hist. MSS. Comm., Middleton MSS.*, p. 172.

[2] R. E. Leader, *Sheffield in the Eighteenth Century*, pp. 84–85. The track was re-laid with iron rails in 1776, according to Smiles, *Lives of the Engineers* (1862), III. 7.

[3] Smiles, *loc. cit.*

[4] *ibid.*

the locomotive was available to draw waggons along them.[1] When George Stephenson had shown, with his second engine in 1815, that steam traction was an economic advantage, it might be thought that the railway would soon be familiar in all parts of the country; but it was ten years before Stephenson was given a real chance, and even after the successful demonstration of the locomotive's capabilities in 1825 the battle had not been won. The directors of the Liverpool and Manchester line hesitated a good deal before deciding that locomotives would be better and cheaper than stationary engines.[2] Indeed, even after the trials at Rainhill in 1829, which settled the question of traction for all but a small piece of that line, the future of the railway as a means of transport was still not quite assured.

Useful as the locomotive had proved to be on the flats of South Lancashire, its powers on a rising track remained to be discovered, and in the meanwhile railway builders might well wonder whether it would be worth while to spend large sums in embanking, in order to keep the track as level as possible, or whether the further improvement of the locomotive would enable it, without a great increase in fuel costs, to climb steeper gradients than those hitherto constructed. It was, moreover, still considered possible in some quarters that steam traction would be found most useful not on special tracks but in town streets and on turnpike roads. Between 1833 and 1836 Walter Hancock had carried over 12,000 passengers in his steam omnibuses plying between Paddington and the City Road[3]; in 1832 and 1833 he ran similar conveyances between London and Brighton; and projects for steam-coach services to Bath and Birmingham were formed. Respectable engineering opinion could be quoted in favour of steam carriages[4]; but

[1] Clapham I. 87.
[2] G. S. Veitch, *The Struggle for the Liverpool and Manchester Railway* (1930), pp. 58–59.
[3] C. E. R. Sherrington, *A Hundred Years of Inland Transport*, pp. 52–53.
[4] Clapham I. 386.

the turnpike trusts strongly opposed them and imposed heavy tolls upon them, fearing, no doubt, that an increase in such traffic would make road maintenance impossibly expensive.

In view of this attitude, engineers interested in rapid transport turned their attention wholly to the special track. This, when constructed, was apt to be regarded in much the same way as a turnpike or a canal; that is, the company owning it was expected to draw its revenue from tolls on the traffic and not necessarily to monopolize ownership of the vehicles plying upon it. Experience very soon showed that it was impossible to run both horse-drawn and steam-propelled traffic on the same lines or to allow both the company's and privately owned locomotives and rolling stock to use them. Accordingly, a Select Committee in 1839 reported that "the safety of the public requires that upon every railway there should be one system of management under one superintending authority. . . . On this account it is necessary that the Company should possess a complete control over their line of road, although they should thereby acquire an entire monopoly."[1] That admission indicates that the railway, as we know it, was already in existence.

The second quarter of the nineteenth century corresponds broadly with the period when the main trunk of the British railway system was constructed; but the bulk of the work was done after 1830, and especially in two active periods, 1835 to 1840 and 1844 to 1848.[2] By the end of the latter year about 4,600 miles of railway were open for traffic. The railway map then showed, as a foundation, a large St. Andrew's cross, with the arms intersecting at Birmingham. London was connected by means of relatively short lines with Southampton, Dover and Colchester. Northwards

[1] Cleveland-Stevens, *English Railways*, p. 11.

[2] The mileages (see Lewin, *Early British Railways*, p. 186 and Clapham II. 181) open at various periods were as follows: 1825—26¾; 1830—97½; 1835—337¾; 1840—1,497½; 1844—2,235¾; 1848—4,646.

the line ran from the capital via Rugby to Birmingham, thence by the Grand Junction to Crewe (whence there was railway connection to Chester and Birkenhead and to Manchester) and onwards by the North Union, cutting across the Liverpool and Manchester, to Warrington, Preston, Lancaster and Carlisle, a point which the railway reached in December 1846.[1] The other arm of the cross may be regarded as starting at Berwick and running south through Newcastle and Darlington to York, and then through Rotherham to Derby, Birmingham, Gloucester, Bristol and even to Taunton and Exeter. Bristol, on the south-western arm of the cross, was connected, through Swindon and Reading, with London. Further north, the eastern and western coasts were connected, though not very directly, by the Hull and Selby line and continuations through Leeds and Manchester to Liverpool; and still further north by the Newcastle and Carlisle line, extended to Maryport.[2] It will be observed that one important branch of the system, the line from Chester to Holyhead, was not finished in 1848, though it was well on the way; the tubular bridge carrying the line over the Menai Strait was opened for traffic in March 1850.[3] Scotland was linked to England by both the eastern and western coasts. The Edinburgh and Glasgow line, opened in 1842, reached Berwick by 1846; but the line was not completely continuous until the Tweed viaduct had been opened in 1850.[4] Carlisle had been joined to Glasgow and Edinburgh in 1848.[5]

A modern reader, three generations later, merely looking at pictures of the earlier railways, with their squat rolling stock and curiously funnelled locomotives, may easily underestimate the magnitude of the achievement. In fact,

[1] For details of the lines ultimately absorbed in the London and North Western, Midland, Great Western and other systems, see Lewin, *op. cit.*, which is provided with excellent maps.

[2] Sherrington, *op. cit.*, p. 114.

[3] Smiles, *Lives of the Engineers*, III. 439.

[4] *ibid.* p. 415.

[5] Sherrington, p. 114.

the effort was titanic. An older generation was wont to measure it by comparison with the energy used in building the Great Pyramid, which was supposed to have occupied at least 100,000 men for twenty years. One railway line alone, the London and Birmingham, was said to represent two and a half times that effort. A single tunnel, at Littleborough on the Midland line, required 23,000,000 bricks and 8,000 tons of cement to line the arch hewn out of solid rock.[1] The Britannia tubular bridge, joining Caernarvonshire to Anglesey, and the high level bridge at Newcastle still impress those who see them with the vastness of the works of which they are a part, and there is, perhaps, no better symbol of the difference between the railway age and its predecessor than a picture of the latter bridge, riding majestically about ninety feet above the old bridge near its feet.

The construction of the railway system was beset with difficulties, physical, technical, political and financial. It had to be discovered by George Stephenson how a railway could be securely based on the vast sponge of Chat Moss, and by him and his son Robert how a tunnel could be cut through unexpected quicksands. To the brute resistance of nature there was added the costlier opposition of landed proprietors and defenders of the old order. Lord Derby's keepers sabotaged the survey for the Liverpool and Manchester,[2] and so did Lord Sefton's. County meetings were held in Northamptonshire, Buckinghamshire, Hertfordshire and Middlesex to resist the London and Birmingham. The town of Northampton, indeed, refused to be on the line and compelled it to go round about and to construct the Kilsby tunnel, at a cost of £300,000. Such opposition may be regarded in part as a phase of the battle between the powers who ruled before 1832 and the new interests for whose dominance the great Reform Bill opened the way; for the supporters of the earlier railway projects

[1] Smiles, *op. cit.* III. 331. [2] Smiles, *ibid.* p. 193.

were especially merchants and industrialists, in Newcastle, Leeds, Manchester, Liverpool and Bristol, interested not merely in railway dividends but in speedy communications and the expansion of trade, and it took some time for the owners of broad acres and their tenant farmers to see that railways were more likely to enrich than to ruin them. It has been computed that in 1832, when the bill for the London and Birmingham was introduced in Parliament, the owners of nearly seven-eighths of the land required for that line were opposed to the bill, which, after an expenditure of £32,000, was rejected. In the following year, after another £40,000 had been spent, it was passed; the opposition had meanwhile been conciliated by the company's agreeing to pay £750,000 for land originally estimated to cost £250,000.[1] When it was perceived that railways increased land values, the appetite for high compensation remained; the Duke of Bedford returned as overpayment £150,000 out of the sum he had received;[2] but such fairness of mind was probably very rare indeed. It is thus little wonder that the cost per mile, in land and compensation, was high; on the Great Western it was nearly £6,700 and on the London and Brighton £8,000.

It might have been expected that the construction of more than 4,500 miles of railway in less than twenty years would require an amount of capital not to be raised without great difficulty; and it is significant that neither in France nor in Germany was it contemplated that such a task could be achieved, as it was in Great Britain, without assistance from the State. The railway capital authorized prior to 1844 amounted to £83,848,000; thence to 1848 another £267,284,000 was authorized.[3] The total, of more than £352,000,000, could perhaps have been raised without any very great strain if it had been possible to spread the operation fairly evenly over the whole period; but railway

[1] John Francis, *A History of the English Railway* (1851), I. 189.
[2] Pratt, *History of Inland Transport and Communication*, p. 254.
[3] Cleveland-Stevens, p. 24,

development was not effectively planned and controlled by the State, and the attempt was made to raise enormous sums in two periods of speculation, the first in 1836–37 and the second, far more frenzied and disastrous, in 1845.[1] In the promotion of the earlier railways the London money market was comparatively little concerned, and the backing was found mainly in the provinces. Behind the Stockton and Darlington stood Pease and his Quaker friends; behind the Liverpool and Manchester the merchant houses of Sandars, Booth, Rathbone and the like; and it is said that seven-eighths of the capital of the London and Birmingham were owned in Lancashire.[2] But in 1836 " blind capital seeking its five per cent." intervened,[3] and nine years later the purlieus of Moorgate Street and Gresham Street poured out schemes which, at best, were impossibly optimistic and, at worst, callously fraudulent. By that time there was a real need for the extension of the railway network, and clear proof, in the dividends of the older lines, that respectable incomes could be earned; money, as the low discount rate in 1843–44 showed, was abundant; the attitude of government was favourable to the multiplication of railways as a corrective of monopoly; and landowners had ceased to be hostile. The result was a burst of promotion and speculation in which " peers and printers, vicars and vice-admirals . . . professors and cotton-spinners . . . attorneys' clerks and college scouts . . . bankers, beer sellers and butlers " took part. Their clamour for railway shares is indicated by the quotations in July 1845, when Midland £100 shares were at £187, Great Western £80 (paid) at £205, and London and Birmingham £100 shares at £243.[4] The peak came in August, reaction in October and widespread ruin thereafter; the shares of the Great Western, which reached £236 during August, fell to £154 by the end of October and £144 by the

[1] In 1846, railway acts authorized a capital of £132,617,000.
[2] Clapham I. 387.
[3] *ibid.* I. 388.
[4] Pratt, *op. cit.* p. 275.

end of November.[1] In 1850 an Act was passed to enable defunct railway projects to be legally buried; in accord with its terms 1,560 miles of projected railway were abandoned, and a further 2,000 miles were abandoned otherwise. Thus, of the 8,592 miles authorized in 1845–7, less than 60 per cent. was actually constructed.[2]

From one point of view, the first phase of railway history may be regarded as ending with the death of George Stephenson in August 1848. His contribution to railway development, when every allowance has been made for the experiments of his predecessors and the work of his contemporaries, was still remarkable. He first made the locomotive, which he found as something between an erratic curiosity and a public nuisance, an economic success; and he was the first effective maker of locomotives for railway purposes. He was also a civil engineer of genius and pertinacity, and the teacher of the first generation of railway engineers, among whom his son, Robert Stephenson, earned a high place by the construction not only of the London and Birmingham but of other lines in this country and abroad. The chief competitor of the Stephensons, and like them an outstanding figure, was Isambard Kingdom Brunel, the engineer of the Great Western and famous as the constructor of the amazing, but commercially unsuccessful, vessel, the *Great Eastern*. Brunel's was the more daring, the Stephensons' the more cautious, mind. He was an innovator, eager to try every new device and aiming at the highest technical excellence; they tended to move more slowly and to introduce technical improvements only when they were satisfied that the shareholders would not lose by them. It is characteristic that George Stephenson, who started his career by tending cows at twopence a day, left behind him a fortune in railway shares, engine works and collieries, and that his son was a millionaire, while Brunel lost a consider-

[1] D. Morier Evans, *The Commercial Crisis 1847–1848*, p. 20.
[2] Pratt, *op. cit.* p. 273.

able sum by investing in failures such as the *Great Eastern*.

The rivalry of the Stephensons and Brunel showed itself especially in connection with two problems, the means of traction and the railway gauge. Brunel believed firmly in the possibility and advantage of using compressed air instead of the steam locomotive. This method, patented in 1840 by Clegg and Samuda, was demonstrated on part of the West London Railway with sufficient success to induce the directors of the Dublin and Kingston line to use it on an extension of their line to Dalkey, but the experience gained from that line, which was less than two miles long, can have had little value. A similar method was used on part of the Croydon railway in 1846, and in September 1847 it was tried out on the South Devon Railway. During six months in 1848 the expenses exceeded the gross income by nearly 10 per cent., and in 1849, with a return to the use of steam locomotives, the history of atmospheric traction ended, not to the advantage of Brunel's reputation.[1]

His other error of judgment, if such it was, took much longer to rectify and had a greater and more prolonged influence on railway development. The Stockton and Darlington had been laid down on a gauge of 4 feet 8½ inches, which was common among the tram roads in its neighbourhood and which avoided the necessity of a new and different type of coal-waggon. Since there was no ground for dissatisfaction with this gauge, it was adopted on the Liverpool and Manchester and the London and Birmingham, and there was naturally an advantage in using it also for all lines which might connect with them. Brunel, however, persuaded the directors of the Great Western to adopt a gauge of 7 feet. The broad gauge may have enabled greater speed to be attained with safety and more comfort to be provided for passengers; but, by requiring more land, it made construction much more costly; and the existence of

[1] On atmospheric traction see Smiles, *op. cit.* III. 369–372 and Sherrington, pp. 92–93.

different gauges hindered co-operation and co-ordination of railway enterprises. One of the first results of the adoption of the broad gauge by the Great Western was the inevitable abandonment of a scheme for a joint terminus at Euston for the Great Western and the London and Birmingham, a step which might have led to the fusion of the two companies. At stations where the broad and narrow gauges met, and especially at Gloucester, confusion frequently prevailed among passengers, and great loss of time and money was entailed for consigners of goods, which had to be transferred from one kind of rolling stock to another. A parliamentary commission on the matter in 1846 reported in favour of the narrow gauge, which had been adopted by the great majority of lines, and an Act of the same year made it the standard railway gauge, though the Great Western was allowed to retain its 7 foot gauge and to adopt it for extensions of its line. Eventually, after experimenting with a third rail, or mixed gauge, the Great Western had to abandon the broad gauge, a process completed by 1892.

The "battle of the gauges" was a phase of the process, active in the middle eighteen-forties, of building a large number of small and unco-ordinated enterprises into a railway system. Uniformity of gauge was necessary to that end, but so also were the fusion of managements and consolidation of ownership. These developments, however inevitable they may seem three generations later, were regarded at the time with some alarm, as extending the scope of monopoly; they also gave rise to the vexed problem of the relation of the State to these new and powerful forms of enterprise. In essence, the fusion of transport enterprises was not new; canal companies, for instance, had been amalgamated in 1784, 1813 and 1821; turnpike trusts had been consolidated in 1819; and railway amalgamation had begun as early as 1834.[1] Public interest in the matter was not actively aroused, however, until the boom period of

[1] Cleveland-Stevens, pp. 10–11, 13–14, 18.

1844–1847, during which several fusions occurred, among them those resulting in the Midland, the London and North Western, the Caledonian, the Lancashire and Yorkshire and the London, Brighton and South Coast railways.

The process of railway amalgamation, and especially the creation of the Midland in 1844, provided a field for the remarkable talents of George Hudson, the "railway king." He was a wealthy linen-draper of York, and was mayor of that city in 1837, during which year also he became chairman of the newly formed York and North Midland Railway Company. Subsequently he developed an interest in other lines and was connected, in one capacity or another, with more than a thousand miles of railway. All the companies with which he had to do were flourishing, largely through his efforts.[1] As his prestige increased, especially after the formation of the Midland, railway boards did as he wished almost without question: "On the 2nd May, 1846 the shareholders of the Midland Company gave their approval to twenty-six bills, which were immediately introduced into Parliament. On Monday following, at ten o'clock, the York and North Midland sanctioned six bills and affirmed various deeds and agreements. . . . Fifteen minutes later he induced the Newcastle and Darlington Company to approve of seven bills and accompanying agreements; and at half-past ten took his seat as a controlling power at the board of the Newcastle and Berwick. During these two days he obtained approval of forty bills, involving the expenditure of about £10,000,000."[2] He was, however, unable to prevent the formation of the Great Northern, from King's Cross to York, authorized in 1846, which diverted a good deal of traffic from the lines in which he was interested; and he had become concerned in the unprosperous Eastern Counties Railway. Failing to earn dividends on this and some other lines, he paid dividends out of capital, a process which

[1] Francis, *History of the English Railway, 1820–1845* (1851), II. 217.
[2] Williams, *Our Iron Roads*, p. 48.

brought him and many shareholders to ruin; but his management of the Midland, his main achievement, was unexceptionable. In respect of that line, at least, he earned a place, with Carr Glyn of the London and Birmingham and the astute Mark Huish of the Grand Junction, as one of the first exponents of the art of businesslike administration without which railway progress was impossible.[1]

THE STATE AND THE RAILWAYS

On the European continent, even in those countries and times when private enterprise was permitted to construct and work railway lines, the state rarely abnegated its powers so completely as in Great Britain. In Belgium, especially, railway development was planned from the beginning in a purposive fashion, with due regard to the needs of the country as a whole; in Germany, where political disunion made wholesale planning at first impossible, the Prussian state, in accord with its nature, acquired a control of the railway system; in France, the government assisted private enterprise in many ways, itself took over one part of the system and subjected the whole to conventions which were designed to end in the transference of the whole network to the State.[2] There can be little doubt that the powers of the State in Great Britain could have been used to more effect in the earlier phase of railway development; they might well have sufficed to save the railway companies from the blackmail levied upon them by landowners, and they could have been used to secure a better planned and more uniform system. Peel's government and Parliament failed to do so, but not because they were irrevocably committed to laissez-faire. Their legislation showed a perception that railway

[1] For an account of Hudson, stressing his capacity and his benevolence, and noting that his business morality was no worse than that of many of his contemporaries, see Francis, *op. cit.* II. 198–241.

[2] On continental railways see Clapham, *Economic Development of France and Germany*, chapters VII and XI; L. McPherson, *Transportation in Europe*, chapter III; Lord Monkswell, *French Railways*, chapter I; W. Lotz, *Verkehrsentwickelung in Deutschland*, chapter XI.

development needed supervision, and authorities for that purpose were created; the trouble was that their creators had no will to use them. In part, the failure to deal consistently with the situation—consistently, that is, from any point of view, whether laissez-faire or the opposite—may be attributed to the parliamentary strength of the railway interest, the shabby tail of the fraudulent George Hudson; but in part it arose from the multiplicity of other matters with which Parliament had to deal, and in part also it was the result of lack of interest on the part of Gladstone after 1845.

The problem was raised in the Commons in 1836 by a far-sighted member, James Morrison, who was convinced of the necessarily monopolistic character of canal and railway companies, and who proposed, since competition could not be effectively secured by legislation, that the State should investigate the affairs of each company, and revise rates and charges, at the end of each period of twenty-one years. Such periodical re-examination of the terms on which monopoly rights were conceded was not new, as various Bank Charter Acts witness, nor was the proposal to limit railway dividends, which Morrison also made, strange; the maximum permitted to the Liverpool and Manchester was 10 per cent., and maxima were prescribed also for the Taff Vale Railway in 1836; but Morrison's bill to make the principle general alarmed the railway interests and was rejected. Nevertheless, though Parliament refused to control railway charges and dividends, it agreed to tax their receipts from passenger traffic, and the State received £112,000 from that source in 1840. It may be noted that in 1838 the government proposed to compel railway companies to carry the mails for nothing, even when special trains and services were necessary for the purpose; but the bill was dropped, and a satisfactory agreement arrived at between the companies and the Post Office. State supervision of railways, after select committees had deliberated on the matter in 1839 and 1840, was provided for by an Act of the latter year, amended in 1842. The Board of Trade was thereby empowered to inspect railways, and without its licence no passenger-carrying line might be opened; the Board could also require information, and, upon the application of either party, could arbitrate in disputes relating to joint traffic. These Acts were desirable in the interest of public safety, but they did not enable the Board to check or to regulate railway monopolies.

In 1844, Gladstone, well-informed with regard to railways, foreseeing the speculative boom and impressed with the strength of such amalgamations as the Midland, considered it necessary to establish some kind of control, and set up a committee to consider it. This committee was very active, and upon the basis of its recommendations Gladstone introduced a bill to permit the government both to revise fares and charges and, after fifteen years, to buy the companies out. His bill was, however, emasculated in its passage through Parliament and, though clauses relating to revision and purchase were allowed to remain, they never became operative. Practically the only good which came of the Act was the "parliamentary fare" of one penny per mile for third-class passengers on a train which every company had to run daily throughout the length of its line. In the same year, in accord with a recommendation of Gladstone's committee, a special railway department of the Board of Trade was established, with Lord Dalhousie at its head. Its main purpose was to examine railway bills and report on them to Parliament. What might have been a useful piece of machinery, however, was made of little account, despite the ability and industry of its members; for the department had inadequate powers, and its reports were sometimes treated as waste paper by Parliament, which continued to discuss railway schemes as though the department did not exist. In fact it came to an end, before it was twelve months old, in 1845.

It was replaced, after further inquiry, by a Railway Commission of five persons, in accord with an Act of 1846; but this body, too, was short-lived, being abolished without opposition in 1851. Had it been erected earlier, it might have served to stem the torrent of railway bills which poured into Parliament in 1845 and 1846 and to impose some order upon the frenzied activity of the time; but by the end of 1846, when the commissioners were appointed, the mischief had been done, and thereafter comparatively few railway projects were put forward. Even so, there were good reasons for keeping the commission intact, to supervise railway activity as it revived; but the stubborn devotion of Parliament to the system of private bill committees meant that the commission could exercise little or no control, and that railway schemes were dealt with in isolation, and not, as the commission would have done, in relation to the railway service as a whole. In the end, therefore, despite Morrison and Gladstone and despite experience of the "railway mania," the British railway network was worked out with little or no governmental interference. It was, nevertheless, not anarchic, for the various lines made arrangements between themselves to ease and extend their business, and, as early as 1842, had founded the Railway Clearing House.[1] This institution, incorporated in 1850, facilitated through traffic and enabled accounts to be kept and balances to or from each company to be settled. Sixty-five companies, including all those of importance except the Great Western, which was excluded because of its broad gauge, were members of it in 1853. The conferences connected with it brought railway managements into contact with each other and that, as Cleveland-Stevens pointed out, may well have helped to bring about amalgamation.[2]

OTHER MEANS OF TRANSPORT

Long before 1850 the railway had beaten the stage-coach.

[1] Francis, *op. cit.* II. 49 *et seq.*

[2] *English Railways etc.*, p. 178.

That conveyance could rarely do better than ten miles an hour, and even that pace was not attainable without a good deal of suffering among horses, which "dropped dead from the effort of a ruptured blood vessel or a heart broken in efforts to obey the whip." The average coach-horse, on some roads, is said to have lasted only two years.[1] It would thus appear that the introduction of the tireless iron horse should count among the humanitarian reforms of the nineteenth century. As for railway speeds, Stephenson had managed 15 miles an hour on the Stockton and Darlington in 1825; 25 and 30 miles an hour were known speeds in 1838[2]; a speed of 45 miles an hour was attained in that year; and by 1850 Great Western expresses were exceeding 50 miles an hour.[3] Inevitably, therefore, there was a rapid and calamitous fall in turnpike revenues as the railway reached one region after another. A toll bar at Eccles, near Manchester, for instance, was leased at £1,700 in 1830; but in 1831, when the railway was open, it would not bring £800. Eight trusts on the road between London and Birmingham had a revenue of £28,500 in 1836; but by 1839 it had fallen to £15,800, which was less than the interest due on money borrowed by the trusts.[4] Apart from railway competition, an Act of 1835, which removed the parochial obligation to perform statute labour or compound for it, caused great losses to the turnpike trusts. In any event, some of them were in a bad way long before the railways began to affect them seriously. The Cumberland trusts, for instance, in 1836 owed £135,000, an amount greater than eight years' income, and those of Devon owed a sum equal to 8·67 years' revenue. Railway traffic was probably partly responsible for the situation in Lancashire, where the trusts owed over £967,000, more than six years' income, and in Yorkshire, with a turnpike debt of £1,119,000, equivalent to 5·9 years' income.[5] In Scotland

[1] Pratt, p. 327. [2] *ibid.* p. 326. [3] Sherrington, p. 105.
[4] Clapham I. 402. [5] *Statistical Journal* I. 545.

railway development was slower, but it meant the same fate for the turnpike trusts. The twenty-two trusts in Lanarkshire in 1851–52 had a total income of £55,776 and a debt of £443,732, including £167,176 on account of interest in arrears.[1]

The road trusts were ruined largely through the passenger traffic which, rather in excess of their expectation, the railways carried. In 1845 nearly two-thirds of their gross receipts came from that source. There was, consequently, plenty of work for the canals to do in carrying goods; but they had to do it much more cheaply. The Aire and Calder Canal, for instance, had to reduce freights from 7s. to 2s. 3d. a ton to compete with the Leeds and Selby line.[2] Down to 1840, nevertheless, efficient canals in regions where traffic was plentiful, and especially in the Midlands, could pay respectable dividends.[3] Thereafter they were less prosperous. Some, by opposing railway bills, were able to compel the railways to pay them compensation or to take them over. The London and Birmingham for instance, in order to prevent the Birmingham canal interests from seeking powers to build a competing railway, agreed to pay the canal company £4 a share on the canal capital and to make good a deficiency in revenue; by 1910 the London and North Western had paid more than £874,000 on this account.[4] Under various Acts passed between 1845 and 1847, the railways took over nearly 950 miles of canal, leaving about 2,750 in independence.[5] These were far less able than the railways to attract capital and to modernize their equipment and services, and they played a much smaller part in the development of transport than they might have done if the canal system had been adequately planned from the beginning.

[1] Sherrington, pp. 109–110. [2] Clapham I. 398. [3] *ibid.* I. 397.
[4] Pratt, pp. 298–299. [5] Clapham I. 398.

STEAM AND SHIPPING[1]

Though steam power by 1850 had conquered on land, it was still a long way from victory on the waters. It was, indeed, not new. As far back as 1788 one steam vessel had travelled on Dalswinton Loch and another on the Forth and Clyde canal; on that canal also the *Charlotte Dundas* plied successfully in 180[illegible]. Nine years later Henry Bell produced his *Comet*, the first passenger steamer in Europe, a paddle-boat 40 feet long and 10½ feet in the beam. A steamer was plying between London and Margate, taking twelve hours for the voyage, in 1815; and in 1821 steam packets were in use between Liverpool and Dublin, though in the summer only. Presumably they offered an advantage in time or in comfort, for the fare was a guinea and a half, as compared with seven shillings by sailing packet.[2] Steam packets were well established on the Thames by 1835, when more than 670,000 passengers were carried between London and Gravesend. By 1844 steam had clearly proved its value in the coasting trade: "Communication is regularly maintained with all the principal neighbouring ports on the continent of Europe. From London vessels proceed to the French coast almost every day; to Holland three times a week; to Belgium as frequently; to Hamburg twice a week; and to Lisbon and Cadiz every week. From the coast of Kent, Sussex and Hampshire, daily departures take place to France. From Hull three vessels depart every week for Hamburg, and one is despatched to Rotterdam; the greater part of the important traffic which formerly was carried on in sailing vessels between those ports is now conveyed through the more quick and certain agency of steam."[3] What Porter regarded as an "extraordinary rapidity of development" is indicated by the following table, showing the number of steamers belonging to the British Empire at various dates:

[1] On this subject see Kirkaldy, *British Shipping*, pp. 33 *et seq.*
[2] Rowland and G. B. Hill, *Life of Sir Rowland Hill* (1880), I. 135, 160.
[3] Porter, p. 320.

Year	England & Wales		Scotland		British Empire	
	Vessels	Tons	Vessels	Tons	Vessels	Tons
1820	17	1,639	14	1,127	43	7,243
1830	203	18,831	61	5,687	315	33,444
1840	560	50,491	129	19,497	824	95,807
1844	679	75,047	137	20,666	988	125,675

An increase of over 1600 per cent. in tonnage in less than a quarter of a century is, at first sight, impressive; but it will be noted that the average British steamer was very small, under 130 tons. Moreover, in comparison with the total tonnage of British shipping, the steam tonnage was very small indeed; in 1847, the year's output of British-built sailing ships was nearly equal to the whole existing tonnage of British steamers.[1]

On the oceanic trade routes the sailing ship was still supreme, though steamers had begun to compete. The American built and owned *Savannah* crossed the Atlantic in 29 days in 1819, but her steam paddles, which were used only for some 80 hours during the voyage, were merely auxiliary, and so were the Boulton and Watt engines of the Canadian *Royal William*, which crossed from Nova Scotia to Portsmouth in 17 days in 1833. Five years later, the *Sirius* and the *Great Western*, the one sailing from London and the other from Bristol, reached America in 17 and 15 days respectively. In the same year two other steamers, the *Royal William* and the *Liverpool*, crossed from the Mersey in 19 and 16½ days. It is thus clear that one of the major problems, the carrying of enough fuel on routes where coaling stations did not exist, was on the way to solution[2]; and also that the steamer, though slower than the sailing ship with a favourable wind, was faster and more regular in

[1] Clapham I. 438.
[2] On the high coal consumption, in relation to tonnage and speed, of early steamers see C. E. Fayle, *Short History of the World's Shipping Industry*, p. 231.

general, being less hindered by contrary winds. Of the four steam vessels which crossed the Atlantic in 1838 only the *Great Western* had been specially designed for the American traffic, as a sort of extension of Brunel's railway; but, despite the ship's good performance, its proprietors did not secure the contract for carrying the American mails. That was awarded in 1839 to the British and North American Royal Mail Steam Packet Company, founded by Samuel Cunard, David Maciver and George Burns; and in 1840, with a government subsidy of £81,000, the company commenced with four ships the service which, as the Cunard Company, it maintains to this day.

At about the same time, quicker communication was established with the East, largely by means of the Peninsular and Oriental Steam Navigation Company. Steamers had already been used for the Spanish mails before an improved service was provided by the Company in 1837, at first to Gibraltar, in 1840 to Alexandria, in 1842 from Suez to India and thereafter to China. In return for its services the Company obtained a subsidy of £210,000 yearly, of which £70,000 came from the East India Company.[1] The gain in speed and certainty of communication was noteworthy, but the Egyptian part of the journey was still overland and slow. Porter, in 1846, had some hope that it was about to be shortened by a railway from Cairo to Suez, or alternatively by a ship canal from the Mediterranean to the Arabian Gulf; but for that the world had twenty-three years to wait. When the Suez Canal was opened, the iron ship was coming into its own. Like the steamer, the iron vessel had been known in the eighteenth century, for John Wilkinson made one in 1787; but the first iron ship to be more than a curiosity was the *Vulcan*, built on the Clyde in 1817. Laird's of Birkenhead made a name by the construction of iron ships, such as the *Garry Owen* of 1834; but many sailormen and others regarded such vessels as unnatural, and the Post

[1] Porter, p. 324.

Office would not trust letters to them. The Admiralty had no iron battleships before 1860.

POSTAL REFORM

The effects of quicker and cheaper transport—in increasing the mobility of labour, stimulating agriculture, expanding industry and commerce, facilitating government, breaking down local barriers, generalizing information and increasing the amenities of life—were too manifold even to be indicated here. It may, however, be noted that the benefits could not be fully gained until the postal service, for which good communications were essential, had been reorganized and considerably cheapened. Administrative reform and improved roads had done something to that end during the eighteenth century; but the situation at the beginning of Queen Victoria's reign was very unsatisfactory. Some places had a local penny post; but the carrying of letters over any considerable distance was hampered by several defects. One was the privilege of franking, which gave some favoured persons, usually of the wealthier classes, the advantage of sending letters and packets free of charge to themselves, but this inevitably meant a heavier charge for other people. Others were the slowness and, in not a few cases, the roundabout routes of the mails. Many letters, which could with advantage have been sent by cross-country roads, were taken to London and then outwards to their destination, and sometimes had to stay in London for a whole day, or even longer at week-ends. Thus, said Rowland Hill, " a letter written at Uxbridge after the close of the Post Office on Friday night was not delivered at Gravesend, a distance of less than forty miles, until Tuesday morning."[1] The greatest defect, however, lay in the very high charges for delivery, charges depending in part on weight, partly on distance and partly on the number of enclosures. There had been some reduction by 1839, but

[1] Hill, *op. cit.* I. 282.

in that year[1] a single letter paid 4d. up to 15 miles, 5d. up to 20 miles, 9d. up to 120 miles and 12d. up to 300 miles. Packets weighing an ounce were charged as four single letters. There were, besides, additional charges on some routes, such as the penny for crossing the Conway Bridge and the same sum for the Menai Bridge.

Such high charges were hampering in many ways. Doctors were less able to deal with smallpox because of the high cost of getting vaccines; commercial firms rarely sought to enlarge their business by sending circulars through the post, and correspondence with their customers was restricted; members of working-class, and even of middle-class, families found it a luxury beyond their means to correspond with their relations; and working men went on tramp in search of jobs which, as they could have ascertained by post, were not to be had, or were anchored to their parishes when cheap postage facilities might have helped them to find work elsewhere.[2] Inevitably, the high postal rates led to wholesale evasion. When postal communication was first opened between Liverpool and New York, the official bag carried five letters and the unofficial bag 10,000. Within the country there was widespread use of cheap and illegal means of delivery; according to Richard Cobden, five-sixths of the letters from Manchester to London did not pass through the post office; and according to a witness from Cirencester " the people in that town did not think of using the post for the conveyance of letters; he knew of two carriers who carried four times as many letters as the mail did."[3]

From 1833 onwards repeated attention was called to the defects of the Post Office by the criticism of Robert Wallace, M.P. for Greenock; but the beginning of public pressure for better facilities came with the publication in 1837 of a pamphlet on Post Office Reform by Rowland Hill, who had

[1] *The Post Office, An Historical Summary* (1911), p. 9.
[2] On the hardship caused to the poor, see Hill, *op. cit.* I. 305 *et seq.*
[3] *ibid.* I. 301.

by then given up the profession of a schoolmaster and was secretary to the Commission for South Australian Colonization. He argued strongly for three principal reforms, namely the institution of a uniform rate, reduction of charges and prepayment of postage. While an energetic propaganda for these reforms was carried on in the country at large by Henry Warburton, Richard Cobden (who was to find the penny post very useful indeed to the Anti-Corn Law League) and others, a parliamentary committee, with Wallace as chairman, had ample opportunities to examine Hill in person. It reported in favour of uniformity and a twopenny rate; but the government, in accord with the real conviction of the reformers, undertook to introduce a penny rate, and this was enacted in 1839. The penny post came into operation in January 1840; the envelopes, with Mulready's symbolical design, fell flat, but the adhesive stamps became popular, after they were made available in May. Rowland Hill, who had been given a temporary post in the Treasury in 1839, in order to carry the reforms through, had many difficulties with the stamps and with other matters, especially the relative smallness of the increase in letters and the consequent loss of revenue. Peel, who followed the Whigs in power, nevertheless regarded the experiment as capable of succeeding, and in his budget of 1842 made no increase in the rate. Hill's appointment was terminated, and the working of his plan, which he had made his life's work, was left in the hands of bureaucrats who had no great enthusiasm for it. When the Whigs returned to power in 1846 Hill was made secretary to the Postmaster-General; but he did not attain independence and sole control until 1854. By that time there could no longer be any doubt as to the success of the penny post; the number of letters[1] posted (exclusive of franks) in 1839 was 76,000,000; in 1840, 169,000 000; in 1847, 322,000,000; and between 1850 and 1855 the average was 410,000,000.

[1] Hill, *op. cit.* II. 86; *The Post Office, An Historical Summary*, p. 10.

RAILWAYS AND ROADS AFTER 1850

During the third quarter of the nineteenth century the railway system developed more rapidly, if less feverishly, than it had during the second. The total length of line rose from 4,600 miles at the end of 1848 to 8,350 in 1858, 13,560 in 1870 and 16,700 in 1886. Amalgamation, however, which had begun in the earlier half of the century, was slow. The North Eastern was constituted in 1854, and by 1865, after swallowing the Stockton and Darlington line and others, it controlled all the railway system in its own area, between the Humber and Berwick. A similar monopolistic position was established by the Great Eastern, amalgamated in 1862, in East Anglia; and in 1865–66 the Caledonian and the North British absorbed some hundreds of miles; but the financial crisis of 1866 arrested further developments of this kind, about which both Parliament and the public felt some alarm. The fear of large-scale railway enterprises inadequately held in check by competition was, nevertheless, not great enough to lend much support to proposals for nationalization, which the Act of 1844 would have permitted and for which Bagehot, in the *Economist*, stated a case. The public complained a good deal about railway charges, and there was some fear of the companies giving preferences to particular customers or towns. On the other hand, governmental action was anything but easy. By 1880 there were some 900 Acts of Parliament relating to railway charges, and a single company might have to refer to more than fifty of them in order to know what it was authorized to charge. In practice, the basis for charging was a classification made by the Railway Clearing House, with rates often below the maxima permitted by the Acts. The difficulties in the way of revision and uniformity, which were required by the Railway and Canal Traffic Act, 1888, are evident from the fact that there were then in force about 13,000,000 rates on the Great Northern and 20,000,000 on the London and North Western.[1] Meanwhile, a Railway Commission, established in 1873 and made permanent as the Railway and Canal Commission in 1888, gave some protection to railway customers, though traders are believed to have submitted to overcharges rather than face the uncertain and costly business of bringing an action against a wealthy railway company.

Travellers, at any rate before 1872, also had good ground of complaint if they belonged to the despised but profitable majority who travelled third class. The coaches provided for them ceased to be open to wind and weather; but third-class coaches were commonly attached only to slow trains. Hence, at one time, "a third-class passenger from London to Liverpool had to spend two days on the journey; and a second-class passenger from London to Liverpool had to stop at Birmingham for the night, or else to proceed by first class at first-class fare."[2] In 1872, however, the Midland, in accord with a policy for which Allport had striven, provided third-class carriages on all trains. The importance of this sort of passenger is indicated by the returns relating to ordinary tickets in 1881[3]:

Class	No. of Passengers	Amount received
First	37,993,944	£3,779,371
Second	64,474,717	3,398,806
Third	520,579,126	15,266,519

The safety of these millions was a matter of special concern to the Board of Trade, the powers of whose inspectors were increased by the Regulation of Railways Act, 1871. The companies themselves did much to avoid accidents by introducing the block system in signalling, though that spread rapidly only after 1870 and was not made compulsory until 1889. In 1876 trials were carried out at Newark with various types of continuous braking systems;

[1] Pratt, *op. cit.* p. 339.
[2] F. S. Williams, *Our Iron Roads*, p. 388.
[3] *ibid.* p. 390.

thereafter, under pressure from the Board of Trade, such braking apparatus came into general use on the important lines, and automatic continuous braking was made compulsory on all in 1889. By the early 'eighties the British railways were remarkably safe for passengers; on the London and North Western, for instance, which carried over 50,000,000 every year, only one had been killed in the three and a half years preceding August 1882.

The turnpike trusts, seriously injured by railway development, sought desperately to maintain their revenues by multiplying toll-gates; but the trusts which provoked the fiercest hostility, in South Wales, cannot have been facing any great railway competition when the Rebecca rioters engaged in wholesale destruction of their property in 1843. Other causes, such as the new Poor Law of 1834 and increasing tithes, as well as excessive and illegal charges[1], helped to produce the insurrection, which was followed by an investigation and a reorganization of the road authorities. County Road Boards, appointed by Quarter Sessions, replaced the trusts throughout South Wales; a government road engineer was appointed to assist them; and, in order to pay off the trust debts, the government advanced at low interest over £200,000, a sum which the Road Boards repaid by 1876. In the remainder of the country the liquidation of turnpike trusts was a long drawn out process. It accelerated from 1871, when a House of Commons Committee on Turnpike Trust Bills decided every year which trusts should be allowed to continue; by 1883, when tolls ceased to be levied in Scotland, only seventy-one trusts remained in Great Britain; by 1890 there were only two, and in 1895 the last toll levied on a public road was collected on the Anglesey section of the Holyhead road. From 1883 onwards the government made grants to relieve taxpayers of part of the cost of maintaining "disturnpiked" roads; the contribution rose from just over £167,000 in 1883 to just

[1] H. Tobit Evans, *Rebecca and Her Daughters*, pp. 4–5.

under £500,000 in 1888. Meanwhile there had been developments with regard to the remainder of the public highways, which in 1838 amounted to more than 104,000 miles, as compared with 22,000 miles under the authority of turnpike trusts. An Act of 1835, repealing most previous legislation relating to public highways, and abolishing the ancient labour obligation of the inhabitants of parishes, in effect handed over the highways to the parishes, with little supervision. Attempts to group them on the basis of poor-law or sanitary-authority areas were not very successful and led to much confusion, and in 1894 there were 5,000 parishes still administering their own roads in their own way at their own will; but the Local Government Act of that year contained provisions, made effective by the end of the century, for merging the road authorities in the rural sanitary authorities.[1]

[1] On roads in the nineteenth century see S. and B. Webb, *Story of the King's Highway*, chapter IX.

CHAPTER III

Agriculture Before and After Repeal

PROGRESS BEFORE 1850

Between the Napoleonic Wars and the accession of Queen Victoria, British agriculture was, in the main, depressed, and was gradually accommodating itself to new conditions, especially to lower price levels. The wars had inevitably stimulated the production of food at home, and the current high prices, made higher still by inflation, made it worth while to grow corn on lands previously on or below the margin. The labour cost of cultivation had not risen proportionately for farmers as a whole, because the poor-law authorities in many parts of the country adopted some variant or other of the Speenhamland bread scale, which kept the wages paid by farmers relatively low, though it increased the pressure on rate-payers. In any event, tenant farmers must, to some extent, have been able to transfer the burden of rates to their landlords, and, as Cobbett held, to substitute for the old-fashioned substantial way of living a new gimcrack magnificence.[1] As the labourers fell into the ranks of pauperdom, the farmers ascended to something like the status of squires. But the foundation of their prosperity was insecure, and in a few years after Waterloo many farmers found themselves in a condition of overwhelming difficulty. Some were embarrassed even before the peace. Richard Cobden's father, for instance, had to sell his farm in 1814; and his neighbours also fared badly. "Cobden was able to say in later years that when he returned to his native place, he found that many of those who were once his fellows had sunk down to the ranks of labourers, and some of them were even working on the roads."[2]

[1] Cobbett, *Rural Rides* (Everyman), I. 265–268.
[2] Morley's *Cobden* (1903), pp. 3–4.

The break in prices was not immediate. For the year of Waterloo the average annual price of wheat was 65s. 7d. a quarter, but it remained well above that level during the following five years, and was especially high in 1817 (96s. 11d.) and 1818 (86s. 3d.). In 1821, the year of the return to the gold standard, the price was 56s. 1d.; and during the next sixteen years it reached the Waterloo level in three years only, in 1825 (68s. 6d.), in 1829 (66s. 3d.) and in 1831 (66s. 4d.). The average for these sixteen years was 56s. 8d., and in four years it was below 50s.[1] Rents, in so far as they were based on the prices obtained in good years, or on the prices which the Corn Laws vainly attempted to secure, were often so high as to make deep inroads into the farmer's profits, or even to swallow them. Some farmers might pay their rents out of capital, but in that case cultivation naturally suffered. Leases for years were unpopular, many farmers preferring yearly tenancies, and, naturally, concentrating rather on getting out of the soil what it would yield with a minimum of expense than on taking care for its improvement. Neither the system of tenure nor the resources of the cultivators as a whole were favourable to any widespread attempt to offset the fall in prices by a better and more scientific technique, and new methods spread only very slowly.

Meanwhile, however, before 1840 two great reforms did something to hasten the day of agricultural improvement. The first was the reform of poor-relief administration in accord with the drastic Act of 1834, whereby the poor rates, which had been £7,870,000 in 1818 and £6,790,000 in 1832, fell to £4,044,000 in 1837. The second was the Tithe Commutation Act of 1836, whereby payment of tithes in money became compulsory, the amount being determined as the equivalent of certain fixed quantities of corn, and the price of the fixed quantity being based

[1] For prices see T. Tooke, *History of Prices*, II. 389; IV. 410–413; Prothero (Lord Ernle) *English Farming Past and Present* (1917), p. 441.

on the average of prices during a period of seven years. The relative fixity of the burden, which was over £4,000,000 in 1835, was an advantage to agriculture because cultivators had previously been deterred from improving their lands or their methods, in not a few instances, by the consideration that part of the increased yield would be gathered by persons who did nothing whatsoever to produce it. It is not likely that farmers were very grateful to the Whig government for the Poor Law Amendment Act; they would have preferred a more effective protection than that offered to them by the existing Corn Law of 1828; but already by 1840 there was in existence the Anti-Corn Law League, which was to play so important a part in the total removal of agricultural protection by Peel's Act of 1846.

When, as a result of that Act, British farmers were subjected to foreign competition, they were able to avoid ruin; that was the result, in part at least, of factors which had been gathering force before Repeal. In the first place, chemistry began to point the way to better cultivation. Sir Humphry Davy's lectures in 1803, and his *Elements of Agricultural Chemistry*, published in 1813, laid a foundation; but widespread interest was aroused only after 1840, the year when a treatise on *Organic Chemistry in its Applications to Agriculture and Physiology* by Justus von Liebig, professor at Giessen, was made available in English. His researches can hardly have had a direct influence on ordinary farmers, but they gave a fresh stimulus to experiments with fertilizers, and those produced at Giessen were widely used in this country.[1] The greatest impetus, however, came from the work of Sir John Lawes, in collaboration with Sir Henry Gilbert, a pupil of Liebig's, at the experimental station at Rothamsted, Hertfordshire, beginning in 1843. They applied the method, now common in scientific inquiry, of checking results by reference to "controls." Thus, for instance, they

[1] R. M. Garnier, *History of the English Landed Interest* (*Modern Period*), p. 433.

grew the same kind of wheat on the same kind of soil with and without fertilizers and demonstrated that well hoed and weeded ground, without manure, would grow wheat crops for ten years in succession without its fertility being so reduced that it could not yield an average of sixteen bushels to the acre, whereas this crop could be doubled by the application of four cwts. of Peruvian guano.[1] It is perhaps significant that the importation of that commodity, which had been merely nominal in 1841, reached 220,000 tons by 1847.[2] In the meantime, Lawes had started a factory for the production of superphosphate manures at Deptford in 1843; seventeen years later he set up a larger works on Barking Creek.

The increasing use of manures naturally gave an added importance to adequate drainage, since it would have been bad economy to allow expensive fertilizers to be washed away by wet weather and floods. Better drainage, moreover, was urgently necessary on heavy clay soils, good for the growing of wheat but apt to be waterlogged and hard to work, so that the crop was often sown and harvested too late. In backward areas, little more was attempted than ploughing so as to raise the level of the strip towards the middle, in the hope that excess moisture would run towards the edges; but in some parts of the country the problem was more effectively tackled by digging ditches, which were part filled with brushwood or heather and covered in again. By a more thorough use of similar means, that is by cutting trenches, 2½ feet deep and 16 to 21 feet apart, filled in with stones, James Smith of Deanston in Perthshire "converted a rush-grown marsh into a garden" in the years following 1823,[3] and pointed the way to many progressive farmers. In some parts of the country, however, stones and their carriage were too costly, and effective drainage had to wait until John Read invented a cylindrical clay pipe in 1843,

[1] J. Caird, *English Agriculture in 1850–51*, pp. 460–461.
[2] Prothero, *op. cit.* 366.
[3] Prothero, p. 364.

and Thomas Scragg, in 1845, invented a machine to manufacture such piping cheaply. Three years later Peel provided State assistance by means of loans, repayable in twenty-two annual instalments at 6½ per cent. In the following years this led to a great improvement of lands in many counties, the more so as the cost of drain pipes was greatly reduced at the same time, in the North Riding, for instance, from twenty-five to fifteen shillings a thousand.[1] Some landlords charged their tenants rather more than 6½ per cent. and thus obtained a profit on the loan as well as the improvement of their land without cost to themselves; others paid a part of the interest and amortization. Under Sir James Graham at Netherby drainage appears to have cost the tenant farmers 3s. 6d., or less, per acre in interest.[2] The value of the improvement, naturally, varied; on one Northumberland farm the wheat crop had been thereby increased twenty per cent.[3]

Despite the relative lowness of agricultural wages in the days of the Old Poor Law, the substitution of machinery for hand labour had already begun. The threshing machine, invented by Andrew Meikle, had reached Lancashire before 1800 and was common in North Wales by 1813; in the eighteen-twenties it was penetrating further into the Speenhamland counties and by 1830 was important among the causes of agrarian disturbance in Kent and other parts of the South. It robbed labourers of the chance of earning from fifteen to twenty shillings a week,[4] and, like the shearing frame and the power loom, was liable to be destroyed by the men whom it displaced. Another machine of Scottish origin was the reaper, invented, after several others had failed, by the Rev. Patrick Bell of Carmyllie in 1827; but, though the machine seems to have worked, it was not widely used. A hay-tossing machine, invented about 1800 by Salmon, of Woburn, was, on the other hand, fairly well

[1] Caird, p. 328. [2] *ibid.* p. 354. [3] *ibid.* p. 374.
[4] Hammond, *Village Labourer*, p. 221.

known, especially in the London region, by 1830.[1] On the whole, and excepting the thresher, machinery made little progress before the days of the Crystal Palace Exhibition. There was, indeed, sufficient demand to keep several firms going, especially in Suffolk. Their ploughs, of which one firm turned out more than three hundred kinds, and harrows may have been largely sold to ordinary farmers, but their threshing machines, and especially their "portable steam engines", were presumably supplied to gentleman farmers. One firm, at Leiston near Saxmundham, employed between 300 and 400 men; another, at Ipswich, employed between 800 and 1,000, but it was an engineering firm, and only about half its men were engaged in making farm implements. Were it not for foreign orders the trade would have been slack in 1851.[2]

One sign of agricultural progress was the formation, and the increasing importance, of societies to foster it. Scotland was early in the field with the Highland Society, which received its charter in 1787 and a grant of £8,000 in 1789; its interests included Gaelic literature and industrial development as well as farming, which it sought to encourage by means of prizes for cultivation, stock-rearing, dairy products, irrigation and the invention of machinery, and by holding exhibitions. England had an equivalent, from 1793 to 1822, in the Board of Agriculture, of which Arthur Young had been secretary. In 1838 the Royal Agricultural Society was founded, and this institution, incorporated in 1840, can now congratulate itself on a century of extraordinary usefulness. Its *Journal* was an important vehicle for the dissemination of new knowledge and practice, as were also its shows, of which the first, held at Oxford in 1839, was attended by 20,000 people. In course of time the endeavours of both societies were assisted by local associations for the encouragement of farming in their own districts. Until recent times there existed very little to supplement the

[1] Clapham I. 140.

[2] Caird, pp. 148–150.

work of the societies by systematic scientific training in agriculture. In this matter, as in others, Scotland led the way, for Sir William Pulteney endowed a chair of Agriculture and Rural Economy in the University of Edinburgh as early as 1790, and the Dick Veterinary College was founded in the same city in 1839.[1] Six years later the Cirencester Agricultural College was opened; it had a farm of 700 acres, a chemical laboratory, facilities for instruction in geology, botany and zoology and for practical training in surveying as well as in the operations of farming. It was intended to "furnish a sound education in scientific agriculture for the sons of tenant farmers," of whom it could accommodate 200; but in 1850 it had only 60 students, the sons of solicitors, clergymen, officers or landed proprietors. Cotswold farmers apparently regarded it with suspicion, believing that "college farming does not pay."[2]

Besides being improved by applied science, agriculture after 1840 was assisted by at least three other factors: the continued growth of population, industrial advance and railway development. The first may be indicated in the following table:

	England and Wales	Scotland	Total Population
1841	15,914,000	2,620,000	18,534,000
1851	17,928,000	2,889,000	20,817,000
1861	20,066,000	3,062,000	23,128,000
1871	22,712,000	3,360,000	26,072,000

It is indeed true that the greater demand for cereals could be met, especially after 1846, by importation; nevertheless, home production increased. Moreover a rising standard of living, which accompanied industrial development and the expansion of markets for British goods, favoured a larger consumption. "With the great mass of consumers," it

[1] J. Mackinnon, *Social and Industrial History of Scotland from the Union to the Present Time*, pp. 69, 71.
[2] Caird, pp. 36–39.

could be written in 1851, " bread still forms the chief article of consumption. But in the manufacturing districts, where wages are good, the use of butcher's meat and cheese is enormously on the increase; and even the agricultural labourer does now occasionally indulge himself in a meat dinner, or season his dry bread with a morsel of cheese."[1] As for the railways, they were for a long time rather an occasional convenience than an acknowledged benefit to the generality of farmers. Improved roads, no doubt, answered many of their needs; but the railway had at least three advantages over the best of roads. In the first place, a railway company was a ratepayer in every parish through which its lines ran and its contribution often kept the rates low.[2] In the second place, it offered good opportunities for supplying the growing towns with perishable commodities, especially milk. This was only slowly realized; Birmingham, as late as 1850, was content to take its milk from the thousand or so cows kept in the town and from farms within a radius of three miles, while Liverpool and Manchester drew their supplies by rail from a distance of thirty miles.[3] Thirdly, there was a great advantage in transporting sheep and cattle by rail. When sent to market by road, they required feeding for a longer time and lost weight considerably during the journey. Thus a drover would take several days to get animals from Castleacre in Norfolk to London, and on the way a sheep would lose 7 lbs. and a bullock 28 lbs. The railway, enabling the livestock to arrive in a few hours and in good condition, saved more than £600 a year for one of the Holkham tenant farmers.[4]

The use of scientific methods, and the consequent expenditure of substantial capital, or what was called " high farming," was to be found at its fullest only on a small minority of estates and farms. An example of it was the practice of the Rector of Sutton Waldron in Dorset, who laid

[1] Caird, p. 484.
[2] *ibid.* p. 125.
[3] *ibid.* p. 228.
[4] *ibid.* p. 169.

the bedding for his cattle on boards six inches above a watertight floor, to keep it dry and to facilitate the draining of liquid into a central tank, whence liquid manure was pumped through pipe lines to convenient positions for spreading it over his fields. He used steam power to thrash and winnow his corn and to grind bones, oilcake and meal, and he cooked and heated the messes for his livestock. More care was spent on them than on many factory workers of the period; milch cows were provided with special quarters for calving; newly purchased animals were kept in quarantine until their freedom from disease was certain; the sheep were weighed once a fortnight, and every care was taken to see that the cattle and sheep houses, and the pigsties, were clean, dry and properly ventilated. The livestock, in short, was treated as a valuable and intricate kind of plant used for food production, either directly in meat and milk, or indirectly in manure, of which not a scrap was wasted.[1] Similar methods were used by Sir John Conroy at Arborfield Hall near Reading,[2] Philip Pusey, M.P.[3] in the same county, and others whom Caird held up as examples in 1851; but it was clearly impossible for the mass of farmers, even had they been convinced that such farming was profitable, to imitate them, except on a very small scale; and many landlords were either too poor or too indifferent to help their tenants, and themselves, by erecting adequate buildings and improving the soil.

Part of the difficulty lay in the system of tenure. The majority of farmers consisted in effect of tenants at will, holding their land from year to year and subject to six months' notice.[4] It is indeed true that even in such conditions tenure might in practice be continuous; under the Wynnes in Denbighshire "father had succeeded son on their farms as regularly as father succeeded son at the princely mansion of Wynnstay. In many instances this succession

[1] Caird, pp. 65–71.
[2] *ibid.* pp. 100–106.
[3] *ibid.* pp. 107–113.
[4] Clapham II. 254; Caird, p. 504.

had continued unbroken from the time of the Tudors or beyond."[1] But the sale of part of the estate, a new landlord and hard times, might mean an end of the old security, and where that was absent, capital expenditure, if not made by the landlord, might rarely be made at all. In some parts of the country, and notably in Lincolnshire, a tenant had a recognized right to compensation, at the end of his term, for improvements made at his own cost. A different, and in Caird's view a better, means to the same end was the concession of a long lease, allowing the tenant time enough to reap, in better crops, the value of his improvements in marling, manuring or draining. In the Scottish lowlands leases of twelve, nineteen and even twenty-one years were common; and that gave progressive farmers adequate scope.[2] But long leases were not, in themselves, enough; a bad farmer on a long lease can work great havoc with the land; and, in any event, there was for many farmers, besides the difficulty of security for capital sunk in the soil, a difficulty in accumulating any considerable capital to sink. In such circumstances, with next to no co-operation among farmers to overcome their difficulties, an obligation lay on the landlords. "If the farmers of England are to be exposed to universal competition," Caird wrote, "the landlords must give them a fair chance. If they refuse to part with the control of their property for the endurance of a lease, they must themselves make such permanent improvements as a tenant at will is not justified in undertaking."[3]

THE CORN LAWS AND THE LEAGUE

Besides contributing to the relief of agriculture by the Poor Law Amendment Act and the Tithe Commutation Act, the government, in the period before 1850, attempted

[1] *The Life and Opinions of Robert Roberts, a Wandering Scholar*, ed. J. H. Davies, p. 74.

[2] Clapham I. 109.

[3] Caird, p. 491.

to give the industry continuous and valuable support by means of the Corn Laws. The earlier history of agricultural protection and corn trade regulation is outside our present purview; but it may be observed briefly that during the seventeenth century the corn laws became less concerned with the interests of the consumer and more with those of the producer, who was encouraged by means of a bounty on export when the price of home-grown wheat was at a level which was not considered adequate. The object of the laws may be conceived as the attainment of a fair price, which would provide a reasonable reward to the grower without imposing an undue hardship on the consumer. It is noteworthy, however, that the price which was considered fair rose from 48 shillings for a quarter of wheat in 1773 to somewhere between 50 and 54 shillings in 1791 and between 63 and 66 shillings in 1804. It is thus hardly possible to deny that "the landlords and farmers were deliberately trying to secure for themselves permanently a range of prices which had been produced by extraordinary circumstances,"[1] namely war, scarcity and inflation. The same undeniable class interest, pursued even further, lay behind the Corn Law of 1815, when the end of the war brought with it the possibility of a fall in prices and rents. It was then enacted that when British wheat stood at 80 shillings a quarter foreign wheat could be imported free of duty, but when home-grown wheat was below that price the import of foreign wheat was prohibited. This law was ostensibly modified by a later enactment in 1822, which excluded foreign wheat while the home price was under 70 shillings, permitted importation—subject to a duty of 12 shillings a quarter—when the home price was between 70 and 80 shillings, and dropped the import duty to five shillings when it was between 80 and 85 shillings. Since, however, those parts of the 1815 Act prohibiting import until home wheat was at 80 shillings had not been repealed,

[1] D. G. Barnes, *A History of the English Corn Laws*, p. 89.

the lower part of this sliding scale was of no effect. In 1828 Huskisson carried through an Act which departed from tradition, first by giving up naked prohibition of import, and secondly by instituting a more gradual sliding scale. Thus:

Home Wheat at	Duty per quarter
52s.	34s. 8d.
53s.	33s. 8d.
54s.	32s. 8d.
—	—
66s.	20s. 8d.
67s.	18s. 8d.
68s.	16s. 8d.
69s.	13s. 8d.
70s.	10s. 8d.
71s.	6s. 8d.
72s.	2s. 8d.
73s.	1s. 0d.

This was the law against which the Anti-Corn Law League was formed to agitate. The controversy was not new, for it had been active in 1814 and 1815, but from 1839 to 1846 it was waged with added force and in a much wider constituency; it was, in fact, important among the means by which the new bourgeoisie worked its way to power in the reformed Parliament and was second only to the contemporary chartist agitation as a means for the political education of the masses. Within four years of the great Reform Act, an Anti-Corn Law Association was formed in London, with twenty-two Members of Parliament among its members,[1] but though some of them, like George Grote, Joseph Hume, J. Roebuck and Sir William Molesworth, were eminent enough, no widespread interest was aroused until in 1838 a Manchester Association was founded. This,

[1] Archibald Prentice, *History of the Anti-Corn Law League* (1853), I. 49–50. Palmerston in 1846 declared that the repeal of the Corn Laws was a consequence of the Reform Act. See Hansard, 3rd Series, lxxxvii, 1057.

uniting in 1839 with similar associations in other places, constituted the League. Leaders in industry and commerce, especially those of Manchester, supplied most of its funds; Richard Cobden gave his time and sacrificed his own concerns for its work, and, where his calm and common-sense arguments did not suffice, the moving eloquence of John Bright succeeded in convincing thousands not merely of the expediency but of the rightness and justice of free trade.

By the eighteen-forties, the way was in several respects easier for the opponents of protection than it had been earlier. In the first place, the authority of political economy was strongly in their favour; there had been time for the classical doctrine of rent to find general acceptance, and that made it easy to convince men that the real purpose of the Corn Laws was to increase rents by means of an artificially produced scarcity, and that, as Ricardo put it, " the interest of the landlord is always opposed to the interest of every other class in the community. His situation is never so prosperous as when food is scarce and dear."[1] In the second place, though industry was still protected, the level of duties had been considerably reduced by Huskisson between 1823 and 1827, so that there was less justification than formerly for protection, on equitable grounds, of agriculture. Moreover, there was room to believe that the opening of the ports to foreign corn would not, as had once been supposed, flood the country with large surpluses from France and the Baltic region;[2] and it was significant that some eminent landowners, who had been protectionists in the Waterloo period, were now favourable to free trade. The League could quote efficient agriculturists on its side, such, for instance, as William Hope, who declared that " high prices are not so very necessary to the farmer as some are apt to imagine . . . in 1836, when wheat was selling at 36s. per quarter, we did

[1] *Principles* (McCulloch edition), p. 378

[2] D. G. Barnes, *op. cit.* pp. 190–191.

well . . . in 1839, with wheat at 72s. per quarter, . . . farmers in East Lothian, myself amongst them, actually lost money."[1]

Naturally, the League made great play with the argument that the Corn Law hindered the development of industry by hampering the export of industrial goods to countries who had nothing but their corn with which to pay for them; moreover, it might be pointed out that flourishing industries would enable the population of Great Britain itself to consume more bread, beef and bacon. The League's propaganda, nevertheless, was not confined to the towns. Its lecturers secured a hearing in the countryside and were able to expose the rifts in the solidarity of the "agricultural interest"; they reiterated the conviction that the tenant farmer gained nothing by laws whereof the main object was the securing of high rents, and that the farm labourer lost more by dear bread than he gained by small and insecure rises in his wages. When intimidation by his masters broke down, Hodge could be found in ominous agreement with the Manchester iconoclasts. In the summer of 1845, for instance, more than a thousand persons, chiefly farm labourers, assembled "under a fine old tree on the green" at Upavon in Wiltshire and listened to facts and opinions which made the Corn Law seem detestable. "The children," said Ozias Lealey, "would jump across the house if they saw a couple of potatoes, and quarrel which should have them. It was enough to drive a man mad. When he came home at night and found them crying for food, and had none to give them, it almost drove him mad; he could not stand it another winter. What would the gentlemen think of this, filled as they were with their roast beef and sherry wine . . . ?"[2]

It is significant also that the League had found an echo in the minds of evangelical Christians. A convention of congregationalist ministers at Saron, near Caernarvon, in

[1] Prentice, *op. cit.* I. 293.

[2] Prentice, *op. cit.* II. 382.

1841, called the Corn Laws unjust and unchristian; a conference of ministers of religion at Manchester in the same year, and a synod of ministers and laymen at Edinburgh in 1842, were overwhelmingly for repeal.[1] On the other hand, the Chartists were frequently opposed to the Corn Law reformers; that was not because chartism was in any sense favourable to the Corn Laws[2] but because the repeal agitation was regarded as a middle-class movement aiming simply at low wages. To the Chartists the price of bread was of little importance since they believed that the workers, until they obtained political power, would in any event only secure bare maintenance, whatever its money cost; and the leaders feared that the fancied benefit of cheap bread might distract the attention of the working classes from the struggle for their real interests. The protectionists also, through the skilful propaganda of George Game Day, were able to make effective use of contradictory statements on wages and prices by members of the League.[3]

Peel, when he came into office in 1841, rejected the view that the Corn Law of 1828 was a major cause of the prevailing distress, which he attributed chiefly to the inevitable depression after the crisis of 1837–38; but he was nevertheless of the opinion that the duties of 1828 were too high and the sliding scale too steep. That scale had been adversely criticized as tending to make the corn trade more speculative than it need have been. This objection had less force against the duties imposed by Peel in 1842, the general principle of which was that the import duty decreased by a shilling for every shilling rise in the price of home wheat.[4]

[1] Prentice, I. 235 *et seq.*, 290.

[2] John Bright inconveniently showed, in the presence of Fergus O'Connor, and by quoting Hansard, that the Chartist leader had defended the Corn Laws as necessary in order to secure an English market for Irish corn. See Prentice, *op. cit.* II. 233–234.

[3] Barnes, *op. cit.* p. 255.

[4]

Home Wheat.	*Duty.*	*Home Wheat.*	*Duty.*
Under 51s. a qr.	20s.	65s. to 66s. ...	7s.
51s. to 52s. ...	19s.	66s. to 69s. ...	6s.
52s. to 55s. ...	18s.	69s. to 70s. ...	5s.
55s. to 56s. ...	17s.	73s. and over	1s.

The Whigs argued for a fixed duty as the only effective method to lessen speculative dealing, and Charles Villiers moved his annual resolution for total repeal, but Peel's bill was carried, with, it will be noted, considerably lower duties than those of 1828. Peel followed this partial removal of protection by reductions of duties on some hundreds of articles in 1842 and 1845, compensating for the loss of revenue by imposing an income tax. Peel's own mind was thus moving more and more towards free trade, and he was subject to the continuous barrage of Cobden's convincing arguments in the House of Commons[1]; but the "agricultural interest" was alarmed, and the high Tories were quite unready to follow Peel when the events of 1845–46 settled the question. The rain in the autumn ruined the corn harvest in Britain, and the potato crop, the staple food of Ireland, was destroyed by blight. Peel, as early as October, saw that the remedy was "the removal of all impediments to the import of all kinds of human food . . . the total and absolute repeal for ever of all duties on all articles of subsistence"[2]; but the majority of his cabinet would not support him even in suspending the Corn Law. Lord John Russell, in November, gave up the Whig plan of a fixed duty and declared for total repeal, but, when Peel resigned, Russell could not form a ministry, and Peel returned, in December 1845, to end at one and the same time a chapter in the unhappy history of privilege and his own ministerial career. A lower scale of duties[3] was imposed, to last until February 1849, from which date the importation of corn was to be free, except for a nominal duty of 1s. a quarter.

[1] Peel in his speech on his resignation recognized that Cobden "from pure and disinterested motives, has, with untiring energy, made appeals to our reason, and has enforced those appeals with an eloquence the more to be admired because it was unaffected and unadorned." Hansard, 3rd Series, lxxxvii, 1054.

[2] Letter to Lord Heytesbury, in Stanhope and Cardwell, *Memoirs of Sir Robert Peel* (1857), II. 121.

[3]

Home Wheat.	*Duty.*	*Home Wheat.*	*Duty.*
Under 48s. qr. ...	10s.	50s. to 51s. ...	7s.
48s. to 49s. ...	9s.	51s. to 52s. ...	6s.
49s. to 50s. ...	8s.	52s. to 53s. ...	5s.
		over 53s. ...	4s.

Three days after the passing of this act Peel was defeated by the irreconcilables of his own party and resigned. His valedictory speech contained one passage which might well serve for his epitaph: "it may be that I shall leave a name sometimes remembered with expressions of goodwill in the abodes of those whose lot it is to labour, and to earn their daily bread by the sweat of their brow, when they shall recruit their exhausted strength with abundant and untaxed food, the sweeter because it is no longer leavened by a sense of injustice."[1]

AGRICULTURE AFTER REPEAL

The passing of Peel's Act naturally led to some discouragement of farming in the years immediately following, but the period between 1846 and 1870 as a whole was by no means unprosperous. The United States, though developing rapidly, from an agricultural point of view, during the Civil War, were not yet ready to pay transport costs on their wheat and still compete strongly in the British market; extraordinary events on the Continent, such as the Crimean War, tended to lessen the possibilities of export to this country; and the gold discoveries of 1849 tended to keep up the prices of agricultural as of other produce. Moreover population was still rising, and the consumption of wheat per head was increasing. The position may perhaps be indicated by the computation, accepted by Caird, that from 1853 to 1861 each person consumed at the rate of 311 lbs. of wheat annually, of which quantity 79 lbs. came from abroad, and that between 1861 and 1869 the consumption per head was 335 lbs., of which 134 lbs. were imported.[2] Certainly, wheat prices declined, but for some farmers there was compensation in the cultivation of oats and barley, the prices of which were not only maintained but, at least in the latter part of the period, increased.

[1] Hansard, *vol. cit.* 1055. [2] *Stat. Journal*, xxxii, 65.

Average Annual Price per quarter of	1837–1846	1847–1856	1857–1870
Wheat ...	58s. 7d.	55s. 4d.	50s. 7d.
Oats ...	22s. 4½d.	22s. 3d.	23s. 10d.
Barley ...	32s. 6½d.	32s. 6d.	34s. 8d.

Moreover, the prices of other produce rose as well. Caird, writing in 1868, held that since 1850 the price of bread had, on the average, remained the same, while the prices of meat, dairy produce and wool had risen by half.[1] In such circumstances, adaptation of land to changing price levels might be expected, and this seems to have occurred. Despite the maintenance of the prices of oats the area under that crop declined, between 1850 and 1867, by about 450,000 acres; the wheat acreage declined by 280,000 acres; on the other hand, 500,000 additional acres were turned over to barley, 300,000 to root crops, 20,000 to clover and perhaps 470,000 to permanent pasture.[2]

Under the stress of competition, and in particularly bad years such as 1865, when the cattle plague caused enormous losses, or 1867, when the harvests were deficient, unfortunate or inefficient farmers were doubtless forced out of business, and there was an opportunity for others to absorb their lands into larger units. In Wales as well as in Westmorland and the southern counties consolidation was reported to be in progress,[3] but available statistics[4] suggest that concentration was to some extent offset by the splitting up of larger units, and was, in any event, too slow to disturb the pattern of agricultural society very markedly. Farms ranging between 50 and 500 acres covered about 75 per cent. of England and Wales in 1851, and farms of about the same sizes accounted for 72 per cent. in 1885. If, however, the proportions of the various sizes of farms did not alter very

[1] *Stat. Journal*, xxxi, 141; cf. *Journal Royal Agric. Soc. 3rd Series* I. 26.
[2] Caird's calculation, *Stat. Journal*, xxxi, 145.
[3] Clapham II. 262.
[4] *ibid.* II. 264.

much, the character of cultivation was changing for the better, not so much because the large-scale cultivators after 1850 were far ahead of their predecessors as because the improvements introduced by the pioneers came into more general use.[1] Old-fashioned methods and implements survived stubbornly. Broadcast sowing was the rule in Wales. The primitive foot-plough was still in use in Skye, and the flail still provided winter employment for labourers even in England; nevertheless, it was giving way to the threshing machine, as the sickle was to the scythe and that in turn to the reaping machine. The steam plough was introduced in 1857, but steam cultivation, even in noted areas of progressive and enthusiastic farming, such as the Scottish lowlands, advanced only very slowly; in the whole United Kingdom only some 200,000 acres were steam-tilled by 1867.[2] Neither the size of British fields nor the lie of the land was suitable for the methods which were so useful in Western America, and, in any event, farmers who had to possess horses for other purposes could hardly afford to use other means of ploughing. The steam-driven thresher, which could go from farm to farm under its own power, was indeed an improvement of which many could share the benefits. The main reason for the increased use of that machine, as well as of others, was no doubt the considerable advance in agricultural wages between 1850 and 1870.[3] Much also should be attributed to the Royal Agricultural Society, which not only offered prizes for improved machines but also, from 1848 onwards, applied dynamometrical tests to those exhibited at its shows. The effect, as the trials became more systematic, was to enable purchasers to form a much better judgment: "neither gaudy paint nor plausible tongues could now induce intelligent farmers to buy anything until they knew what the dynamometer had to say to

[1] *Journal Royal Agric. Soc. 3rd Series* I. 26.
[2] Clapham II. 268.
[3] In the four divisions distinguished in Lord Ernle's tables (*English Farming, Past and Present*, pp. 468–70) they rose respectively by 24 per cent., 32 per cent., 50 per cent. and 26 per cent.

the salesman."[1] At the same time, manufacturers were stimulated by the Society's conditions to produce more economical machines, including steam engines; the coal consumption per horse-power per hour of the prize engine in 1849 was $11\frac{1}{2}$ lbs.; in 1856 it was $3\frac{1}{2}$ lbs., in 1872 $2\frac{3}{4}$ lbs. and in 1887 $1\frac{4}{5}$ lbs.

[1] *Journal Royal Agric. Soc. 3rd Series* I. 263.

CHAPTER IV

The Textile Manufactures

THE GROWTH OF FACTORY PRODUCTION

Of the four chief branches of the textile industry at the opening of Queen Victoria's reign, two, namely, the manufacture of woollen cloth and of linen, had existed since immemorial antiquity. The production of silk and cotton goods, both of which needed a foreign-grown raw material, came later. The former was certainly established by the middle of the fourteenth century,[1] and the latter was known in Lancashire by 1601,[2] though the first cotton fabrics made in this country were mixed, having a linen warp and a cotton weft, until Arkwright's roller-spinning frame enabled a cotton yarn to be spun which was strong enough for warp.[3] All four industries were transformed, in time, by a series of inventions during the eighteenth century and by later improvements of the new machines; but the transformation was still far from complete in 1837. The process may be regarded as beginning with the water-driven machinery containing "97,476 wheels, movements and individual parts" set up in a large mill in Derby by John Lombe, in order to supply organzine, or thrown silk, hitherto obtained from Italy. This process, after the expiry of the patent in 1732, was adopted in other mills in the same town, at Stockport, Glossop, Chesterfield and elsewhere.[4] More important for the textile industry in general were the fly shuttle, roller spinning, the jenny, the mule and the power

[1] Lipson, *Economic History*, I. 318.
[2] Wadsworth and Mann, *The Cotton Trade and Industrial Lancashire*, p. 15.
[3] Baines, *History of the Cotton Manufacture*, pp. 163–164.
[4] Glover, *History . . . of Derby* (1829), pp. 247–8; Smiles, *Men of Invention, etc.* p. 120.

loom,[1] which, when Watt's steam engine could be used to drive them, brought about the transition to factory production, especially in the cotton industry, in which their full effects were most rapidly shown.

In that industry, as in others, the transition came earlier in spinning than in weaving. Cotton spinning must have been largely a factory industry by 1812, in which year, according to a Manchester employer in the trade, two-thirds of the cotton spinning then carried on was accomplished by means of Crompton's mule, which directly employed no less than 70,000 people.[2] Power-loom weaving was then only in its infancy, though Cartwright's invention had been available since 1784. Horrocks and others improved it early in the nineteenth century, and after the boom period of 1824 power looms multiplied. There were perhaps 85,000 of them in England and 15,000 in Scotland in 1833[3]; by 1835 the cotton industry required over 114,000, of which 17,531 were in Scotland.[4] That the steam engine had, nevertheless, not yet won a complete victory is evident from the large number of handlooms, of which there are believed to have been 250,000 used in the cotton industry in 1833[5]; and a member of the Commission on Handloom Weavers was astonished to find in 1840 that the number of people in that unhappy trade was " not only very considerable but . . . almost as great as at any former period." They survived, no doubt, because the craft was easy to learn, very poorly paid, and still necessary for some fabrics which the machines were not yet capable of producing; but the day of the handloom weaver was coming to an end in the cotton industry, though some of the people displaced could find employment in the woollen manufacture. There, power weaving

[1] On these inventions, which are outside the scope of the present volume, see *e.g.*, Daniels, *The Early English Cotton Industry*.

[2] Daniels, *op. cit.* p. 188.

[3] Baines, *op. cit.* p. 237.

[4] For figures relating to power looms, quoted from the Handloom Weavers Commission report, see Knowles, *Industrial and Commercial Revolutions*, p. 55.

[5] Baines, *op. cit.* p. 383.

"remained experimental down to 1830."[1] Five years later, the number of power looms in use was only 5,127, of which 22 were in Scotland. Indeed, as late as 1858 in Yorkshire, the chief seat of the industry, the majority of piece-working weavers remained outside the factories.[2]

Measured by the same standards, progress in the linen industry was even slower. A "mill or machine upon new principles for spinning yarn from hemp, tow, flax or wool" was patented in 1787 by John Kendrew, optician, and Thomas Porthouse, clock-maker, both of Darlington.[3] The first machine of this kind to be used in Scotland was purchased in 1790 by James Ivory of Brigton and was reported in 1791 to be producing a good, marketable yarn. Even earlier a Kendrew and Porthouse machine had been set up near Leeds by several partners, including John Marshall.[4] One of his foreman mechanics, Matthew Murray, made extensive alterations and improvements, and the Marshall works made Leeds the headquarters of flax spinning in England.[5] The output of such firms as Marshall, of Leeds, and Baxter, of Dundee, no doubt stimulated inquiry into the possibility of power weaving, but without any immediate results of importance. On account of the difference in the fibre, Cartwright's loom could not be used for linen; but it is said that power weaving was carried on in a London factory between 1813 and 1832.[6] A manufacturer in Aberdeen claimed to have 200 power looms erecting in 1824-25, and Baxters, in Dundee, commenced power-loom weaving in 1828, though they soon gave it up. In 1836 they started again, with better success, and by 1864 were said to employ more power looms in linen weaving than any other firm in the world. The year 1836 may perhaps be taken to mark the real beginning of the factory produc-

[1] Clapham I. 145.
[2] *ibid.* I. 193.
[3] A. J. Warden, *The Linen Trade* (1864), p. 690.
[4] J. Horner, *The Linen Trade of Europe*, pp. 253–254.
[5] For these works in 1864, see Warden, p. 383.
[6] Warden, p. 710.

tion of linen; in the previous year the total number of power looms in the industry was only 209 (168 in Scotland), or one for every 546 in the cotton industry. By that time, the steam-driven power loom was also in use for weaving the cheaper kinds of silk[1]; but the number for the whole industry in 1835 was only 1714; and twelve years later Porter wrote: "Except in . . . throwing, it has not hitherto been found practicable to apply machinery to any great extent for simplifying the processes of manufacturing the finer kinds of silk goods, or for economizing the cost of their production."[2]

The speeding up and cheapening of spinning was no doubt an advantage for two textile manufactures hitherto not mentioned, namely, the hosiery and lace trades, the former of which became notorious, in the Waterloo period, on account of the destructive activities of the followers of Ned Ludd. Unlike the machine-breakers of Lancashire and the West Riding, however, the Luddites of Nottinghamshire were not sabotaging new and power-driven machinery; they were attempting rather to prevent the use of unapprenticed labour, to stop the manufacture of inferior goods, such as "cut-ups," and especially to remedy abuses in connection with the hiring of the machines with which they worked. The knitting frame, invented as early as 1589,[3] was in 1837 and long afterwards used not in factories but in domestic industry, and largely for the production of stockings and underwear. Cotton knitted goods were produced chiefly in the Nottingham region, woollen goods mainly in Leicestershire and silk hosiery and the like in Derbyshire. In 1844 the three manufactures required about 42,700 knitting frames, of which over 24,800, or 58 per cent., were used in the cotton branch, 14,083, or 33 per cent., in the woollen, and only 3,771, or 9 per cent., in silk.[4] Lace-making by

[1] Clapham I. 196–197. [2] *Progress of the Nation* (1847), p. 224.
[3] Hammond, *The Skilled Labourer*, p. 221. On the Nottinghamshire Luddites, see *ibid*. p. 257 *et seq*.
[4] Porter, p. 209.

machinery began successfully in 1806. The machines, which were simplified and made more rapid in the ensuing forty years, were expensive, and it was exceptional for any one owner to possess more than thirty of them.[1] By 1844 bobbin-net production must have been mainly a factory business, for out of 3,200 machines, 1,750 were steam-driven.[2]

As the textile industries were transformed by machinery and steam power, so their geographical distribution altered, the change, as might be expected, being most noticeable in cotton and worsted. On the evidence picturesquely set out in Petermann's map,[3] of 1851, the woollen industry was widely extended, hardly any part of Great Britain being without some share in it; but the map gives no indication of the quantities produced, of the numbers employed or of the stage of development of the woollen industry in the various districts. In some of them it had little importance and in others was little more than a survival. The North Wales counties, for instance, had a woollen industry of some size in the eighteenth and earlier nineteenth centuries and were especially noted for the manufacture of flannel. Cotton goods also were produced at Holywell, Mold and Llangollen; but both industries suffered from the crisis of 1837, and the construction of railways rather harmed them by bringing English goods in than helped them by carrying Welsh goods out, though yarn was sent to Rochdale, to be woven into Lancashire "Welsh" flannel. The woollen industry did indeed survive, especially in the region of Newtown and Llanidloes, but its output and personnel were small.[4] Areas of much greater importance were suffering at the same time. Wiltshire, where, according to Defoe, "it was no extraordinary thing to have clothiers worth from

[1] Porter, p. 211. There were 837 owners in 1844; of these 717 owned five machines or fewer.
[2] *ibid.* p. 214.
[3] Based on census figures of occupations. For the map see the back of Clapham II; for a caution with regard to it, *ibid.* II. p. 26.
[4] A. H. Dodd, *The Industrial Revolution in North Wales*, pp. 280, 283, 297.

ten thousand to forty thousand pounds a man "[1] in the earlier eighteenth century, found employment for only 7,000 people in the woollen industry in 1851.[2] Scotland, which made contributions of its own to technical progress, such as Melrose's piecing machine and the introduction of the condenser from America by Thomas Roberts of Galashiels, employed about 15,000 people in its woollen industry in 1851. Important among its products were tweeds, the manufacture of which advanced considerably from 1829 onwards. By 1869 it employed 13,600 hands, used 3,400 horse-power and turned out goods worth more than £2,000,000.[3] The woollen industry of Great Britain as a whole had by 1851 almost reached its modern degree of concentration; 56,000 people, or forty per cent. of its whole personnel, were in the West Riding; and if to that county Lancashire be added, the two contained 48 per cent. of the woollen-cloth workers of Great Britain. The worsted manufacture was, by that time, almost entirely an industry of the West Riding. Over 86 per cent. of the spindles and 94 per cent. of the power looms used in it were in Yorkshire.

The silk industry, in Petermann's map, appears to have been widely distributed, being carried on in south-east Scotland, Devon, Somerset, Essex and Suffolk as well as in the better known silk regions of London, the Midlands and Lancashire and the neighbouring counties. This was to be expected, since handloom weaving survived, even in Lancashire, until 1850.[4] Nevertheless, in so far as the manufacture had become a factory industry, it already showed a marked tendency to concentration as early as 1835. Silk factories could then be found in twenty-three English counties; but only in nine of them did the factory workers exceed 1,000, and only three had more than 2,000. Cheshire, with 10,706, Lancashire, with 5,038, and Derby, with 2,725,

[1] *Tour through . . . Great Britain* (Everyman), I. 281.
[2] Clapham II. 27.
[3] D. Bremner, *Industries of Scotland*, pp. 157–158.
[4] Clapham II. 28.

accounted for more than 60 per cent. of the total of 30,000.[1] The linen industry showed much the same characteristics; it was scattered; power-loom weaving came late and slowly; but, in so far as it was a factory industry, concentration was observable by 1835. In that year seventeen English counties, with 152 factories between them, employed a little over 16,000 linen workers of all ages; but more than 3,000 of these were in Lancashire, and over 9,400 in the West Riding. Roughly speaking, about half the "factory" workers in linen were in England and half in Scotland and Ireland.[2] Four years later, when the total number of workers in England had hardly altered, Scotland had taken the lead. It had 183 factories at work, as compared with 169 in England, with more water and steam power to drive them and with more than 17,900 people employed in them.[3] Both countries later fell far behind Ireland; after 1856 the number of spindles in England declined and so also, after 1871, did the Scottish spindles. Ireland in 1874 had over 900,000 spindles, more by 148,000 than the total for Great Britain at its highest.[4]

The classic instance of concentration was the cotton industry. During the eighteenth century it had been carried on, in one form or another, in London, North Wiltshire, Dorset, Gloucestershire, Worcestershire and Herefordshire[5] as well as in the better known and more developed cotton districts of the north and Scotland. By 1838 the English industry was almost entirely concentrated in seven counties, Cheshire, Cumberland, Derby, Lancashire, Nottinghamshire, Staffordshire and Yorkshire[6]; but three of these counties had only 4,500 cotton operatives between them, and more than 96 per cent. of the total for the

[1] Porter, p. 223. Scotland had only 686 workers in its half-dozen silk factories.
[2] Porter, p. 233. Scotland had 13,409 workers, Ireland 3,681.
[3] *ibid.* p. 234.
[4] Porter (ed. Hirst, 1912), p. 357.
[5] Wadsworth and Mann, *The Cotton Trade and Industrial Lancashire*, p. 171.
[6] Chapman, *The Lancashire Cotton Industry*, p. 149. The seven counties contained 217,000 cotton workers. Flintshire, possibly, had 1,000 and there were about 1,200 elsewhere.

English industry lived in what was in fact a single cotton area, in Lancashire, Cheshire, Derbyshire and Yorkshire. The two former counties alone accounted for 86 per cent. The only other cotton district of importance was in Scotland, especially in the counties of Renfrew and Lanark. In 1838 the Scottish industry employed 35,600 hands, or a little under 14 per cent. of the total for Great Britain. Subsequently the numbers in Scotland declined not merely proportionately but absolutely; at the end of the nineteenth century, when Lancashire had 398,100 cotton operatives, Scotland had only 29,000.

It is thus clear that the textile industries as a whole showed a remarkable tendency to concentrate in two chief areas. The southern, and more important, region stretched from Liverpool across the Pennines to Leeds, with cotton mainly at its western end, wool at the eastern and silk in the centre. Similarly in Scotland the textile manufactures were mainly carried on in a belt stretching across the country from Paisley to Forfar, with Glasgow as the chief cotton centre and Dundee as the headquarters of linen and jute. Within these areas there was a further tendency to the concentration of particular processes and specialized products. Thus, for instance, cotton spinning came to be largely confined in Lancashire to the southern part of the county and weaving to the northern, especially to Blackburn, Burnley and Preston.[1] As yet the reasons for the transference of the textile industries from some regions to others are but imperfectly understood and agreed upon; but it would seem that some of the causes were only partly economic or not economic at all. Violent and corrupt municipal politics, for instance, partly explain the incapacity of Norwich to resist the growing competition of West Riding clothiers[2]; on the other hand, the lack of municipal status was possibly one of the factors favouring the industrial growth of

[1] Chapman, *op. cit.* p. 156. This development was only beginning by 1850; it was marked by 1884. See J. Jewkes in *Econ. Hist. Rev.* II. 90 *folg.*

[2] Clapham in *Economic Journal*, xx, 210.

Manchester.[1] Differences in temperament, a matter on which it is easier to be positive than convincing, may have had some effect, in helping ruder and determined northern types, starting with the cheaper and coarser fabrics, to menace, and ultimately to overcome, more conservative southern manufacturers, producing finer and more luxurious wares. No doubt the more abundant water power of Lancashire and Yorkshire gave those regions an advantage over the west of England, and, when the water-wheel yielded to the steam engine, the cheaper coal available in the same areas had a similar effect, but neither its becks nor its coal enabled Cumberland to set up textile manufactures of any great importance. Besides coal, the West Riding had iron and, like Lancashire and the region of the Clyde, engineers; these were factors of importance as textile machinery came to be constructed of iron and steel instead of wood.[2]

The location of industries in times past was, doubtless, partly determined by the existence of local supplies of raw material, but even in the sixteenth century it was possible to base a local industry on wool obtained from a distance. "Halifax men," says a writer of 1588, "occupie a fyne wolle most owt of Lincolneshire" and sell their own coarser wool to the men of Rochdale.[3] With improved communications in the eighteenth century this was easier; and when, in the nineteenth century, Australian wool became available in large quantities, it went to the places where the industry was established and did not call new industries into existence near the ports. On the other hand, Dundee may, in part, have owed its predominance in the linen industry to its convenience for the importation of continental flax.[4] The concentration of the cotton industry in Lan-

[1] Chapman, p. 154.
[2] Clapham, *op. cit.* p. 209.
[3] Crump and Ghorbal, *History of the Huddersfield Woollen Industry*, p. 33.
[4] Between 1838 and 1863 its imports were never below 12,000 tons in the year, and were sometimes over 30,000 tons. See Warden, *op. cit.* p. 633.

cashire has been explained as in part the result of having near at hand one of the best harbours in the world, the Mersey estuary[1]; but this perhaps rather helps to explain the growth of the industry when once established than to account for its beginnings in Lancashire. The raw material was at first imported from the Levant and unloaded in London. West Indian and Brazilian cotton was imported into Liverpool during the last twenty years of the eighteenth century, and, after the invention of Eli Whitney's gin for cleaning cotton in 1794, the importation from the United States increased enormously.[2] By 1810 that country was far and away the most important source of supply. Liverpool and Glasgow were certainly convenient both for importing raw cotton and for exporting manufactured goods, but other ports might have served, if not as well, at least adequately. Whitehaven and Lancaster imported West Indian cotton in the eighteenth century,[3] and Bristol, which had advantages comparable with those of Liverpool, might conceivably have become the port of entry for an important cotton industry in its neighbourhood, for cotton spinning was carried on in Gloucestershire in the eighteenth century.[4]

One circumstance favouring the establishment of textile industries was poverty of soil, or insufficiency of land, which drove small-scale cultivators to find by-occupations. These conditions were not confined, however, to the Pennine

[1] Schulze-Gaevernitz, *Cotton Trade in England and on the Continent* (1895), p. 39; Chapman, p. 153.

[2] The change in the sources of supply is evident from the following table, for which see T. Ellison, *The Cotton Trade of Great Britain* (1886), p. 86:

	Percentage of import from					
	U.S.A	Brazil	British W. Indies	Mediterranean	East Indies	Sundries.
1786–90	·16	7·87	70·75	20·44	·78	—
1796–1800	24·08	11·43	35·23	18·47	8·9	1·89
1806–10	53·14	16·07	16·23	1·28	12·79	·49
1846–50	81·13	3·76	·12	2·04	12·76	·19

[3] Daniels, *The Early English Cotton Industry*, p. 58.

[4] Wadsworth and Mann, p. 172.

slopes and were important only in connection with other factors; they meant that when opportunities for expansion came, the existence of sufficiently skilled labour enabled them to be seized. The cotton industry was, no doubt, established the more easily in Lancashire because the spinning and weaving of flax and wool were already carried on there. Another factor which is believed to have been of special importance in concentrating the same industry in Lancashire was the climate. "The county has to thank the proximity of the sea for something still more important—the damp sea-breezes which envelop the hills and produce rains. The degree of moisture of the air is, in fact, on those heights, only ten per cent. below complete saturation. This dampness was, later, to make it possible to spin cotton to such a fineness here as is impossible elsewhere, or only to be attained by large extra expense."[1] It is said that Americans in 1890 considered the advantage of the damp Lancashire air to be equal to seven per cent. of the cost of production on fine counts of yarn.[2] This factor, however, does not appear to have been of any importance in the early history of the industry, and, according to one authority, it mattered less than the abundance of soft water, free from lime.[3]

THE TEXTILE INDUSTRIES AFTER 1850

The mechanical inventions mentioned at the beginning of this chapter, though they provided a foundation for the factory production of textiles, required innumerable improvements and additions before the modern industry became possible. Among the more important of those additions were the devices[4] which between them brought an end to the ancient and, in its way, aristocratic craft of the woolcomber. Edmund Cartwright, the inventor of the power loom, had patented his Big Ben as far back as 1792; but

[1] Schulze-Gaevernitz, *op. cit.* p. 39; cf. Chapman, p. 153.
[2] Schulze-Gaevernitz, *op. cit.* 40 n.
[3] Wadsworth and Mann, p. 172.
[4] On these machines see James Burnley, *History of Wool and Wool Combing.*

this did not fulfil the claims made for it and, though it showed that the problem could be solved, did not itself provide an adequate solution. A great advance was made by Josué Heilmann, a native of Alsace, who turned his mind to the problem of combing cotton in 1841, and in 1846 took out an English patent for a combing machine on the "nip" principle. In the meanwhile, a greatly improved, but still unsatisfactory, wool-combing machine had been produced by G. E. Donisthorpe; his patent rights were purchased by S. Cunliffe Lister, who, in association with the original inventor and after considerable expense, made the "white elephant" a practicable and profitable machine. Its success depended on the "nip" principle, which Donisthorpe and Lister began to use about 1850, and though they claimed to have arrived independently at the improvements in their machines, Heilmann's representatives successfully sued for infringement of his patent. They also disposed of his English interests to Messrs. Akroyd and Titus Salt, and they sold them to Lister, who was thus able to clear his rivals from the field and to dominate wool-combing in the West Riding. His interests were by no means confined to that region; at one time he had, beside five wool-combing mills in England, four others on the Continent. Later he turned his attention to the problem of working up silk waste, and, after ten years of experiment and an expenditure of £360,000, succeeded there as well. Another inventor, long interested in wool-combing machinery, was Isaac Holden, who in 1847 was associated with Lister in a patent covering various minor improvements. In the following year the two were partners in a wool-combing mill in France, and patented a machine on the principle of "square motion," of which Holden claimed the invention though the patent was in his partner's name. The firm of Isaac Holden and Sons, established in 1859, opened the Alston Mills five years later at Bradford, where, by 1889, it could comb at the rate of more than 31,000,000 fleeces annually. Meanwhile, still another variety of combing machine had been patented in 1853. It was the invention of James Noble, working in conjunction with Lister's partner, Donisthorpe.

In the cotton industry, the major changes were first the introduction of ring spinning and, second, completely automatic weaving. Ring spinning, patented in the United States by J. Thorpe in 1828, and widely used in that country, did not reach Lancashire until about the middle of the nineteenth century and was not widely adopted for some time afterwards. The ring frame could be tended by women and worked at very high speed. Its great advantage was that it made spinning continuous; but it did not suit English conditions as well as it did American, being incapable of spinning a weft yarn good enough for some of the finer fabrics, for which purpose the improved, and increasingly automatic, mule was still necessary. Weaving also was made continuous. Various devices were introduced which caused the loom to stop automatically when the weft yarn broke, and, later, devices for the recharging of shuttles so as to interrupt the weaving as little as possible. In this kind of improvement also Great Britain rather lagged behind the United States, in which the Northrop, or completely automatic, loom was invented in 1892. It was most suitable for weaving plain fabrics and not so well adapted for those produced in Lancashire.

To feed the new and rapid machinery there were required immense quantities of raw materials, which both industries drew from abroad. Australian fleeces, in very small quantities, began to appear in the English market before 1830; but in 1835, when 42,000,000 lbs. were imported, only about one tenth of the quantity came from Australia, while more than half of it came from Germany. By 1850 Australia supplied 39,000,000 lbs. out of a total importation of 75,300,000 lbs., and Germany sent only 9,200,000 lbs.[1] In that year the domestic yield of wool was still far in excess

[1] Clapham II. 7.

of imports. The change during the remainder of the century is indicated in the following table[1]:

	Domestic yield lbs.	Imported lbs.
1850	130,000,000	70,000,000
1870	150,000,000	266,000,000
1900	141,000,000	587,000,000

The cotton industry, in comparison, was unfortunate, since it relied for the most part of its raw material on the United States and, consequently, suffered when the supply was interrupted by the Civil War. The decline, as the following table[2] makes clear, was sudden and profound:

	Imports from U.S.A. in bales.	Total imports in bales.	Total imports in million lbs.	Liverpool average prices of middling Orleans, in pence per lb.
1861	1,841,600	3,035,700	1261·4	9
1862	71,766	1,445,068	533·1	18½
1863	131,900	1,932,200	691·8	24½
1864	197,800	2,587,100	896·1	27¾
1865	461,910	2,755,310	966·4	19¾
1866	1,162,740	3,749,040	1353·8	15⅚

It was realized at the time that, apart from the cotton famine, the early 'sixties would have brought some degree of stagnation, for 1859 and 1860 were years of "terrific prosperity and over-production," stimulated by huge yields of American cotton, with a low price for it, and a large demand for cotton goods in the Far East.[3] Thus by 1861 manufacturers had large stocks on hand which, but for the outbreak of the Civil War, they would have had to sell at very low prices. Once these stocks were disposed of, Lancashire was overwhelmed with disaster. Short time was followed by unemployment on a vast scale. In three years, according to one calculation,[4] employers lost £28,500,000,

[1] Porter (ed. Hirst), p. 333. It will be noted that his figure for 1850 does not quite agree with Clapham's.

[2] Imports, Ellison, *Cotton Trade of Great Britain*, Table 1; prices, W. O. Henderson, *The Lancashire Cotton Famine*, pp. 122–123.

[3] R. A. Arnold, *History of the Cotton Famine* (1865), pp. 29–32.

[4] J. Watts, *Facts of the Cotton Famine* (1866), p. 369.

and the working classes lost £33,000,000 in wages.[1] Savings disappeared and poor-relief expenditure mounted. In 28 cotton districts in 1861 it had been £191,101; it was £231,322 in 1862, £1,469,698 in 1863 and £1,140,655 in 1864. Moreover, without counting private and unrecorded charity, the Mansion House and other funds amounted to more than £1,660,000.[2] It was noteworthy that starving Lancashire remained orderly and that working-class sympathy, despite the distress, was with the liberating northern states. The cotton famine clearly showed what some observers had feared before, the danger of relying on one country for so considerable a proportion of the raw material, and this stimulated inquiry into the possibility of developing other cotton-growing areas. Brazilian and Egyptian cotton were found useful for some kinds of fabric and the short-stapled Indian and Syrian cotton for others; and had the Civil War continued those countries might have become the chief sources, though their cotton could not have been obtained so cheaply.[3] In fact, the southern states continued to supply the bulk of the cotton used in Great Britain; in 1884, out of a total importation of 4,154,700 bales, 2,765,170 came from the United States.[4]

The trouble of Lancashire, as one historian said, was the opportunity of Yorkshire and, as the same authority showed, of Belfast as well. Between 1861 and 1864 the area under flax was more than doubled; the export of linen yarn rose from just under 28 million lbs. to more than 40·5 million and the export of linen fabrics from 116·3 to 209·9 million yards.[5] The impetus to the woollen and worsted trade, though real, was less remarkable.[6] Nevertheless, after the cotton famine, cotton quickly regained and increased its

[1] J. Watts, *Facts of the Cotton Famine* (1866), pp. 462–465.
[2] S. J. Chapman, *op. cit.* p. 68.
[3] Henderson, *op. cit.* pp. 50–51.
[4] Ellison, *op. cit.* Table 1.
[5] Watts, *Facts of the Cotton Famine*, pp. 385-386.
[6] *ibid.*, p. 395. Between 1861 and 1864 the export of woollen yarns rose from 27·5 million to 31·9 million lbs. and the export of woollen and worsted fabrics from 164·4 million to 241·5 million yards.

dominance among textiles. Its position may be appreciated from the fact that in the years 1880 to 1884, when the exports of the United Kingdom were worth £234,000,000, textiles accounted for 46 per cent., and cotton for nearly 32·5 per cent., of that sum.[1] That result was brought about by an enormous increase in spindles and looms and by driving them at greater speeds, thus increasing the productivity of the operatives and decreasing the costs of production.[2] This meant an increasing concentration of the workers in factories, but the number of persons employed in them probably grew less rapidly than the number of machines. The average number of operatives in a cotton factory, which had been 137 in 1838, had only reached 177 as late as 1871. In the same year the average for worsted mills, which had grown more rapidly, was 175, and for woollen mills, which lagged far behind, was only 70 workers.[3]

[1] Clapham II. 29.

[2] This may be shown by the following comparisons, extracted from Ellison, pp. 68–69:

	Yarn Spun, in million lbs.	Spindles	Hands	Production		Wages. per lb.
				Per spindle	Per hand	
1844–46	523·3	19,500,000	190,000	26·8 lbs.	2,754 lbs.	2·3d.
1859–61	910	30,400,000	248,000	30 lbs.	3,671 lbs.	2·1d.
1880–82	1,324	42,000,000	240,000	31·5 lbs.	5,520 lbs.	1·9d.

	Goods, in million lbs.	Looms	Hands	Production		Wages per lb.
				Per loom	Per hand	
1844–46	348·1	282,000	210,000	1,234 lbs.	1,681 lbs.	3.5d.
1859–61	650·9	400,000	203,000	1,627 lbs.	3,206 lbs.	2.9d.
1880–82	993·5	550,000	246,000	1,806 lbs.	4,039 lbs.	2·3d.

[3] Clapham II. 117.

CHAPTER V

THE IRON, COAL AND ENGINEERING INDUSTRIES

IRON AND STEEL

IN 1840 the British iron industry had benefited by more than a century of progress and expansion.[1] Early in the eighteenth century the first Abraham Darby at Coalbrookdale, succeeding where Dud Dudley and others failed, had smelted iron by means of coke, and thus began the emancipation of the foundry from the forests, to which it had been tied by the necessity of charcoal as fuel. His process was not practicable with all kinds of coal, and spread slowly, but the great Carron Works, opened in 1760, were from the first intended to carry on coke smelting, and during the second half of the eighteenth century the new method was rapidly adopted elsewhere. As early as 1788, out of 61,300 tons of pig iron produced, 48,200 tons were coke-smelted; and by 1806 the charcoal iron amounted only to 7,800 tons out of a total output of 258,206 tons.[2] What Abraham Darby did for iron another Quaker, Benjamin Huntsman, did for steel. In or shortly after 1740, at Handsworth, near Sheffield, he worked out the process for producing crucible, or cast, steel. His was a harder and more uniform metal than any which could be made by the older method and, apart from its advantages in the production of clock springs, razors and the like, was of the greatest importance for the making of dies and machine tools, without which the development of engineering was hardly possible. A third step forward in the eighteenth century was the invention of puddling and rolling, perfected by Henry Cort in 1783 and 1784, which

[1] On the technical improvements and the history of the industry in the eighteenth and early nineteenth centuries, see Ashton, *Iron and Steel in the Industrial Revolution*.
[2] H. Scrivenor, *Comprehensive History of the Iron Trade* (1841), pp. 87, 97.

enabled pit coal to be used in the production of a bar iron of high quality. This process, with improvements such as the substitution of a metal for a sand floor, laid the basis of a large new industry, especially in South Wales, where Richard Crawshay, at the Cyfarthfa Works, and Samuel Homfray, at Penydarren, were among the first to introduce it.[1]

With the extended use of pit coal there came other developments, and especially the application of steam power for working the blast, the forge hammer and the rolling mill. It was no accident that James Watt's first engine was set up in Kinneil House for Roebuck, of the Carron Iron Works, in 1769. Another great iron-master, John Wilkinson, had four steam engines to work his blast by 1780, and he was followed by still others in Sheffield, Rotherham, Neath, Penydarren, Dowlais and elsewhere. By 1800 the industry employed 30 Boulton and Watt engines[2]; it was thereby in process of being freed from dependence on inadequate and irregular supplies of water power, and tended more than ever to be concentrated on the coal fields. Its progress was, meanwhile, profoundly influenced by the vast armament demand inevitable in the reign of George III, about half of which consisted of years of war. After Waterloo depression settled down on the industry until the boom years, 1823 to 1825.

At that period James Neilson,[3] manager of the Glasgow Gas Works, was working out his revolutionary theory of the hot blast. It was contrary to the beliefs of iron-masters, who considered that better iron was produced in winter than in summer because the air in the blast was colder; but experiment soon showed the correctness of Neilson's conclusions. His patent was taken out in 1829 and the method tried out at the Clyde Iron Works. Previously,

[1] C. Wilkins, *History of the Iron, Steel, Tinplate and Other Trades of Wales* (1903), p. 277.

[2] J. Lord, *Capital and Steam Power*, p. 175.

[3] On whom see Smiles, *Industrial Biography*, chapter IX.

with coke and cold blast, it took more than 161 cwts. of coal to produce a ton of cast iron; in 1830, by heating the blast to 300 degrees Fahrenheit, the amount necessary was reduced to just over 103 cwts.; by raising the temperature to 600 degrees Fahrenheit and using raw coal instead of coke, a further reduction, to just over 45 cwts., was made possible in 1833.[1] Cheap as coal was in Scotland, this great reduction in the quantity required greatly stimulated the use of the new method, and, with the added advantage of the blackband ironstone, the Scottish industry advanced remarkably in the following period. Its output of pig iron was said to be 37,500 tons in 1830 and over 195,000 tons in 1839.[2]

In 1840 there were ten districts which between them were estimated to produce 1,396,700 tons of iron.[3] Northumberland was then the least considerable of all, with an output of only 11,000 tons; the Forest of Dean did a little better with 15,500 tons and North Wales better still with 26,500 tons. Flintshire and Denbighshire, nevertheless, though the latter had made history in its day, were on the point of losing much of their importance in the iron industry; a few larger works in the neighbourhood of Wrexham survived because of railway development, but the 'forties brought stagnation to the others.[4] Derbyshire in 1840 produced 31,000 tons, and Yorkshire 56,000 tons. The really important districts were, in order of output, South Wales (505,000 tons), Staffordshire (427,650), Scotland (241,000) and Shropshire (82,750). The scale of operations varied considerably between these districts; in 1830, for instance, the average annual output of a blast furnace in Yorkshire was 1,071 tons, in Scotland 1,389 tons and in South Wales 2,457 tons.[5] The number of furnaces to a firm also varied.

[1] Scrivenor, pp. 296–297.
[2] *ibid.*, pp. 298–99.
[3] Porter (1847), p. 272.
[4] Dodd, *Industrial Revolution in North Wales*, pp. 150–151.
[5] For the number of furnaces and the outputs of the districts, see Scrivenor, p. 134.

As late as 1846, except for Cyfarthfa and Dowlais, which had eleven and eighteen respectively, no firm in the country had as many as ten, and the average was under four.[1] The blast furnaces were growing in size by that time, but it is clear that the foundry, as such, was not necessarily a large concern; as late as 1862 it would appear that a Black Country furnace on the average employed 40 people.[2] On the other hand, the leading iron firms, since the eighteenth century, had been integrated, having their own coal and iron mines and being engaged not only in smelting but in refining and rolling iron.[3] In that event, the numbers employed might be very large; Crawshay, with six furnaces and two rolling mills, is said to have employed 1,500 men at Cyfarthfa in 1806.[4] Works on this scale were doubtless exceptional; but a personnel of 300 or 500, not counting colliers and miners, was not at all uncommon in the early nineteenth century.[5] It followed that large capitals were necessary; in 1833, it was estimated, an iron works with a capacity of 300 tons of bar iron a week might cost "anything from £50,000 to £150,000."[6]

In marked contrast to the "heavy" end of the iron industry, as it was carried on in such vast works as those at Dowlais, the hardware and cutlery trades obstinately preserved their ancient small-scale character. Thus in 1841 there were to be found in and about Sheffield over 12,000 persons employed in the cutlery, and nearly 3,000 in the file, trade, the great majority of whom worked either by themselves or in very small establishments.[7] The first factory in which all processes were carried on was erected in 1823, and the production of knife blades by revolving dies began, though not very successfully, in 1827. Saw-grinding

[1] Clapham II. pp. 429–430.
[2] G. C. Allen, *Industrial Development of Birmingham and the Black Country*, p. 90.
[3] Ashton, *op. cit.* p. 100.
[4] Wilkins, *op. cit.* p. 68.
[5] Ashton, p. 100.
[6] *ibid.*
[7] G. I. H. Lloyd, *The Cutlery Trades*, p. 180.

machinery was introduced from America by a Sheffield saw maker in 1858; file-cutting machinery began to be used about 1875; late in the second half of the nineteenth century forging by hand gave way to forging by means of pneumatic hammers, blades were produced by means of presses, and the accessory parts of knives were stamped out of sheet metal.[1] Despite these changes the business unit remained small; as late as 1900 the average number employed in a file-cutting workshop was less than four, and there were, besides, many outworkers, earning their small pay in their own homes. Especially in times of depression, the cutlery trades in general were thronged with what Sheffield still calls "little mesters," who were either factors on a small scale with outworkers in their employment or entrepreneurs hiring a little power and small premises, where they employed from two to six persons on such grinding or other work as they could obtain from factors or factories.[2] Similarly in Birmingham the production of finished goods was on a small scale. The master gunmaker, for instance, was usually a factor who acquired the parts of a gun and distributed them to specialized craftsmen to finish and assemble. The parts were commonly made by little masters, either employing outworkers or having small workshops, or doing both.[3] Nail-making, in 1860, was still a domestic industry, the nailer providing his own tools and fuel and working up, with the help of his wife and children, the iron supplied to him every week by the nailmaster.[4]

In the half century which followed Queen Victoria's accession the history of the iron and steel industry was a story of new markets, new inventions and a changing order of importance in the centres. After Waterloo the armament demand had given way to orders for boilers, machine

[1] G. I. H. Lloyd, *The Cutlery Trades*, pp. 186–187, 198.
[2] *ibid.* pp. 196–197.
[3] G. C. Allen, *op. cit.* p. 116.
[4] *ibid.* p. 125.

parts and gas- and water-piping, though that use of iron was probably not very considerable before reformed municipal government and Chadwick's boards of health had begun to take effect. In the 'forties, the great customers for iron were the railway companies; the new lines opened in 1847–48, it has been calculated, needed about 400,000 tons in addition to their requirements for rolling stock and bridges[1]; and the railway mania "ran the price of Scotch pig iron from 32s. up to £5 10s. 0d. per ton, and Staffordshire bars rose from £5 6s. 0d. to £12 per ton."[2] Once the railway skeleton had been constructed, the demand for iron naturally declined; but new customers arose in the shipyards. In 1850 the net tonnage of iron ships built was only 12,800; it rose to 64,679 by 1860, 255,000 by 1870 and 390,953 by 1877.[3] Each register ton meant, perhaps, half a ton of iron in the hull, and, since about four-fifths of the iron ships built in 1879 consisted of steamers, there would be an additional need of iron for making boilers and machinery. In time, both railway lines and ships came to be made of steel. The former were first laid down by the London and North Western at Crewe in 1861[4], and a further experiment was tried at Camden Town in 1862. A long time was necessary, however, before it became clear that the greater hardness, toughness and durability of the steel rail were worth the higher price that had to be paid for them, and the complete abandonment of the iron rail by the larger companies came only in the later 'seventies.[5] As late as 1886 Sir Lowthian Bell left it on record that a great diversity of opinion prevailed on the comparative capacity of iron and steel rails to stand heavy traffic.[6] For shipbuilding, steel had great advantages in its relative lightness and its higher

[1] Clapham I. 428.
[2] Sir Lowthian Bell, *The Iron Trade of the United Kingdom* (1886; an issue in book form of a statement submitted to the Royal Commission on Depression of Trade), p. 7.
[3] Bell, *op. cit.* p. 43.
[4] *D.N.B.* under Bessemer.
[5] Clapham II. 61.
[6] Bell, *op. cit.* p. 33.

capacity to resist strain, but here also its price was high and, as late as 1880, nine iron ships were built for every one of steel.[1]

The first major step towards the production of cheap steel was the invention of Henry Bessemer, an investigator of Huguenot extraction, whose father, an expert in die sinking, had set up a type-founding establishment in partnership with William Caslon. Several of the younger Bessemer's inventions were connected with printing and with dies; the best known of them was probably the device, for perforating the faces of stamps, which prevented frauds upon the revenue amounting to hundreds of thousands of pounds every year. This at last brought him a knighthood; but more important, as the source of an income which enabled him to carry on experiments in metallurgy, were the processes upon which a flourishing business in bronze powder and gold paint was based. When, after forty years of peace, the Crimean War called the attention of inventors to the defects of British artillery, Bessemer began a course of investigations to discover a better metal and arrived, not without the help of a happy accident, at the essentials of the process which bears his name and which, with many modifications in detail, was covered by a series of patents between 1854 and 1869. The principle was described in a famous paper "On the Manufacture of Malleable Iron and Steel without Fuel" read at the British Association in 1856. At bottom it consisted in running molten pig iron directly into a converter, in which air at high pressure was blown into it, keeping its temperature high and burning out impurities, so that either malleable iron or steel could be produced, according to the degree of elimination of carbon. Though at first eagerly taken up by producers desiring to save the fuel consumed in puddling, the process commonly failed, and much further investigation was required in order to find the causes, the chief one being the use of iron with too high a phosphorus content. In order to carry on his work

[1] Bell, *op. cit.* p. 52.

Bessemer in 1859 opened at Sheffield an iron and steel works in which, for fourteen years, he earned extraordinarily large profits, to which, of course, he added the licence fees paid by other firms, in this country and elsewhere, who set up Bessemer plants.

Meanwhile a beginning had been made with a method of steel production which, before the end of the century, was to overtake the Bessemer process and eventually almost to supersede it in Britain. It was the invention of William Siemens, though he is believed to have owed much to his brother Frederick. They were members of an extraordinarily able Hanoverian family of scientific engineers; a third brother, Werner, was the inventor of the electric dynamo. William Siemens, who came to England at the age of twenty in 1843 to dispose of an electro-plating process, was a pioneer in the investigation of heat economy, and in 1856 took out a patent for the application to furnaces of the "regenerative" principle. In 1857 it was applied to the melting and reheating of steel and was the basis of what is called "open hearth" steel production. One form of the process owed much to Emile Martin of Sireuil, who produced cast steel by melting steel scrap in a bath of molten pig iron. The idea had occurred to Bessemer, who took out a patent for a process of this kind in 1855. Siemens himself, at the Landore works, opened in 1869, did not use scrap steel but a pure ore, which was poured into the molten pig at a high temperature. In comparison with Bessemer's, the Siemens process was slow, for it required six hours or more as against fifteen minutes; on the other hand it permitted a greater range of hardness and mildness to be achieved, was far more exact in its working, and produced a metal which was more uniform and reliable throughout. Bessemer steel was preferred for railway and structural use, open-hearth steel for ship-building, sheets and such purposes as required ductility as well as uniformity.[1] The

[1] J. S. Jeans, *Iron Trade of Great Britain*, pp. 55–61.

relative progress of the two methods may be indicated by the fact that between 1880 and 1885 the proportion of open-hearth steel to Bessemer steel produced rose from about one quarter to about one half.[1]

In comparison with these processes, puddling had an advantage in that it was not restricted to special ores, whereas the new methods of production required haematite ore, of which this country had only limited supplies, in Furness and West Cumberland. Fortunately for the Bessemer plants, however, the iron ores of Spain would serve, and, though the prices of haematite remained substantially higher than those of Cleveland iron, the economy of working was so great that ore could be " brought from Bilbao and converted into steel rails at Middlesbrough at the same or even a less cost than the same article can be made of iron from the ironstone of the Cleveland Hills, lying almost at the gates of the rail-mills."[2] There would, nevertheless, be an enormous advantage in a discovery enabling phosphoric iron ores to be used; and this was at length achieved by the experiments of Sidney Gilchrist Thomas and his cousin Percy Gilchrist, culminating in 1879 at the Middlesbrough works of the Bolckow Vaughan Company. The process consisted in lining the converter with calcareous substances and adding similar material to the charge, in order to get rid of phosphorus, which Bessemer's process could not remove from the iron. Possibly because non-phosphoric ores were easy to import, the new process was only slowly adopted in this country. On the Continent, and especially in Lorraine, where the native ore was phosphoric and haematite could not easily be imported, the basic process enormously stimulated production.

The progress of the industry in the forty years with which we are here concerned may be gauged by the increase in the average weekly " make " of furnaces: 64 tons in 1839, 126 tons in 1860 and 263 tons in 1880. The total annual

[1] See table, Clapham II. 58.

[2] Bell, *op. cit.* p. 17.

"make" of the country rose from 1,243,680 tons in 1839 to 3,826,750 tons in 1860 and 7,749,230 tons in 1880. The changing importance of the districts is indicated in the following table,[1] which brings out the relative decline of Scotland and South Wales and the emergence of the North Eastern, North Western and Lincolnshire and Northamptonshire areas.

	Percentages of total output of pig iron		
	1839	1860	1880
Wales and Monmouth ..	38·80	26·63	12·23
Staffordshire	28·99	16·11	7·87
Shropshire	6.46	3·79	1·14
Scotland	15·70	24·50	13·53
West Riding	4·20	2·58	3·96
Derbyshire	2·73	3·28	4·73
North-Western[2] ..	—	4·42	19·88
North-Eastern[3]	0·04	17·22	31·99
Lincolnshire and Northants	—	0·19	4·99

COAL MINING

Stimulated by the continued growth of population, by improved transport, by the multiplication of steam engines and by the development of the metallurgical industries, coal mining expanded rapidly during the first four decades of the nineteenth century. The total output was perhaps about 16,000,000 tons in 1816, 30,000,000 tons in 1836, and 44,000,000 tons in 1846.[4] One factor contributing to this great increase was Sir Humphry Davy's safety lamp, invented in 1815, which, according to a contemporary,[5] "operated as a complete renovation to many of the collieries which were then in a state of exhaustion," for it enabled mining to be carried on in places previously too dangerous to work in and made it possible to take out coal which other-

[1] Extracted from Bell, *op. cit.* p. 9.
[2] Cumberland and Lancashire.
[3] Northumberland, Durham and North Riding.
[4] Clapham I. 431.
[5] Quoted in Porter, p. 277.

wise would have had to be left underground. The Davy lamp was, however, adopted only slowly. Even in the North of England, where it was most widely used, it was very rarely employed, in 1841, except in "broken" and "pillar working," and in Lancashire and Cheshire, at the same date, it was used only when the workings were tried before the colliers began their labour for the day. The men, it is said, did not like it because it gave a poorer light than candles, and, since they were paid by piece-work, they preferred the naked light despite its danger.[1]

Another factor helping to increase the output was the spread of more thorough methods of winning the mineral. In the nineteenth century, as in the eighteenth, the methods, though there were many local variants, fell into two broadly different categories.[2] Especially in the North of England, the system used was that commonly known as "bord and pillar"; in Scotland it was called "stoop and room"; in Staffordshire, "post and thirl." The "bord," "room," "thirl" or "stall" was the place in which the miner cut away the coal; and between such places it was necessary to leave pillars of coal standing, to take the pressure of the strata above them. Failing any other method of support, and in places where the pressure was considerable, these pillars had to be very wide. Thus, the deeper the pit, the smaller the proportion of coal that could be won. An estimate relating to the North of England suggests that at a depth of 20 fathoms the pillars ought to be 20 feet by 5, and at 300 fathoms, 30 feet by 24.[3] These figures applied, however, only to the first working, and it was calculated that by subsequent operations many of the pillars could be removed, a business which, though still very risky, was made easier by the Davy lamp. In broad con-

[1] R. L. Galloway, *Annals of Coal Mining and the Coal Trade, Second Series* (1904), pp. 306, 309.

[2] On the methods and variants, see Galloway, *op. cit.* chapters XVIII and XIX; also H. Stanley Jevons, *The British Coal Trade*, chapter VIII.

[3] Galloway, *op. cit.* p. 251.

trast to "pillar and bord," long-wall working aimed at extracting all the coal in one operation, leaving, instead of pillars of coal, a packing of stone, slack and rubble to fill the "goaf" or "gob" whence the coal had come and upon which the superincumbent strata gradually settled down. This method, which appears to have taken its rise in Shropshire in the seventeenth century, spread during the eighteenth to Warwickshire, Derbyshire, Lancashire, East Cumberland and even Scotland, Shropshire colliers being sometimes taken to other districts to begin it.[1] About 1820 it reached the Forest of Dean and, in and after 1840, South Wales and Monmouthshire.[2] Though tried before 1800 in the neighbourhood of Newcastle-on-Tyne, and, about 1850, at Monkwearmouth and other pits, the long-wall method has not, to this day, become universal in the coal-fields of the Tyne and Wear.[3] Long-wall working was sometimes begun near the shaft bottom; in other cases the extraction started at the boundary, so that the miner worked towards the shaft. The second variant, called long-wall retreating, was probably safer, since falls of the roof, as they occurred, were behind him and not between him and the shaft; but it meant a large outlay before any coal was raised, and required, therefore, greater capital resources.

As the coal output increased the pits were sunk to greater depths. In the earlier eighteenth century the maximum depth in Northumberland and Durham, where the deepest pits were, was about 400 feet,[4] and coal below 360 feet was ordinarily considered to be inaccessible.[5] By 1793 a pit at the Howgill colliery, Whitehaven, was sunk to a depth of 993 feet, though coal was raised only from 726 feet, and the same colliery contained what was considered the deepest pit in England in 1801, the coal being 894 feet below the

[1] T. S. Ashton and J. Sykes, *The Coal Industry of the Eighteenth Century*, pp. 30–31.
[2] Galloway, *op. cit.* p. 247.
[3] Galloway, *op. cit.* pp. 248, 251; Ashton and Sykes, p. 32.
[4] Galloway, *Annals of Coal Mining* (*First Series*, 1898), p. 231.
[5] *ibid.* p. 248.

surface.[1] In the Midlands and South Wales in 1840 and later there were still many shallow workings; the Tredegar Iron Company, for instance, worked a vein of coal 15 feet thick lying only ten inches down.[2] But in most places, and especially in the northern coal-fields, the deeper measures had to be sought. Up to 1835, indeed, practically all the nation's coal was obtained from pits of less than 1,000 feet depth.[3] Monkwearmouth was exceptionally deep—1,590 feet—for the eighteen-thirties; but in the next decade Lancashire approached this depth. The Arley pit at Ince was sunk down to 1,242 feet in 1849; at Pendleton, near Manchester, one seam at a depth of 1,392 feet had been reached in 1840, and another was worked later at 1,527 feet. Monkwearmouth went deeper still, to the Hutton seam at 1,722 feet, in 1846. The deepest pit of all was at Apedale in North Staffordshire, 2,145 feet.[4] Since the sinking of such deep shafts was too costly to be easily repeated, it became necessary to work the seams to which they led as extensively as possible, and this in turn meant additional outlays on roads, tramways, winding gear and other necessaries. Thus as early as 1830 sums ranging from £10,000 to £150,000 might be spent on single collieries[5]; and by 1838 the Northern Coal Mining Company, which proved unfortunate, was started with a capital of £500,000.[6]

The managements of the larger and deeper pits were inevitably faced with problems relating to ventilation, haulage and winding. The ancient enemies, choke damp and fire damp, the latter of which is still an occasional cause of appalling disasters, were dealt with in several ways[7]; but the

[1] Galloway, p. 355.
[2] *ibid. Second Series*, p. 349. In Sheffield, during the making of new streets, so large a surface of coal was uncovered that bricks for the houses were made from clay got out of the cellars and burnt with coal dug from the same spot. *Ibid.* p. 348.
[3] Galloway, *Annals, First Series*, p. 477.
[4] Galloway, *Annals, Second Series*, pp. 13, 17, 351.
[5] Clapham I. 424.
[6] Galloway, *Annals* II, p. 11.
[7] On ventilation see Galloway, II, chapters XX, XXI, XXII; and K. N. Moss, in *Historical Review of Coal Mining*, chapter IX.

most effective means, almost universally used in the North of England in the first half of the nineteenth century,[1] was to keep furnaces burning at the bottom of the upcast shaft. These, by heating the outflowing air, caused a draught which, starting down the downcast shaft, could, by means of trap doors and brattices, be split and directed to all parts of the mine. This method was not, however, equally practicable everywhere and, even in the best conditions, had its disadvantages; the furnaces were destructive of ropes and tackle, made repair work difficult and, worst of all, entailed some risk of fire and explosion (though this risk could be minimized by means of a dumb drift, bringing the escaping air into the shaft at a point well above the furnaces); moreover, if an explosion did occur, the furnaces had to be extinguished and no ventilation was possible. About 1840 attention was called, both in this country and in Belgium, to a safer method, of heating the air by means of jets of steam at high pressure; it was apparently successful when tried out at Seaton Delaval, but was not widespread, though it was used elsewhere, as for instance in South Wales in 1849. Various mechanical devices also were tried, among them the exhaust fan, invented by William Fourness of Leeds in 1837 and installed in several Lancashire collieries in the earlier eighteen-forties. This fan is said to have been capable of exhausting 4,500 cubic feet of air per minute, at a cost of 1s. to 1s. 6d. a day. His machines, however, were small; larger ones were set up in South Wales about 1849, an air pump by William Brunton and a centrifugal fan by W. P. Struve. From that time onwards, with the improvement of the fan, the modern method of ventilation was evolved, so that air could be forced down one shaft or drawn up by another.

Improvements in the winding and haulage of coal[2] depended mainly on two things, the steam engine and

[1] It was in use in Scotland in 1868; see D. Bremner, *Industries of Scotland*, p. 17.
[2] On which see Galloway II, chapters XXIV, XXV; and E. O. Forster Brown, in *Historical Review of Coal Mining*, chapter XI.

stronger ropes. The old Newcomen engine, which had so greatly facilitated mining in the eighteenth century, continued to be used; it was the usual type in Ayrshire as late as 1840. Elsewhere engines of the Watt type were widespread by that time, though their capacity was small, from 20 to 150 horse-power, and they were often used both for pumping and winding. The latter operation up to 1841 was almost universally carried on, in Northumberland, Durham, Lancashire and Yorkshire, by means of hempen ropes, which were costly[1] and short-lived. In the Harz mountains wire ropes were in regular use as early as 1834, and an English patent for their use in ships' rigging was taken out in 1835. They were used in 1840 in the Blackwall tunnel and thereafter increasingly in collieries. At the same time the raising of tubs of coal and men by means of cages running on guide rods or rails[2] was being rapidly adopted, and safety devices, to prevent the falling of cages, were coming into use. Older methods of raising coal nevertheless persisted. Endless chains were still working in some Lancashire pits in 1865, and the water balance[3] in South Wales in 1861. Steam engines had been used below ground since early in the century, and by 1840 they were commonly used for haulage. They were nevertheless dangerous, and attention had been called as early as 1830 to the possibility of substituting compressed air. The first known instance of transmission of power by that means in collieries occurred at the Govan mine near Glasgow in 1849. An impetus to its employment elsewhere was given by a fire at Darley Main in 1850.

During the following forty years[4] the history of coal

[1] They might cost as much as £300 for 600 yards. See Galloway II. 329.

[2] Corves running on guides in the shaft are shown in the plates at the end of a treatise by John Curr (of Sheffield, Colliery Agent to the Duke of Norfolk), *An Account of an Improved Method of Drawing Coals and Extracting Ores from Mines, etc.* (Newcastle, 1789).

[3] Tubs of coal were raised by letting tubs or buckets of water down into the pit and the water was either allowed to escape through an adit or pumped out of the mine by means of a steam engine.

[4] Clapham II. 99–104, 120–122.

mining is a story of the spread of these improvements, so that by 1890 most of the pits were provided with complete mechanical equipment for ventilation and winding and a good deal for haulage. Despite some experiments with percussion tools and coal-cutting machines, however, the hewer's work was commonly done, as it had been for centuries, with the pick. Meanwhile the pits were being sunk to greater depths; Ashton Moss, near Manchester, reached 2,888 feet. The productivity of the miner and the total output of coal, as the following table shows, increased together:

	Output in tons per annum	Tons per miner per annum
1851	57,000,000	264
1871	117,000,000	373
1891	185,000,000	358

These changes were accompanied by tendencies towards increasing size among colliery undertakings and towards concentration of ownership. In North Wales the average number employed in a coal mine in 1885 was not much more than 100; in West Lancashire it was 213. In most areas the business unit was rarely more than two mines; but Powell Duffryn in South Wales, and Pease and Partners and Bowes and Partners in the North, had more than a dozen, and the Wigan Coal and Iron Company worked twenty-nine. There were, besides, what Professor Clapham has well called feudal enterprises, such as those of Lord Londonderry, who, in 1844, required shopkeepers and tradesmen as well as colliers to accept the authority of "their proprietors and masters," and, in 1850, declared publicly that he would allow no inspector in his pits.[1]

ENGINEERING

Though it is convenient, and for the sake of clearness necessary, to treat of them separately, coal mining, metallurgical industry and transport were interdependent in

[1] S. Webb, *Story of the Durham Miners*, pp. 46, 50.

development. Coal mining could not be carried on effectively without the steam engine and the railway, nor they without the coal; and the railway, in turn, may be counted both a cause and a result of the development of the iron and steel industries. Similarly, the development of each of these was linked with engineering. Indeed, in one sense, the engineer was the essential agent in the economic progress of the nineteenth century; for, though everything that was done might, in some fashion or other, have been done without him, nothing could have been done on such a scale, at such a speed and with such economy as then became possible. For good or evil he changed the way in which fields were cultivated, cloth was manufactured and travellers were carried; the lengthening of human life in reformed municipalities and its sudden termination on distant battlefields alike depended on him. The eighteenth century had given great scope to civil engineers, such as James Brindley and Thomas Telford, in the construction of canals and roads, and to craftsmen, such as Hargreaves, Crompton and James Watt, in the invention of machines. The nineteenth century, with railways, gave even greater scope to mechanical and constructional engineers, such as the Stephensons and Brassey, and made far greater demands on the ingenuity of inventors, such as Donisthorpe and Whitworth. Almost every human activity came to be carried on by means of some process or instrument covered by a patent, and a vast population came to live, more or less consciously, by means of complex arrangements unparalleled in history.

What was characteristic of the new way of living was its increased dependence on precision, uniformity and speed. The first steam engines were largely hand-made, differed from one another in many respects, were imperfect and irregular in their working and could be turned out only very slowly. They were the work of craftsmen who, like their medieval predecessors, were not at their best when required to do the same thing over and over again and, in any event, could achieve only a human degree of accuracy. Craftsmen had indeed known for centuries that the foundation of their arts was measurement: "for there is none artificial nor handicraft that is wrought by man's hand but it is wrought by geometry . . . and there is none instrument, that is to say a tool to work with, but it hath some proportion more or less, and proportion is measure."[1] But the measure, by the nineteenth century, had to be so accurate that it could be made only by a machine; and once the machine had been made, it could, without limit, turn out thousands of parts like one another to the thousandth of an inch.

This precision and speed were greatly advanced by the ingenuity and labour of Henry Maudslay, who began his career in 1783 by making and filling cartridges in Woolwich Arsenal, and laid the foundation of his mechanical skill in the carpenters' shop and later in the smithy of the same establishment. Thence he passed into the service of Joseph Bramah, who had invented a patent lock but was unable to get it made with sufficient exactness. Maudslay, who rose to be chief foreman under Bramah, devised new tools which enabled the parts to be made quickly, accurately and relatively cheaply. He also made Bramah's hydraulic press a practical machine by inventing the self-tightening collar without which it would not work satisfactorily. Dissatisfied with his earnings, Maudslay in 1797 started a workshop of his own which had a double importance in the history of engineering. In the first place he had greater scope for his special gift of inventing machine tools capable of great accuracy; and in the second his shop was a training ground for some of the ablest mechanical engineers of the nineteenth century. Among them were Richard Roberts, the inventor of the self-acting mule, and James Nasmyth, the inventor of the steam hammer; the ingenious Joseph Clement, who worked as draughtsman for Maudslay, also

[1] See Knoop, Jones and Hamer, *Two Earliest Masonic MSS.*, pp. 73–75.

became a trainer of engineers in his own workshop, which he opened in 1817. Maudslay's chief contribution to accuracy in workmanship was probably the invention, or the re-discovery,[1] of the slide-rest, capable of being easily moved in a line parallel with the axis of the work in the lathe and holding a cutting tool with a firmness which human strength and dexterity could not achieve. The slide-rest was improved by others and was made automatic, so that the gearing of the lathe regulated the speed at which the tool travelled; but, even in the state in which Maudslay left it, it was of extraordinary importance, being, as Nasmyth said, the parent of all the engineering tools used in the workshops of the following period. Of similar importance was the planing machine, in the invention or improvement of which several mechanicians[2] were concerned, including James Fox, the founder of a machine-making firm at Derby, Richard Roberts, Matthew Murray, chief mechanic of Marshall's flax mills at Leeds, and especially Joseph Whitworth, who, after serving both Maudslay and Clement, set up on his own account in Manchester in 1833. Both before and after that year he gave a good deal of attention to the production of surfaces as near to a true plane as possible, and his "Jim Crow" planing machine, capable of horizontal, vertical and oblique motion, and of moving the surface to be planed both backwards and forwards, worked with extraordinary accuracy. It was also astonishingly economical in comparison with the laborious method of chipping and filing by hand which had been usual in his youth; in 1856 the planing machine did at a labour cost of less than one penny what had cost twelve shillings thirty years previously. Whitworth had meanwhile carried out improvements in the lathe and in drilling, slotting and other machines; he had also, between 1840 and 1850 devised measuring instruments, and he exhibited one in 1856

[1] On the question of Maudslay's originality see Smiles, *Industrial Biography* (1905), pp. 208–12, 340–2.

[2] Smiles, *op. cit.* chapter XIV,

which, it was claimed, could detect a difference of one-millionth of an inch. The precision of his instruments enabled him to produce his famous standard gauges. At the same time he worked out a uniform system for standardizing the pitch of screws; this, which he suggested as early as 1841, took the best part of twenty years to be adopted.

As measurement became finer, the work to be done became larger, and machine tools of very great size were consequently necessary. The most important of them was probably the steam hammer, which James Nasmyth invented in 1838 for the purpose of forging the enormous paddle shaft then intended to be used in the steamer *Great Britain*. The hammer was, however, first used for forging crankshafts in the Schneider works at Le Creusot, where its inventor saw it in action in 1840. He improved and patented it in the same year, and within a few years this implement which, "while capable of forging an Armstrong hundred pounder . . . could hammer a nail or crack a nut without bruising the kernel,"[1] was installed in all properly equipped heavy engineering works. It was especially useful in the production of steel plates, ordnance and railway wheels. A modification of it, the pile-driver invented in 1843, enormously facilitated civil engineering works, such as the construction of the High Level Bridge at Newcastle.

Concomitantly with these inventions and with the development of steam engines and the railways, there arose the specialized engineer and the engineering crafts. These to a large extent replaced the millwright, who had hitherto commonly supplied such engineering knowledge as was required in the erection and modification of plant. James Brindley, for instance, had been apprenticed to a wheelwright and millwright in 1733, and first showed his capacity by properly carrying out his incompetent master's contract to erect the machinery in a paper mill.[2] At his best the

[1] Smiles, *Industrial Biography*, p. 289.
[2] Smiles, *Lives of the Engineers* (1874), I. 130, 135–7.

millwright was, as Sir William Fairbairn wrote, "an itinerant engineer and mechanic of high reputation. He could handle the axe, the hammer and the plane with equal skill and precision; he could turn, bore or forge . . . he was a fair arithmetician, knew something of geometry, levelling and mensuration . . . could calculate the velocities, strength and power of machines . . . draw in plan and section . . . could build bridges, cut canals and perform a variety of work now done by civil engineers."[1] The emergence of other trades, which took over part of the millwright's large field, is indicated in the names and membership of the earlier trade unions,[2] such as the Steam Engine Makers (1824), the Iron Forgers (1830) and the Boilermakers (1832); several of these were joined together in the Friendly Union of Mechanics (1826), which became the Journeymen Steam Engine and Machine Makers and Millwrights Friendly Society, the parent union of the old Amalgamated Society of Engineers and the modern Amalgamated Engineering Union. In course of time, machine tools meant the division of the personnel of engineering shops into two classes, of skilled craftsmen and semi-skilled machine-minders, but the latter was little developed in 1850, and the former resented the employment of any but apprenticed and trade unionist workmen. Of these the A.S.E. in 1851 contained 11,000 and the Ironfounders another 4,000 or 5,000.[3] The former society thus accounted for about a quarter of the total number employed in the engineering trades at the time.[4]

Trade unionism on the A.S.E. scale showed that the day had gone by when it was relatively easy for an individual to found, on technical and moral qualities alone, an engineering or machine-making works of his own. Richard Roberts had done so, like Maudslay and Clement before him, though

[1] Quoted in A. P. M. Fleming and H. J. Brocklehurst, *History of Engineering*, p. 276.
[2] S. and B. Webb, *History of Trade Unionism* (1898), pp. 187, 190.
[3] *ibid.* p. 195.
[4] Clapham I. 448.

a lack of interest in merely commercial matters brought him to poverty in the end. Nasmyth had his own works at Patricroft, and Whitworth in Manchester; but the capital necessary in 1850 was far more than a mechanic, without special good fortune or backing, could ordinarily secure. At that time, it is true, engineering works were not usually very large; of 677 engine and machine makers, 457 employed less than ten men each, though even then there were fourteen employing 350 men or more.[1]

[1] Clapham I. 448.

CHAPTER VI

Credit and Business Organization

BANKING

One hundred years ago the organization of banking in Great Britain had made considerable progress and the system was shortly to be placed on the foundation on which it rested until 1914. Its working depended mainly on two kinds of institution, the central bank in London and some hundreds of other banks, private or joint-stock, in the metropolitan area and the " country " outside it. The Bank of England, after nearly a century and a half of activity and twenty-five years after the end of a war of unparalleled magnitude, was sound and its influence was very great. It was the government's banker and the custodian of such cash reserves as the other banks did not require in their daily business. Up to 1826 it enjoyed, besides the advantage of limited liability, a monopoly in England of joint-stock banking with the privilege of note issue,[1] which in effect meant a monopoly of all joint-stock banking as it was then understood. It followed that the other banks were partnerships and, if they issued notes, partnerships of six persons at most. Their capitals were thus likely to be small, and it was not possible for them to develop by absorption into more considerable and solid enterprises. Since the Bank of England showed no desire before 1826 to penetrate into the provinces, it was clear that the textile, iron, steel and engineering trades and the canal and railway enterprises of the Midlands and the North had to make such progress as they could with the help of these small, and in practice not uniformly efficient and reliable, institutions. Indeed industrial concerns, especially in the

[1] Under Acts of 1697, 1708, 1716 and 1742.

iron trade, sometimes found it convenient to found their own banks.[1] The number of private banks in the provinces increased rapidly during the Napoleonic Wars, being 230 in 1797 and 940 in 1814. Some of them were conducted with great prudence and entire honesty, but many were carried on by partners who were over-inclined to take risks and insufficient in their understanding of banking business, and the mortality was therefore high in times of crisis. Between 1814 and 1816, for instance, 240 of these banks became bankrupt.

In Scotland the position was different and far better. The Bank of Scotland, founded in 1695, had at first a monopoly of joint-stock banking, but its privilege in that respect expired in 1716; a second bank, the Royal Bank, was chartered in 1727 and a third, the British Linen Company, in 1746. This had by 1793 twelve branches in various parts of the country. It was to this policy of opening branches, which the three older banks, as well as the Commercial Bank, founded in 1810, followed, that much of the superiority of Scottish banking may be attributed. Private banks were not unknown but they did little important business, and the banking system, besides being more uniform, had a greater chance of solidity and safety than in England, since the joint-stock banks had greater resources than the mass of small banks south of the Border. Moreover, the Scottish banks gave greater encouragement to small depositors and easier help to small-scale borrowers of good repute.[2] The size and good management of their resources by these banks gave their notes an excellent reputation, so that it could be claimed that "nine-tenths of the labouring classes of Scotland, if they had their choice, would prefer a one pound note to a sovereign."[3]

After the collapse of the speculative boom of 1825, the

[1] For examples, see Ashton, *Iron and Steel in the Industrial Revolution*, pp. 229–232.
[2] Clapham I. 269.
[3] J. W. Gilbart, *History, Principles and Practice of Banking* (ed. A. S. Michie, 1905). II, 215.

difference in the banking systems of the two countries was reduced by two Acts passed in 1826. In order to give greater security, the formation of joint-stock banks with power to issue notes was made legally possible in England outside a circle of sixty-five miles radius with its centre in London, and the Bank of England was enabled to open branches in the provinces. On the ground that the cause of the collapse in 1825 had been the over-issue of small notes, all further issues of notes of less than £5 were prohibited in England; the pressure of Scottish opinion, and the reputation of the Scottish banks and their one pound notes, were sufficient to exclude Scotland from the scope of that prohibition. These Acts strengthened the banking system, but some doubts remained about the competence of joint-stock banks in the London area, and there were hindrances to the development of adequate currency and credit control. One, a legacy from mercantilist times and even, in one sense, from the Middle Ages, was the legal maximum rate of interest, by this time five per cent. The maximum was not entirely abolished until 1854, but the Bank Charter Act of 1833 removed the restriction so far as it applied to bills and promissory notes payable at or within three months. Previously the Bank of England, if it wished to curtail its advances in times when money was scarce, had to refuse to discount some or many of the bills offered to it; henceforth it was able to raise its discount rate above 5 per cent. as might appear to be necessary. The same Act made Bank of England notes legal tender in England and Wales for amounts over £5, a provision which tended to reduce the drains on its reserves in times of pressure, since other banks and their agents would generally be willing to accept its notes instead of calling for gold. Further, the legality of joint-stock banks within the sixty-five mile radius was made clear. They were prohibited from issuing notes payable at or within six months, but otherwise they could carry on all banking business; and the restriction on note issue was a matter of less importance as their customers became increasingly familiar with the use of cheques.

From 1826 onwards joint-stock banks increased in numbers, and some, such as the Manchester and Liverpool District Bank, began to found branches. In 1833 there were 32 joint-stock banks in England and Wales; there were 99 in 1836 and 115 in 1841. Private banks meanwhile were turning themselves into joint-stock banks, being absorbed or disappearing otherwise; their numbers fell from 781 in 1821 to 321 in 1841. Of the joint-stock banks 91, and of the private banks 287, issued their own notes; those which did not were mainly in the London area, but others, in South Lancashire, Birmingham and Newcastle, made special arrangements with the Bank of England to use its notes exclusively.[1] This increase in the number of joint-stock banks coincided with a period of railway activity and with speculation, especially in American securities, which led to a mild crisis in the winter of 1836–37, and, though the difficulties were surmounted, bad harvests and other causes led to a drain on the Bank of England's reserves in 1839, so that though the discount rate was raised to 6 per cent. the Bank was driven to borrow £2,000,000 in France. There was, inevitably, criticism of the Bank, which discounted too cheaply, and even sent gold to America, at a time when the exchanges were unfavourable. Moreover, though it had been stated by the Governor in 1832 that the Bank's principle was to hold one-third of its assets in coin and bullion,[2] it had actually held only about a fifth in that form during 1835.[3] At the same time, there was also a marked tendency to attribute the situation to injudicious issues of notes by the country banks, and a keen controversy arose between supporters of what were called respectively the

[1] Clapham I. 511–12.

[2] T. E. Gregory, *Select Statutes, Documents and Reports relating to British Banking*, I. 5.

[3] Clapham I. 515.

"banking" and the "currency" principles in relation to note issues.[1]

The former, supported by Thomas Tooke, author of the *History of Prices*, and James Wilson, founder of the *Economist*, stressed the view that the State's duty in the matter was to see that notes were convertible into cash, and argued that the size of note issues might safely be left to the experience of bankers and their knowledge of the needs of industry and commerce. The latter school, of which the best known representative was Samuel Jones Loyd, later Lord Overstone, held that a fixed relation was necessary between the amount of gold in the country and the size of the note issues ; as gold flowed out the volume of the issues should be decreased, and as gold came in the issues should be increased. The question was argued at length before a committee of inquiry of which Sir Robert Peel was a member. He attended regularly when Jones Loyd gave evidence, but was not present to hear Tooke ; he seems to have been impressed with the necessity of regulating the size of the note issue and centralizing it and, when he was in power, passed the Bank Charter Act, 1844, which leaned towards the "currency principle." Briefly stated, the purport of that statute was as follows. The Bank of England was divided into a banking department, to carry on its general banking business, and an issue department, whence the other department was to get bank notes. In exchange for these the banking department was to hand over £14,000,000 in securities, and gold and silver coin or bullion for the remainder, so that, except for the fiduciary issue of notes to the value of £14,000,000, which the Bank could reduce if it chose, the notes issued would correspond exactly with the amount of coin or bullion held to cover them. Not more than one-fifth of the metallic cover was to be in silver. As to the country banks, it was provided that for the future no new privilege of note issue should be

[1] For a summary and discussion of these views see *e.g.*, Andréadès, *History of the Bank of England*, chapter IV ; A. E. Feavearyear, *The Pound Sterling*, pp. 240–251; Gregory, *op. cit.* I. xix–xxiii.

granted. Banks already possessing it might retain it, so long as the number of their partners was not more than six, but a maximum was fixed for their note issues. Should a bank, by amalgamation or otherwise, forfeit its privilege, the Bank of England might add to its fiduciary issue two-thirds of the lapsed issue.

In virtue of the Act of 1844, the aims of the currency school were gradually reached, for the note-issuing banks declined in number and the last of them disappeared in 1921. Meanwhile the fiduciary issue rose, reaching a maximum of £19,750,000 in 1923. It should, however, be noted that the currency school took a restricted view of what constituted currency. Jones Loyd stated unmistakably, in reply to Peel, that by quantity of money he meant "the quantity of metallic coin and of paper notes promising to pay coin on demand," and that he did not count bills of exchange as part of the money in circulation.[1] Similarly he was bound to exclude cheques; but it is now clear that the cheque book serves many of the purposes for which bank notes were formerly used, and it is possible for a bank, by giving its customers power to draw cheques, to do what used to be done by making an advance in the form of notes. It follows that the Act of 1844, though its operation limited and ultimately centralized the note issue, did not thereby subject the banks in general to control in regard to their capacity to extend credit.

It is also clear that, to whatever extent the Act may have helped to ward off crises, as the currency school thought it would, it also tended to make a crisis, when it came, more acute. That was made plain in 1847. The railway mania had locked up a large part of the nation's resources in railway stock at a time when crop failures, which sealed the fate of the Corn Laws, necessitated heavy importation of corn at high prices and led to a large decrease in the Bank of England's reserves. When corn

[1] Gregory, *op. cit.* pp. 28, 30.

merchants, in difficulties through a fall in prices resulting from good harvests in 1847, began to fail in the autumn, and bill brokers were involved as well, a panic set in; but the Bank, because of the low level of its reserves and the restrictions imposed by the Act of 1844, could only be restrictive in turn and, by ceasing to discount, made the position worse. Eventually, after a good deal of pressure, the government advised the Bank to make advances at 8 per cent. and promised that, should it be necessary to exceed the limit of the fiduciary issue, an Act of Indemnity would be passed. Knowledge that the Bank could go beyond the limit set for it was on this occasion sufficient to allay anxiety, and an excess issue of notes was not required. Ten years later, however, in a similar situation that had to be made. The crisis of 1857 came rather suddenly, and was in large part the result of failures in the United States, which placed some English houses in difficulties; moreover the stoppage of the Western Bank of Scotland and the City of Glasgow Bank showed that the vaunted excellence of Scottish banking had its limits. The Bank of England raised the discount rate to 10 per cent., obtained the promise of an Act of Indemnity, and put into circulation bank notes in excess of the limit by £928,000. In the crisis of 1866, connected with the failure of Overend, Gurney and Co., the Bank of England gave ready help to the country banks, and, though the Bank Act was suspended, no excess issue was necessary. The troubles of Baring Brothers in 1890 did not cause a panic; a guarantee fund, operating until the firm's assets could be realized, sufficed to tide over the difficulty.

The increase in the number of banks meant a need for some systematic arrangements for settling accounts between them at short intervals. Some machinery of the kind existed in the seventeenth century, but permanent premises in which "clearing" could be conducted were first acquired in London only about 1773. By 1810, when forty-six banks were members of the Clearing House,[1] the clearing averaged about £4,700,000 daily, differences being paid in notes. The private banks were for a long time jealous of the joint-stock banks, and especially of J. W. Gilbart's London and Westminster Bank, and excluded them from membership; but that caused a good deal of unnecessary trouble for the private banks themselves and led the joint-stock banks to threaten to set up a clearing house of their own. In 1854 the joint-stock banks were admitted, and a rule was adopted that all members should have accounts at the Bank of England, which made it possible to settle differences by cheque instead of in notes. Ten years later the system was completed by the admission of the Bank of England.

LIMITED LIABILITY COMPANIES

To the establishment of an adequate banking system, mainly in the second quarter of the nineteenth century, there was added another achievement, the development and liberation of joint-stock organization, mainly in the third quarter of the century. Joint-stock trade was not in itself new; the East India Company had been a joint-stock concern since its foundation, though the stock was at first subscribed only for a period, and did not become permanent until 1657; but after the collapse of the South Sea Bubble in 1720 the government, by the "Bubble Act" of that year, put great difficulties in the way of company trading, and authoritative opinion was in favour of restricting joint-stock organization to a small number of activities, where very large capitals were required, where the undertaking was of special utility, or where the business was mainly of a routine kind.[2] Neither the law nor opinion did in fact prevent

[1] On which see E. T. Powell, *Evolution of the Money Market*, pp. 305–8; *Gilbart on Banking* (1905), II. 310 *et seq.*

[2] Adam Smith, *Wealth of Nations* (ed. Cannan), II. 246–7. By 1848 it was recognized that Adam Smith's views required qualifying. See J. S. Mill's *Principles* I. ix. § 2.

business from being carried on by associations calling themselves companies; but such companies, however large, were in the eye of the law nothing more than partnerships. They differed from such concerns as the East India Company and the Bank of England in two important respects. In the first place, they could not sue or be sued in their own name or in the person of one of their officers, and in the second, the liability of every partner for the debts of the concern was unlimited, so that it was possible for a partner to lose not only the amount of his investment in the business but the remainder of his assets as well. The incapacity to go to law as a corporate body, which meant that all the partners had to be parties to an action in the courts, was a great disadvantage where the number of partners, as was sometimes the case, ran to hundreds, and where membership of the co-partnery fluctuated. Many concerns, consequently, thought it worth while to seek incorporation by special Act of Parliament; no fewer than a hundred such Acts were passed between 1801 and 1844, many of them being in favour of insurance companies.

Meanwhile, in 1825, the "Bubble Act" was repealed, but it was by no means clear that unincorporated companies, though no longer prohibited by statute, were secure under the common law. The repealing Act did, however, increase the power of the Crown to grant incorporation and also enabled it to prescribe a "regulated" liability instead of the unlimited liability hitherto always associated with corporate status. Another Act, in 1837, further increased the Crown's powers to grant quasi-corporate status, but the Board of Trade was chary in exercising them; and in any event the cost of obtaining a charter remained high. A great step forward was taken in 1844, by the Registration Act; for the purposes of this statute (which did not apply to Scotland or to banks) a joint-stock company was a partnership with more than twenty-five members and having its capital in transferable shares. Registration, which was completed in two stages, enabled the company to sue and be sued in its own name; the liability of partners, however, remained unlimited and even continued for three years after a partner had disposed of his interest. Accordingly, in the view of reformers, it was necessary to press for the extension to business concerns in general of the limited liability which had hitherto been reserved for complete corporations.[1]

Fears of speculative trading, and even of fraudulent promotion (suspicions which might well be entertained in the years following the railway mania), legal and commercial conservatism, pride in a reputation for honesty and in success achieved while liability was unlimited, and perhaps fear of the competition of new firms, all tended to set opinion against general limited liability. On the other hand, as Mill pointed out, large-scale production was hardly possible, and railways of any length would not have been possible at all, without it. The principle was in operation in other countries, which might thereby attract British capital, to the detriment of industries and public utilities at home. Personal, as compared with real, property had notably increased[2], and it seemed prudent to give greater opportunity and security in using it, especially to possessors of small capitals and savings, whose number was increasing. In any event, limited liability in 1850 seemed very much a privilege and as such out of keeping with the ideas of the time. Robert Lowe, President of the Board of Trade in 1856, who believed firmly in the wisdom of granting general limited liability, introduced a bill which became law in that year. It provided that any seven or more persons might form themselves into a company, with limited liability if they chose, by signing a memorandum of association

[1] On the preceding and following paragraphs see the valuable articles by H. A. Shannon, "The Coming of General Limited Liability" (*Economic History*, January 1931) and "The First Five Thousand Limited Companies and their Duration" (*Economic History*, January 1932).

[2] Cf. L. Levi, *History of British Commerce* (1872), p. 334; *Econ. Hist.*, January 1931, p. 286.

declaring the name and objects of the company. They could either make their own rules or adopt model rules set out for them, requiring a balance sheet to be presented to an annual meeting of the shareholders; and shareholders, if representing a fifth of the number and of the capital, could require the company's accounts to be inspected by Board of Trade auditors. A further Act in 1858 made similar provisions applicable to banks, and insurance companies were included when the law was consolidated in an Act of 1862, which, though extended and modified since, is the basis of the law relating to such companies.

What the merchant gild was to the thirteenth century the limited company, in its way, was to the nineteenth; and, indeed, between the two forms of association there was a real, if tenuous, thread of historical connection. Certainly the limited company was in accord with the spirit of the age which produced it, an age in which the "democratization of ownership"[1] might be expected to increase. In theory, also, the joint-stock company might be democratic in structure, with sovereignty in a shareholders' meeting, capable of questioning, criticizing and changing its directing officers. Moreover, as the shareholders individually were independent citizens legitimately pursuing their own interests, so the companies they formed were independent and free to pursue their interests in competition against others of their kind. This willingness to compete, coupled with optimism and considerable inexperience, led to abuses which the *laissez-faire* spirit of the joint-stock acts almost invited. Companies were promoted for the sole purpose, as the Master of the Rolls declared, of being wound up, so that the capital subscribed by an acquisitive or ignorant public could be divided between promoters and lawyers. Some investors became the prey of makers of specious promises; others were ruined by false reports or manipulators of the market. Judgment of the advantages and

[1] A. Marshall, *Industry and Trade*, p. 314.

risks of investment could, in any event, develop only slowly among a large class, and the extension of capacity to read and understand prospectuses, balance sheets and the financial press must, to some extent, have depended on the spread of elementary education, hastened in 1870.

In the later 'fifties and the 'sixties there was, naturally, a growth in the number of limited companies, some of them new and some of them old firms on a new basis. The Overend Gurney crash in 1866 suggests that the growth had been too rapid and that the Act of 1862 came at a time when optimism was over-rife. In any event, as the researches of Mr. Shannon have made clear, among the earlier limited companies a high mortality rate prevailed. Of the large sample of companies, belonging to 1856–1865, which he examined, about 36 per cent. died within five years, and 54 per cent. within seven years, of their promotion. The spread of limited companies, it may be noted, however rapid in some directions, was slow in others. In the woollen industry generally most of the business, as late as 1885, was in the hands of private firms; that was also the case with the trades of Birmingham, the cutlery trades of Sheffield, the silk and lace industries and in parts of the Lancashire cotton district, and even in shipping the large limited companies which existed did not do the greater part of the business.[1]

THE CO-OPERATIVE MOVEMENT

Competition, which, according to both political economy and popular opinion in 1850, made for efficiency and cheapness, did not appear, towards the end of the century, to be either inevitable or so desirable; and by the eighteen-nineties trusts were coming into existence in order to reduce or avoid it. Meanwhile there had been a remarkable strengthening and spread of associations claiming to be based on the different and nobler principle of co-operation.

[1] Clapham II. 139–140.

Joint-stock organization and co-operation were by no means incompatible. Indeed, the joint-stock company had a co-operative aspect, its purpose being association for mutual benefit. At least one of the earlier socialists believed that the problems of production and distribution could be solved by a co-ordination of the efforts of thousands of joint-stock companies "working for a common end and deriving a common benefit from all that is produced."[1] When Bray was writing, the co-operative movement already had a history. Its ideals can be traced back to Bellers' *College of Industry* and even further back in the seventeenth century to the communism of Gerard Winstanley and his Diggers; and practical co-operative enterprises, in baking, milling and shop-keeping, existed in the eighteenth century. Co-operative stores were numerous in the eighteen-twenties; they are estimated to have numbered about 250 in 1830[2]; but they failed to develop into productive societies or communities, and such communities as were founded, as for instance at Orbiston near Motherwell in 1825, Ralahine in Ireland in 1831 and Queenswood in Hampshire in 1840, did not long survive.

The faith which Robert Owen had founded nevertheless lived, and animated the creators of the first modern co-operative society, the Rochdale Equitable Pioneers, which opened for business in Toad Lane in that town in 1844. Its objects included the manufacture of goods by its unemployed members and the foundation of a co-operative community or colony; but the success of the society may be attributed to concentration on a more immediate and realizable purpose, the supplying of its members with unadulterated goods at as near cost price as possible. It started with 28 members and a capital of as many pounds, on which it proposed to pay a fixed interest. Its main contribution to the movement was the establishment

[1] J. F. Bray, *Labour's Wrongs and Labour's Remedy*, 1839 (L. S. E. Reprint), p. 157.

[2] Clapham, I. 599.

of the practice (which, it would appear, the society did not originate) of dividing the surplus or profit on trading among the members in proportion to the amounts of their purchases. The society was thus democratic; the members, who managed its affairs, secured the benefits for themselves. It was also well served, and prospered; between 1845 and 1850 its membership rose from 74 to 600 and its turnover increased from £710 to £13,179. Success of this kind stimulated efforts elsewhere, at first in Lancashire and soon afterwards in the industrial north and midlands and in Scotland. There existed by 1851 about 130 societies on the Rochdale plan and their membership possibly reached 15,000.[1]

Up to that time the growth of such societies was considerably hampered by the state of the law, which regarded them as partnerships; it prevented them from selling their goods to persons other than members and from owning real property except the land on which they carried on business; the investment of their funds was circumscribed, so that one society could not help another with a loan; the liability of each member for the society's debts was unlimited; and there was no effective protection of their property against embezzlement. Largely through the interest and help of the Christian Socialists, especially the lawyers, Thomas Hughes, Vansittart Neale and J. M. Ludlow, the position of the societies was remedied by the Industrial and Provident Societies Acts of 1852 and 1862. The former gave the societies protection similar to that enjoyed by friendly societies and enabled them to enforce their rules on their members; the latter limited the liability of members to the amount of their shares and permitted the application of profits to purposes hitherto not allowed, such as educational work.

Robert Owen, who died in 1858, would not have been satisfied with what had been achieved up to that time.

[1] Clapham, I. 599.

Successful store management was only a beginning of the movement towards co-operative production as a way of life, to which he had looked forward as early as 1816, and which, in one form or another, he had spent time and a fortune to further, both in the United States and, after his return, in the Labour Exchange in Gray's Inn Road. This was an attempt, which failed by 1834, to co-ordinate the co-operative societies then existing. In part, the movement for co-operative production arose out of the business and needs of the store-keeping societies themselves; the Pioneers and other Rochdale societies, for instance, established a corn-milling concern of their own. The chief impetus, however, came from the Christian Socialists, who were aware of French attempts to organize self-governing workshops and who, like J. S. Mill,[1] saw therein the possibility of a new and better economic and social order. A Society for Promoting Working Men's Associations was formed which spent money on propaganda and made loans, supplemented by private advances, to various enterprises, such as the Working Tailors' Association which opened in London in 1850. The latter society proposed to pay 4 per cent. on borrowed capital, to allocate one-third of the net profits to propaganda and extension and to divide the remainder among the members according to their earnings. In the same year similar associations were founded among Pimlico building workers (who had struck against an extension of hours on Saturdays), the London bakers and the working printers. None of these became permanent, though the tailors' association lasted until about 1860. Manchester succeeded rather better with a Working Tailors' Association, started in 1850 and lasting until 1872; a Salford Hatters' Association, which from 1852 onwards shared the same premises, did not die until 1873. The career of most of these societies was much shorter; in part they failed through lack of care in choosing members at the beginning

[1] See *Principles of Political Economy*, Book IV, chapter VII, §§ 4, 5, 6.

and lack of harmony in managing their affairs afterwards; some, in so far as they did succeed, tended to become exclusive in spirit and rather tried to keep a good thing for themselves than to spread the practice of co-operative production. In any event, the efforts of the societies were almost necessarily limited to handicrafts and enterprises requiring only small capitals. More ambitious attempts, arising out of the engineering strike of 1851, to run iron works came to very little; E. Vansittart Neale, who lost a good deal of money by his connection with a project of the kind in Southwark, left it on record that few of the Amalgamated Engineers "had any faith in self-employment as a means of permanently raising their position as workers."[1]

On the surface, at least, the working classes did better with cotton mills. The oldest of them was the Bacup and Wardle Commercial Company, which began manufacturing, i.e., weaving, in 1851, had a capital of £60,000 in 1860, suffered less than other mills in the cotton famine, paid a dividend of 48 per cent. in 1874 and was still in existence, though it was losing money, in 1890. The second was the Rochdale Co-operative Manufacturing Society, founded in 1854; thence to 1890 it was said to have paid an average dividend of 6 per cent.; its capital in that year was £65,855, held by about a thousand persons, mostly working men, and it supplied the Co-operative Wholesale with calicoes to the value of £15,000 or more annually. This kind of enterprise was remarkably popular in Oldham, where the Sun Mill Company, founded (though under another name) in 1858, was the pioneer. Its profits led, in and after 1870, to the promotion of others, of which there are said to have been fifty in the Oldham district by 1874; their capital exceeded £2,500,000, and three-quarters of their shareholders consisted of "bona fide working men, daily engaged in manual labour and in receipt of weekly wages."[2] Neither

[1] B. Jones, *Co-operative Production*, I. 135.
[2] *ibid.* I. p. 294.

these nor their predecessors were, or long continued to be, co-operative in the sense in which Robert Owen and the Christian Socialists understood the word, for though they might, at any rate for a time, give a share of the profits to the workers, or to some of their workers, and though co-operative societies might invest in them and deal with them, the workers did not manage them, and, as their subscription lists were thrown open to people not employed in the mills, the bonuses to labour were apt to be given up. Working men, it was said, preferred to be shareholders in mills other than those in which they were employed; and where employees and shareholders were the same people it was very difficult for the management to maintain authority and efficiency.

In shop-keeping it was easier to preserve the co-operative character of enterprises and at the same time to develop and extend the movement. In the early 'sixties it was being urged in several quarters, and especially in South Lancashire, that a stronger organization was required in order to help the weaker distributing societies and especially to assist them in buying on better terms, a service not the less desirable when the purchasing power of their members was greatly reduced by the cotton famine. The Industrial and Provident Societies Act of 1862 made the way easier and, after a special conference in Manchester in 1863, the North of England Co-operative Wholesale Industrial and Provident Society was constituted and began business in Manchester in the spring of 1864. The Co-operative Wholesale Society, as it is now called, was a *societas societatum*; its capital was provided by the constituent co-operative societies, which received a fixed rate of interest thereon and in addition a dividend in proportion to their purchases. The new society was not everywhere welcomed; some distributive societies preferred to buy, as hitherto, in the open market, and some of their buyers no doubt had some fear of losing their occupations; but progress was uninterrupted. The membership of the customer societies rose from 24,000 in 1865 to 79,245 in 1870, 361,523 in 1880 and 721,316 in 1890; and in the same period the net sales increased steadily from £120,754 to £7,429,073.[1] Inevitably, its concern being chiefly with provisions and apparel, it sought to strengthen its position by producing goods for itself and acquiring its own supplies of raw material.[2] Scotland in 1868 followed the lead of Lancashire by setting up a wholesale society, which began manufacturing its own goods in 1881.

[1] Redfern, *The Story of the C.W.S.*, pp. 418-9.
[2] See below p. 171.

CHAPTER VII

Employers, Employed and the State

With the changes in technique and organization of which some account has been given in the preceding chapters, there came, partly as result and partly as cause, changes in economic, political and social relationships. For want of sufficient information those changes cannot be measured with any exactness; but even superficial observers were aware of them, and many contemporaries found them, for good or evil, significant. Some looked back with longing to an age in which the relation of lord to dependant had been, if more absolute, also more kindly and natural than the bondage of mill hands to cotton lords. Others rejoiced in the breakdown of ancestral and merely traditional dominance, and welcomed a competitive world in which it was possible for the humblest to rise, by virtue of his own gifts and character, to eminence and riches. The one school deplored the passing of chivalry; the other was glad to be rid of servility and monopoly; and Sir Walter Scott made a fortune by recreating the old unreal world of romance for those who lived in the new grim world of reform.

THE EMPLOYING CLASS

By the year of Victoria's accession a new and more or less conscious class of capitalist masters was in the saddle. Its pressure had brought about an alteration of the political constitution to fit a new "balance of dominion," as Harrington called it, in 1832; and the new class was to win a victory against its predecessor, the landed interest, by the repeal of the Corn Laws in 1846. It would, indeed, be incorrect to regard the battle over the Corn Laws as simply a contest with all the landlords on one side and all the industrialists on the other, each considering only its own interests in the narrowest manner. Lord Milton, one of the largest landowners in England had changed his mind about the desirability of protection long before the foundation of the League; and, in any event, it was the Tories who, loyally following Peel, put an end to the Corn Laws. In the House of Commons which carried that measure there were, according to a recent computation,[1] 180 Whig and Radical and 301 Tory landholders, while on the Whig and Radical side there were 132 men with industrial or commercial interests, as compared with 100 Tories of the same kind. It is, indeed, true that the new interests counted for more and more in Parliament after 1832; between 1847 and 1865 the railway representation, for instance, rose from 86 to 160; and between 1832 and 1865 representatives of the landed interest declined from 489 to 436, while the number of votes which might be mobilized for mercantile, industrial and financial interests rose from 248 to 545. Land, in any event, remained important; in 1841, landed property was estimated to be worth, at 25 years' purchase, about £815,000,000 as compared with a total of £2,000,000,000 for personal property.[2] However the economic interests of landowners and industrialists might clash on particular questions, the possessors of both shared equally in the belief that property was especially sacred, and that its owners had a special right to political power and influence. The second Reform Act, in 1867, and the third, in 1884, certainly gave the vote to classes having little or no "stake in the country" in the ordinary sense; but by that time, when Chartism had long been a spent force, it might well be expected that the new voters would generally be content to follow the lead of the "historic" parties.

The victors of 1846 had sprung in many instances from

[1] J. A. Thomas, *The House of Commons, 1832–1901*, pp. 4–7. In these tables a member interested in land and, *e.g.*, railways is counted twice.

[2] Porter (1847), pp. 608, 614–5.

yeoman or peasant stock,[1] and the fact is not strange, since the mass of the population, even in the first half of the nineteenth century, was still largely rural, and the textile and metallurgical industries in the eighteenth century had been rural also. In the transition from domestic to factory production, therefore, there were opportunities for farmers, who often carried on textile production in slack seasons, to set up as cloth manufacturers; others, with a by-occupation in nail making or the like, had a chance to extend their business or to become iron masters. It was, naturally, only a few who, like Sir Robert Peel's father or Richard Crawshay, became founders of large concerns; many, especially in the woollen industry and in the Sheffield and Birmingham trades, became heads of small businesses; but most of the country-bred population which turned to industrial pursuits could hope only to be wage earners. Many who were dispossessed by enclosures entered mills and factories; and when, after 1834, the old system of supplementing farm labourers' wages from the poor rates was given up, many of those whom the farmers could not employ found work in mines, railway construction or other non-agricultural occupations.

The new class of masters was diverse in origin, and its separate elements made different contributions to the organization and development of industry. It contained some inventors and engineers, such as Richard Roberts, George Stephenson and James Nasmyth, whose chief contribution was technical or scientific; others, like Robert Owen, had little or no technical knowledge but possessed a gift for organization and worked out the principles of a new art, that of arranging and governing the labours of large numbers of people working together. Some, like Richard Arkwright, combined technical and administrative qualifications; others, like George Hudson, were strong as business men, with an understanding of finance; and still others, like George Stephenson and Sir Henry Bessemer, combined

[1] P. Mantoux, *The Industrial Revolution in the Eighteenth Century*, pp. 379–80.

scientific or technical ability with shrewdness and business capacity. Inevitably, men with such diversity of gifts and background varied a good deal in their opinions and interests. In general, it is commonly believed, the world was too much with them, and their values were almost entirely monetary ; but such a belief leaves much out of account and tends to idealize their predecessors. Robert Owen, for instance, while gaining a fortune, never lost a profound sense of social obligation, to which he willingly sacrificed his time and money; Richard Cobden placed his public work before the success of his business; Joshua Wedgwood was a man of wide interests and cultivated taste; and the literary and philosophical and other similar societies of Manchester, Liverpool, Birmingham, Sheffield and other towns were evidence that the manufacturers and business men of those places were by no means without interest in matters other than the daily business of their mills and counting houses. Nevertheless, it must be admitted that the pursuit of gain was the prime purpose of many members of the new class and that finer feelings were sacrificed to it. No inventor could rely on his royalties being honourably paid; an organization was formed for the specific and mean purpose of combating Kay's right to payment for the fly-shuttle; Crompton was shamefully deceived by those who agreed to pay him for publicly demonstrating his mule, though the spinning firms, who made fortunes by it, were later willing for him to be slightly compensated, at the cost of the taxpayers. It is clear that the masters were conscious of their economic, and even of their class, interests, and combined, legally or otherwise, to defend them. Price and output agreements were common in the iron and steel industries in the eighteenth and early nineteenth centuries.[1] Formal associations for similar purposes among pottery manufacturers existed from 1770 onwards, and in 1836 the employers formed a combination to resist the trade union,

[1] Ashton, *Iron and Steel in the Industrial Revolution*, p. 177 *et seq.*

which, in their opinion, "destroyed the legitimate control of the Masters."[1] In copper mining, brewing, salt production, silk weaving, shipping and ship-building, combinations were by no means unknown,[2] and the Newcastle coal trade had, in the Vend, a combination whose history stretches from the reign of Elizabeth to that of Victoria and which broke down only in 1845. It is possible that between 1850 and 1875 competition was more active and combination among capitalists less frequent than it had been in the first half of the nineteenth century, and that, but for the necessity of resisting trade unions, employers' organizations would have been fewer still.[3]

FACTORY REFORM

Such tendencies as there were towards combination among employers in the same trade did not in any way lessen the desire of individuals to be undisputed masters in their own works, and to be free from interference on the part of the public authorities. In some instances employers had voluntarily, either out of humanity or intelligent self-interest, diminished or abolished some of the practices prevailing in the establishments of their competitors; but legal compulsion was required to enforce minimum standards on employers in general.[4] The evils of the early factories and mines were partly a *damnosa hereditas* from the days of domestic industry, in which the employment of children and the sweating of women had long prevailed, as they prevailed in workshops long after the factories had been reformed. In part the abuses arose out of the need of labour in places where power abounded but population was scanty, as in the Pennine valleys; the gap was filled by

[1] E. Surrey Dane, *Economic History of the Staffordshire Pottery Industry* (unpublished dissertation, in Sheffield University Library), chapter IV.
[2] Clapham I. 198–200.
[3] Clapham II. 143–144.
[4] On the factory acts see B. L. Hutchins and A. Harrison, *History of Factory Legislation.*

transporting either children, as poor-law "apprentices," or whole families from poverty-stricken areas, a practice which both relieved the ratepayers and suited the millowners. The condition of "apprentices" was improved by an Act of 1802, so far as it was operative, and the employment of children and young persons in cotton mills was restricted by Acts of 1819 and 1831; but factory reform in real earnest started only in 1833, not before it was time.

Before the passing of the Factory Act of that year it was possible for a boy of fourteen to be made to work in a woollen mill for forty of the hours between 1.0 a.m. on Monday and 11.30 p.m. on Tuesday, and then to resume work at 5.0 a.m. on Wednesday.[1] One witness explained that, however humane the adult worker might be, he had no choice but to beat his child assistants: "The machine turns off a regular quantity of cardings, and . . . . . . they must keep with the machine . . . as he (the slubber) must keep up with the machine or be found fault with, he spurs the children to keep up also by various means, but that which he commonly resorts to is to strap them when they become drowsy . . . the effect of piecening upon the hands. . . . It makes them bleed; the skin is completely rubbed off, and in that case they bleed in perhaps a dozen parts."[2] Another gave evidence of the possible consequence of drowsiness among unfenced machinery: "I have known more accidents happen at the fore-end of the day . . . I mean before breakfast time. I was an eye-witness of one . . . a child was working wool . . . but the strap caught him as he was hardly awake, and it carried him into the machinery; and we found one limb in one place and one in another, and he was cut to bits almost."[3] One witness, who had begun to work when under nine years of age, saw his own children suffering the brutalities he had himself undergone, and stated the dilemma in which many

[1] *Report from the Committee on the Bill to regulate the Labour of Children in the Mills and Factories of the United Kingdom* (1832), pp. 26–27.

[2] *ibid.* pp. 96–97.

[3] *ibid.* pp. 108–9.

working-class parents found themselves : " I have been beat with a billy-roller towards night, when I have been particularly drowsy, till I repeatedly vomited blood. . . . I have two children . . . at the mill at present . . . the oldest . . . has had to stop a day or two at home for three successive weeks together, on account of being beat upon the head. . . . My wife has numbers of times upbraided me for suffering them to go (to the mill), but still I thought it was better to allow them to go there than altogether starve for want of bread, and one or other must be the case."[1] Such children were fortunate if they were employed in Benjamin Gott's mill: " Mr. Gott kept . . . a billy set of children ; that is, three children more than was wanted ; and if any one was ill, another was put in its place. . . . By order of Mr. Gott they were only chastised with a ferule if they would not obey ; but no man was allowed by Mr. Gott to do more than use that ; but he did not know the extent to which they carried even that sometimes."[2]

The employment of children under nine, except in silk mills, was prohibited by the Act of 1833, and so was night work for persons under eighteen, except in the lace manufacture. Twelve hours a day and sixty-nine a week were imposed as maxima for all such persons, and, after 1839, a maximum of nine hours a day and forty-eight hours a week for children under thirteen, except in silk mills. The most important provision of the Act, however, was the appointment of State inspectors to see that the regulations were carried out and to confer with each other and suggest further reforms. The Act by no means satisfied the reformers, whose leader in the House of Commons was Lord Ashley, and they continued to press for legislation to institute a ten-hour day. In the meanwhile, Lord Ashley obtained an inquiry into the condition of women and children in mines. Its investigations

[1] *Report from the Committee on the Bill to regulate the Labour of Children in the Mills and Factories of the United Kingdom* (1832), pp. 46-47.

[2] *ibid.* p. 36.

showed[1] that children at seven years of age, and even at lower ages, were commonly employed, and that their hours were long. In the Derbyshire pits they worked sixteen hours out of the twenty-four. Their occupation, when very young, was to open and shut doors, but they were often put to hauling. For this purpose they wore a girdle round the waist, with a ring, to which a rope was attached; this passed between the legs of the human beast of burden, who crept on all fours, dragging behind him a load of coal. "I went down the pit at seven years of age," said one of them. "When I drew by the girdle and chain the skin was broken and the blood ran down. I dursn't say anything. If we said anything they, the butty and the reeve . . . would take a stick and beat us. I have seen many draw at six but they were not able to draw the full day out. If they are put to the work they must do it or be beat." Women were not employed underground in some areas, but in Yorkshire and Lancashire, East Scotland and South Wales their labour was commonly used. In one West Riding pit a girl of 14 was set to hewing at the coal face in a gallery two feet high; but the usual occupation for women, as for children, was hauling. "The road is very steep," said Betty Harris of Little Bolton, "and we have to hold by a rope, and when there is no rope, by anything we can catch hold of. . . . The pit is very wet where I work and the water comes over our clog tops. I have seen it up to my thighs. . . . I am very tired when I get home at night. I fall asleep sometimes before I get washed. . . . I have drawn till I have had the skin off me . . . my feller has beaten me many a time for not being ready. I were not used to it at first, and he had little patience." The physical results of such labour must sometimes have been calamitous. Mary Hardman, who worked in a pit near Leven, illustrated one of them: "I am a married woman, and was married whilst I worked in the coal pits. I have had either three or

[1] The instances which follow are taken from *Reports of the Commissioners for Inquiring into the Employment of Children in Mines and Manufactories* (1842).

four children born the same day that I have been at work, and I have gone back to my work nine or ten days after I lay down almost always. Four out of the eight was stillborn."

The report made a profound impression which probably helped to bring reforms not only in the mines but elsewhere. An Act of 1842 prohibited entirely the employment of women and children below ground; another in 1844 prohibited night work for women and imposed a maximum of twelve hours a day; this was reduced to ten by an Act of 1847, and, in 1850, the reform was made secure by fixing meal times and the hours within which the legal working day must fall. These statutes were based on the view that women, though adults, were not in a position to secure their own interests and that, consequently, the government was bound to come to their assistance. With the hours of men, who were deemed capable of protecting themselves, the State was not conceived as having a right to interfere. Nevertheless, it was well enough known that the limitation of women's labour would in practice often shorten the working day for men as well; and it was possible for men also to reduce their hours still further by collective bargaining. After 1850 factory reform was carried out piece-meal, by extension to one trade after another. An Act of 1867 helped to bring workshops into line with factories, and this was carried further in a consolidating Act in 1878. Within less than half a century of the Reform Act, therefore, many of the evils connected with the industrial employment of women and children had been abolished; and, it may be noted, Forster's Act in 1870 had begun to do effectively what the Factory Acts had attempted with little success, that is to abolish illiteracy among the workers. There were, however, still many thousands, in domestic service, in agriculture, in their own homes and in insanitary workshops, who were not effectively protected or not protected at all, and who were peculiarly liable to contract lead poisoning, tuberculosis or other diseases. Moreover they were often, as in the

East London garment-making trades, shamefully sweated. Regulation of their hours was far more difficult than in the case of factory workers; and though ancient precedents existed for the regulation of their wages, any such principle was contrary to the ideas of the age which passed the first factory acts. Nevertheless, those acts were departures from the more or less rigid *laissez-faire* views which property owners, if not eminent economists, were apt to hold; and the practice of interference, given the socialist trend of opinion in the later nineteenth century,[1] was likely to be carried further, though it was not until the twentieth century that Trade Boards were set up to protect the least organized and most victimized class of workers.

DIRECT AND INDIRECT TAXATION

If in some directions the State, during the second and third quarters of the nineteenth century, interfered increasingly in economic relationships, in others it inclined to greater freedom. Peel's progress towards free trade culminated in Corn Law Repeal; but his disciple, Gladstone, and other chancellors of the exchequer in the Gladstonian tradition, remitted one duty after another. It is true that the revenue from customs did not, on the whole, decline and that the proceeds of the excise increased, as the following table indicates:

	Customs	Excise
	£000	£000
1840	21,584	13,510
1841–50	21,067	13,473
1851–60	22,894	17,054
1861–70	22,713	19,450
1871–80	20,068	26,696.

But the object was almost entirely revenue and not at all the protection of particular industries. For both political

[1] On which see A. V. Dicey, *Law and Public Opinion in England*, lectures VII, VIII.

parties protection was a dead issue in the generation following 1846, and Cobden's principles, which his countrymen in the main accepted, were supreme. They were the basis of the treaty, which he took an important part in negotiating, with France in 1860. It may be taken as marking the optimism of Great Britain in an age before its industrial leadership had been challenged; its desire was for peaceful progress, which the Napoleonic dictatorship in France appeared to menace, and which the triumph of Prussia ten years later was to make uncertain. With peace the Cobdenite era coupled retrenchment and reform; but the two latter were imperfectly compatible, and national expenditure, despite economies, could not be prevented from growing; the annual tax revenue averaged £52,100,000 in 1841–46, £62,900,000 in 1861–66 and £73,800,000 in 1881–86.

It followed, since many duties were abolished or reduced, that other sources of revenue had to be found, and among them the income tax played a much greater part than Gladstone wished. Originally introduced by Pitt to help in meeting the cost of continental wars, the tax was given up on the restoration of peace; but Peel re-introduced it in 1842 as a temporary measure to cover the losses in revenue which were the first effects of his remissions of customs duties. Gladstone, in his budget of 1853, carried it on, hoping that after a period of seven years it would cease to be necessary; but neither he nor his successors, who accepted his view that the income tax ought to be an extraordinary instrument for special needs, were able to get rid of it, though they were able to keep it at rates which, by modern standards, appear to be very low. Peel had introduced it at 7d. in the pound; it was 10d. in 1860, but only 3d. in 1873 and 2d. in 1874 and 1875. The last attempt to abolish it was made when Gladstone went to the country in 1874; but at 2d. in the pound it can hardly have been much resented and, after 1867, there were many voters who did not pay it; in any event, the election, in which Gladstone was defeated, turned on other issues. It may be noted that the yield for each penny of the tax gives some idea of the growth of assessable income in the period. Each penny produced £730,000 in 1842, £850,000 in 1853, £1,750,000 in 1873 and over £2,000,000 in 1884.[1]

THE WAGES OF LABOUR

Between the eighteenth century, when wages were still occasionally fixed by the public authority, and the institution of the Trade Boards in 1909, the wages of labour were entirely determined by agreement between employer and employed. The history of wages in the meantime, therefore, should show how far the workers, without the direct help of the State, were able to share in the undoubted increase in wealth which the changes already described made possible. Unfortunately, the subject bristles with difficulties; information relating to the first half of the nineteenth century is abundant only for certain places, trades and times; little is known about the relation between weekly or daily rates and annual earnings; piece rates are an additional complication in some trades and extra earnings and payments in kind in others; and there are, for want of sufficient information about prices, difficulties in relating money earnings to real wages. It is nevertheless possible to give a general account of the changes, and to conclude that the working classes as a whole, though with some tragic exceptions, improved their condition during the four decades which followed the Reform Act. It will be noted that the period falls into two approximately equal parts; during the former, money wages in general were fairly stable and during the latter they rose.

Agricultural earnings varied from one part of the country to another. A line drawn from Chester south-eastwards to the south of Staffordshire and thence north-eastwards through the north of Warwickshire and Leicestershire to the

[1] Sydney Buxton, *Finance and Politics*, II. 170.

Wash, would, in 1850, have divided the country into a relatively highly paid area to the north and a low-wage region to the south.[1] The difference is largely explained by the fact that coal-mining and industrial labour, north of the line, offered alternative occupations, and farmers had consequently to pay more to keep their men. In the West Riding wages might be as high as 14s. a week, and the average for the northern counties was between 11s. and 11s. 6d.; in the south the average was 8s. 5d., and the wage might be as low as 7s. The general course of wages in the period now under consideration may be summarily indicated in the following table,[2] which shows the average weekly wages of agricultural labourers in four districts:

	1837	1850–51	1860	1869–70	1872
North and North-Eastern Area ...	10s. 4d.	9s. 1d.	11s. 1d.	11s. 3d.	13s. 2d.
South-East and East Midlands	10s.	9s. 5d.	11s. 9d.	12s. 5d.	14s. 10d.
West Midlands and South-West ...	8s. 10d.	7s. 2d.	9s. 11d.	10s. 10d.	13s. 1d.
North and North-West	12s. 1d.	11s. 10d.	13s. 5d.	15s.	17s. 4d.

It is evident that up to 1851 the general tendency was downwards and that in the following period the level rose. The figures in the table, however, apply only to weekly wages and exclude extra earnings at harvest time, on which most farm labourers' families counted, as well as the earnings of women and children and payments in kind, which not infrequently included house room. One observer in 1874 estimated that a Suffolk labourer, whose weekly earnings amounted to 13s., could count on £8 10s. 0d. in extra earnings at harvest time and on an equivalent of 3s. a week in the value of an allotment and low cottage rent, so that he would obtain "a total of 18s. 6d. weekly in money or money's worth, including no extra earnings at hay-time, or from piece-work throughout the year, and nothing for pigs, privileges or perquisites." The same authority calculated that a man and wife with five children could receive the

[1] See Caird's map, reproduced in Clapham I. 467.
[2] Prothero (Lord Ernle), *English Agriculture Past and Present*, pp. 468–70.

equivalent of 36s. a week.[1] On the other hand, some items were received as of grace, and not every labourer could be sure of an allotment; and a cheap cottage might be a fetter as well as an advantage, for the fear of being homeless might bring its occupant to accept terms which he knew to be unfair. In any event, the housing was sometimes appalling. A cottage near Dennington, for instance, had one bedroom, twelve or thirteen feet square; "in this one room slept the labourer and his wife, a daughter aged twenty-four and a son aged twenty-one, another son of nineteen, a boy of fourteen and a girl of seven"; downstairs in the neat living room was a framed certificate that the occupier had been awarded a prize of £2 "for having served as horse-driver thirty-six years upon the same farm or with the same master or mistress."[2] Other evidence suggested that such overcrowding was by no means so exceptional as it ought to have been. Altogether, after allowance has been made for the fact that farm labourers were paid for rainy and frosty days and that old men might be kept on after they had ceased to be worth their whole pay, as well as for the port wine in sickness and the other gifts of ladies bountiful to the poor men at their gates, it would seem that the followers of Joseph Arch had not a little of the right on their side, vain as that advantage might be.

In the other great extractive industry, coal mining, wages followed a similar course, that is, falling in the 'forties and rising, though not to a very high level, thereafter. The trend is illustrated by Bowley's figures for the daily wages of a Lanarkshire miner, which are set at 4s. in 1831–40, 3s. in 1841–50, 3s. 8d. in 1851–60, 3s. 9d. in 1861–70, 6s. 10d. in 1871–75 and 4s. 4d. in 1876–80.[3] The demand for miners' labour was, naturally, affected by the progress of industry and communications, but the miner's occupation was not itself very much altered by mechanical changes. In

[1] F. Clifford, *The Agricultural Lock-Out of 1874*, pp. 243, 244.
[2] *ibid.* pp. 191–194.
[3] A. L. Bowley, *Wages in the United Kingdom in the Nineteenth Century*, p. 107.

that respect, therefore, the miner may be compared with workers in the building industry, the masons, bricklayers and carpenters who continued to ply their tools in much the same way as they had for centuries. In London such artisans earned about 27s. a week in 1830; the wage rose gradually to 30s. in 1844, and remained at that level until 1852, when it rose to 33s. It stayed there until 1864, rose to nearly 38s. by 1866 and touched 40s. in 1872. Labourers' wages in the same trade and place followed the same course at a lower level, rising from 19s. in 1831 to just over 22s. in 1866.[1] Comparisons are far more difficult to make in the trades more directly affected by technical changes, such as textiles and engineering. As crafts became obsolete the pay of those who followed them decreased, a miserable process when, as was the case with handloom weavers, the number of workers did not decline as rapidly as their chances of employment. The wages of their successors, and of spinners, in the cotton industry of Manchester and the surrounding district have been tabulated[2] as follows:

	1832	1833	1839	1846	1849	1859	1870	1877
Power loom weavers								
2 looms	8s.—12s.	—	9s. 4d.	10s.	10s. 2d.	10s. 9d.	10s. 9d.	—
3 looms	13s. 6d.—16s.	—	—	—	13s.	15s. 6d.	15s. 5d.	17s.6d.
4 looms	—	—	16s. 8d.	16s.	16s.	18s.	—	—
Spinners (average)	—	27s. 1d.	22s. 11d.	—	21s. 7d.	24s. 1d.	27s. 8d.	33s.10d.

Without going into further detail with regard to a subject which abounds rather in complications than in certainties, it may suffice to cite, as an indication of the upward trend of money wages, part of a table expressing the averages for certain selected trades as percentages of the level of each in 1891:[3]

[1] See graph in Bowley, *op. cit.* opposite p. 90.
[2] See table in Bowley, opposite p. 118.
[3] *ibid.*, p. 130.

	1840	1850	1860	1870	1880
Cotton	50	54	64	74	85
Wool	74	79	87	97	110
Building	66	69	78	90	98
Mining	61	59	68	72	70
Iron	77	76	80	90	94
Agriculture	75	71	87	92	104

It is not possible to determine to what extent better wage rates were offset by poorer chances of finding work; but there is no lack of evidence to show that the incomes of working-class families must, at certain times, have been considerably reduced by unemployment, and that the assistance of members out of work was the largest item of trade union expenditure.[1] On that account the Friendly Society of Ironfounders paid out, in the period 1831–1888, over £740,000 out of total expenditure of £1,280,000. Similarly the Amalgamated Society of Engineers, between 1851 and 1888, distributed £2,958,000, more than £1,460,000 of it being unemployed benefit. The former society, which was fairly prosperous from 1831 to 1836 and 1843 to 1846, suffered severely between 1837 and 1842 and again in the depression following the crisis year of 1847. The difference between good years, like 1871–76, and bad years, such as 1868 and 1879, is evident from the percentage of members out of work, which, in particular years, was as follows:

1854— 7·6	1862—13·8	1871— 2·4	1874— 3·9	1878—14·6
1857— 9·1	1867—15·9	1872— 1·4	1875— 3·5	1879—22·3
1858—16·0	1868—18·0	1873— 3·2	1876— 5·7	1880—10·9

From the records of other trade unions it would be possible to trace parallel fluctuations; but statistics of this kind have

[1] G. F. Steffen, *Studien zur Geschichte der englischen Lohnarbeiter*, III. 98 folg.

only a very limited value, for they are scarce with regard to the period before 1850 and imperfect afterwards; and, in any event, it is unsafe to assume that they can serve as a measure of unemployment among the large masses of workers who were outside the trade unions. Such workers, very probably, suffered more from unemployment than the minority, who were more skilled, had some hope of postponing dismissal, and possessed, in their organizations, a means of mitigating their condition when out of work.

If, setting particularly good and bad years out of account, it could be assumed that the average chance of employment did not vary very much between 1840 and 1880, it would follow that the working classes as a whole improved their condition between the two dates, for the generally upward trend of money wages was not accompanied by an equivalent rise in the cost of living. From 1840 to 1850 the cost of living fell, perhaps by as much as 30 per cent.[1] It may be noted that Peel's progress towards free trade was marked by the remission of the duty on sugar, enabling it to be sold at 1½d. a pound, and on other imports. The repeal of the Corn Laws ushered in an age of cheap bread, and, though the 4 lb. loaf cost more than 10d. in the middle eighteen-fifties, the Crimean War years, the tendency from that time on was downwards, and, from 1885 to 1890 the price of the 4 lb. loaf remained well below 7½d., the price in the early 'fifties.[2] Gladstone benefited the working classes by repealing the excise on soap in 1853 and reducing the duty on tea in 1863. Meat prices rose and so did house rents; but some of the rise in rent is accounted for by the fact that the housing was better. Altogether, there is reason for believing that real wages rose markedly. One authority[3] put the position as follows:

[1] Clapham I. 559.
[2] Clapham II. 460.
[3] G. H. Wood, "Real Wages and the Standard of Comfort since 1850," in *S.J.* 1909; see table p. 97 and details pp. 102–3. The base year (= 100) is 1850.

Real Wages	1850–54	1855–59	1860–64	1865–69	1870–74	1875–79	1880–84
(*a*) Average Operatives in full work	101	98	107	114	125	135	137
With average lost time	97	92	100	108	122	127	131
(*b*) Operatives of unchanged grade in full work ...	101	96	102	106	114	122	122
With average lost time	97	90	97	100	113	115	117

It should, moreover, be noted that the higher real wage was received, in many cases, for a shorter period of work. In the 'fifties a 63-hour week was common; but by 1861 it had been reduced, for engineers and iron-founders, to 57 and subsequently it fell, for them and for other workers, to 54 or 54½ hours.[1]

TRADE UNIONISM

In order to maintain their standards of living and working conditions, the workers in a variety of trades had, since the early eighteenth century, taken to combining among themselves. In so far as the objects of their societies were provident they could be regarded as laudable, but effective action on trade union lines carried with it a risk of prosecution for conspiracy. The illegality of the early trade unions was a characteristic which they shared with combinations of employers; but these, being generally tacit and formed in the interests of more powerful individuals, were not prosecuted. When frantic fear of French revolutionary principles led to the suppression of political reform societies, associations of manual workers appeared especially dangerous, and the common-law illegality was reinforced by statutes of 1799 and 1800 prohibiting trade unionism under severe penalties. These Acts, though they made trade unions

[1] Clapham II. 448–449.

generally insecure, did not in fact prevent their formation and even their co-operation in the face of persecution ; and when the old fears had somewhat died down, it was possible, largely through the efforts of Francis Place, a working-class politician, and Joseph Hume, M.P., to bring about the repeal of the Combination Acts in 1824, though the repealing Act was modified in 1825. Under the Act of 1825, though trade union action was encompassed with many difficulties, a trade union was not in itself unlawful ; and the promotion of such societies was active, though the collapse of the industrial boom in 1825 meant that their efforts were generally unsuccessful. There followed a movement for the formation of large and powerful federations, in the cotton industry, the building trades and especially in Robert Owen's Grand National Consolidated Trades Union, which at one time included 500,000 members. The organization of such large numbers, however, required an art which had not then been mastered and machinery which had not been created ; and the prosecution of the Tolpuddle martyrs in 1834 showed the opposition which such ambitious trade unionism might expect from the unsympathetic, and at times unscrupulous, public authorities. None of the attempts at large federal unions became permanent ; and during the later eighteen-thirties and the early eighteen-forties such revolutionary feeling as existed showed itself in Chartism, from which the trade unions in general held aloof. In the later 'forties Chartism itself disintegrated, as better trade and cheaper bread made the masses less desperate.

Meanwhile, development of a less dramatic sort was taking place among trade unions. The Stone-masons, Moulders and others, with membership varying from 3,000 to 5,000, were organized in national unions and learning, with difficulty, the habits of book-keeping, correspondence and administration required in managing their affairs through central and branch executives. Difficulties of organization were especially great among the various kinds of engineers. They were organized in societies whose membership to some extent overlapped and whose relations were not such as to help effectively in securing the aims they had in common, such, for instance, as the preservation of their skilled status and the reduction or abolition of systematic overtime. Under the statesmanlike leadership of William Newton, his disciple, William Allan, and their society, the Journeymen Steam-Engine and Machine Makers and Millwrights Friendly Society, a movement for linking up the engineering unions in one strong society was successful in 1850, when the Amalgamated Society of Engineers, now the Amalgamated Engineering Union, was founded. By October 1851 the fusion was complete and the new society was 11,000 strong, with an income of £550 weekly from members' subscriptions. In the two decades which followed, "amalgamated principles" were accepted in other trades, notably, under the leadership of Robert Applegarth in the building industry.

The trade union world was largely guided by the views and experience of a kind of unofficial cabinet, called by the Webbs the "Junta," and known in their own day to their opponents as "the Clique" or the "Dirty Pack." The more important personalities among them were four general secretaries—William Allan of the A.S.E., Robert Applegarth of the Carpenters, Daniel Guile of the Ironfounders and Edwin Coulson of the London Bricklayers—together with George Odger, a London trade unionist and radical politician. Applegarth and Odger were both on the council of the First International in 1870; but in trade unionism, as they understood it, there was little or no revolutionary spirit. In the main they represented the outlook, and stood for the interests, of skilled artisans, for whom they claimed a status comparable to that of professional men, but their allies included Alexander Macdonald, the organizer of the Miners National Union. Their policy may be briefly stated as high rates of contribution, generous benefit scales and the avoidance of strikes wherever possible. The necessity of the strike, and the possibility of the lock-out, as an *ultima ratio* were not denied; but it was believed that the interests of employers and employed could generally be reconciled, so long as the worker was enabled to put a reserve price upon his labour, that is, so long as the provision of benefits freed him from the necessity of taking any job that was offered, and thus made collective bargaining a reality. It was a further object of the Junta to promote the formation of trades councils in all industrial centres and to interest trade unionists in politics, in order to press for legislation amending the law of master and servant and safeguarding the funds of the unions.

The latter was, naturally, a point of the greatest importance to such societies as the A.S.E., with its income of £27,000 or more yearly. The trade unions had considered themselves safe under the Friendly Societies Act of 1855, which enabled such societies, if established for any purpose not illegal, to prosecute defaulting or dishonest officials, but the case of Hornby *v.* Close in 1867 showed that the security was illusory, for the Court of Queen's Bench held that trade unions, though they ceased to be criminal in 1825, were still established for objects which were illegal, as being in restraint of trade; and that, consequently, trade unions were outside the scope of the Act of 1855. Meanwhile, the hostility of employers and of a great part of the public was aroused against the unions by a series of outrages, including arson and murder, committed by trade unionists in the regions of Sheffield and Manchester. The inquiry into these acts of violence made it sufficiently plain that union officials had been concerned, and that payment to the thugs had been made from trade union funds.[1] On the other hand, it was also clear that the "new model" unions, such as the A.S.E., abhorred lynch law and practices like "ratten-

[1] The evidence is set out at large in the *Report presented to the Trade Union Commission, 1867, by Examiners appointed to inquire into acts of intimidation, etc.*

ing," which prevailed only among a few backward unions and, in general, had declined. It was, consequently, urged that the best way to bring about the abandonment of such primitive methods was to give the workers adequate opportunities of forming unions of a better type; and that it was necessary to that end to legalize the unions and to safeguard their resources. With the expert help of Frederic Harrison in stating trade union requirements, and the tenacity of A. J. Mundella and Thomas Hughes in Parliament, the Junta secured from Gladstone's government in 1871 an Act which made the funds of trade unions safe, but preserved the incapacity of unions to sue and be sued. Thus, a union could protect itself against a dishonest official but could not easily be dragged into the courts by a member whom it excluded for blacklegging. On the other hand, though trade union objects were now freed from the reproach of illegality, trade union practices were made dangerous by a Criminal Law Amendment Act which attached penalties to ill-defined offences such as "molestation," "watching and besetting" and the like, and seemed to render valueless a previous Act, of 1859, which expressly legalized peaceful picketing. Gladstone's government refused to consider the repeal of the objectionable Act, and it is possible that the hostility of trade unionists, many of whom had been enfranchized by the second Reform Act of 1867, partly accounted for the liberal defeat in 1874. The conservatives in 1875 gave trade unionists what they had vainly sought from Gladstone; the Conspiracy and Protection of Property Act of that year prevented the prosecution of trade unionists for combining to do anything which would not have been criminal if done by an individual.

In the half century which separated the semi-legalization of 1825 from the full legalization of 1875, therefore, the trade unions had weathered severe storms and made a remarkable advance. The number of trade unionists in the earlier period is not known; at the Trade Union Congress of 1874 it was said to be more than 1,100,000, including 250,000 coal miners, as many cotton workers and 100,000 farm labourers. The latter had entered the movement as the result of the efforts of Joseph Arch and his helpers; but their strength was broken and their numbers greatly diminished before very long. Otherwise, the organized workers were well placed for the defence of their interests in the period of falling prices after 1876. It should, however, be noted that, apart from the miners, trade unionism was mainly confined to skilled workers. The following decades were to witness the spread of this form of organization, but with a different spirit and outlook, among the growing masses of the semi-skilled and unskilled workers.

PART TWO

1875–1914

CHAPTER VIII

Industrial and Commercial Organization

TYPES OF BUSINESS

The late Victorian period may be said to mark the transition from an industrial system predominantly controlled and managed by capitalist *entrepreneurs* to one in which corporate undertakings, joint-stock, co-operative and public, all involving the separation of management from ownership, had become the typical forms of organization. Joint-stock enterprise had, of course, already made considerable headway by the 'seventies. Canals, railways, many of the banks, and some of the great shipping companies had been joint-stock from the beginning; and the conversion of private concerns into companies had made some progress by 1870, especially in the coal, iron and engineering industries. But the great majority of firms in these industries, as well as in manufacturing, ship-building, commerce and the rest, were at that time still private. By 1914, however, the situation had been transformed; the joint-stock principle had become supreme in the industries producing on a large scale, and had permeated many of the smaller trades. Family businesses had been steadily converted into limited companies, from motives of prudence or expansion. New agencies for the flotation of companies, such as company promoters, underwriters and investment companies, multiplied in the 'seventies and 'eighties, and sold large numbers of existing and brand new businesses to the investing public. Joint-stock combines swallowed up innumerable private firms. In 1914 there were, besides the railway and other companies incorporated by special Acts of Parliament, 62,762 registered companies in Great Britain, with a paid-up capital of £2,482 million, compared with 8,924, with a paid-up capital of £482 million, in 1885.

A large proportion of these registered companies, however, were really nothing more than private firms and partnerships that had assumed company form in order to acquire the privilege of limited liability. They had none of the characteristics of the joint-stock company proper, such as the raising of capital by subscriptions from the general public, and the divorce of control from ownership. The modern legal distinction between public and private companies was not made before 1907, but it has been estimated by Mr. H. A. Shannon[1] that about one-fifth of the effective company formations in the years 1875–83 were "private," and that in 1890 the proportion was about one half. Under the Companies Act of 1907 businesses might be registered as private companies provided that their Articles of Association restricted the right to transfer shares, limited the number of shareholders to fifty, and prohibited any invitation to the public to subscribe for shares and debentures. Such private companies could be registered by as few as two persons, as against the seven needed to register a public company, and were not required to file with the Registrar of Companies an annual statement in the form of a balance sheet, so that no publicity need be given to their financial position. Many companies amended their Articles to comply with the legal definition of a private company, about 15,000 of the 48,492 private companies in the register in 1914 having been thus transferred from the "public" to the "private" category. In that year private companies outnumbered public by more than three to one; nevertheless there can be no doubt that the public companies of 1914 were far more important, in respect to capital, employment and output, than the private companies. Unfortunately the annual reports of the Registrar did not distinguish

[1] "The Limited Companies of 1866–1883," *Economic History Review*, 1931, p. 302.

between the aggregate paid-up capital of public and of private companies before 1926; but in that year there were 16,240 public companies, with a paid-up capital of £3,180 million, and 81,348 private companies, with £1,456 million of paid-up capital. Further evidence of the modern dominance of the public company is the fact that in the immediate post-war years 57 per cent. of the profits of all businesses, public and private, are estimated to have been made by public companies.[1] There are still some extensive fields of activity, such as agriculture, retailing and building, where the public company is responsible for only a minor part of the total output. But wherever any considerable capital expenditure is needed the superlative advantages of the joint-stock company—aggregation of small capitals, limitation of liability, transferability of shares, and power to issue several types of share to appeal to different classes of investor—mark it out as the most appropriate form of organization.

Though the joint-stock company has led to a wider diffusion of business ownership, it has been the principal means of concentrating business control. For the general body of shareholders of a large company cannot possibly play any effective part in the management of the concern they own; they are bound to entrust its control to a very small group of directors. Moreover the capitalization of a company can be so devised that the subscribers of a minor part of the total capital own the majority of the voting rights. The bulk of a company's capital may have been provided by the general public, in exchange for debenture bonds and preference shares, but a single shareholder or a small syndicate may nevertheless control its destiny, by acquiring the majority of the ordinary shares. By interposing a holding company between the controlling syndicate and the operating company, the proportion of the latter's capital that

[1] Committee on National Debt and Taxation, *Minutes of Evidence*, Qs. 8848–8851.

the syndicate need provide can be still further reduced. The company form of organization has thus made it possible for the modern captain of industry to wield an economic power out of all proportion to the capital he has invested. It has not resulted, as was at one time expected, in the democratization of industrial control.

Consumers' co-operation, corporate in capitalization but differing from the joint-stock company in having democratic control, went from strength to strength between the 'seventies and the outbreak of the war, as is indicated in the following table.

RETAIL CO-OPERATIVE SOCIETIES IN GREAT BRITAIN[1]

	1881	1900	1914
Number of societies	971	1,439	1,385
Total membership	547,212	1,707,011	3,053,770
Membership per society ...	564	1,186	2,205
Total sales (in £)	15,411,185	50,053,567	87,978,898
Sales per member (in £) ...	28·2	29·4	28·8
Total share capital (in £) ...	5,380,246	20,566,287	39,537,049

The quadrupling of the membership of the average society between 1881 and 1914 is accounted for by a variety of factors—the growth of population, the opening of new branches by existing societies, the magnet of the dividend on purchases, and also, especially in the later years of the period, the amalgamation of societies. For in co-operative distribution, as in other trades, economies arise from large-scale operations; moreover the society with a huge membership can provide economically a range of goods and facilities that is beyond the reach of the smaller societies. Hence, despite the formation of new societies, there has been a progressive decline in the total number since 1909. Until the war the chief strength of the co-operative movement remained in the areas where it had been earliest established. The industrial North of England, the Lowlands of Scotland, and the mining areas generally, with wage-earning populations conscious

[1] F. Hall and W. P. Watkins, *Co-operation*, pp. 141–43 and 202–5.

of their community of interests, became solidly co-operative. On the other hand, the scattered nature of rural communities was unfavourable to co-operative growth; residential districts remained aloof from what was still an essentially working-class organization, and in areas, such as London, with a diversity of local industry and a lack of working-class solidarity, the co-operative movement remained weak. Broadly speaking, co-operation flourished in the same economic environment as trade unionism.

By far the most significant development in the history of co-operation in this period was the extension of its sphere of activity backwards from retailing and wholesaling to the earlier stages of the processes of production. The great majority of retail societies undertook some form of simple small-scale production, such as baking, slaughtering or boot-repairing. But it was through the two wholesale societies that the movement launched out into a wide range of industrial activity. To this extension of the scope of consumers' co-operation there was at first strong opposition from the supporters of producers' co-operation, whose ideal was the self-governing workshop. The principle of consumers' control, however, ably defended by J. T. W. Mitchell, chairman of the C.W.S. from 1874 to 1895, was victorious. Beginning with the acquisition of the Crumpsall biscuit works in 1873, the English wholesale society extended its productive enterprise until it had about fifty factories and depots in 1914, producing such things as clothing, flour, soap, hardware and other household goods. The Scottish wholesale society was a little later in developing its manufacturing activities, but in 1881 it set up two factories for shirt-making and tailoring. Its great achievement was the colony of factories on the Shieldhall site, near Glasgow, developed after 1887. A joint committee of the English and Scottish wholesale societies was established in 1900 to manage their tea, cocoa and chocolate undertakings, and proceeded to acquire tea estates of its own in India and

Ceylon. It also took over in 1913 the Co-operative Insurance Society, founded in 1867 as a federal society to insure the property of the retail societies, and now engaged in general insurance business. Deposit banking was early added to the list of co-operative activities, the C.W.S. opening a department for this purpose in 1872, though only deposits from co-operative societies were accepted until 1910, when individual members, as well as trade unions, were encouraged to open accounts. The progress made by the wholesale societies from 1870 to 1913 may be judged from the following table.

ENGLISH AND SCOTTISH CO-OPERATIVE WHOLESALE SOCIETIES.

Year	Sales	Value of Goods produced
	£	£
1870	782,983	—
1900	21,507,520	4,086,823
1913	40,340,349	10,305,717

Producers' co-operation languished after the fervour of the Christian Socialists had died down, but revived after the formation of the Co-operative Productive Federation in 1882. The number of societies accepting in some degree the principle of co-partnership, *i.e.* giving their workers a share in capital, profits and control, grew from 15 in 1883 to 112 twenty-five years later. Few of these were run as strictly self-governing workshops, with control vested solely in the hands of workers. In practically all of them a considerable part of the capital was subscribed by consumers' retail societies or by sympathetic outsiders, who naturally also shared, along with the workers, in control and management. Compared with consumers' co-operation, this branch of the movement, founded on the principle of workers' control, has failed to make any appreciable headway. It suffers from managerial defects, which appear to be inherent in its structure; for the manager of a producers' society has to perform the exacting dual rôle of master and servant of the members.

A third group of corporate undertakings, those operated by public authorities, grew rapidly in the last quarter of the nineteenth century owing to the enterprise of local authorities, and gave rise to a prolonged political controversy, which is by no means ended even now, over the merits and dangers of municipal socialism. Long enough before the politicians became agitated over the question, however, the municipalities had been quietly extending their trading activities. Even in 1830 there were eleven municipal water undertakings in England and Wales, the oldest of which was that of Tiverton, dating back to about 1250. By 1870 the number had grown to 78, mainly through the acquisition of private undertakings. The gas industry remained almost exclusively the preserve of private enterprise until the middle of the century, when there were only nine municipal gas undertakings in England and Wales, the oldest being Manchester's, established in 1817 by the local Commissioners of Police. By 1870 the number had grown to 37. Scores of towns had also, by that year, established such trading undertakings as market halls, harbours, cemeteries, baths and wash-houses. What distinguished the municipal trading of the later Victorian era was the accelerated pace at which private undertakings were acquired by public authorities, and the extension of public enterprise to such new fields as electric supply and tramways. In the 'seventies gas and water undertakings were municipalized by the score; between 1869 and 1878, for example, 68 private gas companies were transferred to municipal ownership in Britain. In the 'nineties local authorities were busily engaged in establishing their own electricity undertakings and in taking over the property of private tramway companies. The position regarding municipal enterprise in 1913 was, briefly, that four-fifths of the consumers of water and of tramway services were served by public undertakings;

two-thirds of the electricity supplied were generated by local authorities; and municipal gas works supplied two-fifths of the consumers of gas.

Little of this municipal activity was prompted by any doctrinaire belief in the virtues of public enterprise. A variety of motives was at work. Since the public utilities, to which municipal enterprise was almost entirely confined, must necessarily be monopolized if they are to be operated with the maximum of efficiency, municipal ownership was frequently resorted to as a means of safeguarding local consumers against monopolistic exploitation. This was the motive, for instance, that inspired Glasgow Corporation's purchase of two local gas companies in 1869. Some municipalities embarked on their trading undertakings with the object of making profits for the relief of rates or for the provision and improvement of local amenities. Joseph Chamberlain, for instance, then Mayor of Birmingham, announced that this was the purpose of his city's acquisition of the local gas company in 1875. Municipal purchase was also a means of ending the friction that not infrequently arose between private companies and local councils over the opening up of highways and streets. Finally, municipal trading having come to be regarded as the touchstone of civic enterprise, considerations of local prestige led some municipalities to undertake their own lighting, watering or transport.

INDUSTRIAL COMBINATION

The epithet "competitive" can probably be more aptly applied to the British industrial system in the 'sixties and 'seventies than in any other phase of its evolution. Even then there was doubtless a goodly sprinkling of trade associations and informal agreements aiming, among other things, at the regulation of prices. These certainly existed, for instance, in the South Staffordshire and North of

England iron trade, the soap trade, the railway industry and some of the local retail trades. "But," declares Professor Clapham, "the imperfect evidence as yet available suggests that, at any rate during the generally prosperous and dynamic third quarter of the nineteenth century, there was rather less co-operation among 'capitalist' producers than there had been in the more difficult first and second quarters."[1] And in the fourth quarter there began that cumulative tendency towards industrial combination which, with the active encouragement of the State since the war, has made "monopolistic," "planned," or at least "imperfectly competitive," the most appropriate adjectives to apply to contemporary economic organization.

Other industrialized countries have experienced the same unremitting drive towards the regulation of competition. In fact the modern combination movement struck root a decade or so earlier in the United States and Germany than in Britain. Clearly, therefore, its origins must be sought in the basic features of modern industrialism and not in the circumstances peculiar to any one country. The crux of the matter is to be found in large-scale production. Technical progress, the widening of markets as the result of improvements in transport, the development of the art of business management, together with a host of other influences, have combined to induce a continuous increase in the size of the average business unit in nearly every industry. Now the presence in a competitive industry of a number of large firms, each of which is saddled with heavy overhead expenses and striving to enlarge its output in order to secure more of the economies of large-scale production, must inevitably create conditions favourable to industrial combination. There can be no stable competitive price in such circumstances, since each firm, knowing that it can lower its average unit costs if it secures additional sales, has an inducement to cut prices. When once price-cutting has started within a

[1] *Op. cit.*, II. 145.

group of firms producing under conditions of diminishing costs, it can be terminated only by the elimination of all firms but the strongest, or by some form of combination. Further, competition among large-scale producers may involve some loss of potential profits not only by giving rise to price cuttting, but also by imposing on each competitor heavier expenditure than would need to be incurred under conditions of monopoly. Hence combination, especially if it is accompanied by unification of management, may yield such economies as the elimination of competitive marketing expenditure and of cross freights, the specialization of plants within an industry, and the like. In the looser types of combination, such as pools, cartels, and associations for regulating prices or output, the predominant motive as a rule is the desire to establish some kind of monopolistic control over the market; in the closer and more stable forms, such as the trust, holding company and merger, the productive economies of "rationalization" are usually an additional, and sometimes, as in the railway amalgamations of 1923, the sole, motive for combination. The vertical combine, in which the successive stages of a process of production are integrated under a single control, a form of organization that is particularly common in the metal industries, is also prompted primarily by considerations of productive efficiency.

In emphasizing the increasing scale of modern production as the dominant cause of industrial combination, we do not wish to imply that no restriction of competition is likely to appear in small-scale trades. Any group of firms, whether operating on a large scale or not, may find it in their interests to restrict output or control prices. This is particularly likely to occur when the members of the group control the output of some rare raw material, or possess patent rights or other privileges giving them differential advantages over competitors outside the group. But in most small-scale industries the multiplicity of existing firms, and the ease with which new rivals can establish themselves, militate against the formation of stable and successful combinations, unless the State arms the industry with powers to restrict entry and to fix prices, as in road transport and hop-growing.

Of the two main forms of monopolistic combination, "terminable associations," in which the participating firms retain their independence, and "trusts," in which there is some measure of common management within the group, the first was by far the more common in the combination movement of pre-war Britain. There were, of course, many amalgamations, but most of these were undertaken for the internal economies they offered, and had little or no monopolistic intent. Only a few British industries came to be dominated by "trusts" on the American model. On the other hand, associations for regulating prices or output, and pooling agreements, were very widespread, especially in industries catering primarily for the home market. Even in these trades, however, the possibilities of successful monopolistic combination were severely limited owing to the absence of protective tariffs. And the staple export trades, confronted with intensified overseas competition, were in no position to fix prices as they chose. Free-trade Britain, with her economy geared to an extensive external trade, was therefore less over-run by combines than her newly risen rivals, Germany and the United States. In the following paragraphs some brief indication will be given of the extent and forms of combination in the principal British industries.

"No industry has been so much syndicated and combined in all the great industrial countries as that of iron."[1] Vertical integration has long been a characteristic of this industry, for some of the early iron-masters mined their own coal and ore. But the process was greatly facilitated in later Victorian times by the evolution of the limited joint-stock company, which made it possible to raise the millions of pounds' worth of capital required to finance the modern

[1] H. W. Macrosty, *The Trust Movement in British Industry*, p. 24.

giant fusions of the iron and steel industry. The development of John Brown and Co. may serve to illustrate the process whereby many similar vertical combines, such as Armstrong-Whitworths, Vickers, Baldwins, and Guest, Keen and Nettlefolds, were constructed. Established at the Atlas Works, Sheffield, in 1854, John Brown and Co. were converted into a limited company a decade later. They were one of the first firms to undertake the production of Bessemer steel, and acquired a special reputation for the manufacture of rails and armour-plate. In the 'seventies they extended their activities backwards to raw-material production, by acquiring iron-ore mines in Lincolnshire and Spain, and collieries in Yorkshire. By the 'nineties an appreciable part of their output consisted of armour plate, marine shaftings and other shipbuilding materials. They therefore acquired one of the leading shipbuilding concerns, the Clydebank Engineering and Shipbuilding Co., in 1899, to ensure a steadier demand for their output of steel products. The firm thus integrated was able to carry out all the processes involved in the construction of monster battleships and liners, from the extraction of the raw materials onwards. Further expansion followed in the first decade of the twentieth century. Seven-eighths of the ordinary share capital of Thos. Firth and Sons, the Sheffield neighbours of John Brown and Co., and famous for their ordnance and projectiles, were purchased in 1903; four years later, substantial interests were acquired in Harland and Wolff, Ltd., the great Belfast shipbuilding and marine engineering concern, itself a combine with wide ramifications; and in 1909 Browns bought a controlling interest in the Coventry Ordnance Works, Ltd., and in Dalton Main Collieries, Ltd.

Besides these vertical combines, of which John Brown's is a typical example, there were numerous horizontal groupings in the iron and steel industry, some of which were planned to restrict competition in particular products.

Stewarts and Lloyds, for instance, a combination formed in 1902 of the principal tube-manufacturing firms of England and Scotland, and the Rivet, Nut and Bolt Co., a fusion of fifteen Scottish firms in 1900, were in this class. None of these, however, attained the position of a monopolistic trust. Amalgamation in the steel industry, however, by reducing the number of competitors to manageable proportions, did facilitate the formation of price-fixing associations and pools, which arose in nearly every section of the industry. Thus the Scottish Steelmakers' Association was formed in 1886 by the four leading Scottish producers of boiler-plates, ship-plates, and other shipbuilding materials, for which they had something like a local monopoly. It was reconstructed on a much broader basis in 1903, and in the following year entered into an agreement with the North-East Coast Steelmakers' Association, whereby the Scottish and Belfast markets were reserved for the members of the Scottish association in return for their undertaking not to invade the English market. The Scottish Steelmakers fixed minimum prices for their products, and differentiated between home and foreign markets, export prices being lower than domestic prices. In the galvanized sheet trade, intermittent attempts to regulate prices had been made since 1883. From 1905 onwards, when the National Galvanized Sheet Association was formed, controlling about 95 per cent. of the British manufacturers, these attempts met with considerable success, a large proportion of the trade being in the hands of a small number of firms. Another effective combination, formed three years before the war, was the National Light Castings Association, which controlled about 95 per cent. of the British trade in baths, stoves, taps, railings and the like. For many years it encouraged builders' merchants to confine their dealings to members of the Association by offering them deferred rebates, payment of which was conditional on their continued loyalty to the Association. Like many other such rings, it adopted also a pooling scheme, whereby members exceeding their output quotas paid a levy into a pool, which was distributed to those whose outputs fell short of their quotas.

Purely national combines clearly cannot wield any effective monopoly power if they are subject to keen foreign competition. Hence, even before the war, international cartels made their appearance in a number of trades. In the iron and steel industry the most notable example of such international agreement was the International Rail Makers' Association, first formed as early as 1884. Germany, Belgium and Britain, the principal exporters of steel rails, undertook not to compete in each other's home market, and divided the export trade to other countries in agreed proportions, the British share being 65 per cent. The cartel broke down two years later, but was revived in 1904 and renewed periodically until the outbreak of war. France and the United States joined the three original parties to form this later cartel, in which the British share was fixed at 37 per cent. in 1904 and 1907, and at 34 per cent. in 1912. "The general effect of the agreement," according to the Report of the Committee on Trusts, 1919, "was gradually to restrict the activity of the British makers to British Colonial markets."

Coal was much less amenable than steel to monopolistic control. A number of huge undertakings were built up by amalgamation, such as the Fife Coal Company, registered in 1878, which, by absorbing half a dozen other companies, had increased its output to 3¾ million tons in 1909; the Joicey undertaking, which took over Lord Durham's huge colliery and steamship interests in 1896; and the "Cambrian Combine," the work of D. A. Thomas (Viscount Rhondda), which between 1907 and 1910 acquired the control of four South Wales colliery companies with a combined annual capacity of about 3½ million tons. None of these groups, however, controlled a sufficient proportion of the pre-war coal output, of over 250 million tons a year, to be able to regulate prices. Each of the main coalfields had its own association of owners, and occasionally regional attempts were made to regulate prices, as in Lancashire, in 1893–94, and in Durham, in 1894–95; but these were doomed to failure, competition within each field and between the fields being far too vigorous. Even in the narrowly localized anthracite industry it proved impossible, owing to the large number of undertakings, to build up an effective combination, and the projected Anthracite Trust of 1903–4 came to nought.

The last decade of the century produced a rich harvest of consolidations in the textile industries. They were of the horizontal type, and most prevalent in the bleaching, dyeing and finishing sections, where firms were much fewer in number than in the spinning and weaving branches. The largest, in point of capitalization, and the most consistently successful, as judged by profits, was the thread combine of J. and P. Coats. Originally established on a small scale in 1826, this family business had already grown to huge dimensions when it was floated as a company in 1890. Its position was strengthened in 1895–96 by the purchase of its four strongest British rivals; but there still remained a score of competitors in Britain and many more on the Continent. In 1897 the majority of the British group outside the Coats combine united to form the English Sewing Cotton Company, but owing to unsound finance and mediocre management its record was disappointing alongside the dazzling success of its highly efficient Paisley rival. The two groups worked in close association, both their outputs being marketed through the Central Thread Agency. Another cotton amalgamation that met with a considerable measure of success was the Fine Cotton Spinners' and Doublers' Association of 1898,[1] a holding company, which ultimately included forty-five firms. In the fine cotton-

[1] This Association, like the others formed in the textile trades at this period, was a limited liability company, not an "association" in the ordinary sense of the term.

spinning section, unlike the coarse, there were several features favourable to monopoly, such as the comparatively small number of firms, the limited supply of Sea Island cotton, and the preference of buyers for the yarns of proved quality produced by existing firms, which naturally hindered the establishment of new competitors. The year 1899 saw also the formation of another successful textile combine, the Bradford Dyers' Association, comprising originally twenty-two firms, working on a commission basis, which controlled the bulk of the piece-dyeing trade in the Bradford district. Three rather smaller combines in the dyeing branch were the English Velvet and Cord Dyers' Association, and the Yorkshire Indigo, Scarlet and Colour Dyers, both formed in 1899, and the British Cotton and Wool Dyers' Association, engaged in the dyeing of yarns, which was floated in 1900. With an original capital of over £9 million and comprising about sixty firms, the Calico Printers' Association, formed in 1899, was one of the biggest combines in the textile trades. Comparatively small in number, highly localized, and possessing a world-wide goodwill, partly based on trade marks, the calico-printing firms were as favourably placed for the formation of an effective monopoly as the fine cotton spinners. The Calico Printers' Association suffered in its early years, like several other textile combines, from too great a decentralization of management, but its profit-making capacity improved after the thorough internal re-organization effected in 1902. In the textile-bleaching trade, a powerful consolidation, with an original capital of over £8 million, was promoted in 1900 by the fusion of fifty-three firms in the Bleachers' Association. All but a handful of these were located in the Manchester district on sites giving access to a supply of water, a facility that new entrants into the trade would find it difficult to obtain. Here again, therefore, we find a relatively small group of firms possessing differential advantages over outsiders, and consequently having a strong incentive to combine.

The chemical trades were another field in which the forces of combination were especially active. It was, in fact, in the salt industry that the first British trust appeared. Salt prices had fallen to an unprofitably low level in the slump of the mid-'eighties, and a vain attempt had been made by the associated producers in 1885 to restore more remunerative prices by restricting output. In 1888 the Salt Union, a limited company, was formed by the amalgamation of sixty-four firms, which controlled some 90 per cent. of the British salt production. Salt prices were thereupon increased, common salt rising from 2s. 6d. per ton in 1888 to 10s. 6d. in the spring of 1889. This price policy paid the trust for a year or two, but ultimately had the most disastrous consequences, for it stimulated a huge increase in the output of its competitors, both at home and abroad. By 1907 the Salt Union's share in the total salt production of the United Kingdom had fallen to less than half. Intermittent, and not very successful, combinations of salt producers after 1899 culminated in 1906 in the formation of a cartel on the German model. A selling syndicate, the North Western Salt Company, was established, nearly all the British salt producers being members. Output quotas were allotted, and a policy of differentiating between the prices charged in different markets was pursued.

Two firms dominated the heavy chemical industry before the war—Brunner Mond and Company, and the United Alkali Company. The first started its career in 1881, absorbed a number of alkali firms, and was distinguished throughout for its technical and business efficiency. The history of the second was less fortunate. Voluntary association having failed to prevent the price of bleaching powder from dropping to unpleasantly low levels, forty-nine firms, including all the principal users of the Le Blanc process, were combined in the United Alkali Company in 1891. For the production of soda the Le Blanc process was less efficient than the ammonia process, used by Brunner Mond among other firms. But, at the time, it had the advantage, compared with the alternative process, of yielding chlorine, from which was made "bleach," one of the main sources of revenue for United Alkali. Unfortunately for the users of the Le Blanc process, the demand for bleaching powder was declining, while that for soda products was expanding. Hence as time went on the balance of advantage shifted more and more in favour of the ammonia process. Moreover, in 1898 a new electrolytic process, promptly adopted by the German chemical industry, proved to be much more efficient for the manufacture of "bleach."

Of the remaining permanent combinations formed before the war, the most prominent were in the soap, wallpaper, cement, whisky and tobacco trades. The first of these was the best known to the general public, owing to the hue and cry raised in the Press over the working agreement entered into in 1906 by eleven soap-makers, headed by Lever Bros. Foiled by the public outcry, the combine was dissolved for the time being, only to reappear as, one by one, the principal soap manufacturing concerns were absorbed by Lever Bros. In 1914 the United Kingdom Soap Manufacturers' Association, dominated by the Lever group, was formed to regulate the price of soap. It controlled about 80 per cent. of the British soap output. In the general paper trade there were far too many firms for any successful combination to be engineered. But the wall-paper section was in a rather special position. There were only about forty firms manufacturing wall-paper in 1900. Moreover, owing to the difference between the customary dimensions of British and continental wall-papers, foreign competition, though existent, was not a serious bar to successful combination. Hence in 1900 thirty-one firms, controlling, it is said, 98 per cent. of the British output, were merged in Wall-Paper Manufacturers, Ltd. Less successful financially was another combine formed in the same year—Associated Portland Cement Manufacturers. This was one of the few British combines in which an element of natural monopoly was present, for most of the twenty-seven firms comprised in the merger were located in the Thames and Medway valleys, and controlled supplies of clay and chalk of specially suitable quality. The wide distribution of these raw materials, however, enabled cement users to obtain alternative supplies of cheaper, though poorer, cement, thus limiting the power of the combine to charge excessive prices for its output. Several of the leading cement manufacturers outside the combine united in 1911 under the name of British Portland Cement, Ltd., which was promoted, and is controlled, by Associated Portland Cement Manufacturers. The Distillers' Company, formed in 1877 by the fusion of six firms, was one of the earliest examples of a combination leading to the eventual establishment of a strong monopoly. By 1907 eleven other distilleries had been absorbed, or brought under control by the purchase of shares, and the "Scotch Combine," by agreement with its two principal competitors, was able to raise whisky prices. The process of concentration was completed in 1925, when the last two competitors of note were brought within the fold. A huge combine has been built up also in the tobacco trade, but it has never occupied anything like the dominant position of the Distillers' Company, owing to the persistence of the demand for the specialities of the independent tobacco firms. The Imperial Tobacco Company was formed in 1901 by the amalgamation of thirteen firms, then controlling about half of the British tobacco trade, as a defensive alliance against the American Tobacco Company, which was vigorously pushing sales in the British market. After a short period of warfare the two combines reached an agreement in 1902, under which each reserved to itself its domestic market, while the tobacco trade in the rest of the world was to be exploited by an international trust, the British-American Tobacco Company, controlled by the British and American combines,

CHAPTER IX

Foreign Competition and Industrial Fluctuation

BRITAIN AND HER RIVALS

By the end of the nineteenth century it had become clear that Britain was losing the industrial supremacy she had so long enjoyed. With the aid of protectionist policies, her two greatest rivals, Germany and the United States, had developed their basic industries in the last quarter of the century at a pace greatly surpassing that of Britain. France, too, though far behind Britain in most industries, showed in many directions a greater rate of industrial expansion. Thus in the pig-iron industry, the United Kingdom's output of 6·4 million tons a year in 1870–74 had exceeded the combined output of these other three countries, the United States producing 2·2 millions, Germany 1·8 and France 1·2. In 1900–4, however, the United Kingdom, with an annual output of 8·6 million tons, had dropped to the third place, the American output having been increased nearly eight-fold to 16·4 millions, and the German five-fold to 8·9 millions, while the French, at 2·6 millions, had more than doubled. In the United States not only was the aggregate production of pig iron greater than Britain's, but so also was the output per head of population. By 1913, when America was producing 31 million tons, and Germany 16·5, Britain, with 10·3 million tons, was completely outclassed.

A similar re-alignment occurred in steel production. In 1870–74, when the basic process was still undiscovered, the steel industry was of very modest size in all countries; Britain produced about half a million tons annually, Germany 300,000, the United States 140,000 and France 130,000. Three decades later America had secured a comfortable lead with an output of over 13 million tons. She was followed by Germany with over 7 million tons, and by the United Kingdom with just under 5 million tons. The French steel output, 1·7 million tons, was still comparatively small. The German and American steel industries grew to colossal dimensions between 1900 and 1913. America produced 31,300,000 tons in 1913, Germany 17,320,000, while the British output had increased to only 7,660,000 tons. It must be remembered, however, that the greater part of the iron and steel output of Britain's rivals was consumed at home, so that she retained her lead as an exporter longer than her lead as a producer. It was not until 1912 that Germany took Britain's place as the principal exporter, judged by value, of iron and steel products, Germany's exports being £48,800,000, compared with Britain's £48,600,000. At this time, despite the huge output of her heavy industries, the United States' exports of iron and steel were little more than half of Britain's.

Britain lost also her lead in coal production, though she remained by far the principal coal exporter down to the war. Her coal output in the early 'seventies averaged 120 million tons a year, nearly two-thirds of the estimated world production, the next largest producer being the United States with 43 million tons. At the turn of the century Britain's share in the world production of coal had shrunk to about a third, her output of 225 million tons being exceeded by America's 241 million tons. Thirteen years later the output of British coal reached its zenith, 287 million tons, which was just under a quarter of the world's production. The United States, producing 509 million tons, were now by far the greatest source of supply. As in the iron and steel industry, Britain maintained her leading position as a coal exporter longer than her position as a producer, for in 1913 she exported over 98 million tons of coal (including bunker coal for foreign-going vessels), compared with 47 million tons exported by Germany and 24 million tons by the United

States. Coal, in fact, came to the fore as one of Britain's staple exports during the forty years preceding the war. The 16 million tons annually exported in 1871–75 had accounted for only 13·22 per cent. of the British coal output and for only 4·3 per cent. of the value of Britain's total exports ; whereas the 98 millions exported in 1913 were 34 per cent. of the total tonnage raised and 10·43 per cent. of Britain's exports. Some observers of our economic position on the eve of the war found it rather disquieting that we should have come to rely to such a degree on the export of a raw material whose supply was not inexhaustible.

In the textile industries also Britain's leadership was challenged. If we take the number of spindles as an approximate measure of the size of a country's cotton industry, Britain's relative position changed thus : in 1881–84 she possessed nearly 54 per cent. of the world's spinning capacity, in 1900 43 per cent., and in 1913 just under 40 per cent. America was second to Britain with 21·5 per cent. of the world's spindleage in 1913. Cotton consumption per spindle, however, was a good deal less in Britain than in other countries, owing to the relatively high proportion of fine yarns produced by the Lancashire industry. If we take the mill consumption of cotton as a measure of size, Britain was second to America in 1912–13, their respective shares in the world's consumption being 20·3 and 26·6 per cent. No other country had a cotton consumption at all approaching those of the two leading producers; India's share was 7·9 per cent., Germany's 7·8 and Japan's 6·2. The rise of the cotton industry in these other countries reduced their imports from Britain, but had not, before the war, begun to threaten seriously her dominant position in the cotton export trade. And as Britain's cotton markets in China, India and the Near East expanded by more than the European and American markets contracted, her exports of cotton piece-goods continued to grow, in quantity and value, down to 1914, this growth, as the following table shows, being most striking after 1900. The yarn trade,

EXPORTS OF COTTON YARNS AND PIECE GOODS FROM THE UNITED KINGDOM[1]

Year	Cotton Yarns		Cotton Piece Goods	
	Quantity (in million lbs.)	Value (in million £)	Quantity (in million yds.)	Value (in million £)
1870–74	205	15·4	3,446	54·9
1875–79	232	12·7	3,670	49·9
1880–84	249	13·1	4,493	55·3
1885–89	252	11·6	4,833	50·8
1890–94	236	10·3	4,975	50·6
1895–99	242	9·2	5,139	48·5
1900–04	162	7·9	5,295	56·7
1905–09	217	12·4	6,002	73·1
1910–13	217	15·1	6,673	89·8

on the other hand, became relatively less important as Europe, and later the East, equipped themselves with spinning machinery, and it declined absolutely, in quantity, after the late 'eighties. In 1910–13 Britain's share of the world trade in cotton yarns and cotton manufactures, as measured by value, was still 57 per cent., Germany and France being the only other countries with any considerable export trade in cotton goods.

Like its great neighbour across the Pennines, the woollen and worsted industry continued to expand down to 1914, the quantity of wool consumed in the United Kingdom advancing from 453 million pounds in 1870–74 to 846 million in 1909–13. But the bulk of the increased output of the British wool-using industries was absorbed in the home market. With the exception of "tops" and yarns, exports of woollen and worsted goods were declining in the three or four decades preceding the war. Exports of tissues reached their peak figure of 324 million yards in 1870–74; by 1909–13 they had fallen as low as 174 million yards. Exports of other woollen products, such as carpets, flannels and blankets, showed a similar downward trend.

[1] Committee on Industry and Trade, *Survey of Textile Industries*, pp. 146, 147.

The manufacture of wool was developing in most of the countries that had formerly been Britain's best customers; and unlike the cotton industry, the woollen industry had no expanding Eastern trade to compensate for its losses in European markets. Britain was able, nevertheless, to increase her share of the international trade in woollen goods during this period. Of the total exports of wool textile manufactures from the United Kingdom, France, Germany and the United States, the British share was 41·6 per cent. in 1880–84, and 53·9 in 1909–13. The shrinkage of Britain's exports of woollen manufactures was thus not due to their being ousted by competing woollen exports from other countries.

In engineering it is not possible to make any comparison of the physical outputs of the leading producing countries, but there can be no doubt that the British industry, though making steady progress, was expanding much more slowly than the German and American industries. In the early 'eighties, Britain's annual exports of machinery were valued at £11½ million, and accounted for 64 per cent. of the total machinery exports of the United Kingdom, France, Germany and the United States. By 1909–13 Britain's machinery exports had increased to nearly £32 million, but her share in the total for these four countries had dropped to 34 per cent., German and American exports having drawn nearly level with the British. The industry in which Britain's supremacy was most successfully maintained was shipbuilding. She had taken the lead in this industry as iron and steam superseded wood and sail, and in the early 'nineties, with an annual output of 998,000 gross tons, was responsible for just over four-fifths of the gross tonnage of merchant vessels launched in the world. This proportion fell to 58·8 per cent. in the early nineteen-hundreds, though the annual output had increased to 1,358,000 gross tons, but recovered slightly to 60·6 per cent. in 1910–14, when Britain launched an average of 1,660,000 gross tons a year.

This loss or decline of Britain's leadership in most sections of the coal, metal and textile industries was quite inevitable. She had no monopoly of the new industrial technique, nor was she by any means the only, or even the most populous, country possessing natural advantages for the development of these basic industries. Though Britain had acquired a long lead in industrial development in the first half of the century, the world could not be expected to remain for ever dependent on the British workshop alone. Other countries, seeking the profits of industrialism, national self-sufficiency, or greater military strength, followed Great Britain along the path of industrialization, without, however, embracing the Cobdenism that was then associated with it. There was, in fact, a widespread resort to higher tariffs as a means of protecting tender home industries from the killing frost of foreign competition. Germany raised her duties on manufactured imports to a protectionist level in 1879, and made further increases in them in 1885. The Caprivi treaties, negotiated between Germany and a number of other countries in the early 'nineties, involved some moderation of her import duties, but the upward trend was resumed after 1902. France, having for a brief space flirted with the principles of free trade, returned to her old protectionist love after the Franco-Prussian war. The Méline tariff of 1892, in particular, considerably stiffened the protection of French industry. The United States, also, adopted a policy of full-blooded protection in the McKinley tariff of 1890. Moderated a little in 1894, American import duties were further raised by the Dingley tariff of 1897. The self-governing colonies were not content to remain engaged only in the production of raw materials, and pursued moderately protectionist policies. Victoria, in 1878, and Canada, in the following year, set the example, ultimately followed by all the others, of erecting tariffs that were avowedly protective and not simply revenue-raising.

More disturbing than this unavoidable decline in Britain's share of the world output of the older staple industries was her comparative backwardness in some of the newer ones. The mantle of the pioneer had apparently fallen now on other shoulders. In such rising industries as the manufacture of motor vehicles, electrical apparatus, and chemicals, Britain, though contributing towards the inventions that made them possible, was early out-distanced by other countries. French and German inventors were primarily responsible for the internal combustion engine. As early as 1893 France had an output of about 500 motor cars a year. Britain had no motor-manufacturing concern until three years later, when the English Daimler Motor Company was formed. Many other firms, especially those in the cycle industry, took up the manufacture of motor vehicles, but all were still on a comparatively small scale before the war. The most spectacular development in the new industry occurred in the United States, where, starting with the Ford Motor Company in 1908, the methods of mass production were applied. In 1913 the United States were turning out 485,000 motor vehicles a year, their average value working out at less than £190 each. In the same year, the French motor output was 45,000, while in 1912 Britain produced only approximately 25,000 motor vehicles, with an average value of about £325 each.

" Much of the basic scientific work underlying the electrical manufacturing industry was carried out by British scientists. Yet, prior to the war, Great Britain lagged greatly behind other important countries, such as the United States and Germany, in the growth of consumption of electricity for power purposes; and, largely owing to this cause, the electrical manufacturing industry in this country, with the exception of the cable-making section, was in a very unsatisfactory position."[1] It is estimated that in 1913 the value of the output of the British electrical industry was £30 million.

[1] Committee on Industry and Trade, *Survey of Metal Industries*, p. 280.

This compared poorly with the German output of £65 million in the same year, and the American output of £74 million in 1914. The French electrical industry, on the other hand, with an output of less than £8 million in 1913, was a long way behind the British. Several factors, legal and economic, were responsible for the comparatively slow growth of the use of electricity in Britain. When the electric supply industry was taking shape in the 'eighties and 'nineties, the legislature failed to appreciate the area requirements of the new industry. Classifying electricity supply in the category of local public utilities, Parliament assumed that the local-authority areas within which water and gas were supplied would be equally suitable for the newcomer. It therefore allowed the country, under the Electric Lighting Acts of 1882 and 1888, to be covered by an uneconomically large number of undertakings, of which there were about 520 in 1900, many being on far too small a scale to be able to sell electricity on terms that would popularize its use. Not until 1898 did Parliament begin to modify its policy, by establishing power companies authorized to supply electricity in bulk to other undertakings over wide areas. Even then, opposition from existing undertakings succeeded in restricting the power companies' sphere of activity mainly to the more sparsely populated parts of the country. The expansion of the electricity industry was retarded also by our possession of cheap and abundant supplies of steam- and gas-coal. Further, gas undertakings had the immense advantage of being first in the field; in the early 'eighties, before electric supply undertakings had appeared, they had nearly two million customers, increased to over four million in 1903 and to nearly seven million in 1913. For illuminating purposes gas became more and more efficient, especially after the invention of the incandescent mantle in the late 'eighties. Nevertheless, despite these domestic handicaps to its development, the British electrical manufacturing industry exported over £7,600,000 worth of goods in 1913, and was second only to Germany so far as the export trade was concerned.

Of Britain's total export trade in the forty years preceding the war, that with the Empire constituted an increasing proportion. This tendency was encouraged in the first decade of the twentieth century by the preferential treatment of imports from Britain into the colonies. Canada was the first to grant such preference, in 1898; she was followed by

EXPORTS OF MERCHANDIZE FROM THE UNITED KINGDOM

Year	Total Value	Exports to Foreign Countries		Exports to British Colonies and Possessions	
	(million £)	Amount (million £)	Proportion of Total	Amount (million £)	Proportion of Total
			Per cent.		Per cent.
1870–74	290	225	77·5	65	22·5
1880–84	298	210	70·6	88	29·4
1890–94	296	211	71·2	85	28·8
1900–04	350	236	67·5	114	32·5
1910–13	581	396	68·5	183	31·5

South Africa and New Zealand in 1903, and by Australia in 1908. On the import side, however, the increase in Britain's dependence on the Empire was slight; in fact, until the end of the century the general trend was towards an increasing proportion of importation from foreign countries.

IMPORTS OF MERCHANDIZE INTO THE UNITED KINGDOM

Year	Total Value	Imports from Foreign Countries		Imports from British Colonies and Possessions	
	(million £)	Amount (million £)	Proportion of Total	Amount (million £)	Proportion of Total
			Per cent.		Per cent.
1870–74	346	270	78·0	76	22·0
1880–84	408	312	76·5	96	23·5
1890–94	419	323	77·1	96	22·9
1900–04	533	422	79·2	111	20·8
1910–13	718	538	75·0	180	25·0

Joseph Chamberlain, seeking to further the aim of imperial unity by strengthening the economic ties within the Empire, announced in 1903 his conversion to a belief in imperial preference and tariff reform, resigned the office of Colonial Secretary, which he had held since 1895, and conducted a nation-wide campaign in support of his new policy. Although Chamberlain himself had originally pleaded for a protective tariff as a means of giving the colonies preferential treatment in the British market, this part of the programme tended to slip into the background, and his campaign developed into an advocacy of the general protection of home industries. It was symptomatic of the change in Britain's international economic position, and of the hesitant outlook engendered by the growth of foreign competition, that Chamberlain received extensive support from many manufacturing interests, no longer confident of their ability to hold their own in an unprotected home market. The electors, however, decisively rejected protection at the polls in 1906.

INDUSTRIAL FLUCTUATION

It is often supposed that the period 1875–96, commonly called the "Great Depression,"[1] was one of almost unrelieved economic adversity, characterized throughout by severe unemployment, falling prices and ruinous foreign competition; and that economic affairs took a turn for the better in the late 'nineties and continued to prosper until 1914. Such a sharp contrast is scarcely warranted by the evidence. It is true that there were several years in the first period, such as 1879, 1884–87, and 1893, when unemployment was exceptionally severe; that the general level of prices was falling down to the mid-'nineties; and that the situation was serious enough in the 'eighties to lead to the appointment of a Royal Commission on the Depression of

[1] For a critical view see H. L. Beales, "'The Great Depression' in Industry and Trade," *Economic History Review*, October 1934, p. 65.

Trade. Nevertheless, the most authoritative statistical investigations indicate that the rate of real economic progress was greater in the period 1875–96, when prices were falling and recorded unemployment averaged 5½ per cent., than in 1896–1914, when prices were rising and the average unemployment percentage was only just over 3. Dr. Bowley[1] has estimated that the National Income of the United Kingdom increased from £1,090 million in 1880 to £1,400 million in 1891–95 and £1,620 million in 1896–1900; by 1913 it had reached £2,220 million. The average income per occupied person grew from £76·1 in 1880 to £85·8 in 1891–95, £94·1 in 1896–1900, and £110·1 in 1913. But, after allowing for the changes in the purchasing power of money over this period, he calculates that the average *real* income per occupied person (taking 1913 = 100) advanced from 67 in 1880 to 91 in 1891–95 and to 100 in 1896–1900. From 1896–1900 to 1913 there was no increase in the real income of the average occupied person.[2] Thus practically the whole of the 50 per cent. improvement of the standard of living of the occupied population between 1880 and 1913 had been secured in the period usually regarded as "depressed."

This broad conclusion is supported by the investigations of other statisticians. Dr. G. T. Jones, for instance, has shown that in the British cotton, iron and steel, and building industries average real output per head was increasing up to about 1900, and then became practically stationary.[3] Mr. C. Clark, also, has estimated, by means of a comparison between indices of physical productivity and of employment, that the output per head was no greater in 1913 than in 1907.[4] Not only, however, did the output per head apparently cease to grow after the turn of the century, but in addition the terms of international trade ceased to move in

[1] *Wages and Income in the United Kingdom since 1860*, p. 92.
[2] *ibid.* p. 94.
[3] *Increasing Return*, p. 245 *et seq.*
[4] "Statistical Studies of the Present Economic Position of Great Britain," in *Economic Journal*, 1931, p. 361.

our favour. Until about 1900 we were able to obtain an increasing quantity of imported foodstuffs and raw materials in exchange for a given quantity of exports, because import prices were falling more rapidly, or rising less rapidly, than export prices. After that year, however, this sort of gain ceased to accrue to us. The available evidence, therefore, suggests that the growing prosperity of the years 1896–1913 was more apparent than real; money incomes increased rapidly, and a smaller proportion of the population was out of work than during the "Great Depression"; but the production of real wealth per head showed little or no increase.

The reasons for the broad downward trend of the price level from the mid-'seventies to the mid-'nineties, and its subsequent rise until 1913, tendencies that were manifest in other industrial countries as well as in Britain, are probably to be found in the monetary sphere. The annual world production of gold was falling during the 'seventies and early 'eighties, reaching its minimum, for this period, in 1883. When we compare the unexampled expansion of industrial output in Europe and North America with the slow rate of increase of gold stocks in the gold-using countries, there can be no doubt that gold was becoming more scarce, relatively to other commodities, during the 'seventies, 'eighties and early 'nineties. We should therefore expect a tendency for gold to appreciate, *i.e.*, for prices in terms of gold to fall. Moreover there was a huge increase in the monetary demand for gold, which doubtless accentuated this tendency. Several countries adopted the single gold standard in the 'seventies, and imported large quantities of gold for coinage purposes. A gold coinage was authorized in Germany in 1871, though the single gold standard was not established until two years later. Over £50 million worth of gold was coined by Germany in 1872 and 1873. The three Scandinavian kingdoms, by mutual agreement, adopted the gold standard in 1876. Holland indefinitely suspended the coinage of silver in 1875, and established a gold coinage. The United States, one of the principal gold producers, had, until 1878, been a net exporter of this metal; but in that year she began to import gold from Europe in anticipation of the resumption of specie payments on January 1st, 1879, and thereafter continued to import on balance in order to meet the monetary requirements of her rapidly expanding population and trade. Whereas in 1866–75 the United States absorbed only £11,196,000 of gold, in 1876–85 her appetite for gold needed the huge amount of £112,589,600 to satisfy it.[1] As against these factors causing gold to appreciate, it must be remembered that banking systems were expanding rapidly and helping to economize gold by facilitating the use of credit money. But this influence was evidently not enough to counteract the other forces depressing the price level.

The gold factor again was the primary cause of the upward turn of prices in the late 'nineties. The gold deposits of the Witwatersrand, discovered in 1884, were being extensively worked by the 'nineties, with the result, shown in the accompanying table, that the world's monetary stock of gold more than doubled between 1891 and 1911. With its extended gold basis, the British banking system was able to expand its deposits, the principal ingredient in the

CHANGES IN WORLD'S MONETARY STOCK OF GOLD[2]

Year	World's stock of gold available for money (in million £)	Percentage increase in preceding decade
1851	144	—
1861	376	161
1871	544	45
1881	650	19
1891	714	10
1901	1,000	40
1911	1,532	53

[1] *Final Report of Royal Commission on Gold and Silver* (1888), Part I, p. 10.
[2] R. A. Lehfeldt, *Money*, p. 19.

country's supply of money, from about £600 million in 1894 to £962 million in 1913, *i.e.*, by 60 per cent.

Superimposed on these broad trends of the price level were the rhythmic ebb and flow of economic activity associated with the trade cycle. These are illustrated in the accompanying diagrams, of which the first shows the fluctuations in prices and unemployment from 1870 to 1914, and the second the fluctuations in real investment, as indicated by the production of pig-iron and by the exports of capital.[1] Comparison of the series shows that falling unemployment was usually associated with rising prices, expanding foreign investment, and abnormal activity in the heavy industries, and, conversely, shrinking investment, at home and abroad, and falling prices, accompanied rising unemployment. Each boom and each slump had, of course, its distinguishing characteristics; but each possessed also the common features just mentioned.

The boom that culminated in what can fairly be described as the world crisis of 1873 was founded on a great burst of capital expansion, especially in the form of railway construction, in the United States, Germany and many other countries. In the four years 1869–72 about 25,000 miles of railroad were constructed in the United States. Germany, flushed with her victory over France, and having at her disposal the promptly paid French indemnity of £200 million, embarked on a huge programme of railway and industrial expansion. Britain's part in all this feverish activity was a dual one. Her heavy industries, at that time still leading the world, exported immense quantities of railway and other engineering materials, the *real* capital on which the boom was based; and her investors put up a large part of the *money* capital required to finance this constructional activity, by investing huge sums overseas, lending money to foreign and colonial governments and taking up

[1] The graph showing exports of capital is based on C. K. Hobson, *The Export of Capital*, p. 204.

PRICES AND UNEMPLOYMENT, 1870–1914

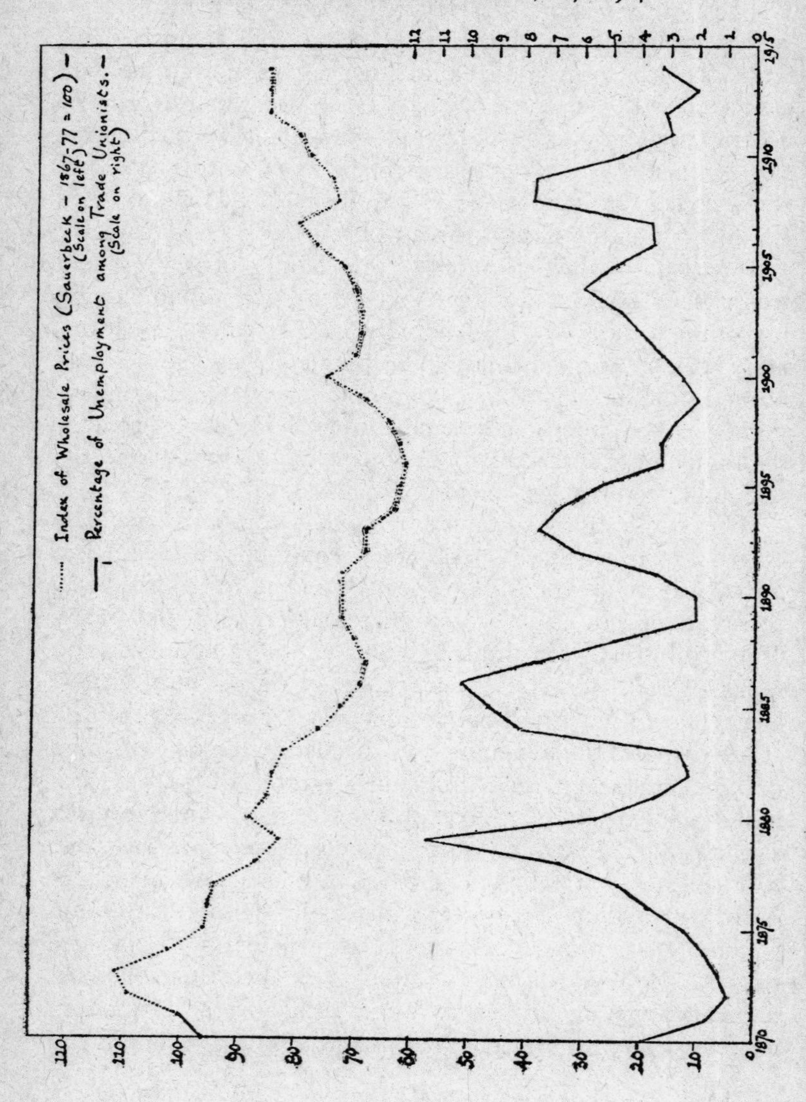

PIG-IRON PRODUCTION AND CAPITAL EXPORTS, 1870–1914

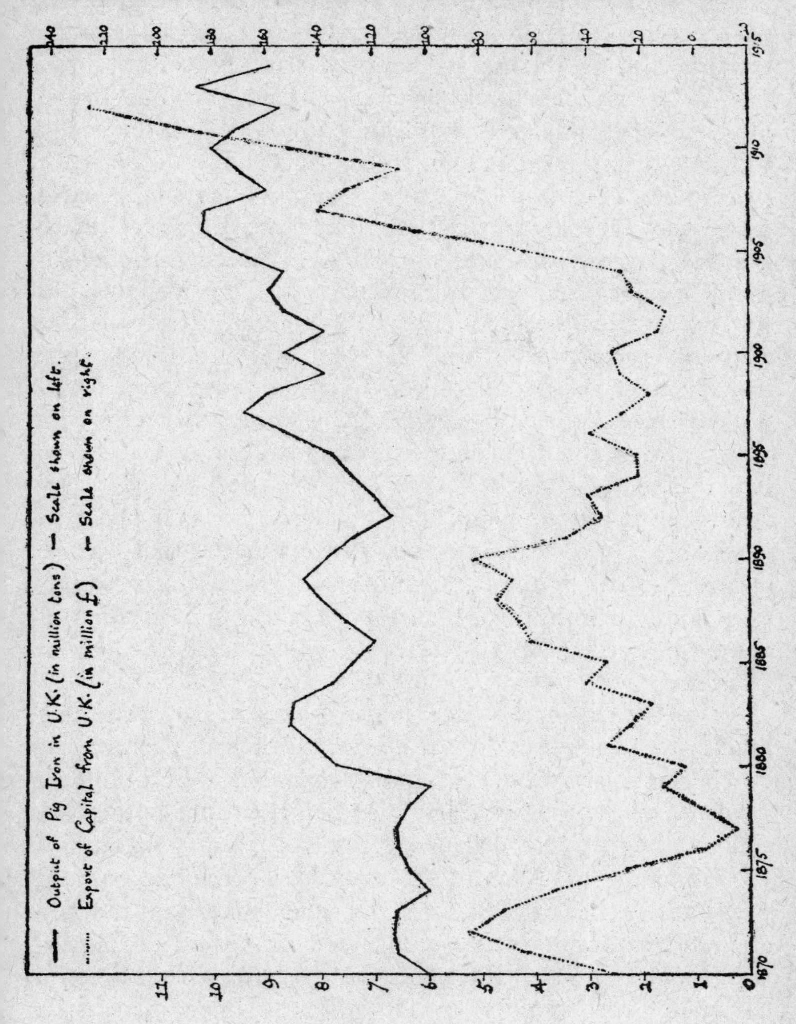

stock in foreign railways. In 1872 alone Britain is estimated to have exported over £83 million of capital, at that time a record figure for foreign investment. The inevitable collapse was ushered in by financial crises in several countries—Austria, the United States, Germany. The British financial system came through unscathed, though Bank rate touched 9 per cent. in November 1873, only 1 per cent. below the conventional crisis level. There followed a depression, deepening until 1879, and affecting particularly the metal industries and agriculture. Recovery came in 1880, though there was but little rise in the price level, and for two or three years Britain's industrial output advanced at a greatly accelerated pace. Between 1879 and 1882 pig-iron production in the United Kingdom rose from 6·0 to 8·6 million tons, *i.e.*, by 43 per cent., and steel production more than doubled, increasing from 1 million to 2·2 million tons. Over a slightly longer period, 1879 to 1883, the annual shipping tonnage built increased by 119 per cent. from 406,000 tons to 892,000, a record figure that was not exceeded until 1899; coal output advanced from 134 to 163·7 million tons, *i.e.*, by 22 per cent.; and cotton consumption grew from 10·5 to 13·4 million cwts. *i.e.*, by 28 per cent.

In 1883 the cycle once more took a downward turn, reaching its lowest ebb in 1886, when a Royal Commission on the Depression of Trade was appointed. Shipbuilding yards turned out in 1886 less than half the tonnage they had built in 1883; cotton consumption fell from 13.4 million cwt. in 1883 to 11.9 in 1885; pig-iron production shrank to 7 million tons in 1886. On the other hand both the steel and the woollen industries continued to expand during the depression. From the trough of 1886 the economic barometer rose rapidly, to the accompaniment of a great burst of investment, of which the lion's share went abroad. South African mines, South American and Australian land, banking and trust companies, were well to the fore among the overseas promotions; at home, breweries and investment companies were specially favoured. Altogether, on home and foreign account, about £422 million of capital were issued in London in the three years 1888–90. The Baring crisis of 1890 marked the end of this boom in company promotion, after which investment flagged for several years. Activity slackened in most of the staple industries, but the slump was less severe than those of the 'seventies and 'eighties. It spent itself in 1893, and gave place to a long period of improving trade, with a gentle, but persistent, upward trend of prices from 1896 onwards. From 1893 to 1899 all the staple industries—coal, metals, and textiles—showed a substantial expansion of output, and in 1899 conditions generally were booming. The volume of new capital issues, however, for both home and foreign investment, was a good deal less than in the boom culminating in 1890. Government borrowing was heavy in 1900 and 1901, in order to finance the South African war, but this was mainly at the expense of other investment, especially foreign investment.

Some slackening of industrial activity followed the termination of this war until 1904, though the reaction was nothing like as marked as those experienced in the 'seventies and 'eighties. Then from 1905 onwards there occurred an extraordinary expansion of foreign investment, far surpassing that of the record year, 1872, even in the two years of slack trade, 1908 and 1909. British investors distributed their funds all over the world, and in all kinds of undertakings. Canada, Argentina and the United States were among the principal recipients; railways, public utilities, plantations and mines, and, in the later years of this foreign investment boom, manufacturing concerns, shared in this flood of capital exports. The process was no more than temporarily slackened by the crisis of 1907. This was world-wide in its incidence, and was heralded by banking collapses in Germany and the United States. London suffered a short spell of high Bank rate, but her money market and banking system, by now well consolidated, weathered the storm without casualties. A general industrial recession followed the crisis, but by 1910 the country's economy had recovered, and until 1914 most of the staple industries were enjoying rising prices and prosperous conditions, apart from the interruptions caused by an unusually severe outbreak of industrial disputes.

CHAPTER X

AGRICULTURE AND ITS PROBLEMS

CHANGING CROPS

IN the 'seventies there began a difficult and protracted adaptation of British agriculture to the new conditions of international competition created by developments in transport. Unfortunately for the farming community, prices in general moved downwards during the first twenty years of this period of adjustment, and the distress of 1874–96 was probably due as much to this fall as to the foreign competition which contemporaries commonly blamed. For when agricultural, along with most other, prices rose from 1896 onwards, moderate prosperity returned to the British countryside, though foreign competition continued. Nevertheless, the most significant and lasting features of this period of agricultural adjustment, namely, the changes in the relative importance of the various branches of farming, must be attributed primarily to the intensification of overseas competition, and not to the temporary fall of the general price level.

Railway construction was opening up vast areas of virgin territory in the new countries of the world, especially the United States, where railway mileage increased from 30,600 in 1860 to 93,600 in 1880 and 156,000 in 1890. At the same time spectacular reductions in railway and shipping freights were enabling overseas farmers to compete in European markets. For example, the combined lake, rail and ocean freight on wheat from Chicago to Liverpool via New York fell from 11s. 6½d. per quarter in 1868 to 5s. 1½d. in 1885 and to 2s. 10½d. in 1902. European farmers thus found their livelihood menaced by a rising flood of agricultural imports. The leading continental powers met the situation promptly by resorting to tariff protection. In Germany moderate duties were imposed in 1879 on a number of agricultural imports, including grain, cattle and meat; the duty on wheat, for example, was equivalent to 2s. 2d. per quarter. As the pressure of imports grew, these duties were stiffened, the wheat duty being raised to 6s. 6½d. in 1885, and to 10s. 10½d. in 1888. France, similarly, assisted her grain producers by imposing import duties on a rising scale; the wheat duty was equivalent to 5s. 2d. per quarter in 1885, 8s. 8d. in 1887, and 12s. 2d. in 1894. Continental Europe was determined to keep up the level of its agricultural output, in order both to preserve national self-sufficiency and to maintain a numerous peasantry as a basis of its conscript armies. Britain alone, of the great powers, adhered to a free-trade policy; her farmers were left to make their own adjustments to the new conditions without any material assistance from the State. She had no interest in the potential supply of conscripts, and felt that she could rely on her unchallenged naval power to protect the overseas trade on which she came increasingly to depend.

In adapting agricultural production to this new overseas rivalry, British farmers followed the elementary rules of a free market; they curtailed the output of those products whose profitability was most reduced, and concentrated more on those crops in whose production they had, as compared with their competitors abroad, the greatest advantages. They still retained the natural protection of distance in producing perishable commodities, such as fresh meat, milk, fruit and market garden produce; while cheap bulky crops, like potatoes, mangolds and hay, could not stand the cost of transport over long distances, so that their home production remained comparatively profitable. On the other hand, grain production became much less remunerative. By the aid of new mechanical appliances grain could be grown on the prairie lands of the new world, with their rich soil and favourable climatic conditions, at such low costs that grain prices tumbled down in European markets. In the 'sixties the average price of wheat in England and Wales had been 51s. 8d. per quarter; it was maintained distinctly above this level in the early 'seventies, and as late as 1877 stood at 56s. 9d. Thereafter it declined steadily to 31s. in 1886, and, after a short-lived recovery, plunged down to a record low level of 22s. 10d. in 1894. Thus in the mid-'nineties the price of wheat had fallen to a level 55 per cent. below that prevailing in the 'sixties. The prices of barley and oats followed a similar, though less ruinous, course; the mid-'nineties' prices of both were about 40 per cent. below the level of the 'sixties.

These changes in the relative profitability of different crops were naturally reflected in changes in the acreage under them. The outstanding feature of the adjustment was the marked shrinkage in the area of arable land, through its conversion to pasture. Arable land (including land under clover and rotation grasses as well as tillage land) amounted to 18,242,000 acres in Great Britain in 1871–75; this represented 58·6 per cent. of the "cultivated area," the remainder being permanent pasture. By 1906–10 the arable area had shrunk to 14,836,000 acres, *i.e.* to 46 per cent. of the "cultivated area."[1] Of this shrinkage in arable acreage the greater part was accounted for by wheat and barley, the wheat area falling by 1,799,000 acres between 1871–75 and 1906–10, and the barley area by 663,000 acres. On the other hand, the acreage under oats, mainly fed to stock, increased by 385,000. The reduced prices obtainable for grain had the further consequence of rendering unprofitable for many farmers the whole course of rotation in which grain was grown; hence followed a

[1] Statistics of the acreages under different crops are given in the annual *Agricultural Statistics*. A useful summary for the period since 1870 is to be found in *The Agricultural Output of England and Wales, 1925* (Cmd. 2,815 of 1927) and *The Agricultural Output of Scotland, 1925* (Cmd. 3,191 of 1928).

diminution of the acreage under other crops figuring in rotations, especially root crops such as turnips and swedes. The turnip and swede acreage dwindled by 564,000 between 1871–75 and 1906–10. Mangolds provided an important exception to this general tendency, showing a considerable increase in acreage; they have certain advantages over turnips, being more resistant to drought, and are valuable in the winter feeding of dairy cattle.

Despite this large-scale conversion of arable land to pasture, the sheep population of the country declined; Britain's flocks numbered 26,675,000 in 1906–10 as compared with 28,790,000 in 1871–75. Sheep may be fed on grass or on green crops grown on arable land; it was in this second class that practically the whole of the reduction in numbers occurred. In the eastern, southern and midland areas of England, where sheep rearing was associated with arable farming, the shrinkage of the arable area was accompanied by large reductions in the number of sheep. In north and north-west England, in Wales and in Scotland, all mountainous areas with extensive tracts of rough grazing, the sheep population was well maintained, and in many counties even increased.

The cattle industry was the one important branch of British agriculture to show an appreciable expansion from the 'seventies onwards, the number of cattle of all kinds increasing from 5,813,000 in 1871–75 to 6,977,000 in 1906–10. Both sections of this industry, namely, dairy farming and beef production, remained prosperous, as compared with arable farming. Milk prices, which had moved up sharply in the 'seventies, sagged after 1879, but in the early 'nineties were still at the same level as in 1871; thereafter they fell by about 20 per cent., but recovered somewhat at the turn of the century. Owing to the growth of population, the increasing milk consumption per head, and the absence of foreign competition in the liquid milk market, the demand for milk grew steadily; consequently

Britain's dairy herd (*i.e.*, cows and heifers in milk or in calf) increased by well over half a million between 1871–75 and 1906–10. How the number of beef cattle varied is not accurately known, but it seems certain that no reduction occurred, and probable that there was some increase. Beef prices had risen in the early 'seventies, and remained above the level of 1871 until 1883; then they dropped quickly, so that four years later they were 18 per cent. lower than in 1871. Thereafter they oscillated round a level about 15 per cent. below that of 1871.

Meat prices were, of course, affected by foreign competition. Before frozen meat became an article of commerce this competition took the form of imports of live animals, mainly from the United States, of canned meat, and above all of cured pig's meat. Though no exact information relating to the British meat supply is available for this period, it is estimated that in the 'sixties Great Britain produced at home 1,036,000 tons a year out of a total of 1,167,000 tons, *i.e.*, 89 per cent. In 1882, when frozen meat imports were still negligible, the home output of meat had expanded slightly to 1,090,000 tons, and the total meat consumption to 1,744,000 tons, so that home producers were now supplying only 63 per cent. of our meat requirements.[1] The frozen meat trade began, so far as Britain was concerned, in 1880, when a small cargo of beef and mutton was brought in good condition from Australia on the *Strathleven*. Two years later New Zealand, and in 1883 Argentina, sent their first consignments of frozen meat to this country. The subsequent development of this trade helped to bring British meat prices down considerably below the level prevailing in the 'seventies. It was, however, much less of a disaster to the British farmer than the overseas competition in grain; for in part, from the 'nineties onwards, the growing frozen meat imports merely displaced imports of live meat. Moreover,

[1] J. T. Critchell and J. Raymond, *A History of the Frozen Meat Trade*, pp. 2, 3. See also the diagram in P. G. Craigie's "Twenty Years' Changes in our Foreign Meat Supplies," *Journal of Royal Agricultural Society*, 1887, p. 471.

despite the cheapness of frozen meat, there remained a large home demand for fresh British meat. It was estimated that in 1893–96 the United Kingdom's annual home production of meat amounted to 1,229,000 tons, which constituted 63 per cent. of the total supply of 1,940,000 tons. In 1905–8 the home output was slightly greater at 1,250,000 tons a year, this being 54 per cent. of the total consumption of 2,313,000 tons.[1] Thus, although the expanding meat requirements of Britain's population were largely met by greatly increased imports, the home production of meat showed some advance during this period of agricultural adjustment.

The production of fruit and fresh vegetables increased remarkably from the 'seventies onwards, largely as a result of rising standards of living. The extraordinary growth of the taste for fruit, together with the development of the jam industry and the revival of the cider trade, led to a great expansion of the acreage under fruit; from 148,000 acres in 1873 the orchard area grew to 243,000 in 1904, *i.e.*, by 63·9 per cent. No accurate returns relating to the acreage under small fruit are available before 1897, but between then and 1913 it increased from 70,000 to 84,000. "The development of the fruit industry has come to the assistance of the farmer most opportunely in certain parts of England, notably in Kent, Middlesex, Worcestershire and Cambridgeshire, and . . . much land which previously grew wheat is now planted with fruit" declared the Departmental Committee on the Fruit Industry in 1905. Market gardening also grew apace, especially in the Thames Valley, Bedfordshire, Huntingdon, the Fen country and the Vale of Evesham. A further notable development of this period was the glass-house industry, producing tomatoes, cucumbers and grapes, and mainly concentrated in the Home Counties. "Fifty years ago the tomato was as great a

[1] Departmental Committee on Combinations in the Meat Trade, *Minutes of Evidence* (Cd. 4,661 of 1909), p. 271; and R. H. Hooker, "The Meat Supply of the United Kingdom," *Journal of Royal Statistical Society*, 1909, p. 318.

rarity in England as an Avocado pear is to-day "[1]; in 1925 47,000 tons of tomatoes were grown in England and Wales.

These adjustments caused much distress to farmers, especially in the arable eastern, midland and southern areas. "Enterprise gradually weakened; landlords lost their ability to help, farmers their recuperative power. Prolonged depression checked costly improvements. Drainage was practically discontinued. Both owners and occupiers were engaged in the task of making both ends meet on vanishing incomes. Land deteriorated in condition; less labour was employed; less stock was kept; bills for cake and fertilizers were reduced."[2] There were two periods of especial difficulty, 1875–84 and 1891–96; in both, a combination of general industrial depression, bad seasons, and foreign competition, exerted a ruinous pressure on British farmers. The second depression was probably the more severe, since by the early 'nineties the working capital of many farmers had become seriously depleted, and years of retrenchment in farming expenditure had lowered the fertility of the soil.

In the late 'nineties, however, the tide began to turn and farming profits to reach more normal levels. Two factors were largely responsible for this—the reduction of agricultural rents, mainly completed by about 1900, and the upward movement of most agricultural prices after 1896. Naturally there was a good deal of delay before rents were entirely adjusted to the new level of agricultural prices; in fact, the aggregate income from the ownership of land, (Schedule A Income Tax assessments) reached a maximum in 1879–80, though 1879 was one of the most disastrous years in the annals of British agriculture, harvests being exceptionally poor, pleuro-pneumonia and foot-and-mouth disease rampant among cattle, and three million sheep lost

[1] Lord Ernle, *English Farming Past and Present* (5th edition), p. 391.
[2] Lord Ernle, *op. cit.* p. 382.

by rot. But as the depression continued landlords were compelled to ease the position of their tenants by rent abatements : and where farms were vacated by bankrupt tenants, only drastic reductions in rents could attract new ones. An interesting minor incident of the agricultural depression was the influx of Scots farmers into Essex, Hertfordshire and Suffolk in the 'eighties, attracted by the cheap terms on which land could be obtained in this stricken area. Aggregate rents from land in England and Wales, which reached their maximum of £52,041,000 in 1879–80, declined to £41,635,000 in 1890–91, and to £37,017,000 in 1901–2, at which level they remained fairly steady until the outbreak of the war.[1] The loss in income to the agricultural landlords of England and Wales, from the peak of 1879 to the new level of 1900, was thus in the neighbourhood of £15 million a year. In Scotland also the income from the ownership of land reached its peak in 1879–80, when landlords collected £7,769,000. From then, Scottish rents fell almost continuously until 1913–14, when they stood at £5,713,000.

While rents remained at this reduced level, agricultural prices recovered from the trough of 1896. According to the Sauerbeck index, the prices of vegetable foods (wheat, flour, barley, oats, maize, potatoes and rice) rose on the average by 30 per cent. between 1896 and 1913, and the prices of animal foods (mutton, pork, bacon and butter) by 35·6 per cent. Though most agricultural prices were still well below the level prevailing in the early 'seventies, the recovery sufficed to restore farming to a condition of comfortable prosperity. A highly competent observer, Mr. (now Sir) A. D. Hall, summing up his impressions of a tour of British agriculture in 1910, wrote : " One could not but conclude that the industry as a whole was in a prosperous condition, and had healthily and stably recovered from the great depression that lay upon it as recently as fifteen years

[1] J. C. Stamp, *British Incomes and Property*, p. 49.

earlier. . . . Of this prosperity the best external evidence was that we could rarely hear of any farms to let, while in every part of the country the good farms were bespoken long before they came into the market."[1]

AGRARIAN LEGISLATION

Wedded to a policy of free trade, the governments of the period of depression were unwilling to introduce any radical measures for the assistance of agriculture, and accordingly pursued the policy usual in such circumstances, namely, the appointment of Royal Commissions, in 1879 and 1893. On the recommendation of these and other advisory bodies, a number of useful, but minor, measures were introduced, none of which, however, counteracted perceptibly the forces compelling adjustment in British agriculture. Farmers were given some protection against the adulteration of feeding stuffs; steps were taken to check animal diseases; and in 1889 the Board of Agriculture was established, its earliest functions being the collection and dissemination of information. Some indirect financial assistance was given to farmers through the development of grants-in-aid to local government services, partly with the object of relieving the rating burdens on agricultural land. The agricultural interest complained, with some justification, that local rates, assessed on the net annual value of real property, imposed disproportionately heavy burdens on an industry whose principal factor of production was land. An attempt to remove this grievance was made by the Agricultural Rates Act of 1896, which relieved agricultural land of half the ordinary rates (other than the sanitary rate, from three-quarters of which agricultural land was already exempt under the Public Health Act of 1848) at an annual cost to the national taxpayer of £1,330,000.

The agrarian legislation of the greatest permanent value,

[1] *A Pilgrimage of British Farming*, pp. 146, 147.

however, was the series of Agricultural Holdings Acts starting in 1875. At common law all agricultural improvements, temporary and permanent, made by the tenant, passed to the landlord at the end of the tenancy, without any compensation being payable. Local customs, such as the "Custom of the Away-Going Crop," had given tenants certain rights to unexhausted improvements, but these were quite inadequate and without statutory recognition. After many years of agitation, dating back to 1843, an Agricultural Holdings Act was passed in 1875, setting forth the circumstances in which a tenant might claim compensation for various classes of improvement. The Act was optional in character, however, and most landlords escaped its provisions by promptly contracting out. It was followed by more effective legislation in 1883, compelling landlords to compensate their tenants for improvements. A further Act was passed in 1906, which among other things conferred on tenants the right to freedom of cropping and of disposal of produce, hitherto commonly restricted in agreements between landlords and tenants, and the right to compensation for damage done by game and for unreasonable disturbance.

The foundation of a system of agricultural education, partly by State aid, was a measure of immense potential value. Before 1890 the provision of agricultural education was left almost entirely to private enterprise. Financial aid was first given by the State in 1888, when the Agricultural Department of the Privy Council (the predecessor of the Board of Agriculture) was authorized to spend up to £5,000 annually in making grants to institutions and societies providing agricultural education. In the course of time the amount of these grants increased, and also the number of institutions receiving them. These included agricultural colleges, special bodies such as the British Dairy Institute and the Royal Veterinary College, and the Universities, which now began to establish agricultural departments. A further important step was taken in 1890, when county councils received large grants, commonly known as "whisky money," for the provision of technical, including agricultural, education. Lecture courses and practical instruction in farm work were provided in local centres; in addition, some county councils co-operated in the establishment of colleges and of university agricultural departments. The Development and Road Improvements Fund Act of 1909 provided additional sums for agricultural education, and made possible the introduction in 1913 of the farm institute scheme; it was impossible to develop this fully, however, until after the war. The final outcome of these measures was a three-decker system of agricultural education, comprising (i) agricultural colleges and university agricultural departments, providing courses of two or three years for intending farmers, land agents, teachers and experts; (ii) farm institutes, providing, under the control of a county organizer, short winter courses for small farmers and others who could not leave their farms for a whole year, and serving also as a centre to which local farmers could turn for advice; and (iii) local day and evening courses provided by the county councils for land workers.

In technique, great advances have been made since 1880, though inevitably there has been a considerable time-lag between advances in theory and improvements in practice. "At no other period in the history of the world," declares Professor J. A. Scott Watson, "has agricultural science made as rapid progress. The farmer's resources in the form of manures, feeding stuffs, crop varieties, implements, etc., have enormously increased, and his costs of production, in terms of human labour, have fallen greatly."[1] Outstanding among the mechanical improvements in the last quarter of the nineteenth century was the reaper-and-binder, an American invention, which came into use in this country in the early 'eighties and was universally employed on farms of

[1] *Baillière's Encyclopaedia of Scientific Agriculture*, p. 43.

sufficient size by 1906.[1] Hay-tedding machinery, though invented at the beginning of the century, did not come into common use until the 'eighties and 'nineties.[2] In dairy farming the greatest mechanical innovation was the milk separator, invented in 1879. Basic slag, an invaluable new fertilizer, especially for pasture land, became available after the invention of the basic steel process in 1879, though it was little used in agriculture until after 1885, when it was discovered that fine grinding was essential for its successful application. Stock-breeding continued to improve, and, with the aid of biology, became more scientific; it was assisted by the formation of numerous breeding societies, and by the introduction, in 1906, of official milk-recording. Great progress was also made in stamping out animal diseases, partly through advances in veterinary science and partly through administrative action (by prohibiting imports of livestock from infected sources, and restricting their movements in infected areas); there has, for instance, been no outbreak of rinderpest in Britain since 1877, and none of pleuro-pneumonia since 1898.[3]

The decline of arable farming and the extension of stock-breeding, dairy farming, market gardening and fruit farming, led to some modification of the size-distribution of agricultural holdings. These tendencies are illustrated in the following tables. Though caution must be exercised in interpreting the official statistics of holdings, there can be no doubt that small and medium farms, especially those of from 20 to 100 acres in extent, became more numerous, while there was a distinct shrinkage of the number of large farms of over 300 acres. The number of agricultural holdings of less than 20 acres is not accurately known, since the official returns are not complete and include much land attached to residential property and not used primarily for agricultural

[1] Clapham III. 90.
[2] W. H. R. Curtler, *A Short History of English Agriculture*, p. 304.
[3] *Baillière's Encyclopaedia of Scientific Agriculture*, p. 45.

NUMBER OF AGRICULTURAL HOLDINGS IN ENGLAND AND WALES[1]

Size of holding (in acres)	1885	1895	1913
Over 1 and not exceeding 5	114,273 (*a*)	97,818	92,302
" 5 " " " 20	126,674	126,714	122,117
" 20 " " " 50	73,472	74,846	78,027
" 50 " " " 100	54,937	56,791	59,287
" 100 " " " 300	67,024	68,277	69,431
" 300	16,608	16,021	14,513
Total	452,988	440,467	435,677

(*a*) Includes holdings of 1 acre.

NUMBER OF AGRICULTURAL HOLDINGS IN SCOTLAND[2]

Size of holding (in acres)	1885	1895	1913
Over 1 and not exceeding 5	21,463(*a*)	20,150	18,418
" 5 " " " 50	32,809	33,921	33,196
" 50 " " " 300	22,327	22,802	23,153
" 300	2,756	2,766	2,621
Total	79,355	79,639	77,388

(*a*) Includes holdings of 1 acre.

purposes. The apparent reduction of the number of holdings in this group is probably to be attributed mainly to the encroachment of urban areas on the small holdings surrounding them, rather than to any decline in the economic suitability of holdings of this type. As Professor Clapham remarks, there is no warrant for describing these changes in the size-distribution of holdings as " a general retreat from large-scale farming."[3] Farms of over 300 acres still accounted for a quarter of the total cultivated area of England and Wales in 1913, and farms of over 150 acres for more than a half. But small and medium-scale farming was certainly more in favour, with both farmers and landlords, than it had been in the years of high farming before 1880. The number of men describing themselves in the censuses

[1] *The Agricultural Output of England and Wales, 1925*, pp. 143, 144.
[2] *The Agricultural Output of Scotland, 1925*, p. 86.
[3] *Op. cit.* III. 103.

as "farmers" increased from 202,400 in 1881 to 208,100 in 1911, while such small-scale cultivators as "gardeners, seedsmen and florists" increased from an estimated 58,900 in 1881 to 121,500 in 1911.[1]

This halt in the tendency to large-scale farming, which had characterized British agriculture since the middle of the eighteenth century, is to be explained largely by the fact that the branches of farming remaining prosperous and expanding after 1880 were those in which small and medium farms provided convenient and economic units; whereas the the declining branches were those in which large-scale farming was dominant. In arable farming, especially grain production, it is generally recognized that the large farm has distinct economic advantages over the small; but where close personal attention to crops and beasts is needed, and where there is little opportunity for the employment of highly specialized mechanical equipment, as in stock-breeding, fruit farming, poultry farming, and so forth, the small farm may well yield greater net receipts per acre than the large. Hence one could reasonably expect, from the nature of the changes in British farming after 1880, that small farms would tend to increase in numbers at the expense of large.

This process was stimulated by legislation as well as by economic forces. There began in the 'eighties, under the Radical leadership of Joseph Chamberlain and Jesse Collings, a movement for the encouragement of small holdings, the main purpose of which was to check the depopulation of the countryside. The reformers secured the passing of the Small Holdings Act of 1892, empowering county councils, recently created by the Local Government Act of 1888, to purchase land for the provision of small holdings; these could be either sold, and paid for by instalments, or, provided the holding did not exceed 15 acres, let. This first experiment disappointed the enthusiasts for small holdings,

[1] A. L. Bowley, "Rural Population in England and Wales," *J.R.S.S.* 1914, p. 610.

only a few hundred acres of land being acquired by the county councils over a period of fourteen years; the councils showed no enthusiasm for the creation of small holdings, and no pressure was applied to them by the Board of Agriculture. Further agitation, however, resulted in much more effective legislation, the Small Holdings and Allotments Act of 1907. County councils were now empowered to acquire land, either by purchase or on lease, for the provision of small holdings; if the land required could not be obtained by agreement, compulsion might be used. Special commissioners were to be appointed by the Board of Agriculture in order to investigate the local demand for small holdings and to induce the councils to make adequate use of their powers. The bias of the earlier legislation in favour of occupying ownership, as against tenancy, was removed by the abolition of the maximum of 15 acres for tenanted holdings. Seven years after the Act had been passed, local authorities had acquired about 200,000 acres of land, of which three-quarters were purchased, and had created some 14,000 small holdings. Whether these can all be regarded as a net addition to the number of small holdings that would otherwise have existed seems doubtful; if the county councils had not catered for the demand for small farms it would probably have been met, in part at least, by private landlords acting on their own initiative. For, as Dr. J. A. Venn points out, the new holdings "predominated in just those districts where their chances of success were greatest. Cambridgeshire, Lincolnshire and Norfolk had established far more than Counties situated in parts of the country remote from access to centres of population or than those on heavy clay-land could have maintained. In other words, it was just in the particular Counties in which small farms were already automatically appearing and prospering that the Act of 1908 created additional examples."[1]

[1] *The Foundations of Agricultural Economics* (1933), p. 133.

THE AGRICULTURAL WORKER

During these years of depression and re-adjustment the agricultural labouring population decreased. The following table shows the number of males, aged fifteen and over, employed in agriculture in Great Britain between 1871 and 1911.[1] It thus excludes the effect of the Education Acts in withdrawing juvenile workers from the industry.

THE MALE AGRICULTURAL POPULATION OF GREAT BRITAIN
(in thousands)

Occupation	1871	1881	1891	1901	1911
Farmers and graziers ...	269·2	251·4	249·4	248·3	252·7
Farm workers	1,028·2	972·9	885·9	800·0	832·1
Market gardeners and horticulturists ...	54·2	76·6	98·0	130·4	147·5
Machine attendants and others...	4·4	7·2	7·5	14·2	19·2
Foresters	10·0	11·1	12·6	16·0	15·8
Total	1,366·0	1,319·2	1,253·4	1,208·9	1,267·3

Male farm workers thus declined in numbers between 1871 and 1911 by nearly 200,000. In part this was offset by the advancing number of market gardeners, horticulturists and other small-scale farmers, many of whom were recruited from the labouring class. Even so the agricultural population as a whole diminished, despite the rapid increase of the total population. In 1911 only one occupied person in twelve got his or her living on the land, as compared with one in eight in 1881.

Several factors doubtless contributed to this decline, but there are wide differences of opinion about their comparative importance. The shrinkage of the arable area and the extension of pasture could be expected to reduce the demand for labour, since, on the average, pasture land provides employment for fewer workers per 1,000

[1] Taken from *Final Report of Agricultural Tribunal of Investigation*, p. 173. Domestic gardeners are excluded from the table.

acres than arable land. Again, the extending use of mechanical appliances in farming was bound to release a part of the supply of agricultural labour; a decline in the agricultural population, relatively to the total, seems inevitable in a progressive community, since the demand for agricultural produce is somewhat inelastic. But we must consider not only these factors operating on the demand for agricultural labour, but also those affecting the supply; for the supply adjusted itself to the demand rapidly enough to prevent any serious decline in money wages in the depressed period 1874–96, and to allow of a broad upward movement of agricultural wages between 1896 and 1914, despite the contraction of the demand for labour. On the supply side a number of influences combined to increase the mobility of the agricultural labourer. The growing industrialization of Britain enlarged the opportunities of alternative employment; the towns, with their bustling activity and variegated life, held an irresistible attraction for the more enterprising spirits of the countryside; the provision of education for the masses, and the development of the Press and of communications, made country dwellers more aware of the opportunities open to them both in the towns and overseas; while the increase of transport facilities made it physically easier to move and take advantage of these opportunities. Another factor possibly contributing to this exodus from the countryside was the deplorable condition of rural housing, in many counties deficient both in quantity and quality. There was very little new building for rural workers during the period we are considering, for the economic rents of new houses were much above the rents most farm workers could afford to pay; in the meantime, the older cottages, frequently insanitary and seriously overcrowded, steadily deteriorated.

These factors, affecting the demand for agricultural labour and its supply, are reflected in the movement of agricultural wages. It is not easy, however, to describe summarily the changes in agricultural earnings, owing to the wide local variations in both cash wages and allowances in kind. Broadly speaking, the further north one went the greater became the proportion of the total wage paid in kind, though there were very many exceptions to this general rule. At the end of the century, few allowances in kind were made in most English counties to ordinary labourers, save those lodged and boarded in farm houses. Beer or cider was frequently given during harvesting, and occasionally cottages were provided free or at low rents. In the northern counties, however, especially in Northumberland and Durham, most ordinary labourers received many such allowances, these including free cottage and potatoes, free carting of coal, and sometimes straw for pigs. Men in charge of animals were allowed cottages and gardens free, and frequently a potato ground, in most districts of England; and in parts of Northumberland it was still the custom to pay shepherds entirely in kind. Allowances in kind were much commoner in Scotland; married men were usually provided with cottages and gardens free, a potato ground or an allowance of potatoes, oatmeal, coals carted free, frequently milk and sometimes straw and manure; while unmarried men were generally lodged in farm houses or bothies and provided with food. In the extreme north of Scotland cash wages accounted, on the average, for less than half of the estimated total earnings. There was, however, a growing tendency in Scotland to pay more of the total wage in cash.

Even when the value of these allowances was added to the cash wages there remained wide variations in total agricultural earnings in different parts of the country. Thus in 1902 total weekly earnings (including payments in kind) ranged from an average of 13s. 7d. in Caithness to 22s. 2d. in Renfrew, Lanark and Durham. The highest earnings (20s. and upwards) were paid in the Lowland counties of Scotland, the northern counties of England, Lancashire and Derbyshire, Glamorgan, Middlesex and Surrey. The lowest (under 16s.) were found in Norfolk and Suffolk, a block of adjoining counties, namely, Gloucester, Oxford, Berkshire, Wiltshire and Dorset, as well as in Cardigan and the extreme north of Scotland. Broadly speaking, earnings were higher in Scotland (19s. 5d. on the average) than in England (17s. 5d.), and higher in the northern half of England than in the southern. On the whole, also, as was to be expected, agricultural wages were highest near the industrial and mining districts of Scotland, the North, South Wales, and London.[1] It is thus evident that no single figure of earnings can adequately describe the diversified economic conditions of the rural labouring class.

With this preliminary caution we can turn to the evidence relating to the movement of the general level of agricultural wages. In 1874–78 the cash wages (excluding extra payments for harvesting, overtime, and allowances in kind) of ordinary labourers on a group of 128 farms in England and Wales are estimated to have averaged about 14s. a week.[2] As the depression intensified they fell steadily to 13s. 2½d. in 1887–88, then recovered to 13s. 10d. in 1892, and after a slight decline in the following two years, moved up to 14s. 11½d. in 1902. Official inquiries showed that in 1902 weekly cash wages averaged 14s. 8d.,[3] in 1907 14s. 9d.,[4] and in 1914 16s. 9d.[5] These changes are brought out more vividly in the adjoining diagram, based on an index number of agricultural money wages.[6] Since the purchasing power of money fluctuated in the period 1880–1914, the course of agricultural *real* wages is also shown in the diagram

[1] See Appendix I to *Second Report by Mr. Wilson Fox on the Wages, Earnings and Conditions of Employment of Agricultural Labourers in the United Kingdom* (Cd. 2,376 of 1905).

[2] These figures for the period 1874–1902 are taken from Wilson Fox, *Second Report*, p. 68.

[3] *ibid.* p. 67.

[4] *Report of an Inquiry by the Board of Trade into the Earnings and Hours of Labour of Work-people in the United Kingdom*, Vol. V (Cd. 5,460 of 1910), p. 23. Total earnings (including payments in kind) were 17s. 6d.

[5] *Report on Wages and Conditions of Employment in Agriculture* (Cmd. 24 of 1919), p. 106.

[6] The index number is taken from A. L. Bowley, *Wages and Income in the United Kingdom since 1860*, p. 9.

THE COURSE OF AGRICULTURAL WAGES, 1850–1914

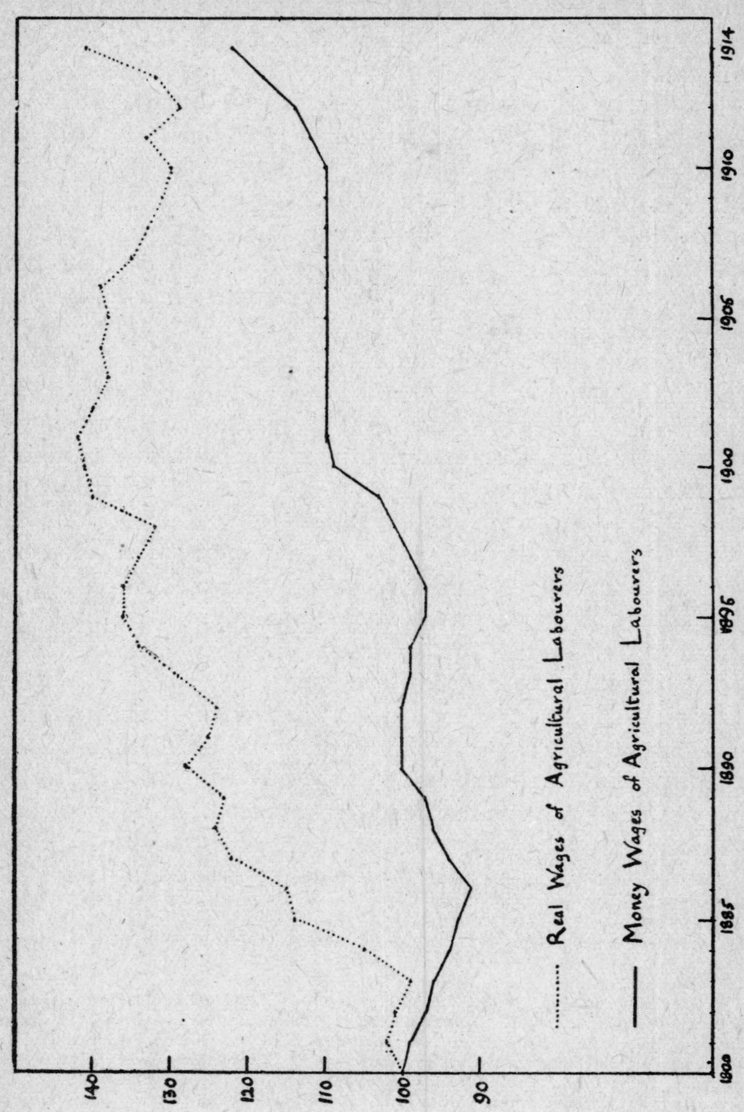

in order to give a more accurate indication of changes in the rural worker's standard of living.[1] It will be noticed that in 1914 agricultural *money* wages were about 20 per cent., and *real* wages about 40 per cent., higher than in 1880; moreover, the two periods of acute depression, the early 'eighties and the early 'nineties, when money wages were dropping, witnessed a marked improvement in the agricultural worker's living conditions, whereas in the period 1900–12, when agriculture was becoming more prosperous, real wages declined somewhat.

[1] In correcting the index of money wages for changes in the cost of living, an index of food prices only (taken from Bowley, *op. cit.* p. 121) has been used, since the great bulk of the agricultural wage is spent on food.

CHAPTER XI

Transport and Communications

RAILWAY COMBINATIONS AND RATES

Nearly all the present main lines of railway are to be found, already completed, on the map prepared in 1872 for the Select Committee on Railway Companies' Amalgamations.[1] Of the few important sections of main line added to the system since then, the chief were the Midland line from Settle to Carlisle, opened for goods traffic in 1875, and the Great Central extension through Nottingham and Leicester to London, authorized in 1893, despite the strong opposition of the other main-line companies, and completed in 1899. The City and South London Railway, the first instalment of the " tube " system, was opened for traffic in 1890, and operated from the first with electric trains. It was followed by the Waterloo and City line in 1898, and the Central London, known for a time as the " Twopenny Tube," from its flat-rate charge, in 1900. Thereafter new underground railways and extensions came thick and fast down to 1914. But, for the country as a whole, the bulk of the additional route mileage constructed after the 'sixties consisted of branch and local lines and of cut-offs for shortening roundabout routes. Of the great feats of railway engineering in this period the most notable were the Severn Tunnel, opened in 1886, which reduced from two hours to one the journey between Bristol and Cardiff, and the Forth Bridge, which, completed in 1890, greatly shortened the route from Edinburgh to Dundee and Aberdeen, and led in 1895 to the " race " between the East and West Coast routes from London to Aberdeen.

[1] There is a photographic facsimile of this map in E. Cleveland-Stevens, *English Railways*, frontispiece, and another map based on it in Clapham II. 184.

Striking increases occurred in the volume of traffic, particularly on the passenger side, in the second half of the Victorian era; these are summarized in the table below.

RAILWAYS OF THE UNITED KINGDOM, 1870–1910[1]

Year	Length of line open for traffic	Total number of passengers, excluding season-ticket holders	Weight of goods and minerals	Gross receipts	Net receipts
	Miles	Millions	Million tons	Million £	Million £
1870	15,537	336·5	*	45·1	23·4
1880	17,933	603·9	235·3	65·5	31·9
1890	20,073	817·7	303·1	79·9	36·8
1900	21,855	1,142·3	424·9	104·8	40·1
1910	23,387	1,306·7	514·4	123·9	47·4

* Figures not available.

The increase of population and the extension of route mileage naturally accounted for part of the additional passenger traffic; but besides these factors there was a steady growth of the travel habit, sedulously encouraged by the railway companies, which vied with each other in offering new facilities for the attraction of passengers. Thus in 1872 the Midland, followed by the Great Eastern, announced that it would provide third-class accommodation on all its trains at the parliamentary fare of one penny per mile. Regarded by most railway managements at the time as a suicidal policy, this bold step paid the Midland handsomely, and was ultimately followed, with minor exceptions, by the other companies. Three years later the enterprising Midland followed up this success by abolishing its second-class accommodation and raising the standard of comfort in its third-class carriages to that of its former seconds (by providing, for example, cushioned seats and backs). It was the Midland also which, in 1874, first introduced the luxurious American Pullman car to British travellers. Other landmarks in the evolution of the railway coach were the use of sleeping carriages in 1873 on the West Coast

[1] *Railway Returns for 1911* (Cd. 6,306 of 1912), p. xx.

route to Scotland, and of dining cars between King's Cross and Leeds in 1879. Corridor trains ran for the first time on the Great Western in 1892. In that year also the Midland introduced the steam-heating of carriages; hitherto passengers had had to make the most of the dubious comforts of hot-water tins and foot-warmers. For the illumination of carriages gas began to supersede oil in 1879, the London and North Western being responsible for this innovation. In the 'eighties several companies experimentally tried electric lighting, but with little success until 1895, when the London and North Western adopted electric lighting for all its principal trains. Owing, however, to the greater cheapness of gas, British railways have been slow in adopting electric lighting as the standard practice. Besides being more comfortable, railway travel became safer, with the general adoption of block signalling and continuous brakes.[1]

Combination among railway companies was much debated throughout the period, and was the subject of government inquiries in 1872 and 1909. A crop of amalgamation bills, the most alarming of which proposed to combine the London and North Western with the Lancashire and Yorkshire, led to the appointment of the first of these committees of inquiry. In its report the committee recognized the inevitability of amalgamations and the failure of committees, commissions and government departments to check the process of railway combination in the past; it admitted that amalgamations, permitting economies in operation, might be in the public interest, and instanced the North Eastern Railway, which, though "the most complete monopoly in the United Kingdom," had "the lowest fares and the highest dividend of any large English railway." Since nothing the legislature could do would maintain effective inter-railway competition, the committee stressed the importance of preserving competi-

[1] See above, pp. 63-64.

tion by sea, river and canal; the recommendation that railways should not be allowed to acquire control of public harbours has not, however, prevented them from becoming the principal dock-owners in the country. In the following year the amalgamation bills whose promotion had led to the inquiry were all rejected by a Joint Committee of the Lords and Commons, and a new Railway and Canal Traffic Act was passed in order to strengthen the public control over railways. This Act established a Railway Commission, with three members, to which was transferred the hearing of complaints, under the Act of 1854, relating to the refusal of reasonable facilities and the granting of undue preference. Certain powers of sanctioning working agreements between railways were also conferred on the Commission. The Act of 1873 further required the railway companies to publish their rates.

After the rebuff of 1873 there were few major railway amalgamations until the Railways Act of 1921. The most noteworthy were the absorption by the Great Western of the Bristol and Exeter in 1876 and of the South Devon in 1878, and the Midland's acquisition of the London, Tilbury and Southend line, with its valuable residential and port traffic, in 1912. A working union, an amalgamation in fact though not in law, was established in 1899 between the South Eastern and the London, Chatham and Dover Railways, the lines being operated as a single system by a Managing Committee. It was the inevitable outcome of a competitive struggle, dating from the 'fifties and, for the shareholders, costly in the extreme, a contest that had degenerated in its later stages into little more than a personal rivalry between Sir Edward Watkin, the ambitious chairman of the South Eastern (and also of the Manchester, Sheffield and Lincolnshire and the Metropolitan lines) and his equally determined opponent, J. S. Forbes, chairman of the Chatham line. Apart from these few large mergers, railway consolidation in the last three decades of the nineteenth century mainly took the form of the unobtrusive extension of control by the main undertakings over the smaller local lines. This was effected by absorption, by lease, or by working agreement, whereby one company acquired the exclusive right to work and manage another company's line. Where two or more of the main companies were interested in a local line, control sometimes took the form of joint ownership or joint lease, the Midland and Great Northern Joint Railway being an example of the first, and the Somerset and Dorset, leased for 999 years to the Midland and the London and South Western in 1875, of the second. By 1911 the twelve leading companies of England and Wales controlled, through ownership, lease, or working arrangement, about 14,000 route miles out of a total of just over 16,000; in Scotland five companies controlled all but about 120 miles of the total of 3,815.

Besides drawing the smaller railways within their orbit, the main undertakings entered into a variety of agreements for restricting competition between themselves. In order to avoid the ruinous cutting of rates to which unrestricted railway competition would have given rise, conferences had been established as early as the 'sixties for the settlement of rates between competitive points. Most of these were on a regional basis, such as the London, Liverpool and Manchester conference, formed in 1860, the English and Scottish conference of 1869, the West Riding conference of 1875, and the Humber Ports conference of 1906; the most important of all was the Normanton conference, formed in 1865, dealing with competitive rates within England and Wales. Competition in facilities, however, continued long after these rates conferences had been established; hence by threatening to transfer traffic, astute traders at competitive points could exact concessions in the form of free warehousing for unduly long periods, of laxity in the enforcement of demurrage charges for the detention of wagons at terminals, or of over-generous treatment of claims for lost or damaged goods. These matters also came to be dealt with by railway agreements, especially after 1900; a Joint Claims Committee, for instance, was formed in 1902.

Another species of railway combination, known since the 'fifties and very much to the fore in the first decade of the present century, was the pooling agreement. Since it enabled the participants to secure economies in their operating costs, it had a special attraction for railway managements after 1896, for most items of working expenditure, such as coal prices, wages and local rates, were rising, while railway rates and charges had become highly inflexible after the passing of the Railway and Canal Traffic Act of 1894. Pooling arrangements generally provided for the division of the receipts from competitive traffic in agreed proportions between the participating companies, an allowance for working expenses being usually deducted from the gross traffic receipts before they were pooled. Having no incentive to divert traffic from their competitors, the members of these pools agreed also to co-operate in working the traffic with the greatest economy. Competitive canvassing, conveyance by circuitous routes, duplication of facilities, and similar sources of competitive waste, could thus be avoided. Pooling might also result in the provision of improved facilities for the public, such as the inter-availability of tickets on different routes and the speedier delivery of consignments through shorter routing. Traffic pools of this type became very common after 1900, the most prominent example being that between the London and North Western, the Midland, and the Lancashire and Yorkshire in 1909. Receipts from traffic with the Channel Islands were pooled between the Great Western and the London and South Western. Three Scottish companies, the Caledonian, North British and Glasgow and South Western, had a pooling arrangement with regard to steamer traffic on the Clyde; and after the failure of a scheme for combining the Great Northern, Great Central and Great Eastern in a working union, these three companies resorted to the looser combination of the traffic pool. The Great Northern and Great Central had agreed in 1907 to form a working union, with a joint managing committee and pooling of receipts; but, on being submitted for the sanction of the Railway and Canal Commission, the agreement was held to be *ultra vires*, this decision being upheld by the Court of Appeal. Thereupon the two companies, together with the Great Eastern, promoted a bill to secure the powers denied them by the Commission, but withdrew it when they realized, from the strength of the opposition, that a long and costly investigation by the Private Bill Committee would be involved.

Traders took alarm at these agreements and proposals for railway fusion, and a Departmental Committee was appointed in 1909 to consider what further safeguards, if any, were needed to protect the public against possible abuses of railway monopoly. In its report, published two years later, the Committee accepted "the growth of co-operation and the more complete elimination of competition as a process at once inevitable, and likely to be beneficial both to the railway companies themselves, and, if properly safeguarded, to the public also."[1] A number of recommendations for the protection of traders were made, such as that railway companies should be required to justify any withdrawal or reduction of facilities, or the making of a charge for any service hitherto rendered gratuitously; but no action was taken by the government on these recommendations.

An earlier agitation by traders on the question of railway rates and charges had succeeded in inducing Parliament to pass protective legislation. The original Railway Acts had generally contained simple classifications of goods, for which maximum tolls and carriage rates were prescribed. These classifications and maximum charges varied from

[1] *Report of Departmental Committee on Railway Agreements and Amalgamations* (Cd. 5,631 of 1911), p. 40.

company to company, so that it was often extraordinarily difficult to ascertain what was the maximum charge for a route through the territories of several separately authorized companies. Moreover it was by no means clear for what services these statutory maxima might be charged; in particular, railway companies and traders disputed for years the legality of making additional charges for the handling of goods at terminals. Impelled by the depression of the 'seventies to seek economies, traders pressed for the overhaul of the railway rates system and for effective protection against exorbitant, and possibly illegal, charges. A Select Committee reported on the matter in 1882, and recommended that a uniform classification be adopted over the whole railway system, that maximum rates be fixed, and that terminal charges be permitted. These principles became the basis of the Railway and Canal Traffic Act of 1888, which required the railway companies to submit for parliamentary approval a revised classification and schedules of maximum rates. After protracted bargaining between the railway companies, trading interests and the Board of Trade, the Provisional Orders embodying the proposed classification and rate schedules were examined, modified and finally confirmed by Parliament, and came into force on January 1st, 1893. The new classification was based very largely on that which the railways had worked out for themselves through the Clearing House; maximum conveyance rates were made to "taper," *i.e.* the rate per ton per mile diminished as the length of the journey increased; and maximum charges were fixed for the use of terminal accommodation and for the work performed in handling goods at stations.

For some traffics the new maximum rates were below the actual rates charged before 1893; but for the bulk of the traffic, which was, and still is, carried at exceptional rates, the maxima were above or equal to the former actual rates. Hence when the new rates legislation came into force and the railway companies charged the maximum authorized rates on practically all classes of traffic, thousands of traders had to pay at higher rates as a result of legislation passed for their protection. The companies defended their action mainly on the ground that they had had insufficient time to overhaul the millions of rates entered in their rate-books, and declared that as quickly as possible new special rates, related to the new statutory maxima, would be put into operation. Some railway managers, however, admitted that they raised rates that were below the statutory limit in order to recoup themselves for losses in revenue where rates had had to be reduced. Though the railway companies were divided in their explanations of their action, traders were unanimous in condemning it as an outrageous step. "Personal experience had done in a week what all the writings of "careful students of the question" could not accomplish in half a century, and had convinced the practical man, whether legislator or trader, that 'fixed maxima are of next to no use in preventing extortion'."[1] Hence fresh legislation was passed, on the recommendation of a Select Committee, in order to restrict the right of railway companies to charge any rates within the authorized maxima. The Railway and Canal Traffic Act of 1894 imposed on railway companies the onus of proving, to the satisfaction of the Railway and Canal Commission, the reasonableness of any increase in a rate made on or after January 1st, 1893, and complained of by a trader; thus the rates existing in 1892 became the effective maxima, except where the companies were able to justify, on the grounds of increased cost for instance, an increase in a rate. The whole structure of railway rates and charges became exceedingly rigid as a result of this enactment, railway managers being shy of making experimental reductions in rates lest they should be debarred from raising them if they proved unremunerative. This position was slightly modi-

[1] Sir W. M. Acworth, *The Elements of Railway Economics* (1924), p. 161.

fied in favour of the companies by the Railway and Canal Traffic Act of 1913, passed as part of the bargain between the government and the companies at the time of the railway strike of 1911; the Act authorized the Railway and Canal Commission to sanction increases in rates where they were needed to compensate for increased wage costs, and the companies at once made an all-round increase of 4 per cent. in their exceptional rates.

THE STAGNATION OF THE CANALS

With the exception of the construction of the Manchester Ship Canal, there is little to record in the history of British canals and waterways in the latter part of the century. Official traffic returns showed that, as a whole, they had stagnated since the 'eighties at least. By far the heaviest

TRAFFIC STATISTICS FOR BRITISH INLAND WATERWAYS[1]

Country	Miles of Waterway	Year	Total Tonnage Conveyed
England and Wales (excluding seaborne traffic on the Manchester Ship Canal) ...	2,416	1888	33,123,666
		1898	34,022,493
		1905	32,340,264
Scotland	153	1888	1,622,713
		1898	1,336,441
		1905	1,171,414

traffic was on the Birmingham Canal system, which carried 7½ million tons in 1905, but even here tonnage had declined slightly since 1888. The Aire and Calder Navigation, with a little under 3 million tons in 1905, had made uninterrupted, though modest, progress since 1858, and a few other canals,

[1] *Fourth and Final Report of Royal Commission on Canals and Inland Navigations* (Cd. 4,979 of 1909), p. 49. These returns relate only to those waterways for which comparable figures are available in all three years. Cargoes conveyed over more than one canal are counted more than once in arriving at the total of "tonnage conveyed."

such as the Leeds and Liverpool and the Grand Junction, carried substantial amounts of traffic.

In a forlorn attempt to revive canal competition and so counter the growing tendency towards railway combination, trading interests, especially in the Birmingham area, urged the need for modernizing the canal system. A Royal Commission on Canals and Inland Navigations was appointed in 1906 and made a most exhaustive investigation, the results of which filled eleven volumes. In its fourth and final report the Commission summarized the condition of canals and waterways thus: "Few improvements and no large extensions of inland waterways (always excepting the Manchester Ship Canal) have been made since 1830, and, on the other hand, there have been many deteriorations and even disappearances of canals which once existed. On a few waterways or sections of waterways, favoured by special conditions, combined in two or three cases with enterprising management, traffic has been maintained and even increased. On other waterways it has declined, on some it has virtually disappeared. Everywhere the proportion of long-distance traffic to local traffic by water has become small. Considered as a whole, the waterways have had no share in the enormous increase of internal transport business which has taken place between the middle of the nineteenth century and the present time."[1]

The canal system had many defects, besides its unavoidable inferiority in speed of transit, to account for this absence of progress. It suffered from a lack of uniformity in the gauge of its waterways and locks, owing to the haphazard mode in which the canals had been originally authorized and constructed. The narrow gauge of a large proportion of the total canal mileage precluded the employment of capacious and economical barges. Moreover, despite canal amalgamations in the pre-railway era, there remained a

[1] *Fourth and Final Report of Royal Commission on Canals and Inland Navigations*, p. 5.

multiplicity of ownership that militated against expenditure on improvement by any one company; there was little point in improving one link in a chain of waterways if the other sections were not brought up to the same standard. The canal companies, though equipped with the requisite legal powers, had failed to develop a clearing house like that which played such a conspicuous part in railway development, so that traders found it difficult to obtain quotations of through rates. Unlike the railway companies, most canal owners had not become carriers, so that they were generally apathetic in this matter of arranging facilities for through traffic. The Commission declined to support those critics who denounced the railway companies, owning about one-third of the canal mileage, as primarily responsible for the relative decline of our waterways; railway canals, on the whole, were no worse maintained than those under independent ownership. On the other hand, railway companies could hardly be expected to go out of their way to encourage traders to consign goods by canal rather than by rail. "It is not just to say, as some have done," declared the Commission, "that railway companies (except perhaps in a few instances) acquired canals in order to strangle them. It is true to say that railway companies having, from various causes, acquired canals, feel, with few exceptions, little desire to do more than their barest legal duty in maintaining them."[1]

The main recommendations made by the majority of the Commission for the removal of these defects were, first, the improvement of the four main canal routes of England so as to form a "cross," providing through transit for barges of 100 tons (or, in an alternative scheme, of 300 tons) between the Thames, Severn, Mersey and Humber estuaries, and with its point of intersection in the Birmingham area. For this purpose these routes were to be vested in a Waterway

[1] *Fourth and Final Report of Royal Commission on Canals and Inland Navigations*, p. 77.

Board, with powers to issue stock for financing the improvements. No legislation on these lines has yet been passed, however, or is likely to be, especially in view of the rapid development of road transport since the Commission reported.

To any generalization about the backwardness of canal enterprise there was one brilliant exception, which gave fresh courage to those who believed that inland navigation still had a future. The construction of the Manchester Ship Canal, a triumph of local patriotism and municipal vision, was authorized by Parliament in 1885, after an expensive contest between its Manchester promoters and their opponents, principally Liverpool and the railway companies. Difficulties in raising the necessary capital, originally estimated at £8 million, delayed the beginning of construction until 1887. As the operations advanced it was realized that the total cost would greatly exceed the estimate, but the Manchester City Council saw the scheme through by lending £5 million to the Company. The Ship Canal, whose thirty-six miles, opened in 1894, had cost some £13 million, stimulated fresh industrial development, especially on Manchester's great trading estate at Trafford Park. In 1913 the Canal conveyed over 5¾ million tons of merchandise, and Manchester, with imports and exports of £56 million, had become the fourth port of Britain.

TRAMS AND BUSES

Urban transport facilities were supplemented in the 'seventies by the provision of tramways, introduced into this country from America, and first tried, with little success, in Birkenhead in 1858 and in London in 1861. Most of them were constructed, by local authorities or private companies, under the Tramways Act of 1870. Those constructed by private companies could be compulsorily purchased by local authorities after twenty-one years. This provision naturally had the effect of discouraging companies from improving tramways, by electrification for instance, when their concessions were drawing to an end. Those constructed by local authorities, which had no powers to operate them, were all leased to private companies until 1882, when Huddersfield, having constructed a tramway and failed to find a lessee, secured powers of operation for itself. In the following years, and especially after 1896, when general powers to operate tramways were conferred on local authorities, the majority of undertakings were taken over by municipal authorities as concessions and leases fell in. Until the 'nineties most trams were hauled by horses, though various kinds of mechanical traction, such as steam, compressed air, gas, and cable, were also utilized. Leeds successfully installed overhead electric traction in 1891, and, with varying time-lags, the other undertakings followed its example, especially after the turn of the century. Tramway mileage increased slowly, the Tramways Act having been on the statute-book thirty years before 1,000 miles had been constructed; then the process was accelerated, so that by 1911 Britain was equipped with 2,530 route miles of tramway.

While tramways were still being extended, their newfangled rival, the motor-bus, which was to replace many of them after the war, had already appeared. The London omnibus companies began to substitute motor vehicles for horse-buses in 1903 and almost completed the changeover in a decade; by 1913 there were 3,522 motor-buses licensed in Greater London and only 142 horse-buses. In the provinces motor-bus services were generally slower to develop, particularly in towns where the council owned the tramways and used its powers as licensing authority to prevent any rivals from competing with it. Where tramways were privately owned, local authorities were naturally less tender of tramway profits, and competitive 'bus services were authorized. Motor cars had begun to appear on British roads in the early 'nineties, their manufacture having been started in Germany by Daimler in 1887, and in France by Panhard and Levasseur in 1889. Motoring was restricted in its early stages by legislation originally intended to regulate traction engines. Under the Locomotives Act of 1865 mechanically driven vehicles were not to run at more than four miles an hour and were to be preceded by a man with a red flag. Though the red flag had been dispensed with in 1878, the low speed restriction remained until 1896, when the limit was raised to fourteen miles an hour. The Motor Cars Act of 1903 extended the permissible speed still further to twenty miles an hour, imposed penalties for reckless and dangerous driving and made the councils of counties and county boroughs responsible for the licencing of all motor cars. In 1904 the licensing returns showed that, after some ten years of motoring development, there were 8,465 private cars in the United Kingdom; in the following ten years the number rose to 132,015. Commercial motor transport made rather less progress than passenger transport, and had hardly begun, by 1914, to threaten the long-distance traffic of the railway companies. For the most part it was confined to short-distance work, hitherto undertaken by horse-drawn vehicles.

PROGRESS IN SHIPPING

It was on the sea that the most striking progress in transport was made in the years 1870–1914. The triumph of steam over sail, of steel over iron, was completed; year by year passenger liners became vaster, speedier, and more luxurious; ships became more specialized in function, and completely new types, such as the tanker and the refrigerating ship, were developed. The following table illustrates the steady decline in sailing tonnage and the huge increase in total tonnage since the 'seventies. In using these figures as a measure of the increase in shipping capacity, it must be remembered that the average steamship, owing to its more

REGISTERED MERCHANT SHIPPING TONNAGE OF THE UNITED KINGDOM[1]

	1870	1880	1890	1900	1910
	tons	tons	tons	tons	tons
Sailing vessels	4,577,855	3,851,045	2,936,021	2,096,498	1,112,944
Steam vessels	1,112,934	2,723,468	5,042,517	7,207,610	10,442,719
Total ...	5,690,789	6,574,513	7,978,538	9,304,108	11,555,663
U.K.'s share in world tonnage	33·94%	32·88%	35·83%	35·50%	33·37%

certain performance, its independence of the winds and its ability to take the shortest routes, can work many more trips a year than the average sailing-ship. "Taking an average of all trades, the annual carrying-power of a modern [steam] cargo-boat is probably at least four times that of a sailing vessel of the same cargo capacity."[2] From about 1890 onwards world shipping tonnage increased more rapidly than British tonnage. Two countries in particular, Germany and Japan, developed very rapidly as maritime powers; German tonnage increased from 1,433,413 in 1890 to 2,903,570 in 1910, and Japan's tonnage from 145,692 to 1,647,629 in the same period. Hence in shipping, as in so many other industries, the British share in total world production was declining.

In the conveyance of mails, passengers and high-class cargoes, for which speed of transit was more important than low freights, the steamship was supreme in the early 'seventies on nearly all routes, the Australian being the principal exception. For many classes of cargo, however, the sailing vessel was still, in the 'seventies and 'eighties, more economical than the steamer. In 1882, for instance, there were 550 sailing vessels engaged in shipping grain from the west coast of the United States to Europe; and nearly a decade later there were still 77 clippers loading wool in Sydney for London.[3] The steady improvement in the

[1] *Tables showing the Progress of Merchant Shipping in the United Kingdom and the Principal Maritime Countries* (Cd. 7,033 of 1913), pp. 58–61.
[2] C. E. Fayle, *A Short History of the World's Shipping Industry*, p. 250.
[3] *ibid.* p. 245.

efficiency of the marine engine, however, resulting in reduced fuel consumption and consequent release of space for cargo, finally gave steam an incontestable advantage over sail for all classes of ocean transport. John Elder's compound engine, which reduced coal consumption by about two-thirds, was followed by the triple expansion engine in 1881 and the quadruple expansion in 1894, effecting still further economies. In the latter year the *Turbinia* was built at Newcastle and fitted with Parsons' newly invented turbine engine, whose superiority, in speed and fuel consumption, over the reciprocating engine was soon recognized. Admiralty vessels ceased to be fitted with reciprocating engines after 1904, and the Cunard line, having tested the turbine in the *Carmania*, on the Atlantic service, had the *Lusitania* and *Mauretania* fitted with turbines in 1907. These improvements in marine engineering led to astonishing increases in the dimensions and speeds of the great passenger liners.[1] The first White Star liner, the *Oceanic*, put into service in 1871, was an iron ship of 3,808 gross tons, with a horse-power of 3,000 and a speed of 14¾ knots. Ten years later the Cunard Company's first all-steel liner, the *Servia*, was built, its tonnage being 7,391 and its speed 16·7 knots. These giants of their own day were very modest in size compared with the *Olympic* of 1910, with its 46,000 tons and 22 knots, or the *Aquitania*, built in 1914 and having a tonnage of 47,000 and a speed of 23 knots.

Steamships can be divided, according to the method of their management, into "liners" and "tramps," the latter being known in politer Victorian times as "seekers." "Liners" sail regularly, in accordance with a published time-table, between specified ports, their owners being common carriers of passengers or goods on those routes. "Tramps," on the other hand, are not tied to a fixed itinerary, but can be chartered, for a particular voyage or a fixed

[1] See the "Diagram showing the Evolution of the Atlantic Liner, 1833–1914" in A. W. Kirkaldy, *British Shipping*, Appendix XVIII.

time, to carry cargo between any ports specified by the charterer. A given ship may, of course, at different times be employed in a liner service or chartered as a tramp. In the days of the sailing vessel there had been a broad division between ships sailing regularly on the same route, the " constant traders," such as the East Indiamen, and those roving freely wherever cargo was to be had, the " free traders." But clearly a liner service in the modern sense of the term, with ships working to a time-table, was out of the question with vessels utterly dependent on wind and weather. The great liner companies, owning fleets of ships, were commonly organized on a large scale from the beginning. Tramp steamers, however, in their early days, were generally owned by individuals or by syndicates taking shares on the " sixty-fourth " system, the management of the ship being entrusted to a member of the group with special qualifications. With the increase in size and capital cost of the steam cargo-boat, ownership by limited companies became increasingly common, many companies owning only one or two boats and leaving their management to a managing owner paid on a commission basis.

In shipping, as in most other industries where overhead expenses are heavy, competition was apt, especially in times of trade depression, to lead to unprofitable rate-cutting, from which shipowners sought to protect themselves by combination. Since the sea was open to all comers, however, and since a large part of the total tonnage consisted of tramps with a multiplicity of owners, monopolistic conditions were much more difficult to establish on the sea than on the railway. Nevertheless, for some classes of traffic the companies providing cargo-liner services were able to restrict competition effectively and to regulate rates through the organizing of a shipping conferences. Like the railway companies' rates conferences, these were on a regional basis, the first being the Calcutta Conference of 1875. It was followed by conferences for the China trade in 1879, the

Australian trade in 1884 and by many others, so that by 1908, when a Royal Commission investigated the activities of the shipping rings, they existed for practically all trades except those of the North Atlantic and the British coast. These conferences fixed uniform rates, which were to be charged to all shippers, and protected themselves from the competition of non-conference lines and tramps, by adopting the ingenious device of the deferred rebate, first applied by the Calcutta Conference, to Manchester piece-goods, in 1877. A merchant who confined his shipments during a stated period (usually four or six months) to vessels belonging to members of the conference became entitled to a rebate, commonly 10 per cent. of the freights he paid in that period. But payment of the rebate was deferred until another similar period had elapsed, and was conditional on the continued loyalty of the trader to the conference during that further period. The conference thus acquired a firm financial hold over the trader, who forfeited rebates he had already earned if he once shipped outside the ring.

The deferred rebate system was most easily applied to those traders, such as the British exporters of manufactured goods, regularly shipping parcels, large and small, to a variety of destinations. It was more difficult, in fact, generally impossible, to apply it to the irregular shipment in bulk of foodstuffs and raw materials from overseas to Britain. For cargoes of this kind, traders preferred to charter ships and secure the benefits of the keen competition between tramps. Hence conferences could more successfully regulate the outward trade from Britain than the inward. There were, however, some high-class homeward cargoes, such as tea from Calcutta and Ceylon, which were subject to the deferred rebate. Railway competition mainly accounted for the absence of a conference for the coasting trade. And in the North Atlantic trade there was so much cargo space available on the regular passenger lines, and rates were so low, that there was little inducement for tramps to compete;

hence there was no need to tie shippers to the liner companies by the offer of a rebate. In 1911 the South African government broke up the deferred rebate system, so far as South African trade was concerned, by withdrawing mail contracts from lines giving rebates. Thereupon the shipowners and shippers devised a new kind of agreement under which, in return for loyalty to the conference, the shipper was assured of regular sailings, and of stability and equality of rates.

The majority of the Royal Commission on Shipping Rings was of the opinion that the Conference system, with its deferred rebates, conferred distinct advantages on traders, such as the provision of regular and fixed sailings, the arrangement of sailings so as to avoid clashing of times, the determination of rates and goods classifications on a stable basis, and equality of rates for all shippers. "Where a regular and organized service is required, the Conference system, fortified by some tie upon the shipper, is as a general rule necessary,"[1] owing to the greater expense involved in providing such regular services. This conclusion was endorsed in the final report of the Imperial Shipping Committee on the Deferred Rebate System in 1923. On the other hand, because the conference system might be abused, for example by fixing excessive rates or by arbitrarily varying rates, the Commission recommended the formation of shippers' associations to bargain on more equal terms with the rings. Apathy and rivalry among traders, however, have retarded the organizing of such associations, only a small number, such as the Manchester Association of Importers and Exporters and the East African Outward Shippers' Conference, having been formed.

THE TELEPHONE

The early history of the telephone system in Britain is largely one of obstructive public control over a private

[1] *Report of Royal Commission on Shipping Rings* (Cd. 4,668 of 1909), p. 78.

monopoly. Two British companies, controlling the Bell and Edison patents, were registered in 1878 and 1879, and amalgamated as the United Telephone Company in 1880. This company supplied the telephone service in the metropolitan area, while the provinces were served by a number of separate companies licensed by the United to use its patents. Owing, however, to a High Court decision that the private transmission of telephone messages was an infringement of the Post Office's telegraph monopoly, these telephone companies could operate only under licence from the Postmaster-General, who naturally wished to protect his telegraph department, already losing heavily, from the unwelcome competition of the newcomer. Until 1884 he issued licences restricting the operation of telephones within a very narrow radius in London and the provincial towns; and even after these restrictions had been relaxed, the telephone companies continued to be hampered by Parliament's refusal to grant them compulsory powers of acquiring way-leaves for their wires. As the result of an agreement between the government and the National Telephone Company, into which the United had turned itself in 1888 on amalgamating with the principal provincial companies, the Telegraph Act of 1892 provided for the Postmaster-General to take over the trunk lines constructed by the company, and to grant to it his way-leave powers relating to local services, which were left to the company. These powers, however, still could not be exercised without the consent of the local authorities concerned, and their consent was sometimes withheld when, as in Glasgow and London, the relations between the local council and the company were inharmonious. A Select Committee of 1895, which investigated the numerous complaints regarding the excessive charges and inefficiency of the National Company, recommended competition as the remedy, and an Act was passed in the following year authorizing municipalities to operate telephone systems. Half a dozen towns set up their own exchanges, but Hull alone was successful in its venture. To the modern generation, accustomed to a State telephone service and regarding it as a public utility that must be monopolized if it is to be economically operated, this recommendation of competition to protect the public against a private monopoly appears particularly fatuous. The problem of how to control this monopoly was finally solved in 1911, when the State acquired it at a price of £12½ million.

CHAPTER XII

Banking and the Money Market

THE CENTRAL BANK

By 1873, when *Lombard Street*, Bagehot's classic exposition of the functions of a central bank, was published, the Bank of England, though still reluctant to admit its special responsibilities, had become the hub of the English banking system. When crisis and panic swept over the money market, the City looked to the Old Lady of Threadneedle Street to act as the " lender of last resort " and to supply the additional currency needed to satisfy the demand for liquidity. The London bankers' practice of keeping part of their cash reserves on deposit with the Bank had been encouraged by an agreement of the clearing bankers, in 1854, to keep accounts at the Bank in order to settle clearing differences by cheque. Already in the mid-'seventies these bankers' balances with the Bank of England amounted to some £10 million, compared with about £1 million thirty years earlier, and they not infrequently exceeded the Banking Department's cash reserve. The Bank of England's discount rate had acquired a special significance, being widely used as an automatic regulator of the interest allowed on deposits ; since the 'fifties the London joint-stock banks had commonly, though without formal agreement, allowed 1 per cent. below Bank rate on deposit accounts, and the Scottish banks had pursued a similar course since 1863.

Besides having to act as guardian of the country's ultimate cash reserve, the Bank was destined to have further greatness thrust upon it, for it became the leading central bank of the international money market, whose development had been enormously accelerated, especially after 1870, by improved means of communication. Balances in London and drafts on London, all constituting a potential drain on Britain's gold stocks, figured increasingly among the assets of foreign bankers and governments. As early as 1878, it is estimated, the Continent regularly held £50 to £60 million of London acceptances.[1] On the Bank of England, therefore, fell the task of managing the gold reserve on which bankers all over the world relied.

As the focal point of this world-wide money market London possessed incomparable advantages, especially a free gold market and unrivalled facilities for accepting and discounting bills. Britain's far-flung commerce had given her merchant bankers contacts throughout the globe, and they had built up a specialized business in the accepting of bills on behalf of traders at home and abroad. These acceptance facilities were extended in the 'seventies, when the London offices of the Scottish banks undertook this type of business, and still more after 1900, when it was embraced by most of the London bankers, hitherto somewhat chary of granting acceptance credits,[2] this being in their opinion too risky a business for a banker. The unique London discount market, reinforced by the formation of the great discount companies in the 'fifties and 'sixties, turned more and more in the last quarter of the century to the financing of bills arising from international trade, partly because there was less business in inland bills. There were several reasons for the decline in the use of the inland bill. First, after the crisis of 1857, partly caused by the country bankers' abuse of re-discounting facilities, "regular re-discounting came to be regarded as the practice of only second-rate banks."[3] Second, the growth of bank deposits, coupled with the consolidation of the banking system, which linked together under a single control areas where deposits

[1] W. T. C. King, *History of the London Discount Market*, p. 270.
[2] The Union Bank of London, however, had over £9 million of acceptance liabilities, out of total liabilities of £19½ million, as early as 1866 (H. Withers, *National Provincial Bank, 1833–1933*, p. 75).
[3] King, *op. cit.* p. 271.

exceeded local credit requirements and areas where the reverse was the position, enabled bankers in industrial districts to provide out of their own resources all the accommodation needed by their customers, without their having to re-discount bills in London. Further, home traders came to prefer the more convenient bank advance, and even more the adjustable overdraft, to the bill of exchange, as a means of obtaining credit. Hence, by the end of the century, the financing of international, as distinct from domestic, trade had become the predominant concern of the discount market, to which flowed sterling bills, " the real cash of international commerce,"[1] from the ends of the earth. Finally, not least among the factors contributing to London's financial hegemony was the certainty, lacking in all other centres of importance, that gold could always be obtained on demand from the central bank.

In order to transact conveniently the growing volume of business they had at the fountain-head of finance, foreign banks began in the 'seventies to open offices in London. Among the first were the Comptoir National d'Escompte de Paris, the Crédit Lyonnais and the Deutsche Bank; these were soon followed by scores of others. Besides engaging in acceptance business, they acquired almost a monopoly of London's foreign-exchange business; for the merchant banking firms, such as the Rothschilds, Barings and Huths, which had formerly been the principal dealers in foreign exchange, were specializing increasingly, in the second half of the century, on accepting and on the issuing of foreign loans. The British joint-stock banks, expanding internally at an amazing pace, were slow to invade the international field, owing to the " general fear that continental branches of the deposit banks would become mobilier banks on the continental model, and lock up English deposits in long-term loans abroad."[2] However, in 1905 the London City

[1] H. Withers, *The Meaning of Money* (3rd. ed), p. 91.
[2] A. S. J. Baster, *The International Banks*, p. 58.

and Midland Bank opened a foreign-exchange department in London, but all its foreign business was, and still is, conducted through agencies and not through overseas branches. The other great joint-stock banks, through their subsidiaries, have acquired foreign branches, the first being Lloyds, which in 1911 absorbed the business of Armstrong and Co., Paris agents of several British banks.

Saddled with new internal and international responsibilities, the Bank of England had to work out an appropriate technique of control. For a time, in the 'seventies and 'eighties, it looked as though it might prove unequal to the task, since it had long ceased to be a giant bank among pigmies. The day was past when a Governor of the Bank could boast, as, with pardonable exaggeration, he did as late as 1864, that "its paid-up capital was so great that it might take in all the other banks with their paid-up capital and 'rest,' and leave them far behind."[1] As the following table shows, the astounding growth of bank deposits had reduced to almost insignificant proportions the Bank of England's share in ordinary deposit banking. The discount market was becoming plentifully supplied with funds by the commercial banks, and the Bank's influence in the market was weakening.

BANK DEPOSITS OF GREAT BRITAIN (in £ million)[2]

Year	Total Deposits (excluding Bank of England)	Total Deposits of Bank of England
1844	50	13·5
1865	200	20·5
1889	568	32·5
1894	600	40·5
1900	734	50·0
1913	962	55·0

In the early 'seventies the Bank began to abandon the rule, adopted in 1844, of "following the market," *i.e.* of adjusting its own rate of discount to the market rate, a

[1] E. T. Powell, *op. cit.* p. 384.
[2] A. E. Feavearyear, *The Pound Sterling*, p. 297.

practice which was incompatible with effective central banking control. Bank rate now normally exceeded the market rate by a fairly wide margin,[1] and in consequence the Bank suffered a serious decline in the volume of its discounting business. Hence in 1878 a further significant change was made in the relations between the Bank and the bill market. The Bank announced that henceforth it would be prepared to discount at the market rate for its private customers, thus recognizing the normal ineffectiveness of its official minimum rate. Though now usually divorced from the market rate, Bank rate was by no means shorn of all significance; it still regulated the interest allowed by the commercial banks, and it was still the approximate rate charged on loans to the bill-brokers whenever the market was "in the Bank." The commercial banks grew restive under this arrangement and threatened to drop the practice of basing their interest allowances on Bank rate; for with Bank rate generally well above the market rate, the margin between what they could earn on bills and what they had to allow on deposits became uncomfortably narrow. Had they carried out this threat, the Bank of England's control over the market would certainly have been seriously weakened; but the inability of the clearing bankers to agree on a common policy prevented this break-away from the leash of Bank rate. They did, however, increase the margin between their deposit rate and Bank rate to 1½ per cent. from 1886 onwards, thus widening still further the usual difference between Bank rate and market rate.

Though content to let the market rate remain below its own official rate in ordinary times, the Bank needed some means of making Bank rate effective whenever it wished to prevent a threatened or actual drain on its reserve. It therefore proceeded to develop the technique of what are nowadays called "open-market operations," which have as their object the variation of the funds at the disposal of the

[1] See the table in R. H. I. Palgrave, *Bank Rate and the Money Market*, p. 33.

money market. Down to 1890 it apparently relied almost entirely[1] on the ancient device, certainly used as early as 1833,[2] of "borrowing on consols," sometimes known as "budla-ing the market."[3] Consols were sold for cash and at the same time bought back for the "account," *i.e.* for the next monthly settlement day of the Stock Exchange, the operation having the effect of temporarily reducing the cash reserves of the commercial banks.[4] This device might, however, and sometimes did, fail to give the Bank effective control when the market was liberally supplied with funds, and other means had to be elaborated for making money scarce. On a number of occasions the Bank induced some of its private depositors to leave on deposit funds that would otherwise have been lent directly in the market, the Bank then either lending them at a stiff rate of interest or withdrawing them entirely from the market. Some of the county councils entered into such an arrangement in December 1889, the India Council in 1890, and the Japanese government in 1905 and 1907. Borrowing "in the market," *i.e.* from the bill-brokers and other financial houses, was continually resorted to after 1890, and in the first decade of the present century co-operation between the Bank and the commercial banks had become sufficiently close for the Bank to borrow directly from the banks, as, for instance, occurred in 1905. The withdrawal of funds from the market by borrowing had, in the years immediately preceding the war, become the usual form of open-market operation.[5] Realizing that, in the last resort, the Bank could force it to establish any rate it wished, the discount market came increasingly to follow the Bank's lead voluntarily. "A helpful hint from the authorities that there

[1] R. G. Hawtrey, *A Century of Bank Rate*, p. 69.
[2] W. T. C. King, *op. cit.* p. 116.
[3] W. F. Spalding, *The London Money Market* (3rd. ed.), p. 87.
[4] The phrases "borrowing on Consols" and "borrowing on securities" may also in the 'nineties have been used to describe the operation of borrowing from bill-brokers and finance houses with securities deposited as collateral. See R. S. Sayers, *Bank of England Operations, 1890–1914*, pp. 27–36.
[5] Withers, *op. cit.* pp. 228–231.

might be breakers ahead came to be almost as effective in Lombard Street as even the most direct disciplinary attempts had often been in the past. For the old 'quantitative' control there had been substituted a more benevolent, and yet more effective, 'moral' control."[1]

The Baring crisis of 1890 did much to establish the moral leadership of the Bank of England, and to convince the banks and the market that it was in their own long-run interests to co-operate with the Bank. In November 1890 the great house of Barings, the oldest of the merchant bankers, got into serious financial difficulties and was on the point of suspending payments. Along with the other issuing houses it had participated in the investment boom of the late 'eighties and had sold vast quantities of securities, some good and others not so good, to the investing and speculative public. Barings had been particularly active in floating issues of Argentine securities. A most inopportune revolution and financial crisis broke out in Argentina in the summer of 1890, and Barings were caught out with several million pounds locked up in unsalable Argentine securities. The firm was far from insolvent, as the Bank discovered on investigating its affairs, but its position was not liquid enough for it to meet its immediate commitments. Approached by Barings for assistance, the Governor of the Bank of England, the resourceful William Lidderdale, arranged for the firm's liabilities to be met in full, by raising a guarantee fund, ultimately amounting to £17,250,000, to which the leading banks subscribed. At the same time the gold reserve was strengthened by the purchase of £1,500,000 of gold from the State Bank of Russia and the borrowing of £3 million of gold from the Bank of France. To minimize the strain on the Bank's resources, Lidderdale induced the banks not to call in their loans from the market. As a result of these co-operative measures the situation was well under control before the

[1] King, *op. cit.* p. 321.

general public got wind of the crisis, and the whole affair passed off without any panic. Barings were liquidated and reconstructed as a limited company, their liabilities being met in full, without any assistance from the guarantors, by January 1895.

A crisis of a very different character affected the City in the autumn of 1907, when a violent financial panic swept over the United States, leaving behind it a trail of ruined banks. While it lasted the American bankers imported over £20 million of gold, of which 85 per cent. came from London. The Bank of England, which had only a £30 million gold reserve when the crisis broke out, was able to meet this terrific strain on its resources by raising Bank rate to 7 per cent. and so attracting gold from the other central banks of Europe. When the abnormal gold flow to America ceased, the Bank's gold stock had been reduced by less than £700,000. Thus despite its somewhat slender reserve, too slender for its international responsibilities in the opinion of some of its critics, the Bank came through this severe test with a greatly enhanced reputation.

In the field of commercial banking, structural, rather than functional, changes were the most conspicuous feature of the four decades before the war. Before considering these, however, one important change in the law relating to joint-stock banking must be mentioned. Down to 1878 many of the leading joint-stock banks had refrained from acquiring the privilege of limited liability, extended to them in 1858, believing that such a step would undermine the confidence of their depositors. But the crash of the City of Glasgow Bank in 1878, the result of the fraudulent operations of its directors and managers, gave a rude shock to the holders of unlimited bank shares, for nearly every shareholder in this bank was reduced to beggary in meeting the claims of its depositors.[1] Legislation passed in the following year, on the suggestion of a distinguished banker, George Rae,

[1] Every shareholder of £100 had to pay £2,750 in the liquidation.

introduced the principle of "reserve liability," under which a company might resolve that a specified part of its nominal share capital should be callable only in the event of the company's liquidation. The remaining unlimited joint-stock banks hastened to take advantage of this compromise device, which enabled them to meet their shareholders' clamour for limitation of liability without, as events proved, forfeiting their depositors' confidence.

The decades that followed witnessed the steady reduction in number of the London private banks and of the country banks, both private and joint-stock, and the building up of a consolidated branch-banking system. Against the competition of his powerful joint-stock rivals, with their superior attractions of published financial statements, greater capital resources, and ability to make large loans, the small private banker was almost defenceless. In 1884 there were still some 200 private firms engaged in deposit banking, having about 440 branches and deposit liabilities estimated at £146 million.[1] By 1914 there were only eight private banks of deposit left, with deposits of £33 million. Absorption by joint-stock banks accounted for most of the reduction, but quite a number escaped this fate by amalgamation among themselves. Of these the most notable example was the group of fifteen Quaker banking firms, with branches stretching from Brighton to Darlington, which, under the leadership of Barclay, Bevan and Co., combined in 1896 and assumed joint-stock status under the name of Barclay and Company Ltd. Further absorptions and extensions raised the number of its branches to 606 in 1914, when it was fifth in size, as judged by deposits, of the great joint-stock banks.

The forceful personality of Edward Holden, "a superb master of the difficult art of banking consolidation,"[2] was mainly responsible for the amalgamations by which the

[1] W. F. Crick and J E. Wadsworth, *A Hundred Years of Joint Stock Banking*, p. 34.

[2] *ibid.* p. 439.

present Midland Bank was built up. From the time of his appointment as joint general manager of the Birmingham and Midland Bank in 1891, the year in which it acquired a footing in London by absorbing the Central Bank of London, to his death in 1919, he devoted himself unsparingly to the extension of the Midland's influence. By 1914, when the Metropolitan Bank of England and Wales, itself a consolidation, was acquired, the London City and Midland Bank, as it was called after the incorporation of the City Bank in 1898, had become the leading British bank, with 1,028 branches and deposits of £126 million. Two others of the present "Big Five," namely, Lloyds and the National Provincial, are also the products of provincial enterprise. The first of these, a Birmingham firm established in 1765, had already absorbed nine banking concerns in the Midlands before it came to London, in 1884, by combining with two banks, hitherto its London agents, under the style of Lloyds, Barnetts and Bosanquets' Bank, Ltd. It assumed the title of Lloyds Bank, Ltd. on amalgamating with the Birmingham Joint Stock Bank and the Worcester and County Banking Co. in 1889. Between then and 1914 it acquired thirty-three banking concerns, stretching from Devon and Cornwall up to Newcastle, and ran the London City and Midland close for the position of the largest bank. In 1914 it had 880 branches and £118 million of deposits. The National Provincial Bank of England had opened a London office at the time of the Overend Gurney panic, thereby losing its note-issuing rights. Already in 1866 it had absorbed sixteen local banks and had built up a widespread branch system, with 122 offices and £13 million of deposits. From then until 1918 its expansion owed little to absorptions, being mainly due to the steady extension of its branches; in 1914 it was the fourth in size of the British banks, with 332 branches and £75 million of deposits. Parr's Bank, with its head office at Warrington, was another of the provincial banks that invaded London, by acquiring in 1891 the London banking house of Fuller, Banbury and Co.

Not all the banking expansion of this period was undertaken by provincial firms. Two notable exceptions were the Union Bank of London and the London and Westminster Bank. The first, founded in 1839, had refused to undertake expansion into the country, but finally admitted the inconvenience of being wholly dependent on the fluctuating rates of interest in the London money market, and amalgamated in 1902 with Smith, Payne and Smiths, originally established in Nottingham before 1688, which had offices in the East Midlands, as well as in London. The Union of London and Smiths, as the combined concern was called, proceeded to extend its system by absorptions, of which the most valuable was that in 1903 of Prescott and Co., private bankers, with many connections in the south of England. The London and Westminster, oldest of the London joint-stock banks, confined its activities to the metropolis even longer than the Union Bank, but in 1909 it amalgamated with the London and County Bank and at once acquired a large provincial connection, mainly in the south. In 1914 the London County and Westminster had 350 branches and deposits of £99 million.

After the Glasgow bank scandal of 1878 there is little to record in the history of Scottish banking, which had already attained a remarkable degree of consolidation in the 'sixties. In 1864 there were only thirteen banks in Scotland, all joint-stock, with 607 branches.[1] Failure of the corrupt and absorption of the weak have since reduced the number to eight. The opening of new branches proceeded steadily, though not as rapidly as in England and Wales, which had much leeway to make up. In 1912, despite the furious competition between the English banks in the opening of branches, the Scottish population was still much more adequately supplied than the English with banking facilities.

[1] Clapham II. 341.

ENGLISH AND SCOTTISH BANKING IN 1872 AND 1912[1]

Country	Number of banking offices		Population		Number of inhabitants to each office	
	1872	1912	1871	1911	1872	1912
England & Wales ...	1,779	6,709	22,712,266	36,075,269	12,766	5,422
Scotland ...	812	1,235	3,360,018	4,759,521	4,137	3,854

The coalescence of the 370 English banks of 1875 into a few huge institutions, each with its vast network of branches, has contributed immeasurably to the stability of the banking system. By spreading their business over a wide range of territory and trades, the banks have been able to spread their risks, and avoid excessive dependence on a single local industry, the main source of weakness in "unit" banking systems. Centralization of reserves has made it easy to meet local fluctuations in cash requirements without any of the strain that would be felt by a purely local bank. Not least among the sources of strength of the amalgamated banks is the psychological advantage of size. The astronomical figures published in bank balance sheets help tc induce a comfortable,though quite irrational, belief in the invulnerability of the banking giants. Further, it can reasonably be contended that without a parallel consolidation of banking, the development of large-scale industry would have been seriously hampered. For the small country banker, even if he had sufficient total resources, could not safely have lent several hundreds of thousands to a single customer; such a loan would have made him unduly dependent on the solvency of that one borrower. On the other hand, the passing of the private banker has by no means been unregretted. It has frequently been alleged that credit facilities were more adaptable to local and personal circumstances in the days of private banking than is possible with the stereotyped large-scale banking of

[1] G. H. Pownall, *English Banking*, p. 72.

to-day. The old banker knew his customers and their affairs intimately, and was prepared, in considering an application for a loan, to rely more on his personal judgment and less on the collateral offered than the modern branch manager is allowed to do. Against this contention, however, it must be remembered that " the attractive phrase ' local elasticity ' sometimes in the past covered undesirable preferences and personal discriminations."[1] Moreover, though amalgamation has doubtless resulted in greater uniformity of practice in the matter of advances, local bank managers have by no means been divested of all discretionary powers. The establishment of local directors has also helped to maintain that closeness of personal touch which characterized the methods of the private banker.

[1] *Final Report of the Committee on Industry and Trade* (Cmd. 3,282 of 1929), p. 48.

CHAPTER XIII

The State and Labour

TRADE UNIONISM OLD AND NEW

Until the mid-'eighties the British trade union movement remained singularly untouched by the ferment of contemporary Socialist ideas, although Karl Marx, the founder of "scientific Socialism," lived for many years in London. The "Junta" and its successors in the leadership of the movement were Liberal in politics. Self help, individualism and *laissez faire* were as axiomatic for them as for the middle classes. Trade unionism was, for the older leaders, not an instrument of class war but a means of improving the condition of wage-earners within the limits of capitalism. A vigorous onslaught on this bourgeois conception of the rôle of trade unions was made in the 'eighties by a group of able young unionists—among them John Burns and Tom Mann—who were much influenced by the teachings of Henry George and Karl Marx. They regarded the older unions as mere friendly societies, ham-strung by their unwillingness to risk losing their friendly benefits, and accordingly called for the adoption of low rates of subscription. This would enable the unions to recruit the lower-paid workers, more interested in an aggressive policy. Their propaganda galvanized the whole trade union movement; many new general labour unions, with low subscriptions, were formed in the late 'eighties to cater for the unskilled who were ineligible for membership of the more aristocratic unions; old unions, too, gained considerably in membership. Unions drew closer together, both by the formation of federations, like the Miners' Federation of 1888 and the Engineering and Shipbuilding Trades' Federation of 1889, and by the establishment of greatly increased numbers of local Trades Councils. An immense stimulus to this "new unionism" was given by the successful strike of London's match-girls in 1888, and still more by the victory of the London dockers, led by Tillett, Burns and Mann, in the following year. The numerical strength of trade unionism increased by leaps and bounds as a consequence of this revival. From 500,000 in 1885 the membership of the unions affiliated to the Trades Union Congress rose to 1,593,000 in 1890.

Declining trade in the early 'nineties brought down the membership below the peak of 1890; for trade-union membership has always been sensitive to the trade cycle, rising and falling as general economic activity has risen and fallen. Demands for wage reductions provoked an outbreak of major industrial disputes in 1893, the worst year of the depression. Some 400,000 English miners were on strike for four months, but had in the end to accept large cuts in their wages. A cotton spinners' strike lasted for twenty weeks; though some wage reductions were imposed in the settlement, they were less than a third of those originally demanded by the employers. As trade picked up in the mid-'nineties, trade-union membership recovered and continued to advance fairly steadily until 1910. During these years trade unionism developed rapidly on its political side. The Trades Union Congress, weaned from its Liberal allegiance, instructed its Parliamentary Committee in 1899 to summon a conference of Socialist societies—the Independent Labour Party, the Social Democratic Federation and the Fabian Society—in order to concert measures for increasing the number of Labour members in Parliament. The Labour Representation Committee, which became the Labour Party in 1906, was the outcome of their deliberations.

By 1910 the trade unions had 2,565,000 members. Three years of acute industrial unrest, flaring up in a series of large-scale strikes, carried the membership to

4,135,000 in 1913. Many currents contributed to the turbulence of these years: syndicalist doctrines from France and industrial unionism from America, both pointing to "direct action"; the grievance of the Osborne judgment, which weakened the political power of the trade unions; and the failure of wage rates to keep pace with the rising cost of living. "The underlying movement," declares G. D. H. Cole, "was a mass movement of sheer reaction against the failure of orthodox Trade Unionism or moderate parliamentarism to secure any improvement in the working-class standard of life."[1] There were numerous sporadic strikes in 1910, many of them unofficial, but none on a national scale. The most serious was that of 30,000 miners of the Rhondda and Aberdare Valleys at the end of the year. On the north-east coast the members of the Boilermakers' Society were locked out for fourteen weeks, and only prompt government intervention averted a general lock-out in the cotton industry. Tempers became still more strained in 1911. In June the seamen and firemen struck successfully for higher wages. Dockers in London, Liverpool and Manchester came out in August, and in the same month the country had its first experience of a national railway strike. Its primary purpose was to secure for the railway unions recognition by the railway companies, which, with the exception of the North Eastern Railway, had hitherto refused to negotiate with the union leaders. With Lloyd George as mediator, the strike was settled in three days. Though the unions were still not officially recognized, the companies had been forced to enter into negotiations with them. Railway trade unionism was immensely strengthened by the outcome of the strike, the total membership rising from 116,000 in 1910 to 337,000 in 1914. Moreover this membership had been consolidated by the amalgamation of three railway unions in

[1] *A Short History of the British Working Class Movement, 1789–1927*, Vol. III, p. 70.

1913 to form the National Union of Railwaymen, with 268,000 members.

The disputes of 1911 were completely overshadowed by those of the following year. In one great strike alone, the miners', there were more men involved than in all the strikes of 1911 put together. For five weeks 850,000 miners, by far the most strongly organized body of workers in the country, fought the owners on the question of a guaranteed minimum wage. It was the first time a national strike affecting all the coalfields simultaneously had been called. The issue was settled, though not with the concurrence of a majority of the men, by the passing of the Coal Mines Minimum Wage Act. There followed a strike of London dockworkers, called by the Transport Workers' Federation, which had been formed in 1910 and was now anxious to try its strength. The collapse of the strike, after it had dragged on for two months, marked the end of the pre-war phase of large-scale industrial conflict.

By 1913 trade unionism was much less concentrated, industrially, than it had been in the 'eighties. The ancient strongholds of the movement—the unions of miners, cotton operatives, engineers and shipbuilders, and skilled building workers—still accounted for a disproportionate part of the aggregate membership. But several powerful new groups had been added to their number. On the railways, where trade unionism had been extremely feeble before 1890, there had, as we have seen, been an immense increase in strength. Other transport workers, too, had flocked into the unions between 1910 and 1913; so also had the general labourers. Black-coated workers were building up effective organizations; there were 113,000 teachers and 235,000 other public employees enrolled in unions in 1913. There remained, however, several trade union "deserts." Except in the dyeing, bleaching and finishing sections, the woollen unions were exceedingly weak; so also were the organizations of agricultural labourers and pottery workers. And, outside the cotton industry and teaching, women workers showed little or no inclination to organize themselves.

After the passing of the Trade Union Act of 1871 the legal position of trade unions seemed assured, until two famous judgments caused an uproar in the labour world. In the first of these, the Taff Vale judgment of 1901, an injunction was granted to restrain the Amalgamated Society of Railway Servants and its agents from watching and besetting the "blacklegs" employed by the Taff Vale Railway to replace men on strike, and from inducing them to break their contracts with the company. Later, damages were awarded against the union for the loss its actions had imposed on the company. It had hitherto been supposed that since trade unions were not legal corporations, though they had certain legal rights, they could not be sued for the tortious acts of their members. The House of Lords, however, acting as the final court of appeal, decided that, though not a corporation, a trade union had the attributes of a corporate personality. Exposed by this judgment to the risk of crippling actions for damages whenever they were involved in disputes, the trade unions pressed for amending legislation, and got it in the Trade Disputes Act of 1906, which removed their liability for any torts committed by themselves or their agents. The second judgment, in the Osborne case of 1909, undermined the political activities of the trade unions and of the Labour Party, for it was decided that a trade union had no legal right to use its funds for political purposes. This restriction was removed by the Trade Union Act of 1913. It provided that before engaging in political activities a trade union must secure the approval of a majority of the members voting in a special ballot; political funds were to be kept separate from the general funds of the unions; and members who objected to contributing to a political fund were to be exempted from doing so, without losing any of their ordinary rights as members.

WAGES AND HOURS

Though unwelcome to employers, the falling price level of the " Great Depression " brought to the working classes a very substantial improvement in their standard of living. Speaking very broadly, we can say that the average wage-earner was able to buy in 1895–96, with the earnings of a normal working-week, about 45 per cent. more of the goods ordinarily consumed by labouring families than he could have done in 1880. His money wages had increased by 15 per cent. between these years, and falling prices had lowered the cost of living by some 20 per cent. This advance of real wages was brought to an abrupt end, however, by the reversal of the trend of prices at the close of the century. Though money wages continued to rise down to 1914, real wages reached their peak in 1899 and then relapsed, so that in 1914 the typical working man was no better off, in terms of real income, than he had been in 1896. These averages naturally mask very unequal rates of change in the earnings of different trades. Builders' money wages showed a steady, unbroken, advance from 1880 down to 1914, with an increase of 23 per cent. over the period as a whole. In the cotton industry, wages rose almost as uninterruptedly, and in 1906 stood 32 per cent. higher than in 1880. Miners' wages, on the other hand, were most unstable, following very closely the fluctuations of coal prices, to which they were frequently tied by the operation of selling-price sliding scales. They stood, for instance, at 141 in 1891, compared with 100 in 1880, and then dropped as low as 117 five years later. From this point they shot up to 163 in 1900, a level not reached again until 1913. As the cost of living rose by 12 per cent. from 1900 to 1913, the miners, suffered an appreciable lowering of their standard of living after the turn of the century. Engineering and ship-building workers experienced still another type of wage variation. From 1880 to 1886 their money wages steadily diminished · they recovered by 1890, but sagged again in the mid-'nineties; by 1898 they had returned once more tc the level of 1880; thereafter they moved forward at an uneven rate, until in 1914 they were 22 per cent. higher than in 1880.[1]

From the official wage censuses taken in 1886 and 1906, and from other sources of information, we can compare the relative earnings of different trades, which are summarized in the following table. Analysis of the distribution of earnings between skilled and unskilled shows that the different grades of worker shared very unequally in the general advance of wages. The skilled worker in most trades secured not only a greater absolute, but also a greater proportionate, increase in earnings than the unskilled. If we range the men workers, other than those engaged in

EARNINGS IN 1886 AND 1906[2]

Industry	Average earnings of males in full week (in shillings)	
	1886	1906
Coal mining	21·2	31·5
Metals, engineering and shipbuilding	23·0	28·1
Textiles	19·4	22·9
Drink	23·0	25·0
Woodworking	21·4	27·1
Gas and water	26·5	26·4
Railways	22·0	25·3
All industries (excluding agriculture)	21·2	26·7
Agriculture	16·3	18·3

mining and agriculture, in the order of their earnings, we find that the median man of the lower-paid half earned 16 per cent. more in 1906 than twenty years earlier, while the median man of the better-paid half earned 26 per cent. more.[3] The inequality in the distribution of earnings was thus becoming more pronounced. As to the share of the

[1] The wage index numbers cited in this paragraph are taken from A. L. Bowley *Wages and Income in the United Kingdom since 1860*, pp. 8, 30.
[2] *ibid.* p. 50.
[3] *ibid.* p. 42.

wage-earning classes in the total national income, Bowley estimates that in 1880 aggregate wages amounted to £439 million, and constituted about 40 per cent. of the nation's income. The national wage-bill rose to £580 million in 1891–95, when it accounted for 41·5 per cent of the national income. From then onwards rising prices had the effect of modifying the distribution of income to the detriment of wage-earners. In 1913 the country's wage-bill, at £857 million, was only 38·5 per cent. of the aggregate income.[1]

Amid the general working-class progress of the last quarter of the century, there remained some black spots, the "sweated" trades, which could be eradicated only by coercive measures. The unfortunate workers in these industries were condemned to a life of incessant toil in order to earn a miserable pittance, which was often not even a subsistence wage. "Sweating" was found where trade unionism was absent, and prevailed particularly among home-workers, women being the chief victims. The chain trade at Cradley Heath, the paper-box trade of the East End of London, tailoring, shirt-making and other sections of the clothing industry, provided some of the worst examples of the "sweating" system. The evidence collected by parliamentary committees in 1888, 1907 and 1908, the introduction of private bills for the suppression of sweating, and the propaganda of the Anti-Sweating League, succeeded in arousing the public conscience. The Trade Boards Act of 1909 was the result. It marked the abandonment of the doctrinaire belief, held by legislators since the repeal of the Statute of Artificers in 1812, in the necessary perfection of an unregulated labour market. In four trades—chain-making, ready-made and wholesale bespoke tailoring, paper-box making, and lace finishing—wages were to be regulated by Trade Boards, consisting of equal numbers of representatives of employers and of employed, together with a few independent "appointed members." After confirmation by

[1] *Wages and Income in the United Kingdom since 1860*, pp. 8, 30.

the Board of Trade, the wage rates fixed by these Boards became the legal minima. The gloomy prognostications of the critics of this legislation proved to be ill-founded; wide-spread ruin did not fall upon the trades selected for the experiment. On the contrary, the necessity of paying the higher wages fixed by the Trade Boards compelled the employers in these industries to improve the efficiency of their organization. The results of the first trial having proved favourable, the Trade Board system was extended in 1913 to four further trades, namely, sugar confectionery and fruit preserving, shirt-making, hollow-ware making, and linen and cotton embroidery. The principle of the legal minimum wage was applied also to the coal-mining industry by an Act of 1912, passed as a means of settling the national miners' strike. It provided for conferences of owners and men, with government representatives, to fix the minimum rates of wages in each district. Unlike the Trade Boards Act, it imposed no penalties for non-payment of the minima, but the aggrieved miner could bring a civil action for recovery of the minimum wage to which he was entitled. The Act made little difference to the general level of miners' wages, but afforded some protection to those working in "abnormal places."

Some shortening of the hours of labour occurred in the period covered by this chapter, but the most resounding victories in this field had been won by the 'seventies. In textile factories, where the length of the working week was determined by the statutory regulations relating to women and "young persons," hours had been reduced from 60 to 56½ in 1874, thus providing the Saturday half-holiday. A further hour had been knocked off in 1901. The eight-hour day, for which the Miners' Federation had fought since 1888, was conceded to the miners by an Act of 1908. This statute was a landmark in the history of labour legislation, for in the nineteenth century Parliament had not directly regulated the working hours of adult men, hitherto deemed capable of looking after themselves. In the engineering trades the 54-hour week, generally adopted in 1871, remained unchanged in most districts until 1919, when 47 hours became the length of the normal week. Builders were commonly working a 50-hour week in 1914, compared with about 54 in the early 'seventies. Parliament tried to ensure a modicum of leisure for young shop assistants, notoriously overworked until very recently, in the Shop Hours Act of 1886. It imposed a maximum of 74 hours a week, but its provisions remained quite ineffectual until their enforcement was entrusted to the local authorities. All shop assistants, adult as well as juvenile, benefited from the Shops Act of 1911, which among other things regulated the early closing of shops.

LABOUR LEGISLATION

In the sphere of labour legislation the outstanding achievement of the pre-war period was the laying of the foundations of a comprehensive social insurance system. Until the end of the nineteenth century wage-earners were left by the State to make what private provision they could to protect themselves from the risk of destitution, which might arise through unemployment, sickness, old age or the death of the breadwinner. Those who failed to make adequate provision and became destitute had no alternative, unless they could engage the sympathies of some charitable society, but to " go on the parish " and stigmatize themselves as paupers. Friendly societies, collecting societies, trade unions and industrial assurance companies, were among the principal forms of mutual aid by which the working classes attempted to stave off this calamity. But with the best will in the world it was impossible for the mass of the people to insure, out of their slender incomes, against all these industrial risks. In 1906 half of the adult male wage-earners in industry were earning less than 29s. 4d. a week;

a quarter earned less than 23s. 4d.; and agricultural labourers were still worse off with average earnings of only 18s. 4d. The one risk that was fairly adequately covered was that of having to incur the expenses of a funeral. In 1910 the industrial assurance companies had some 31 million life policies outstanding, of an average value of just under £10. The collecting societies, such as the Royal Liver and the Liverpool Victoria, had over 7 million members. In addition to these, most of the ordinary friendly societies and trade unions also provided funeral benefits. Insurance against sickness was much less extensive. Of those who came within the scope of the National Health Insurance scheme in 1911, only about one-third were entitled to sickness benefits from friendly societies. Voluntary unemployment insurance was still rarer, since it was undertaken only by the trade unions. In 1903 the number of workers entitled to unemployment benefit fell a little short of a million. As to the risk of widowhood and orphanhood, few members of the working classes could afford to insure their lives for amounts that would provide adequately for their dependants. There was no escaping the conclusion that if destitution was to be prevented, self help would have to be supplemented by some measure of State assistance.

Loss of earnings through industrial accidents was the first of the risks against which the State provided some protection. Before 1880 the right of workmen to claim from their employers compensation for accidents arising out of their work was restricted by the "doctrine of common employment," elaborated in a legal decision of 1837. The employer was liable for any injury caused by his servants to a member of the public, but he was not liable when a servant was injured in an accident caused by a fellow servant. This legal doctrine hit with especial severity the servants of large impersonal employers, like railway companies, since the majority of the accidents that befell them were necessarily due to the mistakes or negligence of fellow workmen. The trade unions, especially those in the mining and railway industries, agitated for the removal of this hardship, and succeeded in 1880 in getting the first Employers' I iability Act through Parliament. It extended the liability of employers to include accidents caused by the negligence of managers, superintendents and foremen, or by the obeying of improper rules. Railway companies were made liable also when their servants were injured through the negligence of signalmen, drivers and pointsmen. Though a step in the right direction, the Act still left workers entirely unprotected against the bulk of the accidents caused by their fellow workmen. It was not until 1897 that the harsh doctrine of common employment was replaced by a new principle of employers' liability, embodied in the Workmen's Compensation Act. Employers in certain dangerous trades (which included factories, mining, quarrying, railways and building) were now made financially responsible for all accidents to workpeople arising in the ordinary course of their employment, whether such accidents were due to the employers' negligence or not. A later Act of 1906 extended the new principle to practically all kinds of employment, and gave workmen suffering from certain industrial diseases the right to compensation.

The question of State pensions for the aged had been thoroughly ventilated, in Parliament and out, for well over a generation before a scheme finally found its way to the statute-book in 1908. Germany, the pioneer in social insurance, had established a contributory pensions scheme, financed on the now familiar tripartite basis, nearly twenty years earlier. In the British scheme the contributory principle was rejected, mainly because it would have meant postponing by many years the date at which claimants could draw their pensions. Instead, old age pensions were financed wholly out of taxation, and the right to draw them was made to depend not on contributions but on need.

Persons aged seventy who could pass certain tests of respectability were entitled to a pension of five shillings a week, provided that their incomes did not exceed £21 a year. Those with annual incomes of more than £21 but not more than £31 received pensions reduced in accordance with a scale. Much criticism was levelled against this income test on the ground that, by penalizing those who had made some provision for their old age, it discouraged thrift among the poor. Any such effect has been minimized by the subsequent amendments to the scheme; for in 1924 the income limit was raised from £21 to £26 5s., plus an allowance of £39 of unearned income. Hence, according to the official scale for computing the income from savings, a claimant may now have as much as £865 of savings before he is disqualified for the full pension of ten shillings a week. A further improvement in the administration of pensions came in 1925, when a compulsory contributory scheme was introduced (in addition to the original non-contributory scheme, which, of course, still remains.) Those insured under this later scheme are entitled to the full pension at sixty-five without any inquiry into their means.

That a man might be unemployed not through weakness of moral character, but through sheer inability to find work, came to be more widely recognized as the nineteenth century advanced and experience of cyclical slumps accumulated. Spasmodic attempts were made to provide some more appropriate treatment for these victims of the industrial system than that meted out by a deterrent Poor Law. Relief works were the remedy commonly applied. With but few exceptions, the most notable being those carefully organized in Lancashire during the cotton famine of the early 'sixties, the results of these relief work schemes were disappointing. They attempted the impossible task of combining "relief" with "work," by making employment on relief schemes less eligible than ordinary wage-work. As a result, the respectable artisan who was temporarily out of work in years of bad trade would have nothing to do with municipal relief works, which he regarded as only one degree removed from poor relief. It was mainly low-grade workers, more often out of work than in, who were employed on relief works. For the chronic under-employment of these people, temporary jobs on relief schemes were clearly no remedy at all. Nevertheless the governments of the period had no other policy for reducing unemployment. Chamberlain issued a circular to local authorities in the bleak year 1886, urging them to embark on relief works, and the same procedure was followed in the slump of 1892–93. In 1905 the Unemployed Workmen Act established Distress Committees in boroughs and urban districts with populations of not less than 50,000. They were empowered to aid emigration and migration, and to provide, or contribute towards the provision of, temporary work for the unemployed. The Act, according to Sir William Beveridge, failed to make "any appreciable impression upon the problem. Its main service has been to demonstrate beyond question its own essential inadequacy and the inadequacy of all measures which, like itself, leave industrial disorganization untouched and deal only with the resultant human suffering."[1]

A common-sense plan for the reduction of unemployment, recommended by both the majority and the minority of the Poor Law Commission of 1905, was the establishment of employment exchanges. Their utility had already been demonstrated in London before they were extended over the whole country under an Act of 1909. Though they clearly could not create additional jobs, they did serve to shorten the average period of unemployment by improving the organization of the labour market. Two years later came the twin unemployment and health insurance schemes introduced in the National Insurance Act of 1911, "probably the most ambitious administrative experiment, and one

[1] *Unemployment—A Problem of Industry* (1930), p. 191.

of the most daring social experiments, ever attempted in this country."[1] Like so much of our social legislation, it retained within a State scheme the voluntary organizations that had done the pioneering work. So far as unemployment insurance was concerned, it combined a compulsory scheme, financed by contributions from employers, employed and the State, with a system of subventions out of State funds to trade unions that paid unemployment benefits to their members. The compulsory scheme applied to about 2¼ million workers in seven groups of trades, selected because they were especially liable to fluctuations of employment. Benefits were at the rate of 7s. a week for a period of not more than fifteen weeks in a year, with the additional proviso that not more than one week's benefit could be paid for every five contributions standing to the credit of the claimant. The scheme was administered through the labour exchanges, but trade unions insuring their members against unemployment could arrange to pay the State benefit along with their own. Further, the State paid to trade unions, whether within or outside the trades compulsorily insured, grants equal to one-sixth of the unemployment benefits paid out of their own funds. This last arrangement had been recommended, in principle, by the Minority of the Poor Law Commission, but the Government declined to rely on it alone, since to do so would have left the great majority of workers uninsured.

Compulsory health insurance, which touched the interests, and evoked the opposition, of the medical profession and of the friendly societies, trade unions and industrial assurance companies, caused a much fiercer controversy than unemployment insurance. The latter opponents, however, were reconciled by their incorporation in the scheme as "approved societies," with responsibility for the administration of all benefits, other than medical and sanatorium benefits, which were entrusted to *ad hoc* local insurance committees.

[1] R. C. Davison, *The Unemployed—Old Policies and New*, p. 75.

" Approved societies " were required to pay certain statutory cash benefits—sickness, disablement and maternity benefits—and might also, if their funds permitted, provide " additional benefits," such as dental and ophthalmic benefits. A tiny minority of persons insured under the scheme could not, or preferred not to, join an " approved society," and became " deposit contributors," their contributions being paid into a special fund from which benefits were paid *via* the local insurance committees.

Factory law grew more elaborate as experience revealed the gaps in existing legislation and the need for additional precautions. For instance, the increasing use of electricity for lighting and power in factories and workshops created new dangers and necessitated extensive additions to the safety code. Special electricity regulations came into force in 1909. But after the great consolidating Act of 1878 there were no changes of note in the principles of the factory code. The most important of the subsequent series of enactments was the Factory and Workshops Act of 1891, which gave the Home Secretary powers, promptly utilized, to issue special regulations for trades that he scheduled as dangerous. There are now forty-three of these dangerous trades, each with its own code of rules.

PART THREE

1914–1939

CHAPTER XIV

Industry and Trade

DECLINING AND EXPANDING INDUSTRIES

Most of the forces that have moulded Britain's economy in the two decades since the war were already becoming conspicuous before 1914. The decline of the birth rate, the growth of foreign competition, the supersession of free competition by combination, and the reaction from *laissez faire*—to mention only a few—did not suddenly affect our economic system for the first time after the war. Nevertheless the most far-sighted observer of our economic situation on the eve of the war could scarcely have anticipated the *scale* of the adjustments that have since been imposed on British industry and trade. An examination of the changes in the industrial distribution of the population provides, perhaps, the best introduction to a study of the main trends in British industry since the war. These changes are illustrated in the accompanying tables. The first gives the census numbers engaged, in the years 1911, 1921 and 1931, in some of the principal British industries, divided according to whether they have expanded or contracted since the war. As these figures include the unemployed, however, they do not show accurately the changes in the distribution of available employment. The second table repairs this defect by showing the changes in the number of insured workers actually employed, in June 1923 and June 1938, in various industries, which are again divided into two groups, of expanding and contracting trades.

It is clear that an immense industrial transference of labour has taken place in the last two decades. Industries such as coal, iron and steel, cotton, wool, shipbuilding and many branches of engineering, which had come to be regarded before the war as the very foundation of Britain's industrial prosperity, have not only declined in relative importance, but have suffered a large absolute diminution of employment. The expanding industries—building, road

INDUSTRIAL DISTRIBUTION OF POPULATION, GREAT BRITAIN

Industry	Number of persons engaged, including those out of work (in thousands)				
	England and Wales			Scotland[1]	
	1911	1921	1931	1921	1931
Expanding:					
Building, decorating and contracting	861	758	1,048	68	102
Woodworking, furniture, etc.	242	228	302	42	45
Bricks, pottery and glass	171	177	214	12	15
Vehicles	197	357	382	18	20
Rubber	24	46	54	8	10
Road transport... ...	291	297	456	38	53
Electrical apparatus ...	80	166	286	10	10
Silk	32	33	70	1	2
Hosiery	59	80	110	15	22
Food, drink, tobacco ...	486	541	717	82	93
Paper making, printing, etc.	285	340	425	46	52
Chemicals, paint, oils ...	133	198	211	18	21
Gas, water, electricity ...	109	163	228	16	17
Local government ...	489	689	911	84	108
Personal service (hotels, restaurants, domestic)...	2,452	2,025	2,406	200	223
Contracting:					
Agriculture	1,230	1,124	1,018	183	177
Coal mining	971	1,133	1,030	163	133
Iron and steel ...	166	239	198	51	37
Engineering and ship-building	637	887	761	245	171
Cotton	628	596	571	25	20
Wool and worsted ...	233	237	228	22	20
Flax, hemp and jute ...	30	27	24	59	54
Lace	44	24	16	3	3
Railways	455	549	496	73	60
Water transport ...	284	330	310	41	50
All industries	16,284	17,178	18,853	2,191	2,221

[1] Comparable figures relating to 1911 are not available for Scotland.

transport, the distributive trades, electrical manufacturing, motor engineering and the rest—have provided more than enough new jobs to compensate for the curtailed employment in the contracting industries, but not enough to prevent a persistently heavy burden of unemployment. Between June 1923 and June 1938 the number of insured workers employed in the expanding group rose from

INDUSTRIAL DISTRIBUTION OF EMPLOYMENT IN THE UNITED KINGDOM, 1923–38[1]

Industry	Estimated Number of Insured Persons aged 16 to 64 in employment in June 1938	Percentage Increase (+) or Decrease (−) since June 1923
Expanding :		
Distributive trades	1,911,218	+ 64·5
Building and contracting ...	1,141,203	+ 63·2
General engineering	591,430	+ 16·8
Hotel, restaurant, etc., service	394,877	+ 71·7
Road transport	385,312	+ 73·1
Motor and aircraft engineering	360,836	+ 109·4
Local government service ...	317,323	+ 49·8
Electrical manufacturing ...	275,120	+ 128·7
Printing, publishing and bookbinding	268,564	+ 27·6
Gas, water and electricity supply	205,177	+ 34·2
Tailoring	190,776	+ 8·5
Laundries, dyeing, etc. ...	168,629	+ 69·5
Professional services	165,608	+ 61·7
Bread, biscuit and cake-making	163,446	+ 15·7
Furniture making	132,422	+ 57·3
Entertainments, sport, etc. ...	127,731	+ 150·5
Contracting :		
Coal mining	701,713	− 41·5
Cotton manufacturing ...	251,184	− 43·2
Woollen and worsted manufacturing	164,731	− 32·3
Iron and steel	152,965	− 17·7
Railway service (non-permanent workers)	149,508	− 14·0
Shipbuilding	139,968	− 4·8
Dock, harbour, etc. service ...	118,270	− 14·6
Boot and shoe manufacturing	111,792	− 11·9
All industries	12,075,268	+ 21·5

[1] *Ministry of Labour Gazette*, December 1938, pp. 486, 487.

6,449,000 to 9,630,000, *i.e.* by 49·3 per cent.; in the contracting group numbers fell from 3,740,000 to 2,671,000, *i.e.* by 28·6 per cent. A significant feature of this industrial redistribution of labour is that the declining group comprises mainly the staple export industries, while most of the expanding trades are engaged solely or predominantly in catering for the home market. The result has been to reduce markedly the relative importance of overseas trade in the economic life of Britain, as is brought out in the following table.

OVERSEAS TRADE IN RELATION TO NATIONAL INCOME[1]

Year	Net National Income (in million £)	Exports of U.K. Produce		Retained Imports	
		Amount (in million £)	Percentage of National Income	Amount (in million £)	Percentage of National Income
1911	2,062	454	22·0	577	28·0
1924	3,600	801	22·2	1,137	31·6
1929	3,868	729	18·9	1,111	28·7
1932	3,313	365	11·0	651	19·6
1935	3,960	426	10·8	70[illegible]	17·7

The decline in the employment available in the old staple industries may be attributed to a variety of influences. Shrinkage of exports, occasioned by the interruption of British trade during the war, by the growth of economic nationalism and by the pressure of competition from abroad; changes in fashion and the development of substitutes; the "saving" of labour by technical progress; these, and many other factors, have played their part in curtailing employment in this group of industries. The interaction of these tendencies may be illustrated from the recent history of the older staple industries.

Britain's coal output has never returned to the pre-war peak, reached in 1913, of 287 million tons, the best year since the war being 1923, when temporary prosperity was restored to the coal industry by the occupation of the Ruhr.

[1] The statistics of National Income in column 2 are taken from C. Clark, *National Income and Outlay*, p. 94, and relate to home-produced income (less government income) plus income from overseas investments.

Since then the general trend of output has been downwards, with short-period upward spurts in years of improving general trade, such as 1929 and 1933–37. Coal exports have dwindled, and in 1938 were only half their pre-war amount. Practically all the countries possessing coal

BRITISH COAL INDUSTRY

Year	Output (in million tons)	Exports (in million tons)	Numbers employed (in thousands)	Annual output per person employed (in tons)
1913	287	73	1,105	260
1923	276	79	1,203	229
1929	258	60	957	270
1932	209	39	819	255
1936	229	35	767	298
1937	241	40	791	304
1938	228	36	†	†

† Not available.

deposits, with the exception of Britain, have increased their rate of production since the war, so reducing their dependence on British exports. World production of coal grew from 1,078 million tons in 1909–13, when the British share was 25 per cent., to 1,280 million tons in 1937, when Britain's contribution had shrunk to 19 per cent. Moreover the countries that still have to import coal take a larger proportion of their supplies from Britain's competitors, especially Germany and Poland, than they did before the war. The demand for coal, on the part of both home and foreign consumers, has been affected also by the extended use of competitive fuels and by the progress made in fuel economy. The world's navies were being rapidly converted to oil-firing before the war, but merchant shipping was slower in turning to the new fuel. In 1914 96·6 per cent. of the tonnage registered at Lloyd's was still coal fired. By 1935 the proportion had dropped to 51 per cent., and will doubtless continue to diminish, since about three-quarters of the shipping tonnage constructed in recent years have been fitted with diesel engines. The Welsh steam coal trade, especially dependent on the bunker demand, has been severely hit by this substitution of oil for coal.

The industrial demand for coal has been affected by the great extension of the use of electric power since the war. Pre-war statistics relating to the amount of electric power used in industry are unfortunately too defective to allow of any satisfactory comparison of the relative importance of mechanical and electrical power now and before 1914. But in the short period 1924–30, when the total power available for use in industry (excluding electricity supply undertakings) increased from 13,403,300 h.p. to 15,322,600 h.p., *i.e.* by 14·3 per cent., the total capacity of electric motors grew from 6,658,600 h.p. to 9,286,100 h.p., *i.e.* by 39·4 per cent.; while mechanically applied power diminished from 6,744,700 h.p. to 6,063,500 h.p., *i.e.* by 10·1 per cent. The degree of electricification varies widely from industry to industry; in the engineering group 95 per cent. of the available power was electrical in 1930, while in the textile industries the proportion was only 38·4 per cent. As some compensation for this diminished industrial demand for coal, British electricity supply undertakings increased their consumption of coal and coke from 6,348,000 tons in 1920–21 to 12,885,000 tons in 1936–37. Owing to fuel economies, however, the coal consumed in the generation of electricity increased nothing like so rapidly as the number of units generated, which grew from 3,890 million kilowatt-hours to 20,524 million over the same period. Thus a five-fold increase in the output of electricity was obtained from a twofold increase in coal and coke consumption.[1]

In the gas industry also improvements in technical efficiency have made possible a considerable increase in the output of gas with practically no increase in the quantity of coal consumed. In 1913 the average ton of coal carbonized

[1] A small quantity of oil and gas is also used in electricity generation, but this does not materially affect the comparison between increased electricity production and increased coal consumption.

in gas works yielded 13·2 thousand cubic feet of gas; by 1936 the yield had been raised to 16·9 thousand cubic feet. Another important coal-using industry, iron and steel manufacture, has also learned how to economize further in fuel consumption, especially by utilizing the gases, formerly wasted, that are generated in coking ovens and blast furnaces. In 1913, for example, nearly two-thirds of Britain's coking ovens were of the bee-hive type, not permitting of the recovery of gas and other by-products. These have now almost entirely disappeared. The increased use of scrap, in place of pig iron, in steel-making furnaces, has greatly reduced the consumption of coke in blast furnaces. In 1913, when Britain produced 10,260,000 tons of pig iron and 7,664,000 tons of steel, the iron and steel industries are estimated to have consumed 31·4 million tons of coal. This had dropped to 23·3 million tons in 1937, when we produced 8,497,000 tons of pig iron and 12,964,000 tons of steel.

Finally, not only have these various influences combined to curtail the output of British coal, but in addition the mechanization of mining has reduced the amount of labour employed in raising the average ton of coal, as is shown in the table on p. 283; so that employment in the coal industry has diminished much more than the aggregate coal output. Compared with other European countries and the United States, Britain has been somewhat slow in installing mechanical equipment for mining, owing partly to the less favourable geological structure of the British seams. At the beginning of the present century a quarter of America's bituminous coal output was cut by machinery, while in Britain only 1½ per cent. was so obtained. By 1924 the percentage of British coal cut by machinery had risen to 19, but in the meantime the corresponding American percentage had risen to nearly 70. Mechanization in British mines has made much more rapid progress in the nineteen-thirties, and in 1937 57 per cent. of our coal output was machine-cut. Mechanical coal conveyors have also been installed at an increasing rate in recent years, 51 per cent. of the total output being mechanically conveyed in 1937, compared with only 17 per cent. in 1930.

The general trend of employment in the iron and steel industry has been downward since the war, though it has fluctuated within a wide range owing to the industry's extreme sensitiveness to changes in the general level of economic activity. In the pig-iron section this curtailment of employment is partly attributable to the permanent contraction of output since the war. Even in the best boom year, 1937, the make of pig iron was only 8,497,000 tons, compared with 10,260,000 in 1913, and in years of slump, such as 1931–32, it did not reach 4 million tons. The increased use of scrap in steel-making furnaces, and the greatly diminished exports of pig iron, account for this contraction of British pig-iron production. Further, technical advances, such as the mechanical charging of furnaces, have immensely increased the output of pig iron per man employed. Hence although the aggregate output of pig iron in 1937 was 14·2 per cent. greater than in 1923, employment among insured workers in the pig-iron industry was 35·6 per cent. less. Except in years of severe depression, Britain's steel output has been greater since the war than in 1913, and in 1937 it reached the record figure of 12,964,000 tons. Nevertheless, owing to the increase in the average capacity of steel furnaces, to the adoption of mechanical charging and to other developments in the arts of metallurgy, which have effected striking economies in labour, employment in the heavy steel industry has tended to decline. It is true that in the peak year, 1937, employment among insured steel workers did return temporarily to a level slightly exceeding (by 1·6 per cent.) that of 1923. But in order to achieve this the output of steel had to be nearly 53 per cent. greater than in the earlier year. And in every year other than 1937 the heavy steel industry has employed fewer workers than in 1923.

The cotton industry, faced with a permanent shrinkage of demand, has been almost continuously in the doldrums since the war. None of the older staples was so dependent as the cotton industry on overseas trade; for about three-quarters of its output, in value, is estimated to have been exported in the prosperous years immediately preceding the war; and none has suffered so severely from the loss of overseas markets since 1918. The accompanying table brings out some of the major features of the decline of this great

BRITISH COTTON INDUSTRY[1]

Year	Production of yarn (million lbs.)	Production of piece goods (million square yards)	Exports of yarn (million lbs.)	Exports of piece goods (million square yards)
1912	1,983	8,050(a)	244	6,913(a)
1924	1,395	6,026	163	4,444
1930	1,047	3,320	137	2,407
1935	1,228	3,386	142	1,948
1937	1,350	— (b)	159	1,922

(a) The figures for 1912 are in linear yards. Since a linear yard, in the post-war years, when both forms of measurement were available, was equivalent to slightly more than one square yard, the contrast between the pre-war and post-war position would probably be heightened if the former were expressed in square yards.

(b) Not available.

industry. At first Lancashire believed that its idle mills would once more hum with activity as soon as the temporary dislocation caused by the war had passed. But by 1925 there were ominous signs that this optimistic outlook would not be justified by events; for the world's consumption of raw cotton had then regained its pre-war level, yet Lancashire was still producing and exporting much less than in 1913. From 1925 until the onset of the world depression, the position of the British cotton industry continued to deteriorate, although in the rest of the world cotton production and exports of cotton manufactures showed a modest expansion. The world slump, with its huge contraction of

[1] *Britain in Recovery*, p. 458. A few slight emendations have been made in the figures of production to make them agree with those of the censuses of production in 1930 and 1935.

international trade, dealt a further staggering blow to Lancashire's staple. A diminutive but welcome recovery of export markets followed the abandonment of the gold standard in 1931, but the general trend of piece-goods exports has been downward again since 1932. In 1938 our exports of cotton yarns had dropped to the lowest level since the cotton famine of the 'sixties (with the single exception of 1918), and our exports of cotton piece-goods had reverted to the level that prevailed in the early 'fifties.

These grievous losses in Lancashire's markets have been due primarily to the growth of domestic cotton industries in countries that formerly imported a large part of their requirements. This tendency towards national self- sufficiency in cotton manufactures was apparent before 1914, but the curtailment of Lancashire's exports during the war gave it a great impetus, which, with the aid of protectionist measures, has continued unabated since the war. But besides suffering from the shrinkage of the volume of world trade in cotton goods, Britain has had to accept a smaller share in the trade that remains. Japan's exports of cotton piece-goods, which in 1910–13 averaged only 156 million linear yards a year, compared with Britain's 6,665 million, have expanded at a remarkable rate. They reached 1,791 million square yards in 1929 and 2,725 million in 1935, since when they have slightly declined. In quantity of cotton exports, though not in value, Japan has out-distanced Britain since 1933. Until 1929 the other chief cotton manufacturing countries, with the exception of Germany, had raised their cotton exports, at Britain's expense, above the level of 1913. But they also, like Britain, have found their external cotton trade declining since 1929. It is in the Indian market, which, before 1914, provided by far the largest single outlet for Lancashire's cotton goods, that the most overwhelming losses have been sustained. In the twelve months ended March 31st, 1914, India imported 3,159 million linear yards of cotton piece-goods, practically all of which (3,068 million) came from the United Kingdom. Despite Lancashire's opposition, India has developed a great cotton industry of her own, so that in the year ended March 31st, 1937, she imported only 764 million yards, of which 334 million were bought from Britain and 417 million from Japan. Thus Britain's annual sales of piece-goods in India have fallen by the stupendous amount of nearly 2½ million yards since 1913. In China, our second largest market before the war, and in other Eastern countries, Lancashire has suffered heavy losses. The market for British exports of cotton manufactures has been maintained best in the dominions and colonies, especially since quotas were applied to textile imports into the latter in 1934.

As a result of this immense shrinkage of our former markets for cotton goods, the character of the Lancashire cotton industry is being transformed. Spinning firms are selling a smaller proportion of their output of yarn to the weavers, and a growing proportion to other industries, such as the manufacture of hosiery and of rubber, whose demand for yarn has been expanding. Of the cotton yarn consumed at home in 1935, nearly one-fifth was utilized outside the cotton industry. Weaving firms, on the other hand, are turning more and more to the weaving of rayon and mixed fabrics, for which the demand is increasing. The mutual dependence of spinners and weavers is thus becoming weaker.

The wool textile industry has been subject, in a less degree, to the same broad influences as the cotton industry. In a world bent on national self-sufficiency, each country has tended to prefer the products of its own industries. The European market for British woollen manufactures was already dwindling before the war, and this tendency has continued. But from 1914 until 1924 compensating markets were found in the Far East, where European dress was being rapidly adopted. Japan had in 1924 become the largest single customer for British woollen and worsted tissues, and China was not far behind. Since then

Japan has developed her own woollen industry, reduced her purchases of British tissues almost to vanishing point, and competed successfully in China and other Eastern markets. The Australian market for tissues has also practically disappeared, and our exports to the United States, and to a smaller extent to Canada, have been markedly reduced. To one country only, namely South Africa, has there been an appreciable expansion of woollen and worsted exports. In contrast to the shrinkage of our overseas trade in tissues and yarns, British exports of "tops" have been well maintained, and in 1935–36 were distinctly above the level of 1913. Since a good half of the pre-war output of woollen

BRITISH WOOLLEN AND WORSTED INDUSTRY[1]

Year	Production (Great Britain)			Exports (United Kingdom)		
	Tops (in million lbs.)	Yarns (in million lbs.)	Tissues (in million square yds.)	Tops (in million lbs.)	Yarns (in million lbs.)	Tissues (in million square yds.)
1912	304	559	550	45	88	224
1924	286	554	443	41	66	217
1930	224	386	315	29	50	114
1935	307	543	408	56	51	110

and worsted manufactures was sold in the home market, the shrinkage of overseas markets has had a much less devastating effect on the wool-using trades than on the cotton industry. The output of the combing and spinning sections was practically the same in 1935 as in 1912, though the yardage of tissues was appreciably reduced. As in the cotton industry, spinners have found a growing market for yarns outside their own industry.

The industries that have expanded in the last twenty years fall into several distinct groups. Some are old-established trades that have grown primarily in response to the increase of population. These include grain-milling, the production of bread, biscuits and cakes, the drink trades,

[1] Based on *Census of Production Reports* and on *Annual Statements of the Trade of the United Kingdom*.

and tailoring. A second group comprises the newer industries, on whose products an increasing proportion of the nation's income is being spent and in which a growing proportion of the population is being employed. Familiar examples are motor and aircraft engineering, motor road transport, the manufacture of artificial silk, and the many branches of the electrical trades. Many, though not all, of these thriving trades, are engaged in producing what may be loosely described as luxuries. In the main, the expanding demand for cars, wireless sets, cinema seats and the like, is simply a symptom of economic progress; as the real wealth per head of population advances there is naturally a tendency to spend relatively less on bread and relatively more on circuses. But this tendency has been accentuated in recent decades by the fall of the birth rate, which has had the effect of reducing the number of dependants maintained by the average occupied person, and has thus increased the proportion of income available for expenditure on comforts and luxuries.

OCCUPIED POPULATION OF GREAT BRITAIN (in '000s)

Year	Males			Females		
	Total population	Total occupied	Per cent.	Total population	Total occupied	Per cent.
1901	17,902	11,548	64·5	19,098	4,763	24·9
1911	19,754	12,930	65·5	21,077	5,424	25·7
1921	20,423	13,656	66·8	22,346	5,701	25·5
1931	21,459	14,790	68·8	23,337	6,265	26·8

In a third division of the expanding group, we find a number of old industries that have been growing, for one reason or another, more rapidly than population. Britain's two largest industries, the distributive trades and the building and allied trades, fall into this class. They have provided a very considerable part of the additional employment since the war. The first of these has grown in response to various stimuli. The geographical redistribution of the population since the war has necessitated the opening of new shops in the towns and suburban housing estates to which population has flowed, while most of the older shops in the areas from which there has been some exodus remain in business. This tendency has been most marked in the retail trades selling goods with demands regularly recurring at short intervals, such as groceries, meat, newspapers, confectionery, tobacco and the like.[1] The rise of new industries has been accompanied by an extension of the distributive mechanism; dealers in cars, petrol, wireless sets and so forth, have established themselves in great numbers. Further, the services incidental to retailing have tended to multiply, so that the number of workers employed by the average dealer is rising. Customers nowadays expect all but the minutest purchases to be delivered to their homes; the extension of credit buying involves some increase in the number of book-keepers employed; and for many durable consumption goods—wireless sets, vacuum cleaners, washing machines—after-sales service has to be provided by dealers.

Building and contracting, together with closely related industries such as stone quarrying and the making of bricks, tiles and artificial stone, increased in size by nearly two-thirds between 1923 and 1938. From the end of the war up to March 31st, 1938, some 3,666,000 houses, roughly equal to 45 per cent. of the number available at the beginning of the period, had been built in England and Wales, of which 1,011,000 were built by local authorities and the remainder by private enterprise. Since 1934 the pace of building has been well over 300,000 houses a year. It may, at first sight, be a matter for surprise that we should undertake this sustained housing effort at a time when the fall of the birth rate has brought our population almost to a stationary condition. But the demand for houses depends

[1] Cf. P. Ford, "Decentralization and Changes in the Number of Shops, 1901–1931," *E.J.*, 1936, p. 359, and "Excessive Competition in the Retail Trades—Changes in the Numbers of Shops, 1901–1931," *E.J.*, 1935, p. 501.

not so much on the rate of increase of the total population as on that of the adult population; and the annual increase of the latter has been greater in the period since the war than ever before. Moreover since it is impossible to transport

AGE-COMPOSITION OF BRITAIN'S POPULATION

Year	Persons under 20 years			Persons of 20 years and over		
	Number	Proportion of total population %	Change in number since previous census	Number	Proportion of total population %	Change in number since previous census
1901	15,743,019	42·6	+ 769,305	21,256,927	57·4	+ 3,202,869
1911	16,376,862	40·1	+ 633,843	24,454,535	59·9	+ 3,197,608
1921	15,921,321	37·2	− 455,541	26,847,875	62·8	+ 2,393,340
1931	14,698,865	32·8	− 1,222,456	30,096,492	67·2	+ 3,248,617

houses from declining to developing areas, internal migration, which has been very pronounced since the war, has required a large amount of new building. Further, owing to the drastic curtailment of building during the war, the housing shortage, already evident before 1914, was greatly aggravated; in 1921 the shortage was probably in the region of a million houses. Since 1932 building on an unprecedented scale has been induced by the combination of lower building costs and lower rates of interest, and also by the local authorities' slum clearance programme, under which, in the five years ending March 31st, 1938, 168,984 houses had been demolished, and 186,755 replacement houses built, in England and Wales.

The industrial redistribution of Britain's population has involved also its geographical redistribution, for, generally speaking, the expanding trades have not been located in the older industrial areas. Some broad indication of the changes in the regional distribution of employment is given in the following table. Whereas in 1923 London and the southern and midland regions provided 46·6 per cent. of the total employment in the United Kingdom, by 1938 their share had grown to 53·9 per cent. Britain's industrial centre of gravity has thus been persistently moving southwards. Coal, by far the most powerful localizing influence in the nineteenth century, has lost much of its magnetic

GEOGRAPHICAL DISTRIBUTION OF THE EMPLOYED POPULATION[1]

Region	Percentage of employed (aged 16–64) in each region			
	June 1923	June 1929	June 1932	June 1935
London ...	18·9	20·7	22·3	22·4
South-Eastern...	5·9	6·8	7·5	8·4
South-Western	6·8	7·2	7·8	7·5
Midlands ...	15·0	15·1	15·1	15·6
North-Eastern	11·2	10·7	10·3	10·4
North-Western	16·8	16·7	16·1	14·4
Northern ...	6·6	5·9	5·1	5·5
Scotland ...	11·0	10·5	10·0	10·0
Wales	5·8	4·4	3·9	3·9
Northern Ireland	2·1	2·1	2·0	1·8
Total	100	100	100	100

"pull," electric power being now readily available in most parts of the country. For the new lighter trades that have developed so rapidly since the war, proximity to large and prosperous consumers' markets appears to have replaced access to supplies of fuel as the main factor determining the choice of industrial location. The populous and prosperous area of Greater London offers, for the luxury consumption goods produced by many of these trades, a much more attractive market than the older industrial regions, haunted by protracted depression and lacking in well-to-do customers. Other factors also have contributed to the growing industrialization of the south. The relative weakness of trade unionism in the south is a strong recommendation for southern sites to employers who fear labour disputes. The high poundage of local rates in the areas suffering from severe unemployment may also have repelled firms selecting

[1] P E P, *Report on the Location of Industry in Great Britain*, p. 45.

new factory sites, but this factor has certainly been of minor importance since the de-rating scheme of 1928 came into operation.

UNEMPLOYMENT SINCE THE WAR

The feature of Britain's post-war economy on which its critics have mainly focussed their attention, and about which an incessant stream of literature has been published, is the persistence of an abnormally high level of unemployment. It is not easy to compare the magnitude of the unemployment problem since the war with that of pre-war decades; for no comprehensive statistics relating to unemployment were available before 1921. But among trade unionists, who may not, however, have been a fully representative sample of the total working population, the range of unemployment in the period 1850–1914 lay between 1 or 2 per cent. at the peaks of trade booms and 10 or 11 per cent. in years of general depression. The average of good and bad years was about 4½ per cent. Since 1920, however, even in the best years, the irreducible minimum of unemployment among insured workers has been about 10 per cent.; and in the worst years it has risen to over 20 per cent. The average for the seventeen years 1921–37 was a little over 14 per cent. The most important single cause of this immense increase in unemployment has undoubtedly been the protracted decline of Britain's staple export trades. Throughout the last two decades it is in this group of industries that a disproportionate amount of unemployment has been concentrated. The supply of labour available for employment in these industries has been steadily reduced, the number of new entrants having year by year fallen short of the losses through death, retirement and transference to other trades. But unfortunately the demand for labour in this contracting group has continued to shrink about as rapidly as the supply, so that the pool of surplus labour has persisted undiminished. Thus, as the following table shows, although the declining industries, as a group, have lost about one million insured workers between 1923 and 1938, they still suffer from an exceptional burden of unemployment.

UNEMPLOYMENT IN THE DECLINING AND EXPANDING INDUSTRIES

	July 1923	July 1929	July 1932	July 1937	July 1938
	'000's	'000's	'000's	'000's	'000's
Declining industries :					
Number insured ...	4,317	3,758	3,649	3,360	3,344
Number unemployed...	577	595	1,253	484	673
Percentage unemployed	13·4	15·8	34·3	14·4	20·1
Expanding industries :					
Number insured ...	7,186	8,336	9,159	10,337	10,776
Number unemployed	737	582	1,668	902	1,146
Percentage unemployed	10·3	7·0	18·2	8·7	10·6
All industries :					
Number insured ...	11,503	12,094	12,808	13,697	14,120
Number unemployed...	1,324	1,177	2,921	1,386	1,819
Percentage unemployed	11·5	9·7	22·8	10·1	13·3

We must not, however, overlook the fact that in the expanding trades also, which for the most part have not had to adapt themselves to a long-drawn-out shrinkage of overseas markets, unemployment has been well above the level that was considered " normal " before the war. To some extent this can be attributed to the recruitment, on a casual basis, of large numbers of general unskilled workers into such industries as building, public works contracting, highway maintenance and the like. These industries have provided insurable employment, at one time or another, for far more workers than they can employ simultaneously even when business is most active. They have attached to themselves an " industrial reserve," which appears to be swelling in numbers. Thus in the summer of 1938, when the building and contracting industry was employing more men than it had ever done before, it had nevertheless about 250,000 unemployed, over a sixth of the total number of insured workers in the industry. Another 60,000 unemployed, mainly navvies and other general labourers, were in the local government service, these being nearly a sixth of the insured workers employed by local authorities.

Unemployment in the expanding industries has been affected also by certain general causes that have conduced to a higher level of unemployment since the war. In the first place, it seems probable that demands are becoming more fickle and unstable, since a diminishing proportion of the national income is being expended upon necessaries and elementary comforts, for which the demands are relatively steady. In a progressive society, with rising standards of living, we can expect a secular tendency towards an increase in that part of aggregate unemployment which is attributable to fluctuations in consumers' demands. Secondly, there is good reason for supposing that "technological unemployment" has become more acute in recent years; for mechanization and rationalization have been proceeding apace over a wide range of industry. Some general impression of the pace of this technical progress can be derived from recent estimates, based on data collected in the censuses of production, of changes in physical production. The physical output per operative employee[1] in a broad group of factory and other trades, employing altogether some five million workers in 1935, is estimated to have increased by 25 per cent. in the short period 1930–35.[2] Between 1924 and 1930 the rate of increase of real output per operative employee was much lower, namely 7 per cent. And for the pre-war decade, we have seen earlier that the evidence points to a stationariness of physical productivity per head.[3]

Because the industries that have borne the brunt of unemployment since the war are strongly localized, depression has lain heavily over certain regions, of which the most sorely

[1] Excluding administrative employees.

[2] London and Cambridge Economic Service, *Memorandum on Output, Employment and Wages in the United Kingdom, 1924, 1930, 1935*, pp. 2, 3.

[3] See above, p.p. 196, 197.

stricken have been South Wales, Durham and Northumberland, West Cumberland and South-west Scotland, now euphemistically described in official parlance as Special Areas. Besides these officially scheduled "special" regions, mainly engaged in coal mining, heavy iron and steel manufacture and shipbuilding, there were many other areas, notably the cotton towns, whose situation was almost as desperate. Even in 1937, when the re-armament boom had induced a partial recovery of the Special Areas, unemployment in the northern half of England, in Wales and Scotland, was twice as heavy as in the thriving south. It has become abundantly clear that it is no transient dislocation from which these regions are suffering, but a permanent contraction of the local industries on which they have hitherto depended for their livelihood.

GEOGRAPHICAL DISTRIBUTION OF UNEMPLOYMENT, 1929–37

Region	Percentage of unemployment among insured workers aged 16–64		
	July 1929	July 1932	July 1937
London	4·7	13·1	5·5
South-Eastern	3·8	13·1	5·0
South-Western	6·8	16·4	6·2
Midlands	9·5	21·6	7·0
North-Eastern[1]	12·6	30·6	11·3
North-Western[1] ...	12·7	26·3	12·9
Scotland	11·2	29·0	16·1
Wales	18·8	38·1	19·9
Great Britain	9·7	22·9	9·9

A solution of the special unemployment problem in these areas can be sought along two lines: either the surplus local population must migrate to areas offering greater opportunities for employment, or new industries must be induced to settle in the depressed areas. Until quite recently the policy of successive governments has been to rely largely on the first of these methods of adjustment, and not to interfere

[1] The areas of these regions have been modified since 1936 by the creation of an additional Northern region.

in any way with the localization of industry. Between 1921 and 1937 it is estimated that some 650,000 people (including dependants as well as wage-earners) have moved out of the Special Areas. Since 1928 industrial transference has been facilitated by the Ministry of Labour, which has given some financial assistance towards the cost of movement: in ten years, about 250,000 workers have been transferred with the Ministry's help. Nevertheless the rate of migration has not been enough to secure an absolute reduction in the number of insured workers available for employment in the depressed areas, so that unemployment has persisted at an intolerably high level. Impelled by the grim tragedy of the decaying areas, the government introduced, in the Special Areas (Development and Improvement) Act of 1934, a small but significant departure from the traditional non-interventionist policy regarding the location of industry. Two commissioners were appointed to organize measures "designed to facilitate the economic development and social improvement" of the Special Areas. Handicapped at first by inadequacy of funds and lack of powers, they have financed the development of three great trading estates at Treforest, Team Valley and Hillington. These are now being tenanted by firms engaged in a variety of the lighter trades. In 1937 the commissioners' powers were greatly strengthened by legislation authorizing them to make grants by way of remissions from rent, rates and taxes.

The trade cycle, temporarily interrupted by the war, has since resumed its sway. Some of its manifestations since the war are recorded in the accompanying diagram. Following the peace of 1918, a brief boom developed, stimulated by the need to renew worn-out equipment, to replace destroyed capital, and to build up stocks to normal peace-time levels. It was supported by a violent currency inflation, about which more will be said in a later chapter. The heavy industries were exceptionally busy, and the tonnage of merchant ships launched from British yards in 1920

INDUSTRIAL FLUCTUATIONS 1913–37

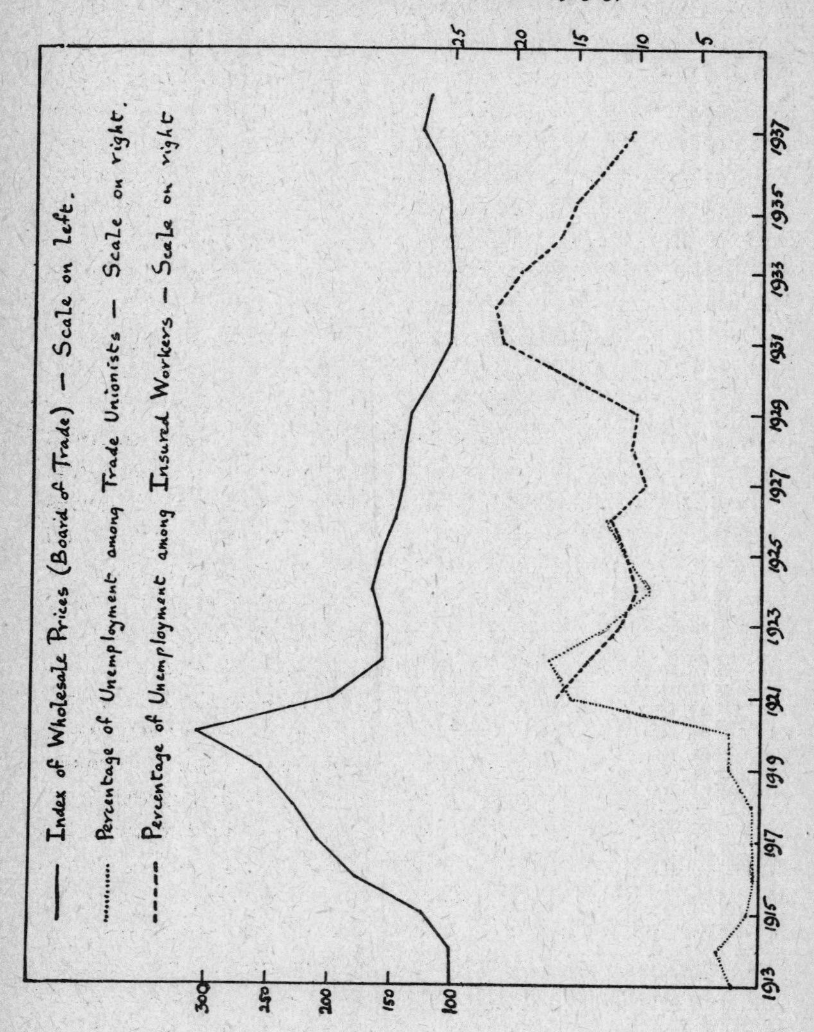

was over two millions, a record output. Unemployment, as indicated by the trade union returns, averaged only 2 per cent. in 1919 and the first half of 1920. Prices reached their peak in the spring of 1920 and then began to descend, slowly at first but at breakneck speed by the end of the year, and continued to fall until the middle of 1922. As prices fell, unemployment mounted until, aggravated by a three months' strike in the coal industry, it reached over 23 per cent. in May 1921. From the spring of 1922 trade began to recover at a somewhat leisurely pace, receiving a temporary fillip in 1923 and 1924 from the occupation of the Ruhr. The year 1924 has since come to be regarded as the first reasonably normal post-war year for British industry and trade. Prices had recovered a little from the low level to which deflation had thrust them in 1922; after an orgy of inflation, currencies were being stabilized in other countries, notably Germany, and trade was less disturbed by unstable foreign exchanges; the heavy iron and steel, engineering and shipbuilding industries, which had been acutely depressed as the result of over-expansion during the war, were fairly busy once more; and the aggregate real national income is estimated by Bowley and Stamp to have returned by 1924 to the level of 1911, though real income per head was 5 to 10 per cent. lower than in the earlier year.[1] On the other side of the picture, however, unemployment, at 10·3 per cent. in 1924, was still greatly in excess of what older generations considered a normal level, though we now regard this figure as a minimum attainable only in years of exceptional industrial activity. The volume of Britain's exports, too, was in 1924 still about one fifth less than in 1913.

From 1924 to 1929 world production and trade were expanding, the former at a surprisingly high rate. Britain shared in this general recovery, but the rate of her economic progress was much less than that of most other countries.

[1] *The National Income, 1924*, p. 56.

According to the Board of Trade's index of production, Britain's industries were producing about 12 per cent. more in 1929 than in 1924; whereas over the same period the United States had increased their output by 24 per cent., France by 29 per cent. and Germany by 47 per cent. The volume of the United Kingdom's exports of domestic produce grew by 8·7 per cent. between 1924 and 1929, but the British share in world exports shrank from 12·94 per cent. to 10·86. Why Britain should have made so little progress in these years of general world economic expansion has been a subject of keen controversy, into which we cannot enter here. Many diseases were diagnosed in the body economic, and as many remedies prescribed. It is generally agreed that our export industries were handicapped by the over-valuation of the pound sterling in the foreign-exchange market from the end of 1924 onwards. This over-valuation certainly made it more difficult to sell British coal abroad, and therefore helped to provoke the catastrophic coal dispute and general strike of 1926, which dealt a further blow to our external trade. British monetary policy at this period can be held responsible also, as is argued in a later chapter, for the maintenance of interest rates at a level that certainly did not encourage business enterprise. Further, the lowering of the domestic price level, which was needed to remove the handicap of an externally over-valued currency, was rendered difficult by the inflexibility of wage rates. This rigidity of wages has commonly been attributed to the greater strength of trade unionism, compared with pre-war years, to the effect of unemployment insurance in preventing standard wage rates from being undermined by the pressure of unemployment, and to the extension of authoritarian control over wages by means of Trade Board legislation.

Foreign critics discerned in Britain's unhappy economic position symptoms of national decadence, of a decline of that spirit of enterprise and innovation which had given

Britain the industrial leadership of the world.[1] The Balfour Committee, which could not be suspected of any bias in favour of this view, found that some of our staple industries, notably coal, coke, iron and steel, were lagging behind their foreign rivals in technique and organization and were in need of re-conditioning and re-equipment. They admitted that in Great Britain the process of " rationalization " had not proceeded so rapidly as in some of the principal competing countries. On the application of science to industry they expressed the following opinion: " Before British industries, taken as a whole, can hope to reap from scientific research the full advantage which it appears to yield to some of their most formidable trade rivals, nothing less than a revolution is needed in their general outlook on science; and in the case of some industries at least, this change of attitude is bound to be slow and difficult, in view of our old and deeply rooted industrial traditions."[2]

Mildly booming conditions prevailed in the years 1927–29, although the general trend of prices was slightly downwards. The capital market was busily engaged in transferring funds from the pockets of hopeful investors to a great variety of concerns, prominent among which were companies manufacturing, or proposing to manufacture, gramophones and radios, artificial silk, films and automatic machines. In 1928 the public subscribed £115 million to some 270 issues made by old and new companies. Five years later the market value of this capital was only £60 million, the slump having intervened and mortality taken its toll of the feebler infant companies (100 of the 221 new companies that made public issues in 1928 had been wound up by April 1933).[3] By the end of 1929 there were unmistakable signs of that intense economic depression which for

[1] e.g., A. Siegfried, *England's Crisis*, p. 58 *et seq.*

[2] *Final Report of the Committee on Industry and Trade* (1929), p. 218.

[3] See " The Results of the 1928 New Issue Boom," *Economic Journal*, 1931, p. 577, and R. A. Harris, " Re-Analysis of the 1928 New Issue Boom," *Economic Journal*, 1933, p. 459.

the next three or four years had the whole world in its grip. Its symptoms were at first more evident abroad than in Britain. The collapse of paper values in the New York stock market in September 1929 was a spectacular harbinger of the slump; a few countries, including Australia and Brazil, embarrassed by the steep fall in the prices of their agricultural exports, had already suspended the gold standard in 1929; the precariously poised German economy, which had hitherto been bolstered up by the flow of American funds, now no longer available, had suffered from shrinking production and mounting unemployment since the middle of 1929. Britain's sharing in this cyclical depression was not, however, long delayed. Throughout 1930, 1931 and the first half of 1932 we were sliding lower into the trough of depression. More than one-fifth of the insured population was out of work in 1931 and 1932, compared with only one-tenth in 1929. Industrial production, as measured by the Board of Trade's index, fell from 111·8 (1924 = 100) to 93·3, *i.e.* by 16½ per cent. This decline of output was very unevenly shared by the various industrial groups. Those mainly engaged in producing goods for export or capital goods—mining, iron and steel manufacture, the textile trades, engineering and shipbuilding—suffered more than the average, while industries catering primarily for consumers in the home market—the food, drink and tobacco trades, boot and shoe manufacture and the like—curtailed their output comparatively little. The slump was more destructive of world trade than of world production, for protectionist measures, defended on a multitude of grounds but having the common effect of strangling international trade, were universally adopted by harassed governments. Britain, typical in this respect, was exporting, in volume, 39 per cent. less in 1932 than in 1929, whereas her industrial output was only 16½ per cent. less. As some compensation for this export loss, the terms of international trade moved strongly in our favour, since the prices of most of the foodstuffs and raw materials we imported dropped much more than those of our mainly manufactured exports.[1]

After 1932, when in most countries the slump reached its nadir, the level of employment and output began to rise, slowly at first and then with gathering speed, until 1937. Over this period unemployment dropped from 21·9 per cent. to 10·6 per cent.; industrial production advanced by no less than 48 per cent., and reached a level 23 per cent. higher than that of the previous best year, 1929. In its earlier stages, recovery owed much to the boom in building, referred to earlier. This stimulus was reinforced later by the re-armament programme, which induced a prodigious expansion of the heavy industries. There were some industries, however, notably the older textile trades, that shared but little in this quickening of economic activity. Without a substantial recovery of their external markets no real prosperity could be restored to these industries. But overseas trade, discouraged by tariffs, import quotas, exchange controls and other regulative devices, failed to expand at anything like the same rate as domestic trade. It is estimated that in 1937, when Britain's industrial output was 23 per cent. greater than in 1929, the volume of her imports was only 9 per cent. greater, and the volume of her exports of domestic produce 13 per cent. less.

[1] London and Cambridge Economic Service, *The Economic Position of Great Britain*, p. 27.

CHAPTER XV

Industrial Reconstruction

THE CHANGING STRUCTURE OF INDUSTRY

Driven by the instability of a rapidly changing world to concert measures for the restoration of economic equilibrium, and encouraged by its experience of government control in war-time, the post-war generation has abandoned most of the cherished economic notions of the Victorians. Monopoly is no longer an ugly monster to be suppressed by every available means. In its modern guises of "rationalization," the approved specific in the nineteen-twenties for most economic ills, and "planning," which replaced "rationalization" in the nineteen-thirties, monopoly has become perfectly respectable. Belief in the virtues of free competition has ceased to be an article of economic faith, both for industrialists and legislators. For we are much more conscious nowadays of the wastes of competition than of its stimulus to efficiency. In industry after industry unrestricted competition has been superseded by planned control. Equally radical has been the change in the general attitude towards State interference in industry and trade. A Mercantilist re-visiting Britain since the war would find himself in familiar surroundings; a Cobdenite would be lost and bewildered. In order to attain such Mercantilist ends as the redressing of an adverse balance of trade and the encouragement of industries of national importance, successive governments have undertaken the regulation of imports by means of tariffs and quotas. Where the method of import regulation is inappropriate, subsidies have been granted, as in agriculture, shipping and aviation. We no longer rely exclusively on the free play of competition and the survival of the fittest in order to ensure that the most efficient forms of organization are adopted. Rationalization is positively encouraged, and sometimes imposed, against the wishes of minorities, by the State. These, and a host of similar, developments are symptomatic of the general discrediting of *laissez faire* in modern times. In the following paragraphs we propose to describe some of the recent measures, public and private, for the control of competition and the regulation of output in a number of leading British industries. Agriculture and transport are left over for treatment in later chapters.

The coal mining industry has been the scene of a pitched battle over the question of compulsory amalgamation. In its report of 1926 the Samuel Commission expressed the view that very substantial economies could be secured from further combination among collieries, but that the initiative of the industry was unlikely to bring about all the amalgamations needed. Though it was opposed to any general measure of compulsory amalgamation, as likely to be mischievous in its effects, it recommended that where desirable amalgamations were held up by dissentient minorities a Coal Commission should be empowered to transfer mining leases from such minorities to the majority group, so that the amalgamation should not be frustrated. The Mining Industry Act of 1926 gave some encouragement to amalgamation by remitting the stamp duties payable on colliery amalgamation schemes and by authorizing the Railway and Canal Commission to coerce unwilling minorities. Its effects on the structure of the industry were, however, slight. Much more significant were the schemes, voluntarily established in 1928 in three coalfields—South Wales, Scotland and the Midlands—for the control of competition. The Welsh scheme provided for the fixing of minimum prices, and the Scottish for the temporary closing down of inefficient collieries, whose owners were to be compensated out of the proceeds of a levy on coal sold in the home market.

The third scheme, commonly known as the Five Counties Scheme, was more elaborate and successful. Those participating in it were allotted basic tonnages and were permitted each month to produce up to a prescribed percentage of these tonnages, fines being imposed on those who exceeded their quotas. Out of the funds raised from these fines and from a levy of 3d. a ton on all coal raised, subsidies were paid on export coal.

The comparative success of this regional coal cartel induced the government to extend its basic principles to the whole coal mining industry under Part I of the Coal Mines Act of 1930. A central council, representing the coal owners, was set up to regulate the output of the industry as a whole. It allocated standard tonnages to each of the districts and, in accordance with its estimates of the demand for coal, prescribed periodically the percentage of the standard tonnage that the districts might produce. Within each district was an executive board, representing the local owners, which divided the standard tonnage of the district between the individual collieries, and fixed minimum prices for all classes of coal. Penalties were imposed on firms exceeding their output quotas or failing to observe the schedule of minimum prices. Quotas were made transferable, so that enterprising, expanding, firms could buy from the less efficient concerns the right to produce more coal. Many amendments have since been made to the details of the scheme, as a result of the experience gained from its operation, but the basic principles of collective control over output and prices remain. Since 1934 the quotas have been applied only to coal produced for sale in the home market, and the export trade has been released from quantitative control. This change was made in order to meet the complaint that export districts, with permitted tonnages exceeding the amounts they could sell in their normal markets, were utilizing this surplus to invade and spoil the inland markets of other districts. Similar difficulties arising from inter-district competition have made it necessary to empower the central council to co-ordinate the district minimum prices.

Part I of the Coal Mines Act of 1930, which put the owners in a position to obtain higher coal prices than they would have done under conditions of unregulated competition, was intended as a temporary palliative, to tide the industry over its difficulties until permanent internal reconstruction had restored it to health. Reconstruction was to be achieved under the provisions of Part II, which set up a Coal Mines Reorganization Commission, with powers to promote, and even to enforce, amalgamation. The coal owners, while accepting the jam of Part I, have been most reluctant to swallow the pill of Part II. They have, in fact, vehemently contended that this particular pill would do the industry more harm than good. Having failed to persuade the owners to move very far in the direction of voluntary amalgamation, the Reorganization Commission began in 1932 to use its statutory powers, and called upon the owners in four areas to prepare amalgamation plans. It encountered the most strenuous opposition. In the hope of securing more support from the owners it therefore modified its policy by encouraging schemes for "partial amalgamation," in which there was some provision for joint control over sales, without complete fusion of the separate concerns. A partial amalgamation scheme of this type was proposed for West Yorkshire and submitted for the sanction of the Railway and Canal Commission in 1935. It was rejected, on the ground that it did not fulfil the exacting conditions laid down in the Coal Mines Act. Thereupon the activities of the Commission were suspended by the government while it considered what legislative amendments were needed to meet this situation.

A government bill was introduced in 1936 to strengthen the powers of the Reorganization Commission, but was dropped owing to the storm of protest raised by the owners.

Finally in 1938 a new Coal Act was put on the statute-book after an exciting passage through Parliament. It provided for the nationalization of mining royalties, and set up a Coal Commission to take over and administer Britain's coal resources. On this Commission was placed also the responsibility for promoting compulsory mining amalgamations. The Commission must first convince the Board of Trade that voluntary amalgamation is not proceeding rapidly enough in a particular area and that compulsion is desirable. The Board of Trade then lays before Parliament an Order authorizing compulsory amalgamation. If Parliament approves this Order, the Coal Commission will prepare a detailed amalgamation scheme, which must be submitted for the sanction of the Railway and Canal Commission. Thus any proposals for compulsory amalgamation will in future have to run the gauntlet of so many sanctioning authorities that it will be surprising if they are not all stillborn. While this fight over compulsory amalgamation has proceeded, control has been slowly becoming more concentrated by voluntary combination. Between 1926 and 1936 56 voluntary mergers, involving 424 pits and about 250,000 men, were effected. It is estimated that in 1937 77 per cent. of the total output of British coal was produced by 129 of the thousand colliery undertakings.[1]

Voluntary combination has achieved a much greater measure of concentration in the iron and steel industry than in the coal industry. A dozen or so huge groups, built up by amalgamation, exchange of shares, or extension of financial control by purchase of shares, are now responsible for the bulk of the output. None of these groups, however, even remotely approaches in size the monster steel trusts of the United States and Germany. The United States Steel Corporation, for instance, has a capacity far exceeding that of the whole British iron and steel industry. During the war, when the capacity of the industry was strained to the

[1] *Britain in Recovery*, p. 240.

utmost, the tendency towards vertical integration was greatly strengthened, for obvious benefits accrued to those producers who controlled guaranteed supplies of raw materials. Since the war, and especially since 1932, extensive measures of financial and technical reconstruction have been carried out. Nominal share capital has been drastically written down. Combination has made possible a greater specialization of plants and a scrapping of surplus capacity. For instance, Colvilles took over in 1934 Beardmore's business in steel plates, sections and rails, leaving the latter firm to concentrate on steel forgings. Stewarts and Lloyds also, in 1933, transferred to Colvilles their Scottish steel plate business. Competition between rival groups has sometimes been ended by transferring certain branches of production to jointly controlled subsidiaries. Thus Vickers and Armstrong-Whitworths, the two leading British armament firms, established in 1927 a joint subsidiary, Vickers-Armstrong, Ltd., to which they transferred the whole of their armament and naval shipbuilding businesses, the parent companies agreeing not to engage in any of these transferred activities. A more recent instance of the same kind of co-operation was the formation in 1934 of Firth-Vickers Stainless Steels, Ltd., a merger of the stainless steel businesses of the English Steel Corporation (jointly controlled by Vickers-Armstrong and Cammell Laird) and of Thomas Firth and John Brown, Ltd.

Since 1932 the leading steel concerns have done much to remove the reproach that the industry was far behind its foreign competitors in technique, huge sums having been spent on modernization of plant and equipment. This reconstruction has been stimulated by the granting in 1932 of tariff protection, which made the home market sufficiently stable and profitable to induce firms to undertake the risks of heavy fresh capital expenditure. In recommending a tariff on iron and steel, the Import Duties Advisory Committee made it clear that the industry must adopt some central scheme of reorganization, otherwise its protection would be withdrawn. After prolonged discussion of rival plans, a majority of the producers adopted in 1934 a scheme, which was accepted, without much enthusiasm, by the Import Duties Committee. The scheme established the machinery through which central reorganization might be carried out, but did not commit the industry to any specific plan of reconstruction. The British Iron and Steel Federation, with a distinguished chairman, Sir Andrew Duncan, appointed from outside the industry, is the central body for coordinating policy. To it are affiliated the many sectional price-fixing associations with which the iron and steel trades are honeycombed. With the aid of import duties temporarily increased for bargaining purposes, the Federation reached an agreement in 1935 with the European Steel Cartel for the regulation of the international trade in iron and steel products. In the same year the Federation promoted the British Iron and Steel Corporation, which undertakes the centralized purchase of iron and steel imports and the sale of exports. Reorganization has thus resulted in the creation of a quasi-monopolistic national authority, with extensive powers of control over the imports, exports and prices of iron and steel products. But there is as yet little evidence that the Federation is setting the pace in the matter of technical reorganization. What has been achieved in this direction is apparently the result of the enterprise of individual firms, and not a part of a centrally planned scheme.

The problem of surplus capacity, which, in varying degrees, has harassed all the declining industries, has been boldly tackled in the shipbuilding industry. National Shipbuilders' Security, a private company, was promoted in 1930, with the financial assistance of the Bankers' Industrial Development Company, to squeeze out the redundant capacity. Its shareholders included nearly all the shipbuilding firms of the country. They undertook to pay a levy of 1 per cent. of the contract or sale price of the tonnage built after November 1st, 1930, the proceeds of the levy being used to buy and dismantle redundant or obsolete shipyards. Up to March 1935, 27 yards, with an annual capacity of a million tons, had been closed down in this way. Since then, owing to the revival of shipbuilding under the stimulus of rearmament and trade recovery, the process of scrapping obsolete yards has been brought almost to a standstill.

"Nearly every regulatory device of which British ingenuity has been able to conceive has made its appearance in cotton textiles, from simple price-fixing to the control of capacity, from loose agreements to complete unification, from private regulation to control by parliamentary edict."[1] The structure of the cotton industry, with its multiplicity of firms—there were some 3,000 in 1924—and its sharply demarcated sections—spinning, weaving, finishing and merchanting—whose interests are by no means always identical, has rendered the task of reorganization extremely difficult. To nearly all the schemes proposed for rehabilitating Lancashire's staple, there has been opposition from substantial minorities. Furthermore, such monopolistic devices as price maintenance and restriction of output, which have served many industries well, are generally inappropriate where, as in the cotton industry, loss of export markets is the main source of difficulty. Only cost-reducing measures can confer any permanent benefits in such a situation. After the collapse of the post-war boom, during which many spinning mills were re-capitalized at grossly inflated figures, the industry reverted for several years to organized short time, the traditional expedient in temporary spells of bad trade. As the industry began to realize that the contraction of its markets was likely to be permanent, more comprehensive measures were suggested. A Cotton Yarn Association was organized by the American

[1] A. F. Lucas, *Industrial Reconstruction and the Control of Competition*, p. 146.

spinning section in January 1927. It fixed minimum prices and allocated output quotas to its members. Before the end of the year it had been dissolved, undermined by the competition of outside firms. The industry then turned for its salvation to large-scale amalgamation, hoping thereby to concentrate the available business in the most efficient mills and so strengthen its competitive position. Three such combines were promoted in 1929—the Lancashire Cotton Corporation, in the American spinning section, Combined Egyptian Spinners in the fine spinning section, and the Quilt Manufacturers' Association. Of these, by far the most ambitious was the first, which acquired 140 spinning mills, about half of which it has scrapped as obsolete. Unfortunately the high hopes with which the Lancashire Cotton Corporation was launched have not been realized. The market for Lancashire's wares has continued to shrink since 1929. And experience has shown that one firm alone cannot grapple successfully with the problem of redundant capacity. In attempting to do so, the Lancashire Cotton Corporation saddled itself with a crippling burden of deadweight capital, and had to undergo financial reconstruction in 1936, when its capital was reduced from £12,100,000 to £4,500,000.

Surplus capacity continued to depress the spinning section until 1936, when a sufficient majority was secured for a plan, embodied in the Cotton Industry Reorganization Act and based, like the shipbuilders' rationalization scheme, on the principle of the "reconstruction levy." A Spindles Board was set up under the Act, with powers to buy up redundant spindles, to raise a loan for financing these purchases, and to make an annual levy, over a period of fifteen years, on all spindles for the purpose of meeting its loan and administrative charges. Still more comprehensive, because it is intended to apply to all sections of the industry, is the scheme contained in the Cotton Industry Enabling Bill, which, at the time of writing, is working its way through

Parliament. If passed, this measure will provide the cotton industry with a central Board, which would initiate and encourage reorganization schemes for the whole industry and its various sections. It is expected that the Board would deal with such matters as the elimination of surplus capacity, the regulation of production and prices, the formation of pools and quota arrangements, and similar matters of internal organization. Any schemes prepared by this Cotton Industry Board and approved by the Board of Trade and by Parliament would become legally binding.

We have described in a little detail the measures of reorganization adopted in the coal, iron and cotton industries, because it is here that we find in its most fully developed form the modern conception of capitalist planning, with its industrial boards equipped by the State with coercive powers. But it must not be assumed that the desperate remedies devised to meet the desperate situations of these declining trades are typical of what is being done over the whole range of British industry. No special measures of State assistance or control have been called for in most of the expanding trades, which have not had to solve such problems as how to eliminate surplus capacity or how to effect technical reconstruction in the face of declining markets. Road transport has been subjected to public control, for reasons discussed in a later chapter, but for the most part the thriving, expanding industries have remained unregulated by the State. There are few industries, however, in which the free play of competition has not been voluntarily restricted by trade associations or other forms of combination. The heavy chemical industry, in which combination had already gone far before the war, is dominated by one of Britain's biggest concerns, Imperial Chemical Industries, formed in 1926 by the merging of the four leading firms engaged in the manufacture of chemicals, dye-stuffs and explosives. Most sections of the engineering and electrical trades have their associations, some of which, like the

Electric Lamp Manufacturers' Association, the Cable Makers' Association, the Saw Manufacturers' and Edge Tool Manufacturers' Associations, are able to exercise a firm control over prices. Strong combines, some of which were established before the war and were described in an earlier chapter, exist also in the soap, tobacco, cement, wall-paper, match, glass-bottle, rubber-tyre and oil trades.

One other highly significant development in the sphere of industrial organization must be mentioned, namely the public corporation. We now have several examples of this interesting species, among them being the Central Electricity Board, the British Broadcasting Corporation and the London Passenger Transport Board. The management of public utilities by bodies representing the public, but not constituted as departments of the central or local authorities, is not an entirely post-war development. About a third of our ports and harbours were controlled before the war by "public trusts," whose members were elected or nominated by the various organizations interested in the provision of port facilities. The Mersey Docks and Harbour Board, established under an Act of 1857 to take over the management of the port from the Corporation of Liverpool, and the Port of London Authority, constituted in 1908, are well-known examples of this type of public enterprise. It is claimed for the non-political public board or commission that it combines the advantages of control in the interests of the users of a public utility, management on sound commercial lines, and freedom from political interference; hence its frequent adoption as the domain of the public utilities is extended. Thus the construction and management of the electricity "grid," through which the generation of electricity has been concentrated in a comparatively small number of huge interconnected stations, was rightly regarded as primarily an engineering, and not a political, matter, and was therefore entrusted in 1926 to a Central Electricity Board, appointed by the Minister of

Transport but not directly responsible to Parliament. The British Broadcasting Corporation, similarly, is governed by a body appointed by the Crown on the recommendation of the Postmaster-General, who answers parliamentary questions on general broadcasting policy, but accepts no responsibility for the internal administration of the service. In a still more independent position is the London Passenger Transport Board, described in a later chapter. Its members are selected by certain "appointing trustees," who are the holders of various distinguished professional and business positions, so that it is not directly answerable to any public authority. Other instances of public boards removed as far as possible from the arena of party politics are the Coal Commission, responsible for the management of Britain's nationalized coal resources, and the Forestry Commission.

COMMERCIAL POLICY

Free trade, in the unadulterated form that existed before 1914, has never been entirely restored in Britain since the war. Until 1931, however, when British fiscal policy was completely re-cast, the lapses from the strict tenets of Cobdenism were but slight, and were, indeed, condoned by the more moderate free traders. Mr. McKenna was responsible for the first breach in 1915, when he imposed duties, most of which were at the rate of 33⅓ per cent. *ad valorem*, on certain luxury imports, including private motor-cars, musical instruments and cinematograph films. Although these customs duties were not offset by any equivalent excise, they were levied not for protective purposes but primarily to strengthen our foreign-exchange position by cutting down unessential imports. They were not abolished, however, when the war-time emergency had passed, except temporarily by the Labour Government in 1924, so that such industries as motor manufacturing were able to develop under the shelter of a substantially protective tariff. Prohibition of importation, except under licence, had been extensively resorted to during the war in order to support the exchanges and save shipping space. Most of these prohibitions were removed in September 1919. But, for the products of certain "key industries," such as dye-stuffs, drugs, scientific instruments, gauges, magnetos and hosiery latch needles, for which we had hitherto depended almost entirely on imported supplies, the prohibitions were continued in order to encourage their production at home. A High Court decision declared that these import prohibitions were illegal, and fresh legislation had therefore to be passed. Dye-stuffs were separately dealt with by an Act of 1920, which prohibited their importation, except under licence, for a period of ten years. As a result the British dye-stuffs industry rapidly developed, so that by 1927 it was able to supply 80 per cent. of Britain's requirements. The other "key industries" were protected by 33⅓ per cent. duties under the Safeguarding of Industries Act, 1921.

This Act authorized also the imposition of duties not exceeding 33⅓ per cent. on commodities whose importation at artificially low prices was attributable to the depreciation of a foreign currency. A very small number of commodities, including fabric gloves, glassware, hollow-ware and gas mantles, imported from Germany, were dealt with in this way. In 1925 the conditions in which safeguarding duties might be imposed were, in some respects, widened. Any industry applying for the levying of such a duty had to satisfy a committee of inquiry that, among other things, it was suffering from exceptional competition caused by currency depreciation, subsidies, bounties, or other artificial advantages, or by inferior conditions of employment abroad. Under this modified procedure a small number of second-rank industries were given some measure of protection. They included the manufactures of pottery, cutlery, lace, buttons, and a few others. One or two of the larger industries, notably the manufactures of wool and of iron and steel, applied for safeguarding duties but failed to prove their case.

The slump of the early nineteen-thirties succeeded where the arguments of the tariff reformers had failed. It stampeded the electors in 1931 into returning a government with a "doctor's mandate" to try any remedy for the country's economic distress. Foremost among the specifics advocated by the Conservative Party, which had a huge parliamentary majority, was protection. Its use was recommended on a variety of grounds. First, so far as the immediate emergency was concerned, it was claimed that a tariff would correct the adverse balance of trade, which had contributed largely to the financial crisis culminating in Britain's abandonment of the gold standard. Until 1930 Britain still had a net credit on the current, as distinct from capital, items affecting her balance of payments. But, as the accompanying table shows, the intensification of the depression converted this "favourable" balance into an "unfavourable" one of just over £100 million in 1931. The visible trade balance (*i.e.* the excess of imports of merchandize over exports) had become more adverse because other countries' demands for our manufactured goods were declining more than our demand for their foodstuffs and raw materials. Our income from overseas investments was severely curtailed, owing to the reduction of the profits earned by companies abroad in which British nationals had invested, and to default on the part of foreign debtors: and our earnings from the sale of financial and shipping services to foreigners were adversely affected by the contraction of world trade. In the free-trade camp, however, the clapping on of a general tariff in order to correct this adverse balance of payments, after the gold standard had been suspended and sterling allowed to depreciate, was commonly regarded as a work of supererogation. But besides this special argument for a tariff, which in any case provided no basis for permanent protection, other more familiar arguments were brought forward. Protection, it was contended, would reduce unemployment and prevent the workers' standard of living from being undermined by the competition of low-paid foreign labour. It would give us, further, a weapon for use in commercial bargaining with other countries.

Having obtained its mandate from the electorate in October 1931, the National Government immediately secured the passing of temporary legislation, the Abnormal Importations (Customs Duties) Act, to cut down our imports. This Act was replaced in the following year by the Import Duties Act, which set up the framework within

BRITAIN'S BALANCE OF PAYMENTS—BOARD OF TRADE ESTIMATES (in £ million)

	1913	1923	1929	1931	1932	1933	1935	1937
Excess of imports of merchandize and silver bullion and specie ...	145	208	381	408	287	263	261	443
Estimated excess of Government payments made overseas ...	(*a*)	25	—	—	24	2	2	4
	145	233	381	408	311	265	263	447
Estimated excess of Government receipts from overseas ...	(*a*)	—	24	14	—	—	—	—
Estimated net national shipping income ...	94	133	130	80	70	65	70	130
Estimated net income from overseas investments	210	200	250	170	150	160	185	220
Estimated net receipts from short interest and commissions	25	30	65	30	25	30	30	35
Estimated net receipts from other sources ...	10	10	15	10	15	10	10	10
Total	339	373	484	304	260	265	295	395
Estimated total credit (+) or debit (−) balance on items specified above	+ 194	+ 140	+ 103	− 104	− 51	—	+ 32	− 52

(*a*) Not separately estimated.

which our subsequent fiscal policy has been elaborated. First, as a basis, duties at the rate of 10 per cent. *ad valorem* were levied on all imports, except those, mainly certain foodstuffs and raw materials, contained in a free list. Additional duties might be levied on the recommendation of an Import Duties Advisory Committee established by the Act. In practice most manufactured imports were subjected to 20 per cent. duties, but higher rates than these have been imposed on a number of luxury imports and on certain commodities, notably iron and steel, home producers of which were deemed to have a specially strong case for adequate protection.

This building up of a tariff wall enabled Britain to develop the policy of imperial preference more fully than was possible when she levied only a narrow range of revenue duties. The sentimental bonds within the Empire had been strengthened by war-time co-operation, and Britain was induced to drop the somewhat doctrinaire opposition, rigidly maintained since 1860, to colonial preference. In 1919 preferential rebates were granted on certain imports of produce from the British Empire, the preferences in most instances being one-sixth of the full duty. Empire goods were also exempted from the duties levied under the Safeguarding of Industries Act. Many subsequent changes were made in the scheme of imperial preferences, which we need not recount here. Suffice it to say that before 1932, owing to Britain's refusal to impose customs duties on foodstuffs, apart from certain minor exceptions, the range of preferences accorded to the Empire was so narrow that only a small part, 6 to 8 per cent., of British imperial trade was affected by them.[1] This was all changed by the Import Duties Act of 1932, and the representatives of Britain and of the Dominions foregathered at Ottawa to conduct some hard bargaining. In return for tariff concessions granted by the Dominions, Britain now accorded the Empire a greatly

[1] J. H. Richardson, *British Economic Foreign Policy*, p. 137.

widened range of preferences. Under the Ottawa agreements Britain increased the preferences for Empire wines, tobacco and coffee, and imposed new or additional duties, from which Empire countries were exempt, on a number of foodstuffs, including wheat, maize, butter, cheese and other milk products, eggs, and apples. Further, Britain agreed that in undertaking the quantitative regulation of meat supplies, she would give Empire producers an expanding share of imports. This development of a full-blooded policy of imperial preference, together with certain other influences, such as the comparative stability of the exchanges within the sterling group of countries, has greatly enlarged the share of the Empire in Britain's total imports, and, to a less extent, the proportion of total British exports destined for the Empire.

OVERSEAS TRADE OF THE UNITED KINGDOM

Year	Imports			Exports		
	Total	From Empire[1]	Percentage of Empire to Total	Total	To Empire[1]	Percentage of Empire to Total
	£ million	£ million		£ million	£ million	
1913	769	192	25·0	635	209	32·9
1924	1,277	337	26·4	941	305	32·4
1931	861	211	24·4	454	148	32·6
1933	675	231	34·2	417	150	35·9
1935	756	266	35·2	481	190	39·5
1937	1,028	384	37·4	597	238	39·9

The Import Duties Act authorized the Treasury to grant tariff concessions to particular foreign countries, and to impose additional retaliatory duties on goods from countries that discriminated against any part of the British Empire. Retaliatory duties have been but little used, the brief tariff war with France in 1934 being the most notable example. But the power to make reciprocal tariff concessions has been extensively utilized in a long series of commercial agreements, negotiated on a bilateral basis. By offering to reduce

[1] Excluding Eire.

duties, to continue most-favoured-nation treatment, or to import not less than certain quantities of specified commodities, Britain has secured from other countries undertakings to increase their purchases from us or to reduce their tariffs on British goods. A common feature of many of these agreements, one which some Mercantilists would have understood and approved, is the emphasis on the " particular balance of trade " between the pair of negotiating countries, accompanied by pressure on the country with the favourable balance to increase its purchases from the other. As a means of liberalizing and extending world trade, the substitution of bilateral, for triangular, trade is of very doubtful value; and it certainly has the effect of reducing the gain from a given volume of international trade. On the other hand, so far as these agreements have led to mutual concessions, extended to third parties by the operation of most-favoured-nation clauses, they are to be welcomed.

CHAPTER XVI

Agriculture during and after the War

FOOD PRODUCTION

The urgent need for an increase in home-produced food supplies during the war imposed on British agriculture a temporary reversal of the tendencies operating in the previous forty years. Despite improvements in agricultural technique, the number of people fed on the produce of British soil had declined since the 'seventies, owing to the conversion of over three million acres of arable land to pasture; for an acre of arable land yields on the average many times the quantity of food produced on an acre of pasture.[1] Sir Thomas Middleton has estimated, on the basis of an annual food consumption averaging one million Calories per head of population, that "the cultivated land of the United Kingdom supplied the needs of about 21,500,000 inhabitants in 1831–40 as compared with 16,872,000 who could have been fed on the million Calorie standard in 1909–13, and with 15,440,000 who were then actually maintained on the higher standard which the people of the United Kingdom reached before the war."[2] As the following table shows, Britain, in the years before the war, was importing four-fifths of her wheat supplies, and two-fifths of her meat supplies; moreover, her home-produced meat was obtained partly with the aid of imported feeding stuffs. On the other hand, much the greater part of the supplies of milk and of vegetables (including potatoes) was produced at home.

[1] It is estimated that 100 acres of land under wheat will on the average maintain 208 persons; under oats, 172; under potatoes, 418. Whereas 100 acres of the average of meat-producing pastures will feed only 9 persons, and of milk-producing pastures, 41 (T. H. Middleton, *Food Production in War*, p. 83).

[2] *ibid.* pp. 97, 98.

ESTIMATED FOOD SUPPLY OF THE UNITED KINGDOM[1]
YEARLY AVERAGE, 1909–13

Foodstuff	Quantity (in thousands of metric tons)		
	Home-produced	Imported	Total
Cereals	891	3,855	4,746
Meat	1,615	1,070	2,685
Poultry, eggs, game and rabbits	234	161	395
Fish	715	133	848
Dairy produce	4,704	528	5,232
Fruit	341	930	1,271
Vegetables	4,788	694	5,482
Sugar, cocoa and chocolate...	—	1,657	1,657
Total (excluding farm consumption)	13,288	9,028	22,316

For the first two years of the war no special steps were taken by the government to increase the home production of food, beyond extending the provision of allotments and advising farmers to increase the wheat acreage. But as the submarine campaign become more deadly and shipping losses increased, the need to produce more food at home became urgent, and a food production policy was launched in December 1916, its main object being the extension of the arable acreage. In each county the War Agricultural Committee, established in 1915 to organize the supply of agricultural labour, fertilizers, machinery and feeding stuffs, and to examine the possibilities of increasing the output of food, was required to set up an Executive Committee, which became the local agent of the Board of Agriculture. Extensive powers were conferred on these Executive Committees; they could issue instructions to farmers concerning the crops they might grow, and could require them to plough up grass land; they were empowered to take over uncultivated or badly cultivated land, and either farm it themselves or arrange for some competent farmer to cultivate it; and they were authorized to undertake manuring, to supply fertilizers

[1] Taken from A. W. Flux, "Our Food Supply before and after the War," *J.R.S.S.*, 1930, p. 541.

at cost price, and to require farmers to use more manure on their land. At the centre, a Food Production Department of the Board of Agriculture was formed in January 1917 to administer the government's tillage policy. Besides setting the pace for the Executive Committees, by allotting quotas of the increased arable acreage to be secured for the harvest of 1918, this Department became the central source of supply for the agricultural industry, providing on a large scale labour, machines, fertilizers, seeds and other farm requisites.

The decision to adopt the "plough policy," though taken too late to have much effect on the harvest of 1917, was triumphantly vindicated in the following year. Two-and-a-half million additional acres of arable land not in grass were cultivated in the United Kingdom in 1918, as compared with the average of the years 1904–13; the wheat crop amounted to 11,640,000 quarters in 1918, as against 7,090,000 in 1904–13, the oats crop to 31,510,000 quarters as against 21,560,000 and the potato crop to 9,220,000 tons, as compared with 6,590,000. On the other hand, it is estimated that the ploughing up of pasture land, and the reduction of the area under fodder-stuffs for stock, involved a loss in 1918 of about 100 million gallons of milk and 100,000 tons of meat.[1] In terms of calories the food supply was increased in 1918 by 24 per cent. compared with the decade preceding the war. This was accomplished in spite of a shortage of men, machines and materials, and in the face of widespread criticism of the alleged folly of ploughing up good grass land.

Farmers could not be expected to break up pastures unless they were assured that the resulting grain crops would be remunerative. Accordingly the Corn Production Act of 1917 guaranteed certain minimum prices: for wheat these were to be 60s. per quarter in 1917, 55s. in 1918–19, and 45s. in 1920–22; and for oats 38s. 6d. in 1917, 32s. in

[1] Middleton, *op. cit.* p. 321.

1918–19 and 24s. for the next three years. These provisions were inoperative, however, since actual market prices were well above the minimum. Landlords were prohibited, under the Act, from taking advantage of these guarantees by raising rents; and—most startling innovation of all—agricultural labourers were assured of certain minimum wages. A central Agricultural Wages Board, composed of equal numbers of farmers' and labourers' representatives, together with neutral members appointed by the Board of Agriculture, and assisted by District Committees of similar composition, was set up to fix legal minimum wages. These were to be "adequate to promote efficiency and to enable a man in an ordinary case to maintain himself and his family with such standard of comfort as may be reasonable, in relation to the nature of his occupation"; they were not, however, to be less than 25s. a week. The lowest rates fixed by the Board for any district were 30s. in 1918, 36s. 6d. in 1919, 42s. in April 1920 and 46s. in August of the same year.

The Corn Production Act, an emergency measure, was followed by more ambitious legislation, the Agriculture Act of 1920, embodying the government's permanent peacetime policy for the rehabilitation of British agriculture. In order to encourage the home production of cereals, largely for military reasons, farmers were guaranteed for their wheat and oats certain minimum prices, which were to be revised each year by a commission, according to changes in costs of production. Cultivation in accord with the rules of good husbandry could be required of farmers, and if they defaulted the Minister of Agriculture was empowered to cultivate their land under a receiver. Further, the machinery for fixing minimum agricultural wages was retained. Finally, the law relating to tenant-right was amended in favour of the tenant; in effect, any tenant turned out of a holding by his landlord, unless on account of bad farming, now became entitled to compensation for disturbance, amounting to not less than one year's rent and not more than two.

This Act had scarcely been inscribed on the statute-book before the short-lived post-war boom collapsed; agricultural prices fell headlong from the dizzy heights they had reached in 1920, and the government hastily abandoned the agricultural policy to which it had so recently committed itself. The wheat harvest of 1920 had been sold at an average price of 86s. 4d. per quarter; in the following year the price was only 49s., and in 1922 40s. 9d. Oat prices, similarly, dropped from an average of 45s. 7d. for the harvest of 1920 to 28s. 4d. for that of 1921, and to 26s. 6d. in 1922. With market prices at these low levels, adherence to the policy of the Agriculture Act would have involved the subsidization of grain producers on a scale much greater than the government was prepared to finance. Accordingly the guarantee of minimum prices for wheat and oats, together with the provisions relating to minimum agricultural wages, the continuance of which was considered to be conditional on the maintenance of the guarantee, was swept away by the Corn Production (Repeal) Act of 1921. For the time being the policy of *laissez faire* in relation to agriculture was largely restored.

TRENDS IN AGRICULTURE

The drop in agricultural prices that caused this reversal of policy continued until 1923. Then for two or three years agricultural prices remained steady; thereafter they fell slowly until 1930, when their decline was greatly accelerated by the world economic depression. The lowest point was reached in 1933 when the agricultural price index was only 6 per cent. above the pre-war level; since then agricultural prices have slowly recovered. Thus from 1920 to 1933 British farmers were selling on a falling market, with disastrous landslides of prices in 1920–23 and 1930–33. Nevertheless so far as price movements were concerned, the farming community fared a little better than most other industries; for the general price level, as measured by the Board of Trade's wholesale price index, fell rather more steeply than agricultural prices. In other words, the purchasing power of agricultural produce in terms of other commodities was greater in 1933 than in 1913, and much greater than in 1920. Moreover, the prices of such raw materials as feeding stuffs and fertilizers declined more than those of finished agricultural produce.

On the other hand, the important item of wages cost has, since 1925, been much heavier than before the war, both absolutely and relatively to agricultural prices. The average rate of wages (including allowances in kind) for ordinary male farm labourers advanced from 18s. in July 1914 to 46s. 10½d. in 1920. With the collapse of prices and the repeal of the legislation concerning minimum agricultural wages, the average dropped to 27s. 10d. in December 1922 and to 28s. in 1923 and 1924. In these latter years, therefore, agricultural wages were only 55 per cent. higher than in 1914, whereas agricultural prices were still about 60 per cent., and the cost of living about 80 per cent., higher than before the war. Since 1925, however, the average wages of farm workers have generally exceeded 31s. and have never been less than 30s.; in the meantime, of course, agricultural prices have fallen, so that in 1933 the money wages of the farm worker were about 70 per cent. greater than in 1914, while the produce of his labour fetched a price, on the average, only 6 per cent. greater than in 1914. Since labour costs, relatively to total costs, are heaviest in arable farming, the improvement in agricultural wages has probably contributed to the continued decline of the arable acreage since the war. It must also be held partly, though by no means wholly, responsible for the continued decline of the agricultural population. In 1911 1,497,000 persons earned their living on the land in Britain; by 1921 the number had fallen to 1,318,000, and by 1931 to 1,198,000. Thus in two decades agriculture provided occupations for practically 300,000 fewer persons.

The relative improvement in the condition of rural labour was largely the result of the Agricultural Wages (Regulation) Act of 1924, which restored the State regulation of agricultural wages. A Wages Board was established for each county, consisting of equal numbers of representatives of employers and workers, together with neutral members appointed by the Minister of Agriculture. These Boards determine the standard and overtime rates, which, after confirmation by a Central Agricultural Wages Board, become the statutory minima. Though agricultural wages are still low, compared with industrial wages, the Agricultural Wages Boards have helped the rural labourer to narrow the wide gap that existed in 1924 between his standard of living and that of the town worker. After ten years of minimum wage regulation, agricultural earnings had increased by about 4s. a week, whereas industrial earnings had fallen slightly, as shown in the following table. Nevertheless,

COMPARISON OF AGRICULTURAL AND INDUSTRIAL EARNINGS[1]

	Average earnings (shillings per week)			
	1906	1924	1931	1935
Industrial workers (men and boys)	27·0	57·6	55·7	56·9
Agricultural workers (men)...	18·3	31·5	35·0	35·7

compared with the years before the war, the agricultural worker in 1935 had not improved his economic condition quite as much as the industrial worker ; between 1906 and 1935 industrial earnings more than doubled, whereas agricultural earnings rather less than doubled.

This improvement in agricultural wages was accompanied by a considerable increase in the productivity of the average farm worker, owing to the striking progress in agricultural

[1] A. L. Bowley, *Wages and Income in the United Kingdom since 1860*, p. 51.

technique. "It appears that in the ten years 1925–34 the physical output of farms increased by 18½ per cent. During the same period the number of farm employees returned in the Ministry of Agriculture's annual statistics declined by 14 per cent. Hence for England and Wales as a whole the volume of the output per worker rose by nearly 40 per cent. in these ten years, or at the rate of approximately 4 per cent. per annum."[1] Mechanization of farming has proceeded apace since the war; the internal combustion engine has been the chief factor, though the electrification of farming has been making much headway in recent years. There were 80,605 oil or petrol engines on British farms in 1931, compared with 20,050 in 1913; electric engines increased in number from 314 in 1913 to 887 in 1925 and 2,896 in 1931. A small proportion of this additional oil, petrol and electric motive power has merely replaced older steam and gas engines, now used much less than before the war. Probably the most characteristic feature of the technical revolution in agriculture in most parts of the world has been the rapidity with which motor tractors have come into general use. Before the war the number of these on British farms was very small; in 1925 there were over 18,000 and in 1939 about 50,000. Of the new agricultural implements, the most amazing is the combine harvester, an American invention, which cuts, threshes and bags crops as it moves along. In dairying, the milking-machine, introduced just before the war, is now widely used, and has contributed much to the greater cleanliness of our milk supplies.

Besides mechanizing farm operations, agriculturists have crowded into the years since the war many other improvements in the arts of husbandry. "Perhaps the most notable example of agricultural progress in the past generation"[2]

[1] R. McG. Carslaw and P. E. Graves, "The Changing Organization of Arable Farms," in *E.J.*, September 1937, p. 489.

[2] J. A. Scott Watson, "Some Impressions of British Farming, VI" in *Journal of Ministry of Agriculture*, August 1934, p. 466.

has been the improvement of pastures, the result of scientific plant-breeding, pioneered by Sir George Stapledon, and of increased skill in the management of grazing. One of the most promising innovations is the bail system of milk production, introduced by Mr. A. J. Hozier, in which the cows graze on open pastures all the year round, being machine-milked and fed on concentrates in a bail that is moved every few days so as to give the herd access to fresh pastures. Owing to these improvements in the quality of grassland, to the control of grazing, and to the grading up of herds by careful breeding, financially assisted by the State, the milk yield of the average cow has greatly increased. In the short period 1925–31 the average lactation yield per cow is estimated to have risen from 482 to 539 gallons a year, *i.e.*, by 12 per cent.[1] Similar advances have been made in other branches of agriculture; in 1930–31 the average hen laid 120 eggs a year, compared with only 75 in 1913; the scientific principles of pig feeding have been established and widely adopted in practice; potato growers have been supplied with improved strains of seed, immune from disease. Thus the popular and superficial urban view of the British farmer as governed wholly by tradition, antiquated in his methods and impervious to new scientific ideas, is very wide of the mark. Doubtless in farming, as in other occupations, there are unenterprising as well as progressive concerns; but in the agricultural industry as a whole the post-war period has been one of solid and considerable technical progress. Britain has begun to harvest the fruits of years of patient research and agricultural education.

Little need be said concerning post-war changes in the relative profitability of different crops, since for the most part the broad trends of the period 1874–1914 have been continued. The arable acreage of Britain has contracted in each year since the war, with the solitary exception of 1934; grain prices have dropped more than most other agricultural

[1] *The Agricultural Output of England and Wales, 1930–31*, p. 22.

prices, and the use of root crops for stock-feeding has greatly declined, farmers relying more on hay and concentrates. Only one arable crop has shown any considerable expansion of production, namely sugar beet. Established experimentally on a small scale before the war, the sugar-beet industry owes its rapid post-war development to the generous financial assistance it has received from the State. In 1922 a measure of protection was accorded by the remission of the excise duty on sugar, but this was not enough to stimulate the infant industry. Accordingly a subsidy was granted for a period of ten years, starting from 1924; home-produced sugar was now subject to duty, but, like that from the Empire, at only half the standard rate. During the ten years 1924–33 the subsidy cost the tax-payer about £30 million, and in addition £10 million were remitted in duty. With this encouragement, the acreage under sugar beet in Great Britain increased from 22,000 in 1924 to 404,000 in 1934, the home output of sugar in the latter year being nearly a quarter of our total consumption. Since 1934 the policy of subsidy has been continued in spite of the majority recommendation of the Greene Committee that it should cease. The Sugar Industry Re-organization Act of 1935 set up a Sugar Commission, which is responsible for determining the rate of subsidy and for supervising the fixing of contract prices for sugar beet; the Act also amalgamated all the sugar factories into a single semi-public undertaking, the British Sugar Corporation, three of the directors of which represent the government.

While the outputs of most arable products have continued to diminish since the war, those of dairy produce, poultry and eggs, vegetables, glass-house and horticultural produce, have continued to expand. The production of milk has been one of the most profitable branches of agriculture. Milk prices, which were regulated by a Permanent Joint Milk Committee, composed of representatives of producers, distributors and manufacturers of milk products, from 1922 until the establishment of the Milk Marketing Boards in 1933, have kept up much better than most other agricultural prices. The output of milk has steadily expanded, the sales of milk and milk products accounting in 1930–31 for 27 per cent. of the value of the agricultural output of England and Wales, and for 20 per cent. of that of Scotland. Rising standards of living, the education of the public in the elementary principles of nutrition, and the development of the canning trade, have greatly increased the demand for fresh vegetables, the vegetable acreage increasing from 126,517 in 1922 to 226,215 in 1936, *i.e.*, by 79·4 per cent. Poultry farming is another branch of agriculture that has greatly enlarged its output since the war. In 1913 Britain had about 33 million fowls; by 1934 there were over 69 million. Since the latter year the poultry population has declined somewhat, owing partly to the spread of disease and partly to greatly increased imports of eggs, especially from Australia and New Zealand.

The meat section of the livestock industry has remained

BRITAIN'S MEAT SUPPLIES[1]

	1909–13	1927–31
	million cwt.	million cwt.
Beef and veal:		
Home produced ...	12·6	12·4
Imported	11·1	15·0
Mutton and lamb:		
Home produced ...	5·6	4·9
Imported	5·7	6·5
Pig meat:		
Home produced ...	5·3	5·6
Imported	6·4	10·3
All meat:		
Home produced ...	23·5	22·9
Imported	23·2	31·8
Total	46·7	54·7

[1] *Report of the Reorganization Commission for Fat Stock for England and Wales*, 1934, p. 10. Import figures relate to the United Kingdom, and figures of home production to Great Britain; but since meat imports into Ireland are small, this does not seriously affect the comparison. See also *Report on the Trade in Refrigerated Beef, Mutton and Lamb*, 1925, p. 58, for statistics of the United Kingdom's meat supply from 1901 to 1924.

the most important branch of British agriculture, as judged by the value of its output, which in 1930–31 was 32 per cent. of the total agricultural output in England and Wales, and nearly 54 per cent. in Scotland. But the home production of meat was, at that time, slightly less than before the war, as the table opposite shows. In 1909–13 Great Britain (as distinct from the United Kingdom) produced at home about half her total meat requirements, but in 1927–31, owing to the slightly curtailed home output and the continued expansion of imports, the proportion had fallen to 41 per cent. The level of livestock prices made meat production distinctly less profitable than dairy farming, until the quantitative regulation of meat imports, beginning in 1933, and the provision of the cattle subsidy, in 1934, restored a more attractive margin of profit. As a result of these measures, the production of meat in Britain rose from 22·9 million cwt. in 1927–31 to 25·8 million in 1935–36.[1]

We have, in the preceding paragraphs, emphasized the continuance since the war of the pre-war trends in British agriculture. There is, however, one highly significant breach in this continuity, namely the very pronounced reversal of the tendency for tenant farming to increase at the expense of occupying ownership. In 1913 11·19 per cent. of the agricultural holdings, and 10·7 per cent. of the area of agricultural land, in England and Wales, were farmed by their owners; this latter figure shot up to 20 in 1921, and to 36 in 1927. There has been a corresponding change in the conditions of land tenure in Scotland; in 1931 32 per cent. of Scotland's agricultural land was owned by its occupiers, as against 11 in 1914. This decline in tenancy is to be attributed not so much to a growth of desire on the tenants' part to become the owners of their holdings, as to anxiety on the part of landlords to sell. The tendency showed itself first in the years immediately after the war, when land commanded exceptionally high prices and far-sighted landowners

[1] *Britain in Recovery*, p. 207.

sold out, the tenant often being given the option of buying or quitting. But this can be only a small part of the explanation; for the acquisition of land by tenants persisted long after land prices had dropped from the abnormal level prevailing in 1920. The main explanation is probably to be found in the heavy burden of taxation since the war, especially in the form of estate duties, resulting in some break-up of landed estates and in the more or less "forced" acquisition of holdings by tenants. Whatever its causes, this extension of occupying ownership must have the effect of exposing an increasing section of the farmer class to more extreme fluctuations of fortune than they would otherwise have experienced; for the traditional functions of the landlord in the English agricultural system include not only estate management and the provision of fixed capital, but also the protection of the tenant from the worst shocks of agricultural depression, by remissions or abatements of rent in hard times. Those farmers who had exchanged their landlords for mortgagees were particularly handicapped during the period of falling agricultural prices.

The increase in the number of owner-occupiers has made more urgent the long-standing problem of agricultural credit, since land purchase must deplete a farmer's financial resources. An attempt to meet the need for further credit facilities has been made in two Agricultural Credits Acts. The first, passed in 1923, authorized the Public Works Loan Commissioners to make long-term loans to farmers who had purchased their land while the Corn Production Act was in force (April 1917 to June 1921); this facility was extensively used by farmers. The Act aimed also at stimulating the co-operative provision of short-term credit, on the lines of the continental Raiffeisen banks; the government would advance funds to agricultural societies at the rate of one pound for every pound share on which five shillings had been paid. Apathy on the part of farmers, however, rendered this provision of the Act practically a dead letter. The second Act, passed in 1928 and based on Mr. R. R. Enfield's *Report on Agricultural Credit*, sought to make the joint-stock banks the principal channel through which farmers could obtain both long-term and short-term credits. It established the Agricultural Mortgage Corporation, whose share capital of £650,000 is held by the Bank of England and the principal joint-stock banks (except the Midland Bank); the Treasury advanced, free of interest, a sum equal to the share capital, and contributes £10,000 a year towards expenses. Loans on mortgage are made for periods of up to 60 years, applications for loans being submitted through the joint-stock banks. For Scotland, a similar institution, the Scottish Agricultural Securities Corporation, was set up in 1933. The credit facilities provided by the Agricultural Mortgage Corporation were quickly and extensively utilized, but the Corporation has been somewhat handicapped through having borrowed the bulk of its funds, by the issue of debentures, at much higher rates of interest than prevail at the present time. The Act also authorized farmers to obtain short-term loans from banks on the security of fixed or floating charges on farm assets. These charges must be recorded at the Land Registry, to which the public have no access; the publicity attaching to the bill of sale, which has made it practically useless as a source of agricultural credit, is thus avoided. Nevertheless little use of this new facility has so far been made by farmers, lack of understanding of the "chattel mortgage" and a preference for tradesmen's credit being apparently mainly responsible.

Though co-operative credit societies have made very little headway in Britain, rather more success has been achieved with other forms of agricultural co-operation. Before 1900 "British agricultural co-operation was a mere blank, darkened by a few failures."[1] In that year the Agricultural Organization Society was formed, and, with the aid of a parallel Scottish Society founded in 1905, led the movement

[1] C. R. Fay, *Co-operation at Home and Abroad* (1908), p. 106.

for the extension of co-operation in agriculture until 1923, when its functions were taken over by the National Farmers' Union. By 1913 381 agricultural co-operative trading societies had been established in Britain, with a membership of nearly 37,000 and sales of over £2,400,000. Ten years later there were over one thousand societies, 145,270 members and sales of over £11,700,000. Since 1923 the number of societies has been practically halved; membership has declined slightly, but sales have been well maintained, and in recent years considerably increased. In 1936 there were 514 societies, with 138,541 members, and sales amounting to some £16,400,000. Of these sales the larger part (about £9½ million) arose from the supply of farming requisites, such as seeds, manures, utensils and the rest, to members; the remainder consisted of sales of farm produce, the principal items being livestock, eggs and poultry, dead meat, and milk and dairy produce.

The marketing of produce is the sphere in which co-operation might be expected to offer the greatest advantages, especially to small farmers; yet it is precisely here that the movement has been most disappointing. "Co-operative marketing in England and Wales occupies a comparatively insignificant position in the total volume of agricultural trade. The share of the produce which it handles is small and it has made as yet but little contribution to the marketing organization of the country as a whole."[1] The reasons commonly given for the backwardness of agricultural co-operation in Britain, in comparison with the continental, and especially the Danish, movement, are first, the fact that there is little export of British agricultural produce, which is therefore not marketed through a few principal centres; secondly, the individualism of most British farmers, and their tendency to regard co-operative societies as a means of disposing of produce of poorer

[1] Ministry of Agriculture, *Report on Co-operative Marketing of Agricultural Produce in England and Wales* (1925), p. 165.

quality, the better being privately marketed; thirdly, the absence in Britain of a concentration of small holdings comparable to that found on the continent; and finally, it has been suggested by Dr. Venn that British farmers have been less sorely afflicted by depressions than continental farmers, and have not therefore been compelled to resort to co-operation as a means of survival.[1]

THE NEW AGRICULTURAL POLICY

For the economic historian of the future the 1930's will almost certainly mark the beginning of a new phase in the development of British agriculture, the substitution of a positive State policy in relation to agriculture for the predominantly *laissez faire* view that held the field from 1846 to 1931. Admittedly liberalism in agriculture was beginning to wear a little thin in the first decade after the war: the infant sugar-beet industry was nourished out of State funds; agricultural land and buildings were relieved of local rating burdens under the de-rating scheme of 1928; the encouragement of small holdings was continued, first by the Land Settlement (Facilities) Act of 1919, under which some 17,000 ex-servicemen were settled on small farms, and secondly by the Small Holdings and Allotments Act of 1926 and the Agricultural Land (Utilization) Act of 1931, which facilitated the provision of "cottage" holdings by county councils; some financial assistance was also given by the State for the provision of agricultural credit, as described above; and finally a patriotic preference for British produce has been fostered by the propaganda of the Empire Marketing Board, established in 1926, and by the "National Mark" scheme, authorized by the Agricultural Produce (Grading and Marking) Act of 1928. Compared, however, with the complete re-orientation of policy that followed, these

[1] *Foundations of Agricultural Economics* (1933), pp. 338–352.

measures were but minor breaches of the broad policy of leaving agriculture to stand on its own feet without artificial aids.

The new policy of agricultural planning is intended to achieve a variety of ends. In part it aims at making British agriculture both more profitable and less subject to fluctuations of prosperity; the arrangements for regulating home production and imports are devised to give protection from the embarrassing consequences of gluts and to maintain agricultural prices at remunerative levels. Besides this economic motive, however, the new agricultural programme has political objectives. In order to strengthen the economic ties between the constituent parts of the British Empire, agricultural imports have been regulated, by tariffs or quotas, so as to give preferential treatment to the Dominions. Further, the new policy aims at reducing our dependence on imported food supplies. On the other hand it involves some sacrifice of the end that formerly determined our agricultural policy, the procuring of the cheapest possible supplies of food.

The methods employed to attain these ends have been adjusted in a piecemeal fashion to the varying economic circumstances of the different branches of farming. Tariffs, import quotas, subsidies, the regulation of home production and the fixing of prices, are the principal weapons in the industry's new armoury. The most thorough-going form of planning is provided for by the Agricultural Marketing Acts, the first of which, passed in 1931, authorized the establishment of a compulsory scheme for controlling the marketing of any agricultural product, provided that two-thirds of the producers concerned, who must also be responsible for two-thirds of the productive capacity, voted in favour of the scheme. Owing, however, to the absence from the Act of any powers to regulate imports or total home sales, most farmers were sceptical about its value to them, and only one scheme, that for the hops industry, which was already protected by duties, was prepared under the 1931 Act alone. In 1933, a protectionist government having been returned to power in the meantime, a second Agricultural Marketing Act was passed, which removed this obstruction to agricultural organization by authorizing the government to regulate both the importation and the home supplies of any agricultural product. Under the two Acts together, the marketing boards, elected by producers, may exercise very extensive powers, including buying, selling and processing, the quantitative regulation of production, the fixing of prices and of the terms on which a product may be sold, and the grading, marking, packing, and transport of a product. So far, marketing schemes have been set up for hops, milk, pigs, bacon and potatoes.

Aided by a 50 per cent. *ad valorem* tariff, the Hops Marketing Board has attained a strong monopolistic position, being the sole agency through which home-grown hops can be marketed. It regulates production by allocating quotas to growers, and in 1934 entered into an agreement with the Brewers' Society, whereby the average selling price of hops sold by the Board was fixed at £9 per cwt. for a period of five years. The Potato Marketing Board is responsible for a crop whose yield is extremely variable, but the demand for which is inelastic; it aims therefore at maintaining remunerative prices by regulating the quantity of potatoes released for sale. By prohibiting the sale for human consumption of potatoes that pass through a riddle of prescribed gauge, it can vary the proportion of the total crop that is put on the market. In addition, over-production is discouraged by allotting "basic acreages" to registered growers and by making a levy of £5 per acre on all additions to basic acreage. These measures for regulating the home production of potatoes have been supplemented since 1934 by the quantitative control of imports through the issue of licences to importers.

In the pig and bacon industries, the main objects of policy

have been the stimulation of home production at the expense of foreign, and the stabilization of the total supply of bacon coming on the home market. The proportion of British bacon requirements produced at home steadily diminished after the war, so that in the early 1930's we had become dependent on imports for about 90 per cent. of our supplies. In November 1932 the British government negotiated with the principal countries concerned a voluntary 15 per cent. reduction of our bacon imports, and in the following year imposed a further compulsory curtailment by 16 per cent. After the establishment of the Pigs and Bacon Marketing Boards in 1933, the government aimed at adjusting the foreign imports of bacon, by means of quotas, so as to fill the gap between an assumed normal consumption of about 10,670,000 cwts. a year, and the estimated supplies from home and Empire sources. These measures induced a rapid expansion of home production; the curers registered under the marketing scheme produced 2,757,000 cwts. of bacon in 1936 compared with 1,736,000 cwts. in 1934; in 1936 the United Kingdom produced about one-third of its bacon requirements. On the other hand, consumers have had to pay greatly enhanced prices for their bacon, especially for Danish bacon, and the difference between the prices of British and Danish bacon has been practically eliminated. So far the Pigs and Bacon Boards, whose main function is to negotiate the terms of the contracts between the pig producers and the curers, have had exceedingly chequered careers, as is perhaps only to be expected where semi-monopolistic control is established in each of two successive stages in a process of production. If bacon-pig prices are fixed low enough to enable curers to earn reasonable profits, pigs are diverted by farmers to the alternative pork market, where prices are uncontrolled, and the supply of bacon pigs then falls short of the curers' requirements. If, on the other hand, attractively high prices are fixed for bacon pigs, the curers are likely to be involved in losses, as happened in the first year of the scheme's operation. In short, "control in this industry is caught between two millstones."[1] These difficulties came to a head at the end of 1936, when the Bacon Board exercised its right to declare void the contracts for 1937, because the producers had contracted to deliver only 1,700,000 pigs, compared with the minimum of 2,200,000 required by the curers. For the following two years the marketing scheme was in abeyance; it was reconstructed in August 1938.

Most debated of all the marketing schemes are those, instituted in 1933 and 1934, for the milk industry.[2] From 1922 onwards milk prices had been unofficially, but on the whole quite effectively, regulated by agreements between the National Farmers' Union and the National Federation of Dairymen's Associations, negotiated through the Joint Milk Council. Separate prices were fixed for milk sold in the liquid market and in the manufacturing market, the first of which, except in the years 1923 and 1928, was the more remunerative. Manufacturing prices were based, in accord with a formula, on the price of imported cheese, so as to take account of overseas competition in the home market for dairy produce. Unfortunately for the stability of the milk industry, the deepening of the world depression after 1929 was accompanied by a steep fall in cheese prices, and manufacturing milk prices accordingly dropped from the 8d. to 9d. a gallon of the 1920's to about 4½d. in 1931 and 1932, the liquid price, at about 9½d. a gallon, being then more than double the manufacturing price. With this widened price differential, those farmers who had hitherto sold a good deal of their milk for manufacturing purposes—in both England and Scotland it was the western farmers who were mainly in this position—began to invade the liquid milk market. The delicately poised differential price structure was thus in danger of collapse. It was to maintain it, and to

[1] A. F. Lucas, *Industrial Reconstruction and the Control of Competition*, p. 252.

[2] There are separate schemes for England and Wales, Scotland (South of Grampians), Aberdeen and District, and the North of Scotland.

preserve the profitableness of the liquid market, that marketing schemes for England and Wales and for southern Scotland were established in 1933.

The Milk Marketing Boards, composed of farmers' representatives, are empowered to fix the terms of the contracts between producers and distributors, and the minimum prices at which distributors may resell. Differentiation of manufacturing and liquid prices has been continued, but by means of somewhat complicated pooling agreements the same average price is paid to all farmers in the pool area, whatever the purpose for which their milk is used. Under the English and Welsh scheme there are eleven regional pools, with an inter-regional compensation levy on liquid sales in order to keep within narrow limits the discrepancy between the pool prices of regions mainly supplying the liquid market and of those supplying large quantities of manufacturing milk. The main Scottish scheme, on the other hand, has a single pool for the whole of its area. Heartened by the success of these schemes in keeping up milk prices at a level comparing very favourably with that of most other agricultural prices, farmers greatly increased their output of milk, and the Boards found themselves saddled with the task of discovering outlets for these increased supplies without spoiling the remunerative liquid market. They turned to the manufacturing market for a solution of the difficulty; whereas in 1933–34 only 25 per cent. of the milk sold under the English and Welsh scheme was used for manufacturing, two years later 35 per cent. was being thus utilized. Manufacturing milk prices, however, suffered in the process, and the government had to come to the aid of the industry with what amounted to a guarantee of minimum prices. Under the Milk Act of 1934 advances were made to the Marketing Boards to fill the gap between actual manufacturing prices and the "standard prices" of 6d. per gallon in winter and 5d. in summer, repayment of these advances being contingent on the "cheese milk price" exceeding the " standard price " by more than 1d. in any of the 42 months, subsequently extended to 54, beginning April 1936.

The Boards, in conjunction with the government, have attempted also, with a considerable measure of success, to stimulate the demand for liquid milk; with the aid of a subsidy, milk has been supplied since October 1934 to school children, at about half the ordinary retail price; in certain distressed areas, such as Rhondda and Jarrow, milk has been experimentally sold to needy persons at half the retail price, and consumption has increased in response by 61 per cent.[1]; the Boards have also undertaken an extensive publicity campaign. Further, farmers have been encouraged to improve the quality of their milk, both by the Accredited Scheme, under which producers of " accredited" (formerly " Grade A ") milk receive from the funds of the Marketing Boards a bonus of 1d. per gallon, and by the Attested Herds Scheme, which provides a bonus of 1d. per gallon, payable by the Exchequer, for producers whose herds pass certain stringent tests. But the policy of lowering retail prices all round, by rationalizing the distribution of milk and narrowing distributors' margins, which has been continually urged on the government by the critics of its present milk policy, has not yet been tried.

Wheat production, though accounting in 1930–31 for less than 2 per cent. of the value of the agricultural output of England and Wales, has been an object of special government solicitude. The price of wheat dropped far more than most other agricultural prices in the world depression, reaching in 1931 a level 24 per cent. below that of 1911–13. The bounty of Nature, especially in 1928 and 1929, together with the protective measures stimulating wheat production in some of the great consuming countries, such as France, Germany and Italy, were the main causes of this unremunerative level of wheat prices. Since it was feared

[1] Viscount Astor and B. S. Rowntree, *British Agriculture*, p. 292.

that the revival of the Corn Laws would be highly unpopular both at home and among Empire farmers,[1] Britain resorted in 1932 to the alternative stimulus of a wheat subsidy ; she thus joined the ranks of nations that protected their farmers from the unpleasant consequences of world plenty by measures adding still further to it. Under the Wheat Act of that year, the subsidy was paid to bridge the gap between the average sale price of wheat in a given year and the standard price of 10s. per cwt. (*i.e.*, 45s. per quarter). This deficiency payment, however, was to be made on an output of not more than 27 million cwt. (increased to 36 million cwt. in 1937) ; if the annual output exceeded this figure, the deficiency payment per cwt. was to be reduced by the proportion between the excess and the actual output. Hence farmers were not guaranteed a price of 10s. per cwt. for all the wheat they chose to produce ; the more they increased their output beyond the figure stipulated, the smaller became the proportion of the deficiency (excess of standard, over actual, price) they received. The source of the funds for the payment of this subsidy is a levy on all flour delivered for consumption at home, whether milled from home-grown or imported wheat, the levy being passed on to consumers in the form of higher prices for flour and bread.

Thus encouraged, Britain's farmers increased the acreage under wheat from the record low level of 1,247,000 in 1931 to 1,832,000 in 1937, *i.e.*, by 47 per cent., this expansion being mainly at the expense of oats and barley. The growers of these latter cereals, however, received a small instalment of government assistance in the Agriculture Act of 1937, which provided deficiency payments for the growers of oats and barley when the market price of oats dropped below 8s. per cwt. This subsidy was payable on only 6 cwt. per acre, the quantity assumed to be normally sold off the farm ; the scheme also provided for a proportionate reduction of the

[1] A small duty of 2s. per quarter has been levied on *foreign* wheat since November 1932, under the Ottawa Agreements Act.

deficiency payment if more than a standard acreage were cultivated. In May 1939 the Minister of Agriculture announced a more generous subsidy for the growers of oats and barley. This may amount to as much as £2 6s. 8d. per acre, the assumed basic yield having been raised from 6 to 14 cwt. per acre.

Finally, the livestock industry has been helped through the period of depression and recovery by import quotas and subsidies. Under the Ottawa agreements of 1932, imports of frozen beef, mutton and lamb from foreign countries were reduced by over one-third, and the principal Empire meat producers, Australia and New Zealand, have agreed to the voluntary regulation of imports from them. Imports of chilled beef have also been regulated by agreements with the countries concerned. These measures sufficed to raise the prices of fat sheep well above the low level of 1923; but the prices of fat cattle continued to fall until in 1934 they were about 7 per cent. below the level of 1913. The government then came to the rescue of the industry with a temporary measure, the Cattle Industry (Emergency Provisions) Act of 1934, which provided for the payment of a subsidy at the rate of 5s. per cwt. for live animals, and 9s. 4d. per cwt. for carcases. In the three years 1934–37 £11,400,000 were paid in subsidy to cattle producers. The government's long-term programme for the assistance of livestock producers was contained in the Livestock Industry Act of 1937, which further developed the subsidy policy by differentiating, in the rates of subsidy, between home-bred and imported animals, and between animals of different quality. Some contribution towards the cost of this subvention is derived from import duties of ¾d. per lb. on chilled beef and veal, and of ⅔d. per lb. on all other beef and veal. The rate of subsidy, however, is in no way dependent on the revenue from these duties. The method of the guaranteed minimum price, applied to wheat, oats and barley, was extended to sheep in May 1939. Any deficiency below 10d. per lb.

for sheep sold for slaughter is to be made good by the Exchequer, subject to the proviso that if the sheep population should rise above 27 million the guaranteed price will be proportionately reduced.

Thus in the short space of less than a decade we have witnessed the complete reversal of an agricultural policy that, for nearly a century, had provided the industrial workers of Britain with cheap food. On the other hand, it condemned the country dweller to a life devoid of most of the simple comforts enjoyed by the townsman, and aggravated the effects of the various factors tending towards rural depopulation. Whether, in order to improve the countryman's standard of living, check the urbanization of the people, and reduce Britain's dependence on overseas food supplies, it is worth while to subsidize agriculture at the expense of the taxpayer, make food dearer, and curtail the activities of the export and shipping industries, we cannot discuss here. To answer the question would require the weighing of imponderables, and the comparison of incommensurables. We merely record the fact that the ends of agricultural policy have undergone a complete revaluation.

CHAPTER XVII

Means of Transport Old and New

RAILWAY POLICY

Though still undecided before the war whether to regard railway amalgamations as a blessing or a curse, Parliament was converted by 1921 to the view that they were in the public interest, and proceeded to put its faith to the test by passing the Railways Act. Seven years of government control had helped to crystallize opinion on the question of State railway policy. During the war a Railway Executive Committee, composed of the general managers of the principal lines, operated the railways as a unified system. The companies were guaranteed, by the government, incomes equal, broadly speaking, to their net earnings in 1913, so that inter-railway accounting and inter-railway competition became pointless, and therefore ceased. Many operating economies were secured in consequence, perhaps the most noteworthy being those arising from the pooling of railway-owned wagons under the "common user" arrangement, first instituted by the Great Northern, Great Central and Great Eastern Railways in 1916, and made general by the Railway Executive Committee in the following year. Impressed by this experience gained under unified control, the Select Committee on Transport declared in its preliminary report of November 1918 that the railways could not be allowed to return to their pre-war position and, without committing itself on the question of public or private ownership, recommended their ultimate unification. The Ministry of Transport, established in 1919, hammered out its policy with regard to the State control of railways, amalgamations, and railway labour conditions, and published an outline of its proposals in June 1920. These became the basis of discussions between the government, the railway companies, railway unions and trading interests, from which emerged, as practically an agreed measure, the Railways Act of 1921.

This great landmark in railway development was a typical example of the British fondness for compromise. The government was not prepared to nationalize the railways, nor would it consolidate them into a single privately owned undertaking, since the State would almost certainly, after a short interval of time, have had to acquire such a private railway monopoly, as it had ultimately had to nationalize the telephone service. On the other hand, to restore the pre-war railway system would have meant depriving the country of the undoubted benefits of unified railway control. Hence the Act provided for the amalgamation of all the principal, and most of the minor, railways, numbering 120 altogether, into four groups, which would be able to secure most, if not all, of the economies of unification. Within the greater part of its territory each of the amalgamated groups had a monopoly of rail transport; but there remained considerable areas, which happened to include some of the heaviest traffic flows, where the groups overlapped and provided competitive facilities. As Sir William Acworth summed up the position, "the effect of the new statutory grouping is to leave the bulk of the territory of Great Britain non-competitive, but the bulk of the traffic competitive."[1]

In order to safeguard the public against excessive charges or inefficient services, the amalgamated companies were subjected to a more rigorous State control than had ever before been applied to the railways. The fixing of standard rates and fares, the alteration of the classification of merchandize, the determination of the conditions of carriage and of packing, together with many other regulative functions, were entrusted to a Railway Rates Tribunal, composed of three members appointed by the Crown. Exceptional rates

[1] "Grouping under the Railways Act, 1921," *E.J.*, 1923, p. 31.

could be quoted by the railway companies, but if they were more than 40 per cent., or less than 5 per cent., below the standard rates, they had to be approved by the Tribunal; and even if they were within those limits, they could be referred by the Minister of Transport to the Tribunal, which could cancel or modify them or alternatively revise the standard rates. Further, every trader had the right to apply to the Tribunal to fix a new exceptional rate or to cancel or vary an existing one. These various charges were to be fixed by the Tribunal so as to enable each company to earn, "with efficient and economical working and management," a "standard revenue," based on the net earnings in 1913 of the company's constituent undertakings, and including also allowances for capital expenditure not fully remunerative in 1913 or incurred since that year, and a share in the economies secured by amalgamation. Since the imposition of an upper limit to profits might have weakened the incentive to efficiency on the part of railway managements, it was provided that if in any year a company earned more than its "standard revenue," the Tribunal was to modify charges so as to hand back to the public, in subsequent years, 80 per cent of the surplus, the remainder being retained by the company. This last provision, however, has been inoperative, since none of the companies has yet earned its "standard revenue." In the interests of economical working, the Act also authorized the Minister of Transport to require the railway companies to standardize their equipment and to adopt schemes for the co-operative working or common user of rolling stock and of other facilities. But the companies were prohibited from entering into pooling agreements or other forms of combination, without the consent of the Minister of Transport.

Finally there was included in the Act a conciliation scheme, already agreed upon by the companies and the unions, for the regulation of the wages and conditions of service of railwaymen. It was one of the most comprehensive schemes of its kind, with its hierarchy of negotiating bodies for each company, its Central Wages Board, composed of equal numbers of representatives of the companies and of the employees, and its National Wages Board, consisting of an independent chairman nominated by the Minister of Labour, and of representatives of railway users, companies, and unions. Until 1933 this negotiating machinery worked, on the whole, admirably. Then, on the companies' proposing further reductions in rates of pay, the National Board became hopelessly divided, and issued six separate reports. Thereupon the railway companies gave notice to terminate the Central and National Boards. New negotiating machinery was instituted in 1935; the Central Wages Board has been replaced by a Railway Staff National Council, with similar composition but greater authority, and the National Board by a Railway Staff National Tribunal, with three members, one nominated by, but not representing, each of the two parties, and a chairman appointed by agreement between the two parties, or, in default of such agreement, by the Minister of Labour. The parties do not, however, undertake beforehand to accept the awards of the Tribunal as binding.

Underlying the Railway Acts was the assumption that the railway companies were regional transport monopolies, needing close supervision by the State. At the time the Act was passed road transport was developing rapidly, but it was still regarded mainly as a substitute for horse-drawn transport, a feeder to the railways rather than a competitor. But by the "appointed day," January 1st, 1928, when the provisions relating to railway charges came into force, motor transport had made such immense strides that the railways were being subjected to competition from bus, coach, lorry and the ubiquitous private car, at practically every point in the system. Road competition has had the most profound effects on railway finance and railway policy. It has reduced the volume of railway traffic, both passenger and freight, despite the increase in the physical volume of national production and the continued growth of population. Moreover, in order to retain this reduced quantum of traffic, cheap fares have had to be so extended that nowadays less than one passenger in fourteen pays the full standard fare. Exceptional rates have had to be applied to an increasing proportion of freight traffic; since the "appointed day" about 1½ million new special rates have been introduced, and it is estimated that at least 80 per cent. of the volume of goods traffic is now conveyed at less than the standard rates.[1] Road competition has, in fact, undermined the whole structure of railway rates, which from the very beginnings of rail transport have been based on the principle of differential charging. They have, that is to say, been adjusted to what each class of traffic will "bear," so that goods of high value per ton have, broadly speaking, been charged greater rates than those of low value. Such a system of charging is practicable only under conditions of monopoly or of very imperfect competition. The appearance of a competitor whose charges are based primarily on cost of transport and not on the value of the consignment has therefore rendered it increasingly difficult for the railways to maintain their differential rates structure. In particular, they have lost a considerable proportion of their high-class traffic, owing to the quotation of lower rates by road hauliers. In passenger transport the most severe losses have been sustained on short-distance and cross-country traffic, for which the road vehicle can provide more convenient, and frequently speedier, services than the rail.

By standardizing equipment, rationalizing construction and repair shops, closing down unremunerative branch lines and improving the methods of working traffic, striking economies have been obtained in railway expenditure; but it has not been possible to reduce it to the same extent as receipts, since a large part of the cost of working a railway

[1] H. M. Hallsworth, in *Britain in Recovery*, p. 293.

consists of overhead expenses that cannot easily be reduced when traffic declines. In fact, in order to counter road competition by offering more attractive facilities, the railways have had to provide a steadily increasing amount of passenger-train mileage. The following table summarizes for the years 1913, 1923, 1929 and 1937, the financial and traffic position of the railways. Since the volume of production and of employment was greater in 1937 than in 1929, and greater in 1929 than in 1923, the decline in traffic over the period as a whole can be attributed mainly to road competition and not to trade depression. But it must be remembered that the reduction of some traffics, especially that in coal, has been caused primarily by protracted depression.

TRAFFIC OF THE BRITISH RAILWAYS[1]

	1913	1923	1929	1937
Passenger Receipts (£ million) ...	54·5	94·1	80·0	75·2
Freight Receipts (£ million)	64·3	109·8	106·5	94·6
Gross Railway Receipts (£ million) ...	119·8	205·8	188·2	171·4
Railway Expenditure (£ million) ...	75·7	166·0	146·9	136·1
Net Railway Receipts (£ million) ...	44·1	39·8	41·3	35·3
Number of Passengers (million) ...	1332·4	1431·0	1267·7	1295·4
Tons of coal, coke, and patent fuel (million)	225·6	222·2	207·1	188·1
Tons of other merchandise (million) ...	138·8	121·0	122·4	109·0

Under the impact of this competition the railway companies have introduced many new facilities and improved services. They were criticized by the Royal Commission on Transport in 1931 for not making the most of their advantage in speed, but in recent years, and especially since 1935, there has been a notable acceleration of passenger trains. In 1938 there were 107 trains booked to run at speeds of 60 miles an hour and over, compared with 25 in 1934 and only 4 in 1914. Electrification of suburban lines, allowing of more intensive services and at the same time yielding economies in operating, has proceeded steadily, particularly

[1] *Railway Returns.*

on the Southern Railway where conditions are specially favourable for electric traction. Speedier delivery of consignments has been secured by running a greatly increased number of express freight trains at times advertised to traders. Containers, providing door-to-door transit without intermediate handling, have been introduced, 13,845 of these being in service at the end of 1937. Another new facility that has been extensively provided is "railhead distribution," whereby goods are despatched in bulk to a railway depôt and stored there until their owners instruct the company to deliver them in the surrounding district. Country lorry services have also been instituted to link up outlying agricultural areas with railway centres.

Since 1928, when the railway companies acquired powers to invest in road transport undertakings and to provide road services of their own, they have become, directly or through their subsidiaries, road operators on a large scale. On the passenger side, where consolidation of bus and coach companies had already gone far, the railways' policy was mainly one of acquiring financial interests in existing undertakings, private and municipal; some £9½ million have been invested in this way. This policy has made it possible to co-ordinate road and rail services in many areas by, for example, arranging time-tables so as to provide convenient connections between bus and train services, or by making road and rail tickets inter-available. On the goods side, the multiplicity of road undertakings and the absence, before 1933, of any public control over their number at first prevented the railway companies from extensively pursuing the same policy as that adopted with the bus companies. But in recent years they have acquired interests in a number of road haulage firms; in 1934, for instance, they absorbed two of the leading road transport concerns, Pickford's and Carter Paterson's. A new type of rate, the "agreed charge," with which the railway companies had already been experimenting in their efforts to recover traffic from the roads, was legalized in the Road and Rail Traffic Act of 1933. It consists of a flat rate of so much per ton or other traffic unit, applying to all of a particular trader's traffic irrespective of the distances the individual consignments are sent, and is quoted subject to the condition that the trader shall forward all his traffic by rail. Finally the railway companies have recently decided to apply to Parliament for the removal of those statutory restrictions on their charging powers which, they allege, put them at an unfair disadvantage compared with their rivals of the road.

THE STATE AND ROAD TRANSPORT

In the last two decades the internal combustion engine has not only added a new nation-wide branch to our transport facilities, but has profoundly modified the social life of the people. It has enormously increased the mobility of the population ; country-dwellers can get into the towns quickly and cheaply, and town-workers can conveniently reside in rural areas. Travel is now numbered among the indispensable comforts of life by many millions of people ; remote parts of the country have been made accessible to the urban population. There is, however, another side of the picture ; some 200,000 persons are annually involved in road accidents, about 6,500 fatally. The development of motor transport since the war is illustrated in the following table.

NUMBER OF MOTOR VEHICLES LICENSED IN BRITAIN
(November 30th in each year)

Type of vehicle	1922	1929	1932	1937
	000's	000's	000's	000's
Cars taxed on h.p.	294	899	1,014	1,677
Motor-cycles ...	352	516	434	387
Motor hackneys ...	72	81	72	74
Goods vehicles ...	159	325	360	492

Motor hackneys, which include buses, coaches and taxis, have increased less rapidly than other classes of vehicle, owing partly to the declining demand for taxis and partly, since 1930, to the restriction of the number of public service vehicles by the Traffic Commissioners set up under the Road Traffic Act of 1930. Motor cycles have been less numerous since 1930 owing to the raising of the age for driving licences from fourteen to sixteen, to the introduction of compulsory third-party insurance, and to the competition of "baby" cars. The phenomenal increase in the number of private cars is attributable to a variety of factors. Improvements in the technical efficiency of the internal combustion engine, and the application of the methods of mass production in the motor engineering industry, have progressively lowered the cost of motoring and brought car-ownership within the reach of the lower-paid middle classes. Though it is not easy to compare the retail prices of cars over a period of time, owing to changes in vehicle design and fittings, it is reliably estimated that car prices were halved between 1924 and 1937.[1] At the same time the rising level of real income per head and the diminution in size of the average family have enlarged the margin available for luxury expenditure; and the devices of salesmanship, together with the attractions of the instalment system, have succeeded in diverting a large part of this margin to the motor trade. Commercial motor vehicles, some two-thirds of which belong to ancillary users, possess manifold advantages, especially for short-distance work. Free from the restrictions of a specialized track, they have a flexibility that the railway and canal can never acquire ; they provide a door-to-door service that saves the cost, damage and loss of time associated with the intermediate handling of goods.

Motor transport has been subject to statutory control since its birth. Down to 1930 this control was exercised primarily in the interests of public safety, except for the regulation of hackney carriages by local licensing authorities, under legislation dating from the Town Police Clauses Act of 1847. The road legislation of the 1930's, however, is

[1] L. F. Duval, 'The Motor Industry,' in *Britain in Recovery*, p. 321.

based on a much broader view of the scope of public control. It is founded on the assumptions that unregulated competition in road transport is wasteful, that it fails to provide regular, co-ordinated, services, and that existing transport operators are entitled to protection against the intrusion of superfluous competitors. The railway companies, in particular, have stressed the wastefulness of allowing the introduction of additional road services if, in the opinion of a public authority, the existing transport facilities are adequate. These economic considerations have been supported by the further argument that the keeping of unnecessary vehicles off the roads would reduce accidents, relieve traffic congestion and keep down highway costs. These views commended themselves to the Royal Commission on Transport,[1] which recommended, in its second Report, sweeping changes in the licensing system relating to public service vehicles, and had the satisfaction of seeing them promptly embodied in the Road Traffic Act of 1930.

The licensing of public service vehicles was transferred under this Act from the local authorities to three Traffic Commissioners appointed for each of the thirteen traffic areas (reduced to twelve in 1934) into which Britain was divided. Firms proposing to operate public passenger services by road must obtain from the Traffic Commissioners two kinds of license: a public service vehicle licence for each vehicle, which must first pass certain tests of fitness, and a road service licence, which authorizes its owner to provide a particular type of service, stage carriage, express carriage or excursion, over a specified route. In deciding whether to issue a road service licence, the Commissioners are required to take into account such factors as the suitability of the proposed route, the extent to which its needs are already adequately served, the extent to which the proposed service is necessary or desirable in the public interest, the traffic

[1]*The Licensing and Regulation of Public Service Vehicles* (Cmd. 3416 of 1929), especially pp. 23, 24.

needs of the area as a whole, and the co-ordination of all forms of passenger transport, including transport by rail. Applications for the issue of licences may be opposed by those who are already providing transport facilities in the area of the proposed route. Further, the Commissioners may, and commonly do, attach various conditions to licences; they may, for instance, fix the fares to be charged and draw up the time-table of the service. Licence-holders are also required by the Act to pay "fair wages," *i.e.*, wages not less than those that government contractors would be required to pay under any "fair wage" resolution of the House of Commons. The general effect of the control thus established has been to restrict severely the development of road passenger transport. It is exceedingly difficult for new operators to secure licences, since they have to satisfy the Commissioners that the existing services are inadequate. The railway companies have naturally made the most of their right to oppose applications for licences, especially those for express carriage services, and have secured a considerable measure of protection from the Commissioners. Passenger transport by road has thus become practically a closed industry; stability is assured by the Commissioners for those who are within the charmed circle, but those who are outside must remain outside. Public service vehicles declined in number from 52,648 in 1930 to 45,656 in 1933; they have since increased to 49,574 in 1937. Long-distance coach services are the class that has been most curtailed.

Control by licensing was extended to the transport of goods by road, on the recommendation of the Conference on Rail and Road Transport, by the Road and Rail Traffic Act of 1933. The Chairmen of the Area Traffic Commissioners set up under the Road Traffic Act of 1930 were made the licensing authorities. Goods vehicle licences are of three kinds: "A" licences issued to public carriers, "B" licences issued to limited carriers, *i.e.*, firms using vehicles in connection with their own businesses but sometimes also acting as public carriers, and " C " licences issued to private carriers, whose sole use of vehicles is ancillary to their own businesses. The granting of all these licences is subject to the fulfilment of certain statutory conditions relating to the fitness of vehicles and the observance of regulations concerning speed, loading, drivers' hours and so forth. Provided these conditions are fulfilled, " C " licences cannot be withheld from ancillary users. But the issue of " A " and " B " licences, since the expiry of the first licencing period, has been entirely at the discretion of the Commissioners, who may withhold them if they consider that the existing facilities, in the areas the applicants propose to serve, are adequate. Rival operators of any form of transport have the right to oppose applications for " A " and " B " licences. In one significant respect the control exercised over road hauliers is less extensive than that over the operators of passenger services; the Commissioners have no powers to regulate the rates charged for goods transport. Traders are considered to be sufficiently safeguarded against excessive road transport charges by the existence of competing transport agencies and by their freedom to operate road vehicles of their own. In any case there is as yet no fully developed structure of road rates that could serve as a basis of control by a public authority. As on the passenger side, the establishment of statutory control over road haulage has had the effect of closing the industry to outsiders, who, in order to secure a licence, must satisfy the Traffic Commissioners not only that there are traders who are prepared to utilize their services but also that the existing transport facilities of all kinds are deficient relatively to the public need.[1] The number of vehicles operated under " A " licences was reduced from 100,182 in September 1935 to 91,101 in June 1937, and under " B " licences from 55,558 to 53,775;

[1] See G. J. Ponsonby, "The New Conditions of Entry into the Road Haulage Business," *Economica*, 1937, p. 184.

ancillary vehicles, on the other hand, operated under " C " licences without discretionary control by the Commissioners, increased from 303,886 to 362,380 in the same period.

London's transport problem, which had been the subject of periodical government inquiries since 1863, became particularly acute after the war, owing to the variety of competing agencies serving the public. In 1933, before the London Passenger Transport Act came into operation, London's population was served by the consolidated " Underground " group (including four tube railway companies, the London General Omnibus Company and several tramway and motor coach companies), the four main-line railways, the Metropolitan Railway, fourteen municipal tramway undertakings, and 54 bus companies and a score of coach companies running independently of the L.G.O.C. Yet despite this welter of competition, London's transport facilities were inadequate. New tube railways were urgently needed, especially in North and East London, the roads being too congested for adequate services to be provided; but owing to the unrestricted competition from surface transport facilities, extensions of the underground system could not be expected to pay financially. It was finally recognized that if there was to be any orderly development of London's transport services, competition must be superseded by monopoly. Unification was achieved in 1933 by the transfer to the London Passenger Transport Board of all passenger transport undertakings in the London traffic area, with the exception of the main-line railways, whose receipts from suburban traffic are pooled with those of the Board.

The consolidated undertaking is unique among the growing number of Britain's public corporations, for it is managed by a Board which is appointed neither by a public authority nor by a body of shareholders, but by certain " appointing trustees," namely the Chairmen of the London County Council and of the Clearing Bankers' Committee, the Presidents of the Law Society and of the Institute of

Chartered Accountants, and a representative of the London and Home Counties Traffic Advisory Committee. Parliament has attempted to avoid the dangers both of political interference through ministerial control and of public exploitation through shareholder control. The result is a Board in a position of unusual independence. It is, however, subject to some external regulation ; it cannot raise its fares without the sanction of the Railway Rates Tribunal ; the Traffic Advisory Committee can make representations to the Board regarding inadequacy of facilities and can lay complaints before the Minister of Transport ; and if a " standard rate " of dividend (5½ per cent.) is not paid on the " C " stock in each of any three successive years the stockholders have the right to appoint a receiver. Unification has already made possible a considerable extension and modernization of London's passenger transport facilities. In 1935 a programme of new works, involving a capital expenditure of £40 million, was drawn up by the Board and the main-line railways in collaboration with the government, which guaranteed the principal and interest of a loan for that amount. When the new works are completed, London will have seventeen additional miles of railway, with eleven new stations, and forty-five of the existing stations will have been reconstructed. London's trams are steadily being superseded by trolley-buses, about half of the original tramway mileage having been thus converted by 1938.

THE SHIPPING SLUMP

In shipping, as in most of the other industries on which Britain's nineteenth-century economic leadership was based, the years following the war brought a relative decline in Britain's position. From 39·2 per cent. in 1914 the United Kingdom's share in the world's merchant shipping tonnage fell to 29·4 in 1930 and to 26·4 in 1937. Until 1930 world tonnage continued to increase, while British tonnage remained practically stationary ; since then, however, shipping tonnage has declined absolutely in the world as a whole, the reduction being proportionately greater in Britain than in the rest of the world. Britain lost nearly 8 million gross

MERCHANT SHIPPING TONNAGE
(in million gross tons)

Country	1914	1921	1930	1937
Great Britain and Ireland ...	19·3	19·6	20·4	17·5
British Empire	21·0	22·1	23·4	20·6
United States	5·4	17·0	13·9	12·4
Japan	1·7	3·4	4·3	4·5
Norway	2·5	2·6	3·7	4·3
Germany	5·5	·7	4·2	3·9
World Total	49·1	62·0	69·6	66·3

tons during the war, but by 1921 she had restored her pre-war tonnage, partly through the activity of her own ship-building industry, especially during the boom of 1919–20, and partly by acquiring enemy tonnage as reparation payments. Meanwhile other countries, deprived of the services and the competition of the British mercantile marine, had enlarged their own fleets. The United States, appealed to by the Allies to build more ships during the war, increased her tonnage by nearly twelve million in the years 1914–21, and regained her mid-nineteenth century position as a close competitor of Britain for the carrying trade of the world. Japan, also, had practically doubled her merchant navy between 1914 and 1921.

Hence after the post-war boom had ended, the world found itself supplied with a greatly expanded shipping tonnage, although the volume of international trade remained below the level of 1913 until 1928. Accordingly tramp shipping freights collapsed from 602 in March 1920 (1913 = 100) to 141 in November 1921, and continued to fall until in 1928, before the world slump set in, they were only 10 per cent. above the level of 1913. Yet despite the existence of this surplus shipping capacity and the consequent low level of freights, world tonnage continued to grow. Part of the additional tonnage consisted of oil tankers for which there was a steadily expanding demand; part was due to the replacement of Germany's lost mercantile marine; and part was the product of shipping subsidies, prompted by the aspirations of economic nationalism. Unaided by the State, British shipping was thus already in a depressed condition when still heavier burdens were imposed on it by the great slump of the early 1930's. In the years 1933–34 the quantum of world trade was about 25 per cent. less than in 1929, shipping freights were about 20 per cent. lower than in 1913, and over 3 million tons of British shipping were laid up in British ports. Ships were able to earn little more than enough to cover their running costs, so that colossal arrears of depreciation were piling up.

Determined to maintain a mercantile marine adequate for national defence, the government granted a temporary subsidy to tramp shipping, the worst-hit section of the industry, under the British Shipping (Assistance) Act of 1935. The subsidy was not to exceed £2 million a year, and was to be scaled down as shipping freights approached the level of 1929, which was taken as a normal year. At the same time a Tramp Shipping Administrative Committee was established under the Act to regulate competition within the industry and improve the level of freights. Minimum freight schemes have been applied to the grain trade from Australia, Canada and the Argentine to Europe, and foreign shipowners have become parties to these schemes. At the end of 1937 the subsidy and the Administrative Committee were discontinued, but the latter's functions have been taken over by a committee voluntarily established by the shipping industry.[1] The government has recently announced its intention to introduce fresh legislation for the subsidizing of British shipping.

Assistance has also been given by the government to the

[1] See *Sixth Report of the Tramp Shipping Administrative Committee* (Cmd. 5750 of 1938).

Cunard Company in the form of a loan, on exceptionally favourable terms, to finance the construction of two new liners, the *Queen Mary* and the *Queen Elizabeth*. Without this aid, the construction of the first would not have been completed and the second would not have been laid down. In order to ensure that these vessels should operate under the most favourable conditions, the government required the Cunard and White Star lines to amalgamate and so restrict competition in the North Atlantic. History thus repeated itself in a curious fashion, for twenty years earlier the Cunard Company had received from the government a loan of £2,600,000 and an annual subsidy of £150,000, to facilitate the construction of two liners, the *Mauretania* and *Lusitania*. On that occasion the assistance had been given to prevent the Cunard fleet from passing under American control, it being a condition of the loan that the Cunarders should remain under British control and be put at the disposal of the government in the event of war.

AIR TRANSPORT

Commercial air transport is an entirely post-war development, the first regular services being introduced by two companies in 1919 between London and Paris. The subsequent expansion of this arm of transport can be judged from the following table. Several British companies at first

BRITISH CIVIL AVIATION[1]

Year	Aircraft mileage flown	Number of passengers	Tons of cargo
	000's		
1919	104	870	30
1922	717	10,390	215
1925	806	11,030	550
1928	916	27,300	813
1931	1,354	23,800	769
1934	4,557	135,100	1,422
1937	10,773	244,400	3,961

[1] These statistics relate to regular air services within Great Britain, between Britain and the Continent, Africa, Malay States and Hong Kong, and between Bermuda and New York (*Statistical Abstract for the U.K.*, Cmd. 5903 of 1939, p. 349).

competed for the traffic on the continental route, but they amalgamated in 1924 to form Imperial Airways Limited, which has since built up a world-wide system of air communications. From the first, these continental and imperial services have had to be subsidized by the government, which has been willing to assist this infant industry primarily in the interests of national defence. Internal air services were much slower in developing, mainly because Britain is too small a country for the aeroplane to show much saving in over-all time, as compared with the express train, on even the longest journeys. The first was introduced in 1922 between Manchester and London by Daimler Airways Limited, but was not a financial success. In 1930 Imperial Airways experimented with a service between London, Birmingham, Manchester and Liverpool, but this was soon abandoned. And in 1931 there was not a single internal service recorded. Since then considerable developments have taken place, so that by 1937 there were fourteen companies providing regular air services, during part or the whole of the year, over some 4,500 miles of route. The railway companies obtained powers in 1929 to construct aerodromes and operate air services, the first being run between Bristol and Cardiff by the Great Western in 1932. Railway Air Services, Limited, was promoted in 1934 by the four grouped companies, in conjunction with Imperial Airways, to pioneer further services, among which was one between London, Birmingham, the Isle of Man and Glasgow. Of the services operating within the British Isles, the most successful have been those involving a journey over the sea, since it is on these routes that air transport can show the greatest saving of time compared with other transport agencies. Municipalities have been encouraged and assisted by the government to construct aerodromes, and of the 98 aerodromes licensed in 1937, 35 were municipally owned.

CHAPTER XVIII

Monetary Policy

INFLATION AND DEFLATION

The imminence of war at the end of July 1914 produced a critical situation in the London money market. The banks, discount houses and bill-brokers held three or four hundred million pounds' worth of bills accepted by London accepting houses and joint-stock banks on behalf of merchants and others abroad.[1] Many of these foreign debtors found it impossible to remit funds to London, for the abnormal pressure to purchase sterling caused a breakdown of the foreign exchange market. Hence there was a danger of a general suspension of payments by the accepting houses, and of a consequent collapse of the discount market. The banks, expecting a rush of the public to withdraw cash, took the precautionary measure of calling in loans from the discount market, which was compelled to resort to the Bank of England for credit accommodation. Bank rate was rapidly raised and reached 10 per cent. on Saturday, August 1st. At the same time masses of securities were unloaded on the Stock Exchange, several members of which were "hammered"; in self-defence the Committee closed the Stock Exchange on July 31st.

The August Bank Holiday, which fell on Monday the 3rd, was extended by three days to give time for the preparation of emergency measures. Among these was a moratorium for certain classes of debtor, including the acceptors of bills, thus meeting the immediate difficulty of the discount market. Subsequently the Bank of England agreed to advance funds to the accepting houses so that they could honour the bills they had accepted, the principal of these loans not being repayable until one year after the end

[1] A. W. Kirkaldy (ed.), *British Finance during and after the War*, p. 4.

of the war; the government guaranteed the Bank against any loss under this arrangement. In order to supply the banks with the additional currency that they were expected to need, the Currency and Bank Notes Act, passed on August 6th, authorized the Bank of England to increase the fiduciary issue beyond the limit prescribed by the Act of 1844, and empowered the Treasury to issue legal-tender currency notes in denominations of one pound and ten shillings. Legally, these Treasury notes were convertible on demand into gold coin at the Bank of England; in fact, however, they were inconvertible notes, since insuperable difficulties were placed in the way of those demanding gold. No requirements were laid down in the Act regarding the maintenance of a cash reserve against the issue of currency notes.

The original issues of these notes were made as loans to the banks; but the public's demand for additional currency proved to be much less than had been expected, and the banks soon repaid the advances. Thereafter they paid for the currency notes they acquired by transferring deposits at the Bank of England to the Currency Notes Account, the government subsequently borrowing the funds paid into this Account and substituting its own securities. Though government apologists claimed that the issue of currency notes was not inflationary, because the method of issue ensured that their amount was merely adjusted to the monetary requirements of the public, nevertheless it played an essential part in the inflationary financial methods pursued during the war. For the ease with which additional supplies of notes could be obtained, and the absence of any upper limit to their amount, removed the brake that normally prevented the unlimited expansion of bank credit. Briefly, the inflationary process worked as follows:[1] first, the Bank of England advanced large credits to the govern-

[1] Cf. *First Interim Report of the Committee on Currency and Foreign Exchanges after the War* (Cd. 9182 of 1918), p. 4.

ment; through the cheques paid to government contractors and employees these credits were transferred to the joint-stock banks, whose cash reserves were correspondingly enlarged; and on the basis of these augmented reserves the banks were able to expand credit, by lending more to their customers (e.g., for the purchase of War Loan) and by investing in more government securities, especially Treasury Bills. Under pre-war conditions any such expansion of credit, by raising the price level, increasing the demand for currency, and causing an adverse movement of the exchanges, would have set up an internal and external drain on the cash reserve of the Bank of England, which would have been compelled to restrict the creation of credit. From 1914 onwards, however, the banks could meet the increasing demand for currency arising from the credit expansion by simply drawing on the unlimited reservoir of the Currency Notes Account. As a result of this elasticity of currency, the volume of purchasing power in circulation increased by about 125 per cent. between 1914 and 1920. The amount of currency in circulation, *i.e.*, gold, silver, copper and bank notes, in 1914, is estimated to have been £128 million; at the beginning of 1920 it was £393 million. Bank deposits, excluding those of the Bank of England, were £2,300 million in 1920, compared with £1,070 million in 1914.[1] Inevitably the general level of prices was raised by this plethora of money, the cost of living index at the beginning of 1920 registering an increase of 126 per cent. compared with 1914, and the *Economist* wholesale price index an increase of 184 per cent.

The gold standard was not officially abandoned until April 1st, 1919, when an embargo was placed on the export of gold. But, in effect, the free, uncontrolled, gold market of pre-war years had already disappeared by the beginning of 1917.[2] Gold coins had vanished from circulation, having

[1] R. McKenna, *Post-War Banking Policy*, pp. 2, 3.
[2] Feavearyear, *op. cit.* p. 307.

been either surrendered in exchange for currency notes or withdrawn into hoards. The melting down of gold coin, which became profitable through the appearance of a premium on gold, was prohibited in December 1916 under the Defence of the Realm Act. Further, owing to shipping losses, higher freights, and the government's refusal to insure gold cargoes, the risk and cost of exporting gold had greatly increased, thus lowering very considerably the gold export point. Finally, by mobilizing American securities and borrowing in America, the government was able to "peg" the sterling-dollar exchange artificially at 4.76½ dollars to the pound, so that, for a time, there was little external depreciation of sterling to reveal the breakdown of the gold standard. When the exchanges were "unpegged," in March, 1919, the London–New York rate rapidly sank to its "natural" level, falling as low as 3·22 dollars to the pound in February 1920.

British currency policy in the years immediately following the war was largely based on the recommendations of the Cunliffe Committee, appointed by the Treasury and the Ministry of Reconstruction in January 1918 to inquire into the currency and exchange problems that were likely to arise after the war. In August 1918 it presented an interim report in which it declared that "after the war the conditions necessary to the maintenance of an effective gold standard should be restored without delay,"[1] and recommended the adoption of certain measures to that end. These included, first, the cessation of government borrowing and the reduction of the floating debt as soon as possible after the war; second, the restoration of the use of Bank rate to check the expansion of credit and the foreign drain of gold; and third, the limitation of the issue of fiduciary notes. On this last point, the Committee recommended that until the Bank of England's gold reserve had risen to £150 million and a satisfactory foreign-exchange position had been

[1] *Interim Report*, p. 11.

maintained for at least a year, the government should follow the policy of cautiously reducing the uncovered note issue. This having been done, the actual maximum fiduciary issue in one year should become the legal maximum issue for the following year. The Committee was opposed to the early resumption of an internal gold circulation, but recommended that the Bank of England, under whose control all the country's gold reserves should be concentrated, should be obliged to provide gold for export in exchange for its notes. Finally, after the fiduciary currency note issue had been reduced to an amount consistent with the maintenance of a gold reserve of £150 million, the outstanding currency notes were to be replaced by Bank of England notes, and the combined issue was to be regulated in accordance with the maximum fiduciary principle, subject to emergency provisions whereby the Bank, with the consent of the Treasury, might temporarily exceed the fiduciary limit. Thus the main features of our subsequent currency policy, namely deflation, restoration of the gold standard, and amalgamation of the Bank of England and Treasury note issues, were all in conformity with the recommendations of the Cunliffe Committee.

It is probable that the deflationary process which started in 1920 would have occurred in any case, as a reaction from the preceding boom. Once industry had raised its depleted stocks to more normal levels, caught up the arrears of capital renewals, and adapted its equipment to the expected level of peace-time demand, some slackening of the feverish activity of 1919–20 was inevitable. That this is at least an important part of the explanation of the post-war collapse of prices is confirmed by the more or less simultaneous appearance of the same phenomenon in many other countries, especially the United States. At the same time, there is no doubt that deflation in Britain was assisted, accentuated and prolonged, by the policy pursued by the government and the Bank of England. Bank rate, which had stood at 5 per cent. for the greater part of the war period, was raised to 6 per cent. in November 1919 and to 7 per cent. in April 1920. It was maintained at this penal level for the unusually long period of twelve months. The Treasury Bill rate[1] was raised in October 1919 from 3½ to 4½ per cent., in the following month to 5½ per cent., and in April 1920 to 6½ per cent. By thus resorting to the traditional instrument of credit control, the monetary authorities were able to help in reversing the movement of the price level, and, though this was no part of their plan, in inducing a severe industrial depression. In further support of this policy a Treasury Minute of December 15th, 1919, directed that the actual maximum fiduciary circulation of currency notes in any year should be the fixed maximum for the following year, this step having been recommended in the Final Report of the Cunliffe Committee, presented a fortnight earlier. From a total of over £320 million in 1919 the fiduciary Treasury note issue was reduced to about £248 million in 1924.

Commodity prices began their precipitous decline in the spring of 1920; the *Economist* index of wholesale prices dropped from the peak of 323 (1914 = 100) in March 1920 to 197 twelve months later, and to 168 at the end of 1921. As the price level fell, the external value of sterling rose, the American exchange improving from 3·22 dollars to the pound in February 1920 to 4·34 a year later and to 4·69 in February 1923. Bank rate, having accomplished its invidious task, was gradually lowered from the crisis level of 7 per cent. to 3 per cent. in July 1922. It was raised to 4 per cent. in July 1923, but not made effective at that level until a year later; then in March 1925 it was raised again to 5 per cent. This stiffening of the rate of discount, together with the speculative purchase of sterling in anticipation of a return to gold, brought sterling back in the spring of 1925

[1] *I.e.* the fixed rate of discount at which Treasury Bills were offered, without any limit to their amount, from April, 1915, to April, 1921.

almost to its pre-war parity with the dollar. Accordingly the government, which had been advised in February 1925, by the Committee on the Currency and Bank of England Note Issues, to announce forthwith that its irrevocable policy was an early return to the gold standard, decided in April that the moment had come to take this step. Mr. Winston Churchill, in his Budget speech of April 28th, announced that gold for export would henceforth be obtainable from the Bank of England in exchange for legal tender money, and an Act was passed shortly afterwards making full arrangements for the functioning of the restored gold standard.

To the man in the street the monetary system established by the Gold Standard Act of 1925, bore but little resemblance to that with which he had been familiar before the war. There was no gold coinage in circulation; the holder of Bank notes and Treasury notes could not demand gold coin in exchange at the Bank of England; nor could the possessor of gold bullion, except the Bank of England, take it to the Mint to have it assayed and coined. The link of sterling with gold was re-established merely by the legal obligation of the Bank of England to sell bars, each containing approximately 400 ounces troy of fine gold, at the fixed price of £3 17s. 10½d. per ounce of standard gold (= approximately 85s. per fine ounce), and to buy at the price of £3 17s. 9d. per ounce. Britain returned, in short, to a gold bullion standard, not to a gold specie standard.

Three years later came the last of the measures advocated by the Cunliffe Committee, namely the transfer of the Treasury note issue to the Bank of England, under the Currency and Bank Notes Act of 1928. The Bank thus became the sole note-issuing authority in England and Wales, though the Scottish banks still retained their rights of issue. Before the transfer the Bank's fiduciary issue stood at £19,750,000, the maximum that was possible under the provisions of the Act of 1844; this figure had been reached in 1923 after the last of the English note-issuing banks, Fox Fowler and Company, lost its right of issue by amalgamating with Lloyds. The Act of 1928 prescribed £260 million as the new upper limit to the fiduciary issue; beyond that amount all notes issued had to be backed by an equivalent reserve of gold. But an important modification of the method of note regulation, amounting, in fact, almost to an abandonment of the maximum fiduciary principle, was made by introducing an "elastic limit." With the consent of the Treasury, the Bank was authorized to exceed the prescribed limit for a period of up to six months; this sanction could be renewed until two years had elapsed from the date of the original excess, after which the approval of Parliament was required. The Treasury was also empowered to direct, at the request of the Bank, that the fiduciary issue should be reduced.

In effect, therefore, the Bank and the Treasury were now authorized to ignore, or at least evade, the maximum fiduciary principle, and to regulate the note issue in accordance with what they conceived to be the currency requirements of the country. The Bank could be empowered to issue additional notes without having any corresponding gold backing; it could, on the other hand, "sterilize" any acquisitions of gold by lowering its fiduciary issue. These powers have not been allowed to rust through disuse. In August 1931 the fiduciary issue was raised to £275 million in order to compensate for the contraction of the note issue, caused by gold losses during the financial crisis. This excess was continued until March 1933, by which time gold was flowing back to the Bank in large quantities as a result of the operations of the Exchange Equalization Account. In December 1936, when the Bank of England acquired £65 million of gold from the Exchange Equalization Account, the Treasury authorized the Bank to reduce its fiduciary issue to £200 million, in order to avoid what it considered would be an undue expansion of the currency. And in January 1939, when the Exchange Equalization Account withdrew £200 million of gold from the Bank, the fiduciary issue was raised to £400 million.

Still another change in the regulation of the note issue was made by the Currency and Bank Notes Act of March 1939. The Bank's gold, hitherto valued for accounting purposes at the old Mint price of £3 17s. 10½d. per standard ounce, is now revalued each week at its market price. The maximum fiduciary issue, which can still be varied with the consent of the Treasury, has been reduced to £300 million in order to offset the increase of nearly £100 million in the book value of the Bank's gold. If, at any weekly revaluation, the gold reserve is less than the excess of the note issue beyond the fiduciary limit, gold is transferred from the Exchange Equalization Account to the Bank; and conversely, if the Bank has more gold than it needs as backing for the note issue the excess can be transferred to the Account. By thus transferring gold between the Bank and the Account, it is now possible to adjust the gold reserve to the note issue instead of, as was formerly the practice, adjusting the note issue to the gold backing. This latest legislation, therefore, frankly abandons the cardinal principle of the Act of 1844, namely the automatic regulation of the note issue by gold movements. The currency is now officially recognized to be a "managed" one.

THE GOLD STANDARD

The return to the gold standard in 1925, described by the Macmillan Committee as "one of the turning points in the post-war economic history of the world,"[1] was destined to be but a brief interlude. From the beginning it was the subject of a lively controversy. "It may, indeed, be said," declared the Macmillan Committee, "that at no time since the termination of the historic disputes which followed the Napoleonic wars and which led to the passing of the Bank

[1] *Report of the Committee on Finance and Industry* (Cmd. 3697 of 1931), p. 6.

Act of 1844 has the monetary organization of our country been the subject of so much criticism as in recent times."[1] The critics contended that sterling was re-linked to gold at a rate which overvalued the pound by about 10 per cent., and that British exporters were consequently handicapped in competing with overseas firms. This contention was accepted as valid by the Macmillan Committee. It was urged, further, that the policy the Bank of England felt obliged to pursue, in order to protect its gold reserve and maintain the gold standard, was having the most disastrous effects on Britain's industry and trade. With a gold reserve of little more than the minimum of £150 million suggested by the Cunliffe Committee, the Bank of England could not, or dared not, pursue the expansionist credit policy that was needed, according to industrialists, to resuscitate depressed British industry. " The rise of Bank rate to 5 per cent. in 1925 was the beginning of a continuous regime of dear money lasting with little relief for five years. There was an interval of nine weeks at 4 per cent. in the autumn of 1925, but otherwise the rate remained at either 4½ or 5 per cent. till still higher rates were imposed in 1929."[2] That this maintenance of high interest rates, with its discouraging influence on investment and enterprise, was the direct outcome of the restored gold standard, cannot be doubted. For after the abandonment of the gold standard in 1931, an unprecedented era of cheap money was ushered in, Bank rate having stood at 2 per cent. since June, 1932. Finally, quite apart from the discussion of the special difficulties encountered by Britain as the result of her return to gold, the gold standard as a system was widely condemned, in Mr. Keynes' famous phrase, as " a barbarous relic." To the embarrassment of industry, it caused the level of prices to fluctuate in accordance with purely accidental factors affecting the supply of, or the demand for, the yellow metal,

[1] *loc. cit.*
[2] R, G. Hawtrey, *A Century of Bank Rate*, p. 134.

and forced any country adhering to it to sacrifice the more important objective of stability of prices to the less important one of stability of exchanges.

There were few regrets, therefore, when in 1931 Britain once more cut herself adrift from the monetary standard to which she had so arduously and hopefully returned. The breakdown of the gold standard was brought about primarily by the world depression. In the first place, by curtailing Britain's exports, receipts from shipping and from financial services, and income from overseas investments, it caused the balance of payments to become adverse. This in itself was bound to put pressure on sterling and induce an unfavourable movement of the exchanges. But further difficulties were added to this basic disturbance. There was, before the crisis developed, a serious lack of balance between Britain's short-term liabilities to foreigners and her short-term foreign assets. On March 31st, 1931, according to evidence collected by the Macmillan Committee, deposits on foreign account with British banks and accepting houses, together with sterling bills held on foreign account and advances made by foreigners to the London discount market, amounted to over £407 million. Against this liability, British banks and accepting houses had claims on foreigners, in respect of acceptances, amounting to nearly £153 million, together with an unknown volume of deposits in foreign banks, which, however, was hardly likely to make up anything like the whole of the balance. This excess of short-term indebtedness to foreigners was in marked contrast to the position before the war when, it was generally believed, London's liquid international assets at least equalled her short-term overseas liabilities. High bank rate had played a by no means unimportant part in the drawing of these liquid funds to London.

With this unbalanced short-term position, it required only some incident necessitating the repatriation of foreign balances, immobilizing British short-term assets abroad, or disturbing confidence in sterling, to induce a large-scale withdrawal of foreign funds from London, thus setting up a terrific pressure on the exchanges and a drain on the Bank's gold reserve. And of such incidents there was no lack in 1931. In May a financial crisis broke out in Austria, with the revelation of the financial difficulties of the Kredit-Anstalt, and spread to Germany, where the banks had to suspend or restrict payments. This crisis in Central Europe reacted on the London money market in several ways; it led foreign bankers to withdraw balances from London in order to increase the liquidity of their own position; it embarrassed the accepting houses, which were unable to recover at once the large sums, estimated at £45 million, owed to them by German firms in respect of acceptances; and it created a panicky and gloomy atmosphere abroad through which the features unfavourable to sterling were seen in their blackest hues. At home we were descending lower into the trough of industrial depression, and expenditure on unemployment relief was mounting rapidly, so that a budgetary deficit was in prospect. On July 31st the May Committee presented its report, describing in somewhat alarming language the parlous condition of Britain's finances, and estimating the deficit in the budget at £120 million. Since unbalanced budgets have often led to inflationary finance, especially in post-war Europe, there was a widespread apprehension, abroad much more than at home, of a depreciation of sterling.

In mid-July there began a vast withdrawal of foreign funds from London. It is estimated that £200 million of these were repatriated in the three months July, August and September. Bank rate was raised, in short stages, from the 2½ per cent. to which it had been reduced on May 14th, 1931, to 4½ per cent. on August 6th, and remained at this level, unusually moderate for a time of crisis, until the suspension of the gold standard. The Bank of England supported the exchanges by borrowing on August 1st £50 million from the Bank of France and the Federal Reserve Bank of New York. These credits having been exhausted, the Treasury raised further loans of £80 million in Paris and New York on August 28th. Meanwhile a National Government had replaced the Labour Government on August 24th, and proceeded to introduce a supplementary budget imposing additional taxation and severe cuts in expenditure, it being hoped that this would serve to restore foreign confidence in sterling and "save the pound." Foreign opinion, however, was by no means assured that these cuts would be accepted by the British public; an unfortunate affair at Invergordon, blazoned forth in the continental press as a "mutiny in the British Navy," appeared to justify these doubts, and the run on London continued. On Saturday, September 19th, the credits raised by the Treasury were practically exhausted; the government had failed to secure further loans from the bankers in Paris and New York, and the Bank of England was losing gold. Accordingly, the government authorized the Bank on the following day to suspend the convertibility of its notes into gold, this action being regularized by the Gold Standard (Amendment) Act passed on September 21st. Sterling promptly depreciated, being about 20 per cent. below its former gold value when the market settled down on Thursday, September 24th, and about 30 per cent. below at the end of the year.[1]

The fall of the pound, though represented before the event as a tragedy to avoid which almost any sacrifice was worth while, soon proved to be a piece of good fortune for British industry. It released Bank rate policy from the strait-jacket of the gold points, and permitted the cheapening of credit that had been impossible during the interregnum of gold. Bank rate, raised to 6 per cent. on the day gold was

[1] Opinions differ widely about the relative significance of the factors contributing to the breakdown of the gold standard. For more detailed discussion see P. Einzig, *The Tragedy of the Pound*; G. Cassel, *The Downfall of the Gold Standard*; T. E. Gregory, *The Gold Standard and its Future*; L. Robbins, *The Great Depression*; F. Benham, *British Monetary Policy*, and H. F. Fraser, *Great Britain and the Gold Standard*.

abandoned, and maintained at that level for five months, was then speedily lowered to 2 per cent. in June 1932, at which rate it has since remained. At the same time, the cash basis of the banking system was broadened by expansive open-market operations on the part of the Bank. Bankers' deposits at the Bank of England rose from the £60–65 million they had averaged in the years 1928–31 to over £80 million in 1932 and £100 million in 1933. As a result, short-term rates of interest fell to phenomenally low levels; the rate of discount on three months' bank bills, for instance, has fluctuated within the limits of ½ and 1 per cent. since the summer of 1932. Long-term rates fell in sympathy with short-term, their decline being assisted by the government's huge conversion operations in 1932, notably the reduction of War Loan interest from 5 to 3½ per cent., and by the banks' large purchases of securities, which raised their investments from £300 million in the last quarter of 1931 to £564 million in the last quarter of 1933. Abandonment of the gold standard also insulated Britain from the depressing deflationary process, which continued unabated in the countries still on gold; here the downward trend of the general price level immediately ceased.

Since the breakdown of the gold standard, the monetary authorities have no longer used Bank rate for the purpose of regulating the exchanges; instead, a new technique of control through exchange funds has been developed. The British Exchange Equalization Account, controlled by the Treasury and operated by the Bank of England, was set up in July 1932 with resources of £175 million, mainly in the form of Treasury Bills; this amount was raised to £375 million in 1933, after the United States left the gold standard, and to £575 million in 1937. Officially the purpose of this fund is to eliminate fluctuations of the exchanges occasioned by purely transitory influences, such as speculation and the shifting of short-term funds from one financial centre to another, but not to counteract "real" causes necessitating changes in the long-term trend of the exchanges. Whether this intention has been strictly adhered to seems open to doubt, since the operations of the fund resulted, down to the spring of 1938, in the acquisition of large amounts of gold. Exchange funds play the leading part in the working of the much modified type of gold standard set up in September 1936, under the Tripartite Agreement. The French, British, and United States governments declared their intention to co-operate in the stabilization of the exchanges between their currencies, and followed up this announcement by each agreeing to release gold for export to the others; that is to say, each Treasury undertook to buy with gold, through its exchange fund, any of its own currency that the other funds had acquired during the preceding day. Subsequently Belgium, Holland and Switzerland joined this co-operating group. Thus gold movements were re-established between the Treasuries of these six countries, as a means of settling temporary balances of payments, but each Treasury retained a perfectly free hand regarding internal monetary policy.

THE BANKS AND INDUSTRY

Turning now to the structure of the banking system, we find the amalgamation movement continuing during the later years of the war and in the immediate post-war years, and then coming almost to a standstill. Of the handful of private banks that still survived in 1914, only one, Hoare's Bank, founded in 1673, now remains to remind us of the origins of English banking. The purely "local bank" has entirely disappeared, but there remain a few regional banks, each with several hundred branches, such as the District Bank and the four independent Scottish banks, which have escaped affiliation to the banking giants. The last stages of the amalgamation process took the form of fusions of huge banks, themselves the results of long series of mergers.

Thus on the last day of 1917 the National Provincial Bank and the Union of London and Smith's Bank joined forces. In 1918, the *annus mirabilis* in the history of bank amalgamations, an unprecedented number of monster fusions was effected; the London City and Midland Bank combined with the London Joint Stock Bank, and altered its name for a few years to London Joint City and Midland, until in 1923 it assumed its present brief title, the Midland Bank; Lloyds absorbed the Capital and Counties Bank, so acquiring some 470 additional branches, mainly in areas where Lloyds had not hitherto been established; Barclays, which two years previously had acquired the United Counties Bank, with numerous branches in Lancashire, Yorkshire and Midlands, continued its expansion by absorbing the London, Provincial and South Western Bank; the National Provincial and Union Bank, its appetite whetted by the fusion of the previous year, absorbed Coutts and Co., whose banking record goes back to 1692; and finally the London County and Westminster amalgamated with Parr's, becoming the London County Westminster and Parr's until 1923, when it abbreviated its name to Westminster Bank. These mergers had the effect of concentrating the great bulk of English banking business in the hands of five banks, dubbed the "Big Five" at the time of the Peace Conference.

Industrial and commercial interests became perturbed over this concentration of financial power, fearing that banking competition might be entirely eliminated and a "money trust" established. A Treasury Committee on Bank Amalgamations was appointed in 1918 to investigate the matter. It reported that, though fusions of big banks might confer some benefits on the community, such as the spreading of credit over larger areas and the making of much larger individual loans than small banks could undertake, nevertheless further amalgamations might prejudice the public interest, by opening the way to joint agreements concerning rates and policy. It therefore recommended that, in future, banking amalgamations should take place only with the consent of both the Treasury and the Board of Trade. A bill implementing this recommendation was dropped, the banks agreeing voluntarily to submit amalgamation schemes for government approval. Since then the process of consolidation has been rounded off by the absorption of the remaining country banks, but the " Big Five " still remain five.

The Scottish banks, reduced to eight, have not escaped the tentacles of the expanding English undertakings; four of them have become affiliated, the Clydesdale Bank to the Midland in 1920 and the North of Scotland Bank to the same bank in 1924; Barclays acquired a controlling interest in the British Linen Bank, and Lloyds in the National Bank of Scotland, both in 1918. Though controlled by their southern purchasers, these four Scottish banks remain in existence as separate legal entities, and retain their note-issuing rights. The other four, the Royal Bank of Scotland, the Bank of Scotland, the Commercial Bank of Scotland and the Union Bank of Scotland, still survive as independent regional banks. Lancashire, which before the war successfully resisted amalgamation schemes that would have deprived it of locally controlled banks, is still served by banks with predominantly Lancashire interests. In 1918 the Bank of Liverpool acquired one of the oldest London banks, Martin's, and in 1928 the combined concern absorbed the Lancashire and Yorkshire Bank. Martin's Bank, therefore, though one of the London clearing banks, is much more regional in its interests than any of the " Big Five." Williams Deacon's Bank, rooted in Lancashire, has escaped the frying-pan of the " Big Five " but fell, in 1930, into the fire of the Royal Bank of Scotland; however, it still retains its nominal independence. The remaining Lancashire banks, the District and the County, combined in 1935.

In the field of banking policy, perhaps the most debated

topic since the war has been that of the relation between the banks and industry. In particular, the bankers' refusal to modify what has long been a cardinal principle of British deposit banking, namely the avoidance of long-term loans and of industrial investments, came under a heavy fire of criticism. If depressed industries were to be rationalized and re-equipped, the banks, declared the critics, would have to play a more active part in putting up the necessary finance. German "industrial banking" was commonly held up as a model of what British banking should be. In reply, the bankers stressed the paramount importance of maintaining liquidity and of avoiding risky investments if banking stability was to be assured, and the Macmillan Committee, while emphasizing the need for institutions engaged in the provision of long-dated capital, agreed that it would be unwise for the banks to depart from their traditional banking sphere.

The banks, however, under the enterprising leadership of the Bank of England, have gone some way towards filling this gap in British financial facilities. In 1929 the Bank set up a subsidiary private company, the Securities Management Trust, with an expert staff, whose functions are to investigate and advise the Bank on schemes needing finance and to co-ordinate arrangements for raising the capital for approved schemes. In the following year, the Bankers' Industrial Development Company was formed, its share capital being subscribed by the joint-stock banks, the merchant bankers and the Securities Management Trust, the last of which has a majority of the voting rights. It has assisted in the financing of a number of rationalization schemes, such as those of National Shipbuilders Security, the Lancashire Cotton Corporation, Stewarts and Lloyds, and John Summers and Sons, Ltd. The Bank of England also acquired, in 1930, a large shareholding in the United Dominions Trust, which is engaged in financing hire purchase for producers. Credit for Industry, a subsidiary of the

United Dominions Trust, was promoted in 1934 to provide long-term loans for small and medium-sized concerns. Perhaps the most startling recent departure from banking traditions was the participation of the banks in the financing of Richard Thomas and Company's reconstruction and extensions at Ebbw Vale in 1938. Of the £6 million required by this concern to complete the programme it had started, £5½ million were raised by issuing Prior Lien Debenture Stock to the joint-stock banks and other financial institutions, and the remainder by issuing ordinary shares, which were taken up by the Securities Management Trust. It is just possible that these unorthodox financial activities of the Bank of England and the commercial banks may mark the beginnings of "industrial banking" in Britain; but it is much too early yet to make any safe prophecy in the matter. If we may judge by the pronouncements of bank chairmen, "Kathleen Mavourneen" loans,[1] which may be for years and may be for ever, are still anathema to the banks. Thus Mr. E. Fisher, chairman of Barclays Bank, addressing the shareholders' meeting on January 19th, 1939, declared: "It is not for us as bankers to provide permanent or long-term capital for agriculture or for any other industry, for should we do so, we should be lessening our general usefulness to the community and exceeding our proper functions."

[1] W. Leaf, *Banking*, p. 157.

CHAPTER XIX

Labour Conditions Since 1914

INDUSTRIAL RELATIONS

An almost complete cessation of hostilities on the labour front followed the outbreak of war in 1914. On August 25th the trade unions proclaimed, unilaterally, an "industrial truce"; and in March 1915 they agreed to relinquish the use of the strike weapon while the war lasted, and to relax their rules so as to allow of the "dilution" of labour in the munitions industries. In return, the government undertook to limit war profits and to use its influence, after the war, in securing the restoration of pre-war trade union practices. Legal sanction was given to the terms of this agreement by the Munitions of War Act, 1915, which among other things prohibited strikes and lock-outs, and imposed compulsory arbitration, in all industries engaged upon war work. The Committee on Production, originally set up to investigate problems of labour supply in engineering and shipbuilding establishments, became the principal arbitration tribunal. Strikes did not entirely cease, but those that occurred were for the most part small, local and unofficial. The most serious was that of 200,000 South Wales miners who successfully defied the law forbidding strikes. After the Armistice the prohibition of strikes and lock-outs was promptly repealed, but the regulation of wages remained subject to statutory restriction for a further period of twelve months. Employers were not to pay less than certain "prescribed" rates, namely the standard rates prevailing on the date of the Armistice; but in order to allow for possible changes in the cost of living during this transitional period, it was provided that new rates might be substituted for the "prescribed" rates, either by agreement between the parties, or by an award, legally binding on the parties, of a specially constituted Interim Court of Arbitration.

Meanwhile the Whitley Committee, one of many appointed to draw up plans for reconstruction after the war, had been studying the problems of industrial relations. For industries in which both employers and employed were well organized, it recommended the establishment of Joint Industrial Councils, together with District Councils and Workshop Committees, possessing a much wider range of functions than those of the ordinary conciliation board. "We are convinced," reported the Committee, "that a permanent improvement in the relations between employers and employed must be founded upon something other than a cash basis. What is wanted is that the workpeople should have a greater opportunity of participating in the discussion about, and adjustment of, those parts of industry by which they are most affected." Hence the Councils were to consider, besides wage matters, such questions as the participation of workpeople in industrial control, the better utilization of the practical knowledge and experience of the workers, technical education and training, and legislation affecting industry. The less adequately organized industries were to set up Joint Industrial Councils, too, but government representatives were to sit on these Councils in an advisory capacity. In a third group, the unorganized industries, the Committee recommended the setting up of Trade Boards, which were ultimately to be replaced by Joint Industrial Councils when these industries had become well enough organized. On the question of arbitration, the Committee flatly rejected any schemes for the compulsory settlement of industrial disputes, but recommended that the State should set up a voluntary arbitration court and arm itself with powers to hold a public inquiry into the circumstances of any industrial dispute.

This series of recommendations was accepted in its

entirety by the government. The Trade Boards Act of 1918 authorized the establishment of Trade Boards in industries having no adequate machinery for the effective regulation of wages, and by 1921 Boards had been set up, to the great advantage of the workpeople concerned, in forty trades, employing about 1½ million workers. Then came the slump, and with it criticisms, by employers, of the Boards and of their rate-fixing policy. The Cave Committee investigated these complaints in 1921–22 and, while appreciating the beneficial effects of the Trade Board system, recommended a number of amendments, including one to restrict the application of the system to trades in which there was not only a lack of negotiating machinery but also an unduly low level of wages. No amending legislation has been passed, but the extension of the Trade Board system has been very much slowed down, only six new trades having been brought within it since 1921, the latest being the baking and rubber manufacturing industries in 1938. The Whitley Committee's recommendations relating to arbitration were implemented in the Industrial Courts Act of 1919. This set up a permanent Industrial Court to which disputes might be referred with the consent of both parties, and empowered the Minister of Labour to appoint a Court of Inquiry to investigate any industrial dispute. The Industrial Court has been used mainly by industries of the second rank, the major industries preferring to rely on their own negotiating machinery. In this restricted sphere the Court has proved a useful agency for the settlement of disputes, especially those relating to the interpretation of agreements. No legislation was needed to establish Joint Industrial Councils, which were set up, generally with government help, in seventy-three industries. Of these, about fifty survive, most of them in industries where labour is not very strongly organized, such as the pottery, wool textile, grain milling, hosiery and silk industries. The "Whitley" Councils, mainly concerned with the negotiation of wage agreements, have disappointed those who hoped that they might open the door to some measure of joint industrial control.

The legal enforcement of collective agreements in certain industries is an interesting recent development in the State regulation of wages. Until 1934 the collective bargains made between a trade union and an employers' association were not, in general, enforceable in the courts. There was nothing, therefore, except the feeble sanction of business morality, to prevent individual employers from ignoring such agreements and paying less than the agreed rates. When this happened extensively, firms remaining loyal to the agreement naturally found themselves at a competitive disadvantage. It was to prevent the "unfair" competition arising from the cutting of wages that the Cotton Manufacturing Industry (Temporary Provisions) Act was passed in 1934, authorizing the Minister of Labour to make collective agreements legally binding on all employers in this industry. In the road transport industry, too, the non-observance by many firms of the decisions of the National Joint Conciliation Board led to the Road Haulage Wages Act of 1938, which provides that the wage rates recommended by a Central Wages Board shall, after confirmation by the Minister of Labour, be the "statutory remuneration."

Acute and widespread industrial unrest, in origin partly political and partly economic, characterized the years immediately following the war. Violently jolted out of their accustomed way of life by the war, the working classes had become more receptive to socialist ideas and more critical of social injustices. They had been encouraged to look forward to the construction of a brave new world, only to be disillusioned as government pledges were broken. While the boom lasted, with its rapidly rising prices, many strikes were called to secure for wage-earners some share in its specious prosperity. Among these were strikes, in 1919, of cotton workers in June, Yorkshire miners and the Police Union in July, and railwaymen and iron-founders in September; and in 1920 came a national miners' strike. When slump and deflation brought demands for wage reductions, a fresh series of disputes was provoked; miners and cotton workers were locked out in 1921, and engineers in the following year. Their resistance failed to stem the downward sweep of wages.

In membership, the trade union movement was far stronger in the years immediately after the war than it has ever been, before or since. The 4,135,000 trade unionists of 1913 had been increased to 6,533,000 in 1918 and to 8,334,000, the peak figure, in 1920. Every industry shared in this advance, but it was among the lower-paid workers that the greatest gains were recorded. General labour unions increased their membership from 375,000 in 1913 to 1,353,000 in 1920. Agricultural workers, usually difficult to organize, were infected by this rapid growth of trade unionism and encouraged by the establishment of machinery for fixing minimum agricultural wages under the Corn Production Act, 1917; in consequence, the membership of agricultural unions rose from a mere 22,000 in 1913 to 211,000 in 1920. A series of amalgamations further consolidated the forces of trade unionism. The majority of iron and steel trade unionists were brought within a single organization, the Iron and Steel Trades Confederation, in 1917; the old Amalgamated Society of Engineers, together with a number of other craft unions, combined in 1920 to form the Amalgamated Engineering Union, with a membership of over 400,000; nearly all the unions recruiting dock and road-transport workers were fused in the Transport and General Workers' Union of 1921, and in the same year three societies of bricklayers and masons amalgamated to form the Amalgamated Union of Building Trade Workers; most of the general labour unions were progressively combined to form the National Union of General and Municipal Workers in 1924. In spite of this " rationalization " of the trade union world, however, there remained (and still remains) a good deal of overlapping between rival unions and a reluctance on the part of skilled workers to merge themselves in unions recruited on an industrial, as distinct from a craft, basis. Thus, despite the formation of the powerful Amalgamated Engineering Union in 1920, no less than fifty engineering unions were involved in the lock-out of 1922; in the cotton industry there are still 164 unions, mainly of the craft type.

The emergence of the General Council of the Trades Union Congress as a co-ordinating body, or general staff, for the whole movement was a momentous development in the world of labour. It was set up in 1921 to replace the old Parliamentary Committee, which had little power of initiative. Among the duties entrusted to it were those of watching and initiating labour legislation, of adjusting inter-union disputes, and of promoting common action on questions of wages and hours. To these an important addition was made in 1924, when the General Council was authorized to intervene in industrial disputes and to organize moral and material support for the unions concerned. In May 1926 the strength of this central organization was put to the test. The general strike, called by the General Council in support of the miners, revealed on the one hand the remarkable solidarity and loyalty of the rank and file, and on the other the lack of determination of their leaders. After nine tense days, during which the country's industries were practically at a standstill, the General Council, faced with a firm refusal of the government to make any concessions, capitulated and called off the strike. The Cabinet had won hands down in this battle of wills.

In order to restrict the use of the strike weapon, the Trade Disputes and Trade Unions Act was passed in the following year. Sympathetic strikes and strikes " designed or calculated to coerce the government either directly or by inflicting hardship upon the community" were declared illegal. Unions of civil servants were required to sever their connection with the rest of the trade union movement. Further, the law relating to the political funds of trade unions was amended by providing that no member of a union could be called upon to pay a political levy unless he had first signed a form stating that he was willing to contribute.

Checked by the collapse of the general strike and by the final defeat of the miners, the trade union movement has since been quiescent. Disputes were a little more numerous in the mildly booming year 1929, and also during the worst years of depression, but, compared with the titanic struggles of 1919–26, the disputes since the general strike have been insignificant. Trade union membership, which had dropped from over 8 million in 1920 to 5,219,000 in 1926, continued to fall until 1933, when it stood at 4,392,000, little more than the figure for 1913. It has since recovered to 5,851,000 in 1937.

SOCIAL INSURANCE

In contrast to its launching, which generated an extraordinary amount of heat, the subsequent history of the Health Insurance scheme has been uneventful. Changes have been made in the scope of the scheme and in the rates of contribution and of benefit. Sanatorium treatment, a benefit provided under the original scheme, has since become the responsibility of the local authorities. But the basic principles laid down in 1911 have remained essentially unchanged. Absence of change does not mean, however, that the scheme as it now stands is universally approved. Criticism is directed mainly against the lack of uniformity of the "additional benefits" provided by the approved societies, and against the administrative waste caused by the overlapping and competition of these societies. There is a strong demand, too, for the extension of the scheme to the dependants of insured workers.

The most serious gap in the system of social insurance was filled by the Widows', Orphans' and Old Age Contributory Pensions Act of 1925. It provided for the payment of widows' pensions at the rate of 10s. a week, together with allowances of 5s. for the first dependent child and 3s. for each subsequent child. For orphans up to the age of 14 (or of 16 if at school) pensions of 7s. 6d. a week were provided. The Act also met the main criticism levelled against the original old-age pensions scheme, by providing insured workers and their wives with old-age pensions at 65 without any test of means. In 1937 the "Black-coated Workers' Act" extended these pensions—widows', orphans' and old-age—on a voluntary basis to the lower-paid middle classes, hitherto excluded either because their incomes were above the limit of £250 a year, or because they were not in insurable employment. The voluntary scheme is open to people in business on their own as well as to employees, provided that their incomes do not exceed £400 a year, if they are men, or £250 if they are women.

Unlike the health and pensions insurance schemes, unemployment insurance has been the subject of prolonged and acrimonious political controversies. Its history from 1920 to 1934 is largely one of retrogression "from insurance by contract to relief by status."[1] The scheme established by the Act of 1920, which extended unemployment insurance to practically all industries, except agriculture and domestic service, was based, like its model of 1911, on strictly actuarial principles. Its rates of contribution and of benefit, and its relating of benefit periods to the number of contributions paid, were devised to keep the Insurance Fund financially self-supporting. The purpose of the scheme was limited to tiding a worker over a temporary spell of unemployment, fifteen weeks' benefit being originally the most that could be

[1] Sir W. Beveridge, *Unemployment—A Problem of Industry* (1930), p. 288.

drawn in any insurance year; it was not intended to provide benefits for indefinite periods. No sooner had the Act of 1920 come into operation than the boom of 1919–20 broke, and prolonged unemployment was imposed on hundreds of thousands of workers. Two alternative courses were now open to the government; they could either adhere rigidly to the principles of the insurance scheme, and leave the Guardians to maintain those who exhausted their benefits or failed to qualify for them; or they could extend the scheme by prolonging the period for which benefits were payable. They considered it socially expedient to choose the second. From March 1921 onwards "uncovenanted" benefits, later called "extended" benefits, were paid in addition to the "covenanted" or "standard" benefits. These extra benefits, payable at the standard rates, were an enormous drain on the Insurance Fund, which soon lost the surplus of £22 million it had in 1920 and accumulated a mounting debt.

An attempt was made in the Act of 1927, based on the recommendations of the Blanesburgh Committee, to rid the scheme of the "extended" benefit, by greatly easing the conditions to be fulfilled for the standard benefit. The "one in six rule," relating benefit weeks to contributions, was abolished, along with the maximum of 26 weeks' benefit in any insurance year. It was now provided, instead, that any claimant who could show, at each quarterly review of his case, that he had thirty contributions to his credit in the preceding two years, could continue to draw his standard benefit for an indefinite period. Those who could not fulfil these very easy conditions were ultimately to be left to the Guardians. But during a "transitional period," which was extended year after year, benefits at the standard rate were payable to those with only eight contributions to their credit in the last two years or thirty at any time. Thus the "extended benefit," which the Act was intended to abolish, reappeared in the new guise of "transitional" benefit, the conditions for standard benefit having at the same time been made much easier of fulfilment.

The budgetary difficulties of 1931 were responsible for a bitterly resented innovation, the "needs test." Public assistance authorities were made responsible for the administration of "transitional benefits," whose cost was borne by the Treasury, and were instructed to assess the needs of claimants as though they were applying for public assistance. It was an arrangement that had many drawbacks, among them a lack of uniformity in administration and a divorce of administration from financial responsibility. Most local authorities regarded the administration of the unpopular "means test" as a thankless task; some refused to carry out the instructions of the Minister of Labour and were replaced by commissioners. Finally came the Unemployment Act of 1934, which introduced administrative order into the muddle of unemployment relief. Unemployment insurance was now sharply differentiated from unemployment assistance. The first was pruned of the excrescences that had grown on it since 1920, and reconstructed on a sound actuarial basis, with benefit weeks related to contributions. An Unemployment Insurance Statutory Committee was set up to watch over the finances of the scheme and to recommend any changes that might be needed to keep it financially self-supporting. Those able-bodied unemployed who could not fulfil the conditions for unemployment benefit or had exhausted their benefits, and who were within the scope of the contributory pensions scheme, the most comprehensive of our social insurance schemes, were transferred to a newly constituted unemployment assistance service. This is administered, with a "needs test" as its basis, by a hierarchy of officials carrying out the regulations of an *ad hoc* Unemployment Assistance Board.

WAGES AND HOURS

Money wages rose to undreamed-of heights between

1914 and 1920. Nevertheless their advance barely sufficed to compensate for the increased cost of living, so that the average worker was no better off in 1920 for all the additional paper money he was then handling. During the greater part of the period of inflation, in fact, money wages had failed to keep pace with the rising cost of living. At the crest of the wave, in November 1920, the cost of living index was 176 per cent. above the level of 1914, and weekly full-time rates of wages had advanced to an approximately similar extent. Deflation brought some increase in *real* wage rates, since money rates fell less rapidly, for a time, than the cost of living. But by the summer of 1922 this lag had been eliminated, and from then until the end of 1924 real wage rates were a little below their level in 1914. For 1924 as a whole, weekly full-time rates are estimated to have been 70 to 75 per cent. higher than in 1914, while the cost of living had increased by 75 per cent.

Earnings, however, do not necessarily move in the same direction, or to the same extent, as wage rates, especially in industries where piecework prevails. They are affected by overtime and short-time, by special allowances, and, where piece rates are paid, by changes in the rate of output. For industry as a whole, average earnings may be affected also by the re-distribution of workers between industries possessing different wage levels. The wage census of 1924 made possible some broad comparison of earnings before and after the war. Its results indicated that while wage rates were 70 to 75 per cent. higher in 1924 than in 1914, average earnings were about 94 per cent. higher. With the cost of living index 75 per cent. above its pre-war level, the average worker in employment must therefore have been about 10 or 11 per cent. better off, in terms of real income, than the average worker of 1914. There were, however, very wide deviations from this average improvement. Unskilled workers in nearly all trades secured, during the war, larger proportionate wage advances than skilled workers; for flat-rate bonuses, rather than percentage increases, were the means commonly adopted to compensate wage-earners for the increased cost of living. In 1924 the real wage rates of skilled workers are estimated to have been about 6 per cent. less than in 1914, while those of the unskilled were about 6 per cent. more. Women workers improved their position more than men; their average earnings in 1924 had increased by 112 per cent. since 1914, whereas men's earnings had advanced by only 90·6 per cent. In mining and quarrying, agriculture and the engineering trades, earnings had increased less than the average; while in the paper and printing trades, the woollen and worsted industry, the clothing trades, transport and the public utilities, they had increased a good deal more than the average. Broadly speaking, wages had risen most in the "sheltered" trades, dependent on the home market, and least in the export trades, exposed to foreign competition. But there were some notable exceptions to this generalization; in both the cotton and woollen industries, for instance, male workers had in 1924 fared better than the average.

Since 1924 the variations in wage rates have been very slight compared with the upheaval of 1914–24. Almost stationary from 1924 to 1929, money wages then moved down as the depression became more intense, until in 1933 they were 6 per cent. below the level of 1924. Meanwhile the cost of living had declined by just over 20 per cent., so that real wages must have risen by almost 18 per cent. from 1924 to 1933. Reviving trade restored the 1924 level of money wages by 1937, but owing to the more rapid rise of the cost of living real wage rates declined a little from 1933 to 1937. The wage position in 1937 can be summarized thus: average earnings had just about doubled since 1914, while the cost of living had risen by only 55 per cent.; hence the standard of living of the average employed worker was about 30 per cent. higher in 1937 than before the war. Some general impression of the changes in the relative earnings of different industries during the past thirty years is given by the following table.

RELATIVE WAGES SINCE 1906[1]

Industry	Average weekly earnings (in shillings)					
	Males			Females		
	1906	1924	1935	1906	1924	1935
Coal-mining	31·5	53·0	44·8	—	—	—
Metal manufacture	—	59·9	61·5	—	24·5	28·0
Engineering	—	51·1	55·0	—	26·3	28·0
All metal industries	28·1	56·4	58·8	10·7	25·2	26·9
Textiles	22·9	51·0	49·2	13·4	28·6	27·5
Clothing	24·2	54·8	54·3	11·2	26·9	27·8
Food, drink and tobacco ...	23·4	58·0	56·6	9·7	27·9	26·6
Paper and printing	27·2	70·7	75·4	9·9	28·0	28·1
Building and woodworking ...	27·4	59·0	55·9	12·4	26·3	28·1
Transport	—	69·5	65·1	—	30·8	28·3
Total	27·0	57·6	56·9	11·8	27·5	27·3
Agriculture	18·3	31·5	35·7	—	—	—

This increase in average real earnings has been accompanied by a general reduction of the hours of labour since 1914. The most substantial gain secured by the trade union movement in the stormy years after the war was the almost universal adoption, in organized trades, of the 48-hour or 47-hour week. For many workers this represented a very considerable reduction of working hours. In the iron and steel industry, for instance, the men were working 12-hour shifts until 1919, when the 8-hour shift was introduced. Railwaymen had their hours reduced from 60 in 1914 to 48 in 1919. The normal working week of engineers and shipbuilders was reduced from 54 hours to 47, and that of cotton and wool-textile operatives from 55½ to 48. In building and coal mining still shorter hours were established; builders obtained a 44-hour week (41½ in winter), and the length of the miners' working day was statutorily reduced from 8 hours to 7. Altogether, nearly 7 million workers had their hours of labour shortened in 1919 and 1920, the average reduction

[1]A. L. Bowley, *Wages and Income in the United Kingdom since 1860*, p. 51.

being about 6 hours a week. In the following slump, some of these gains were lost. Building operatives had to accept an increase to a 46½-hour week (44 in winter) in 1923, and legislation was passed during the mining stoppage of 1926 to restore the 8-hour day for underground workers. This latter has since been reduced, by the Coal Mines Act of 1930, to 7½. In most industries, however, there was very little change in hours after 1920 until 1936, when a new move towards shorter hours began. The normal working week of boot and shoe operatives and of printers has been reduced from 48 to 45, and that of flour millers from 47 to 44. Agricultural workers, paper-box and paper-bag makers, and seamen, have also benefited from recent reductions of hours.

TAXATION AND REDISTRIBUTION

The share of the wage-earning class in the net national income (including income from overseas investments) has been 38 or 39 per cent. since the war, tending to diminish slightly in years of booming trade and to increase in bad years. Perhaps the most significant feature of the changes

DISTRIBUTION OF THE NATIONAL INCOME[1] (in £ million)

Income	1911	1924	1929	1932	1935
Home-produced income ...	1,842	3,320	3,553	3,138	3,745
Income from overseas ...	220	280	315	175	215
Total income	2,062	3,600	3,868	3,313	3,960
Distribution of total income:					
Wages	728	1,399	1,486	1,333	1,520
Percentage of total ...	35·3	38·9	38·4	40·2	38·4
Salaries	288	841	944	890	937
Percentage of total ...	14·0	23·4	24·4	26·9	23·7
Profits and interest ...	843	1,114	1,136	765	1,164
Percentage of total ...	40·9	30·9	29·4	23·1	29·4
Rents	203	246	302	325	339
Percentage of total ...	9·8	6·8	7·8	9·8	8·5

in the distribution of income since the war has been the growth of the salaried class. In part, of course, this increase

[1] Adapted from C. Clark, *National Income and Outlay*, p. 94.

is more apparent than real, merely reflecting changes in the form of business organization; many concerns organized as private firms before the war and yielding "profits" to their heads, have since been converted into companies, public or private, whose directors and managers are now paid "salaries." But in part the increase in the ratio of salaries to total income is attributable to the employment of a growing proportion of the population in commerce, administration and the professions.

We must remember, however, that by no means all of this income is left, in Gladstone's phrase, "to fructify in the pockets of the people." A growing proportion is extracted in order to finance the services of public authorities. In 1913 the revenue raised from national taxes and local rates amounted to £264 million, which accounted for about 12 per cent. of the national income (home-produced *plus* overseas). Since the war the huge increase in public expenditure on the debt service, defence and the social services, has made it necessary to raise revenues equal to between a quarter and a third of the national income. In 1924, for instance, the revenue of public authorities, at £926 million, represented over 25 per cent. of the national income; and in 1932, when income had shrunk and national expenditure increased, the public revenue of £998 million swallowed up nearly 30 per cent. of the nation's income. Clearly, when national revenue and expenditure are on this scale there arises the possibility of substantially modifying the distribution of incomes through the tax system. Calculation of the share of different income classes in the burdens of taxation and in the benefits of expenditure is by no means easy; there are many pitfalls even for the expert statistician. But reliable estimates indicate that there has been a modest transference of income from the richer classes to the poorer since the war.

On the revenue side, the most marked change since 1914 has been the evolution of a highly progressive tax system.

By steeply graduating the income tax (including surtax) and estate duties, the tax burdens falling on the rich have been increased much more severely than those falling on the poor. It is estimated, for instance, that a family of man, wife, and three children, with an earned income of £100, paid 5·4 per cent. of it in taxation in 1913–14, and 10·9 per cent. in 1930–31; an equal-sized family, with an income of £50,000, paid only 8·4 per cent. in the earlier year and 53·2 per cent. in the later.[1] Until the adoption of protection, which greatly extended the burden of taxation on the poorer classes, the heavy post-war rates of direct taxes, together with their severe graduation, had the effect of reducing considerably the proportion of the total tax revenue raised from the working classes. Taking a pre-war income of £160 a year, and a post-war of £250, as marking the upper limit of the working class, Mr. Clark estimates[2] that £90·2 million, *i.e.*, 34·3 per cent., was the working-class share of the total burden of central and local taxation in 1913–14; by 1925–26 the working class was contributing a greatly increased amount, £265 million, but this constituted only 28·7 per cent. of the total. Since 1931, however, protection has modified the distribution of tax burdens unfavourably to the working class, which in 1935–36 paid £338 million in taxation, *i.e.*, 33 per cent. of the total.

On the expenditure side, a similar analysis can be made of the distribution of benefits. First, some of the services financed by public authorities confer benefits exclusively or mainly on the working classes; these include unemployment benefits and allowances, old age pensions, public assistance, education, housing, certain health services and a few others. The expenditure on these social services has increased at a staggering rate—from £63 million in 1910 to £503 million in 1935. Secondly, there are some items of expenditure whose benefits accrue mainly to the well-to-do;

[1] U. K. Hicks, *The Finance of British Government, 1920–36*, p. 385.
[2] *National Income and Outlay*, pp. 145, 146.

the most important are interest on the National Debt and highway maintenance. Thirdly, there is a group of services conferring common benefits on the whole community, rich and poor; these cannot, except quite arbitrarily, be allocated between social classes. They include defence, the diplomatic service, the judicial system, and the like. For the year 1913 Mr. Clark[1] computes that the expenditure on services conferring special benefits on the working class amounted to £75½ million, while the taxation paid by this class amounted to £90 million. Before the war, therefore, it would appear that the workers paid for the whole of the *special* benefits they derived from the State, and in addition contributed something towards the common benefits. In 1925–26 the working classes benefited from public expenditure to the extent of £310 million, and their share of taxation amounted to £265 million; they thus contributed nothing towards the cost of common benefits, and in addition received from the well-to-do classes a transfer estimated at £45 million. In 1935–36, when working-class taxation had increased to £338 million and special benefits to £429 million, the transfer from the richer class to the poorer had advanced to over £90 million. Thus the main developments in the field of public finance since the war—heavier direct taxation, steeper graduation, and greatly increased social expenditure—have been on balance favourable to the working classes, though as yet only a small proportion of the total national income is transferred through the financial system from the rich to the poor.

[1] *National Income and Outlay*, p. 147.

SELECT BIBLIOGRAPHY

I. General

Bowley, A. L., *Some Economic Consequences of the Great War* (1930).

Clapham, J. H., *An Economic History of Modern Britain*, 3 vols. I. *The Early Railway Age, 1820–1850* (1926); II. *Free Trade and Steel, 1850–1886* (1932); III. *Machines and National Rivalries (1887–1914) with an Epilogue (1914–1929)*, 1938.

Cole, G. D. H., *British Industry and Trade Past and Future* (1932).

Cunningham, W., *The Growth of English Industry and Commerce in Modern Times*, Part II, *Laissez Faire* (1917).

Dearle, N. B., *An Economic Chronicle of the Great War for Great Britain and Ireland, 1914–1919* (1929).

Dodd, A. H., *The Industrial Revolution in North Wales* (1933).

Ensor, R. C. K., *England, 1870–1914* (1936).

Fay, C. R., *England from Adam Smith to the Present Day* (1928).

Halévy, E., *A History of the English People in 1815*, Vol. I, Book II, *Economic Life* (1924).

Knowles, L. C. A., *The Industrial and Commercial Revolutions in Great Britain during the Nineteenth Century* (1927).

Layton, Sir W. T., and Crowther, G., *An Introduction to the Study of Prices* (1938).

Mackinnon, J., *Social and Industrial History of Scotland from the Union to the Present Time* (1921).

Mantoux, P., *The Industrial Revolution in the Eighteenth Century* (1928).

Marwick, W. H., *Economic Developments in Victorian Scotland* (1936).

McCulloch, J. R., *A Statistical Account of the British Empire*, 2 vols. (1839).

Porter, G. R., *The Progress of the Nation*, ed. F. W. Hirst (1912)

Woodward, E. L., *The Age of Reform, 1815–70* (1938).

Memoranda, Statistical Tables, and Charts . . . on British and Foreign Trade and Industrial Conditions (1903).

Second Series of Memoranda, Statistical Tables, and Charts . . . on British and Foreign Trade and Industrial Conditions (1904).

Statistical Tables and Charts relating to British and Foreign Trade and Industry (1854–1908), 1909.

Committee on Industry and Trade, *Factors in Industrial and Commercial Efficiency* (1927); *Further Factors in Industrial and Commercial Efficiency* (1928); *Final Report* (1929).

Statistical Tables relating to British and Foreign Trade and Industry (1924–30), 2 vols. (1930–31).

II. Agriculture

Astor, Viscount, and Rowntree, B. S., *British Agriculture* (1938).

Caird, J., *English Agriculture in 1850–51* (1852); *The Landed Interest and the Supply of Food* (1878).

Carslaw, R. M., and Graves, P. E., " Recent Changes in the Physical Output of Arable Farms," *Economic Journal*, 1935; " The Changing Organization of Arable Farms," *Economic Journal*, 1937.

Clifford, F., *The Agricultural Lock-Out of 1874* (1875).

Cobbett, W., *Rural Rides* (Everyman edition), 2 vols.

Craigie, P. G., " The Size and Distribution of Agricultural Holdings in England and Abroad," *Statistical Journal*, 1887.

Curtler, W. H. R., *A Short History of English Agriculture* (1909).

Ernle, Lord, and Hall, Sir A. D., *English Farming Past and Present* (1935).

Flux, A. W., " Our Food Supply before and after the War," *Statistical Journal*, 1930.

Fussell, G. E., " Welsh Farming in 1879," *Cymmrodorion Transactions*, 1938.

Garnier, R. M., *History of the English Landed Interest*, Vol. II (1893).

Green, F. E., *A History of the English Agricultural Labourer, 1870–1920* (1920).

Hall, Sir A. D., *A Pilgrimage of British Farming* (1912); *Agriculture after the War* (1916).

Hammond, J. L., and B., *The Village Labourer, 1760–1832* (1911).

Hasbach, W., *A History of the English Agricultural Labourer* (1908).

Levy, H., *Large and Small Holdings* (1911).

Middleton, Sir T. H., *Food Production in War* (1923).

Orwin, C. S., " Observations on the Open Fields," *Economic History Review*, 1938.

Venn, J. A., *Foundations of Agricultural Economics* (1933).

Royal Commission on the Depressed Condition of the Agricultural Interest, *Reports* and *Evidence* (1881–82).

Royal Commission on Agricultural Depression, *Reports* and *Evidence* (1894–97).

Report by Mr. Wilson Fox on the Wages and Earnings of Agricultural Labourers in the United Kingdom (1900).

Second Report by Mr. Wilson Fox on the Wages, Earnings and Conditions of Employment of Agricultural Labourers in the United Kingdom (1905).

Report on the Decline in the Agricultural Population of Great Britain, 1881–1906 (1906).

Report of an Enquiry into the Earnings and Hours of Labour of Workpeople in the United Kingdom, Vol. V (1910).

Report on the Wages and Conditions of Employment in Agriculture, 2 vols. (1919).

Final Report of the Agricultural Tribunal of Investigation (1924).

The Agricultural Output of England and Wales, 1925 (1927).

The Agricultural Output of Scotland, 1925 (1928).

The Agricultural Output of England and Wales, 1930–31 (1934).

The Agricultural Output of Scotland, 1930 (1934).

The Ministry of Agriculture has published an Economic Series since the war, too numerous to be listed here, containing a wealth of information about crops, marketing, etc.

III. Organization of Industry and Trade

Andrews, P. W. S., "Post-War Public Companies: A Study in Investment and Enterprise," *Economic Journal*, 1937.

Carr-Saunders, A. M., and others, *Consumers' Co-operation in Great Britain* (1938).

Carter, G. R., *The Tendency towards Industrial Combination* (1913).

Darwin, L., *Municipal Trade* (1903).

Fay, C. R., *Co-operation at Home and Abroad*, Vol. I (1936).

Fitzgerald, P., *Industrial Combination in England* (1927).

Hobson, J. A., *The Evolution of Modern Capitalism* (1917).

Holyoake, G. J., *The History of the Rochdale Equitable Pioneers* (1893); *The History of Co-operation*, 2 vols. (1906).

Hunt, B. C., *The Development of the Business Corporation in England, 1800–1867* (1936).

Jones, B., *Co-operative Production*, 2 vols. (1894).

Knoop, D., *Principles and Methods of Municipal Trading* (1912).

Levi, L., "On Joint Stock Companies," *Statistical Journal*, 1870;

" The Progress of Joint Stock Companies with Limited and Unlimited Liability in the United Kingdom, 1869–84," *Statistical Journal*, 1886.

Levy, H., *Monopolies, Cartels and Trusts in British Industry* (1927).

Lucas, A. F., *Industrial Reconstruction and the Control of Competition* (1937).

Macgregor, D. H., " Joint Stock Companies and the Risk Factor," *Economic Journal*, 1929.

Macrosty, H. W., *The Trust Movement in British Industry* (1907).

Marshall, A., *Industry and Trade* (1919).

O'Brien, T. H., *British Experiments in Public Ownership and Control* (1937).

Potter, B., *The Co-operative Movement in Great Britain* (1930).

Redfern, P., *The New History of the " C.W.S."* (1938).

Robson, W. A. (ed.), *Public Enterprise* (1937).

Shannon, H. A., " The Coming of General Limited Liability," *Economic History*, 1931 ; " The First Five Thousand Limited Companies," *Economic History*, 1932 ; " The Limited Companies of 1866–1883," *Economic History Review*, 1933.

Todd, G., " Some Aspects of Joint Stock Companies, 1844–1900," *Economic History Review*, 1932.

Webb, C., *Industrial Co-operation* (1936).

Joint Select Committee on Municipal Trading, *Report* and *Evidence* (1900).

Report of the Committee on Trusts (1919).

IV. Industrial Fluctuation and Commercial Crises

Beales, H. L., " ' The Great Depression ' in Industry and Trade," *Economic History Review*, 1934.

Beveridge, Sir W. H., *Unemployment : A Problem of Industry* (1930).

Burton, N. H., *Financial Crises and Periods of Industrial and Commercial Depression* (1908).

Clay, H., *The Post-War Unemployment Problem* (1929).

Evans, D. M., *The Commercial Crisis, 1847–1848* (1848) ; *The History of the Commercial Crisis, 1857–1858* (1859).

Hirst, F. W., *The Six Panics and other Essays* (1913).

Hyndman, H. M., *Commercial Crises of the Nineteenth Century* (1908).

Jevons, W. S., *Investigations in Currency and Finance* (1884).
League of Nations, *The Course and Phases of the World Economic Depression* (1932).
Mitchell, W. C., *Business Cycles* (1927).
Robbins, L., *The Great Depression* (1934).
Robertson, D. H., *A Study of Industrial Fluctuation* (1915).
Royal Commission on the Depression of Trade, *Reports* and *Evidence* (1886).

V. Industries

Allen, G. C., *The Industrial Development of Birmingham and the Black Country, 1860–1927* (1929); *British Industries and their Organization* (1933).
Arnold, R. A., *History of the Cotton Famine* (1865).
Ashley, W. J. (ed.), *British Industries* (1903).
Ashton, T. S., *Iron and Steel in the Industrial Revolution* (1924).
Ashton, T. S., and Sykes, J., *The Coal Industry of the Eighteenth Century* (1929).
Baines, E., *History of the Cotton Manufacture in Great Britain* (1835).
Beales, H. L., " Studies in Bibliography, IV. The ' Basic ' Industries of England, 1850–1914," *Economic History Review*, 1935.
Bell, I. Lowthian, *The Iron Trade of the United Kingdom* (1886).
Birkett, M. S., " The Iron and Steel Industry during the War," *Statistical Journal*, 1920; " The Iron and Steel Industry since the War," *Statistical Journal*, 1930.
Bowker, B., *Lancashire under the Hammer* (1928).
Bremner, D., *The Industries of Scotland* (1869).
British Association, *Britain in Depression* (1935); *Britain in Recovery* (1938).
Burnley, J., *History of Wool and Woolcombing* (1889).
Chapman, S. J., *The Lancashire Cotton Industry* (1904).
Chapman, S. J., and Ashton, T. S., " The Sizes of Business, Mainly in the Textile Industries," *Statistical Journal*, 1914.
Chapman, S. J., and Marquis, F. J., " The Recruiting of the Employing Classes from the Ranks of the Wage-Earners in the Cotton Industry," *Statistical Journal*, 1912.
Clapham, J. H., *The Woollen and Worsted Industries* (1907).
Cox, H. (ed.), *British Industries under Free Trade* (1903).

Crump, W. B., and Ghorbal, G., *History of the Huddersfield Woollen Industry* (1935).

Daniels, G. W., *The Early English Cotton Industry* (1920).

Daniels, G. W., and Jewkes, J., " The Crisis in the Lancashire Cotton Industry," *Economic Journal*, 1927 ; " The Post-War Depression in the Lancashire Cotton Industry," *Statistical Journal*, 1928.

Ellison, T., *The Cotton Trade of Great Britain* (1886).

Felkin, W., *A History of the Machine-wrought Hosiery and Lace Manufactures* (1867).

Fleming, A. P. M., and Brocklehurst, H. J., *A History of Engineering* (1925).

Galloway, R. L., *Annals of Coal Mining and the Coal Trade*, 2 vols. (1898).

Henderson, W. O., *The Lancashire Cotton Famine* (1934).

Horner, J., *The Linen Trade of Europe* (1920).

Jeans, J. S., *The Iron Trade of Great Britain* (1906).

Jevons, H. S., *The British Coal Trade* (1915).

Jevons, W. S., *The Coal Question* (ed. A. W. Flux), 1906.

Jones, G. T., *Increasing Return* (1933).

Jones, J. H., *The Tinplate Industry* (1914) ; " The Present Position of the British Coal Trade," *Statistical Journal*, 1930.

Lloyd, G. I. H., *The Cutlery Trades* (1913).

Miall, S., *A History of the British Chemical Industry, 1634–1928* (1931).

Mining Association, *Historical Review of Coal Mining* (1924).

Neuman, A. M., *Economic Organization of the British Coal Industry* (1934).

Plummer, A., *New British Industries in the Twentieth Century* (1937).

P E P (Political and Economic Planning), *Report on the British Iron and Steel Industry* (1933) ; *Report on the British Cotton Industry* (1934) ; *Report on the British Coal Industry* (1936) ; *Report on the Supply of Electricity in Great Britain* (1936) ; *Report on the Location of Industry in Great Britain* (1939) ; *Report on the British Gas Industry* (1939).

Schulze-Gaevernitz, G., *The Cotton Trade in England and on the Continent* (1895).

Scrivenor, H., *A Comprehensive History of the Iron Trade* (1841).

Smiles, S., *Industrial Biography* (1878).

Southey, T., *The Rise, Progress and Present State of Colonial Sheep and Wools* (1851).
Wadsworth, A. P., and Mann, J., *The Cotton Trade and Industrial Lancashire, 1600–1780* (1931).
Warden, J., *The Linen Trade, Ancient and Modern* (1864).
Watts, J., *Facts of the Cotton Famine* (1866).
Wells, F. A., *The British Hosiery Trade* (1935).
Wilkins, C., *The History of the Iron, Steel, Tinplate and other Trades of Wales* (1903).
Reports of the Censuses of Production, 1907, 1912, 1924, 1930 and 1935.
Report of the Committee on the Iron and Steel Trades after the War (1918).
Report of the Committee on the Shipping and Shipbuilding Industries after the War (1918).
Report of the Committee on the Textile Trades after the War (1918).
Royal Commissions on the Coal Industry, 1919 and 1925, *Reports* and *Evidence*.
Committee on Industry and Trade, *Survey of Metal Industries* (1928); *Survey of Textile Industries* (1928).
Economic Advisory Council, *Report on the Cotton Industry* (1930)
Report of the Import Duties Advisory Committee on the Present Position and Future Development of the Iron and Steel Industry (1937).

VI. Commerce and Commercial Policy

Ashley, W. J., *The Tariff Problem* (1903).
Barnes, D. G., *A History of the English Corn Laws from 1660 to 1846* (1930).
Bowley, A. L., *England's Foreign Trade in the Nineteenth Century* (1905).
Burnett-Hurst, A. R., "Lancashire and the Indian Market," *Statistical Journal*, 1932.
Critchell, J. T., and Raymond, J., *A History of the Frozen Meat Trade* (1912).
Ellinger, B., "Japanese Competition in the Cotton Trade," *Statistical Journal*, 1930.
Fay, C. R., *The Corn Laws and Social England* (1932).
Fuchs, C. J., *The Trade Policy of Great Britain and her Colonies since 1860* (1905).

Hobson, C. K., *The Export of Capital* (1913).
Hoffman, R. J. S., *Great Britain and the German Trade Rivalry, 1875–1914* (1933).
Jenks, L. H., *The Migration of British Capital to 1875* (1927).
Levi, L., *History of British Commerce* (1872).
Loveday, A., *Britain and World Trade* (1931).
Morley, J., *Life of Richard Cobden*, 2 vols. (1881).
P E P, *Report on International Trade* (1937).
Prentice, A., *History of the Anti-Corn-Law League*, 2 vols. (1853).
Richardson, J. H., *British Economic Foreign Policy* (1936).
Taussig, F. W., " The Change in Great Britain's Foreign Trade Terms after 1900," *Economic Journal*, 1925.
Thomas, D. A., " The Growth and Direction of our Foreign Trade in Coal during the last Half Century," *Statistical Journal*, 1903.
Annual Statements of the Trade of the United Kingdom.
Committee on Industry and Trade, *Survey of Overseas Markets* (1925).

VII. Transport and Communications

Acworth, Sir W. M., *The Railways of Scotland* (1890) ; *The Railways of England* (1900) ; " Grouping under the Railways Act, 1921," *Economic Journal*, 1923 ; *The Elements of Railway Economics* (1924).
Baldwin, F. G. C., *The History of the Telephone in the United Kingdom* (1925).
Campbell, C. D., *British Railways in Boom and Depression* (1932).
Cary, J., *New Itinerary or an Accurate Delineation of the Great Roads, etc.* (1821).
Cornewall-Jones, R. J., *The British Merchant Service* (1898).
Chester, D. N., *Public Control of Road Passenger Transport* (1936).
Cleveland-Stevens, E., *English Railways : Their Development and their Relation to the State* (1915).
Evans, H. T., *Rebecca and Her Daughters* (1910).
Fayle, C. E., *A Short History of the World's Shipping Industry* (1933).
Fenelon, K. G., *The Economics of Road Transport* (1925); " British Railways since the War," *Statistical Journal*, 1933 ; " Road Transport in Great Britain since the War," *Statistical Journal*, 1935.
Forbes, U. A., and Ashford, W. H. R., *Our Waterways* (1906).

Francis, J., *A History of the English Railway* (1851).
Grinling, C. H., *The Great Northern Railway, 1845–1902* (1903).
Hill, Sir R., and G. B., *The Life of Sir Rowland Hill and the History of Penny Postage*, 2 vols. (1880).
Jackman, W. T., *Transportation in Modern England*, 2 vols. (1916).
Jones, C., *British Merchant Shipping* (1922).
Kirkaldy, A. W., *British Shipping* (1914).
Kirkaldy, A. W., and Evans, A. D., *The History and Economics of Transport* (1927).
Leigh's New Pocket Road Book of England and Wales (1837).
Lewin, H. G., *Early British Railways, 1801–1844* (1925).
MacDermot, E. T., *History of the Great Western Railway*, 2 vols. (1927–31).
Mogg, E., *Paterson's Roads, etc.* (1829).
Pratt, E. A., *A History of Inland Transport and Communications in England* (1912).
Robertson, W. A., *Combination among Railway Companies* (1912).
Sherrington, C. E. R., *The Economics of Rail Transport in Great Britain*, Vol. I (1928) ; *A Hundred Years of Inland Transport, 1830–1933* (1934).
Smiles, S., *Lives of the Engineers*, 3 vols. (1861–62).
Stretton, C. E., *The History of the Midland Railway* (1901).
The Post Office, An Historical Summary (1911).
Tomlinson, W. W., *The North-Eastern Railway* (1914).
Veitch, G. S., *The Struggle for the Liverpool and Manchester Railway* (1930).
Webb, S. and B., *The Story of the King's Highway* (1920).
Williams, F. S., *Our Iron Roads* (1885).
Departmental Committee on Railway Amalgamations, *Report* and *Evidence* (1911).
Royal Commission on Canals and Inland Waterways, *Reports* and *Evidence* (1907–11).
Royal Commission on Shipping Rings, *Report* and *Evidence* (1909).
Royal Commission on Transport, *Reports* and *Evidence* (1929–31).

VIII. Banking and Currency

Acres, W. M., *The Bank of England from Within*, 2 vols. (1931).
Anderson, J. L., *The Story of the Commercial Bank of Scotland Limited* (1910).

Andréadès, A., *History of the Bank of England* (1924).

Bagehot, W., *Lombard Street* (1873).

Beach, W. E., *British International Gold Movements and Banking Policy, 1881–1913* (1935).

Benham, F., *British Monetary Policy* (1932).

Buxton, S., *Finance and Politics*, 2 vols. (1888).

Crick, W. F., and Wadsworth, J. E., *A Hundred Years of Joint Stock Banking* (1936).

Einzig, P., *The Tragedy of the Pound* (1932).

Feavearyear, A. E., *The Pound Sterling: A History of English Money* (1931).

Gilbart, J. W., *The History, Principles and Practice of Banking*, ed. A. S. Michie (1905).

Graham, W., *The One Pound Note in the History of Banking in Great Britain* (1911).

Grant, A. T. K., *A Study of the Capital Market in Post-War Britain* (1937).

Gregory, T. E., *Select Statutes, Documents and Reports relating to British Banking, 1832–1928*, 2 vols. (1929); *The Gold Standard and its Future* (1932); *The Westminster Bank through a Century*, 2 vols. (1936).

Hawtrey, R. G., *A Century of Bank Rate* (1938).

Kerr, A. W., *History of Banking in Scotland*, ed. F. H. Allan (1926).

King, W. T. C., *History of the London Discount Market* (1936).

Kirkaldy, A. W. (ed.), *British Finance, 1914–1921* (1921).

Lloyds Bank Limited, Its History and Progress (1914).

Matthews, P. W., and Tuke, A. W., *A History of Barclay's Bank* (1926).

Munro, N., *History of the Royal Bank of Scotland* (1928).

Palgrave, R. H. I., *Bank Rate and the Money Market* (1903).

Powell, E. T., *The Evolution of the Money Market, 1385–1915* (1916).

Rait, R. S., *The History of the Union Bank of Scotland* (1930).

Sayers, R. S., *Bank of England Operations, 1890–1914* (1936).

Sykes, J., *The Amalgamation Movement in English Banking, 1825–1924* (1926).

Thomas, S. E., *The Rise and Growth of Joint Stock Banking*, Vol. I (1934).

Withers, H., *National Provincial Bank, 1833–1933* (1933).

Royal Commission on Gold and Silver, *Final Report* (1888).
Interim Report of Committee on Currency and Foreign Exchanges after the War (1918).
Committee on Finance and Industry, *Report* and *Evidence* (1931).

IX. Labour Conditions and Trade Unionism

Amulree, Lord, *Industrial Arbitration in Great Britain* (1929).
Askwith, Lord, *Industrial Problems and Disputes* (1920).
Beer, M., *History of British Socialism*, 2 vols. (1919–20).
Bowley, A. L., *Wages and Income in the United Kingdom since 1860* (1937) (containing bibliography) ; *Wages in the United Kingdom in the Nineteenth Century* (1900).
Cohen, P., *The British System of Social Insurance* (1932).
Cole, G. D. H., *The World of Labour* (1913) ; *Short History of the British Working Class Movement, 1789–1937* (1937).
Cole, G. D. H., and Arnot, R. P., *Trade Unionism on the Railways* (1917).
Crook, W. H., *The General Strike* (1931).
Davison, R. C., *The Unemployed : Old Policies and New* (1929) ; *British Unemployment Policy* (1938).
Edwards, N., *The History of the South Wales Miners* (1926).
Fay, C. R., *Life and Labour in the Nineteenth Century* (1920).
Fisher, A. G. B., *Wages and their Regulation in Great Britain since 1918* (1926).
Hammond, J. L. and B., *The Age of the Chartists, 1832–1854* (1930).
Hedges, R. Y., and Winterbottom, A., *The Legal History of Trade Unionism* (1930).
Hutchins, B. L., and Harrison, A., *History of Factory Legislation* (1926).
Hutt, A., *The Post-War History of the British Working Class* (1937).
Jewkes, J., and Gray, E. M., *Wages and Labour in the Lancashire Cotton Spinning Industry* (1935).
Johnston, T., *History of the Working Classes in Scotland* (1920).
P E P, *Report on the British Social Services* (1937).
Kiddier, W., *The Old Trade Unions* (1931).
Kirkaldy, A. W. (ed.), *British Labour, 1914–1921* (1921).
Mess, H. A., *Factory Legislation and its Administration, 1891–1924* (1926).

Milne-Bailey, W., *Trade Union Documents* (1929); *Trade Unions and the State* (1934).

Postgate, R. W., *The Builders' History* (1923).

Robertson, D. H., " A Narrative of the General Strike of 1926," *Economic Journal*, 1926.

Rowe, J. W. F., *Wages in the Coal Industry* (1923); *Wages in Practice and Theory* (1928).

Sells, D., *The British Trade Boards System* (1923).

Steffen, G. F., *Studien zur Geschichte der englischen Lohnarbeiter*, 3 vols. (1901–05).

Webb, S. and B., *The Story of the Durham Miners, 1662–1921* (1921); *Industrial Democracy* (1920); *The History of Trade Unionism* (1920).

Williams, G., *The State and the Standard of Living* (1936).

Wood, G. H., " Real Wages and the Standard of Comfort since 1850," *Statistical Journal*, 1909.

Yates, M. L., *Wages and Labour Conditions in British Engineering* (1937).

Report from the Committee on the Bill to regulate the Labour of Children in the Mills and Factories of the United Kingdom (1832).

Reports of the Commissioners for inquiring into the Employment and Conditions of Children in Mines and Manufactories (1842).

Report from the Poor Law Commissioners on . . . the Sanitary Condition of the Labouring Population (1842).

Committee on Industry and Trade, *Survey of Industrial Relations* (1926).

Reports of Inquiries into Earnings and Hours in 1886, 1906, 1924, 1928, 1931, and 1935. All but the first two of these were published in the *Ministry of Labour Gazette*.

X. Population and Wealth

Bowley, A. L., *National Progress in Wealth and Trade* (1904); *The Division of the Product of Industry* (1919); *The Change in the Distribution of the National Income, 1880–1913* (1920).

Bowley, A. L., and Stamp, Sir J., *The National Income, 1924* (1928).

Carr-Saunders, A. M., *The Population Problem* (1922); *World Population* (1936).

Clark, C., *The National Income, 1924–1931* (1932); *National Income and Outlay* (1937).

Giffen, Sir R., *Economic Inquiries and Studies*, 2 vols. (1904).
Holland, G. C., *Vital Statistics of Sheffield* (1843).
Macdonald, D. F., *Scotland's Shifting Population, 1770–1850* (1937).
Marshall, T. H., "The Population of England and Wales from the Industrial Revolution to the World War," *Economic History Review*, 1938.
Redford, A., *Labour Migration in England, 1800–1850* (1926).
Stamp, Lord, *British Incomes and Property* (1916); *The National Capital and other Statistical Studies* (1937).
Welton, T. A., "On the Distribution of Population in England and Wales and its Progress in the Period of Ninety Years from 1801 to 1891," *Statistical Journal*, 1900.

INDEX